樋 口 大 輔

What is a talent?
Is it a special power?
Is it something only the chosen ones can have?
But, what does it mean to be a chosen one to
begin with?
What is the difference between ordinary and
extraordinary?

A talent is something one has, which others don't
have. Finding that unique something, and nurturing
it to blossom. I think that's what talent is.

– Daisuke Higuchi

Daisuke Higuchi's manga career began in 1992 when the
artist was honored with third prize in the 43rd Osamu
Tezuka Award. In that same year, Higuchi debuted as
creator of a romantic action story titled *Itaru*. In 1998,
Weekly Shonen Jump began serializing *Whistle!*
Higuchi's realistic soccer manga became an instant hit
with readers and eventually inspired an anime series,
debuting on Japanese TV in May of 2002.

WHISTLE!
VOL. 12: IN THE DISTANCE

The SHONEN JUMP Manga Edition

STORY AND ART BY
DAISUKE HIGUCHI

English Adaptation/Drew Williams
Translation/Naomi Kokubo
Touch-up Art & Lettering/Jim Keefe
Cover, Graphics & Layout/Sean Lee
Editor/Ian Robertson

Editor in Chief, Books/Alvin Lu
Editor in Chief, Magazines/Marc Weidenbaum
VP of Publishing Licensing/Rika Inouye
VP of Sales/Gonzalo Ferreyra
Sr. VP of Marketing/Liza Coppola
Publisher/Hyoe Narita

Printed in the U.S.A.

Published by VIZ Media, LLC
P.O. Box 77010
San Francisco, CA 94107

SHONEN JUMP Manga Edition
10 9 8 7 6 5 4 3 2
First printing, July 2006
Second printing, March 2007

PARENTAL ADVISORY
WHISTLE! is rated A and is
suitable for readers of all ages.

RATED
A
ALL AGES

VIZ MEDIA
www.viz.com

THE WORLD'S
MOST POPULAR MANGA
SHONEN JUMP
www.shonenjump.com

WHISTLE!™

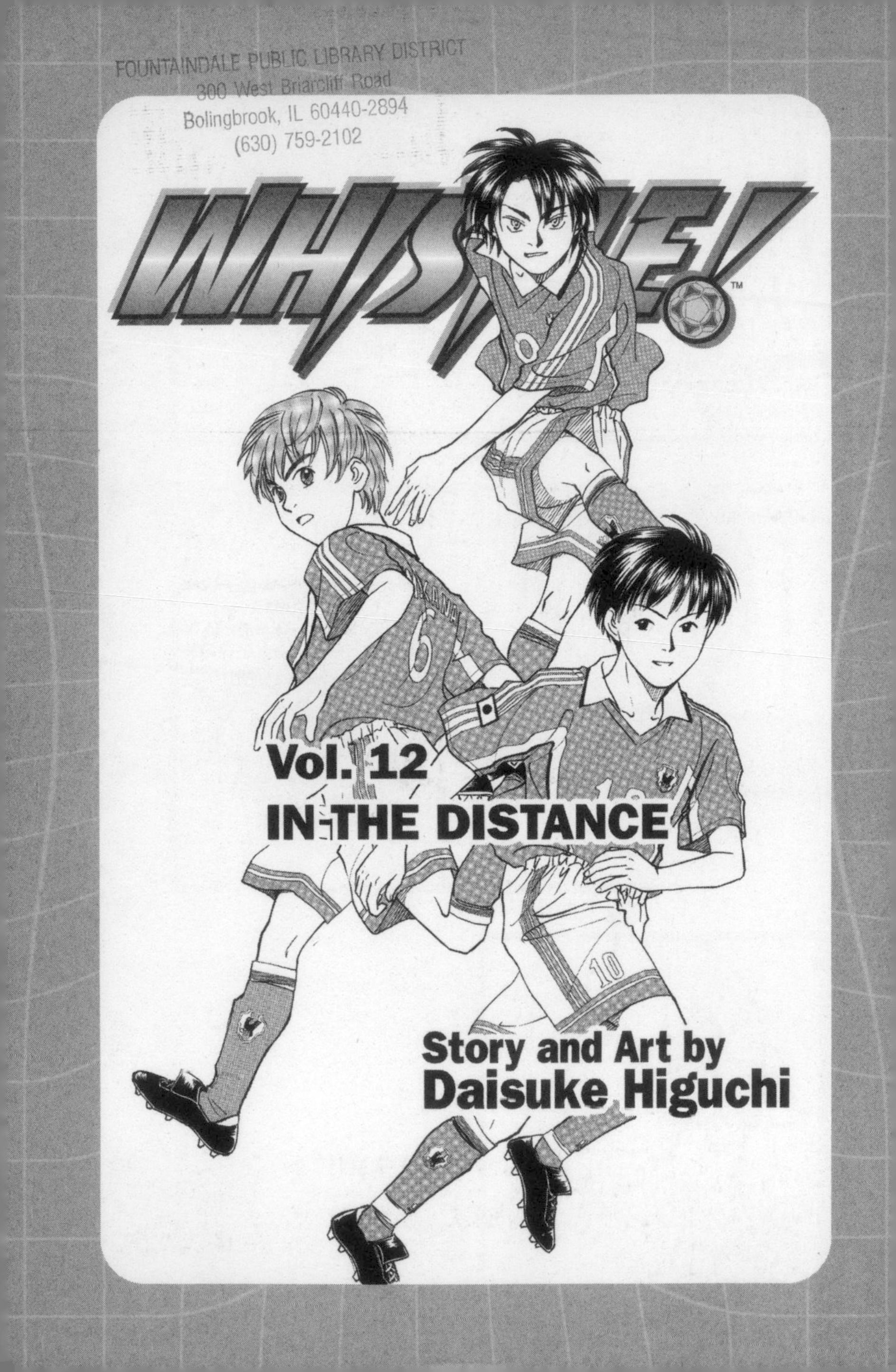

Vol. 12

IN THE DISTANCE

Story and Art by
Daisuke Higuchi

CHARACTERS

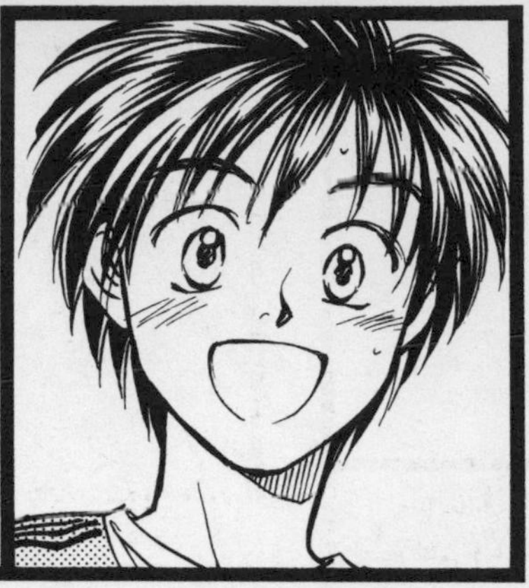

SHŌ KAZAMATSURI

● JOSUI JUNIOR HIGH SOCCER TEAM FORWARD

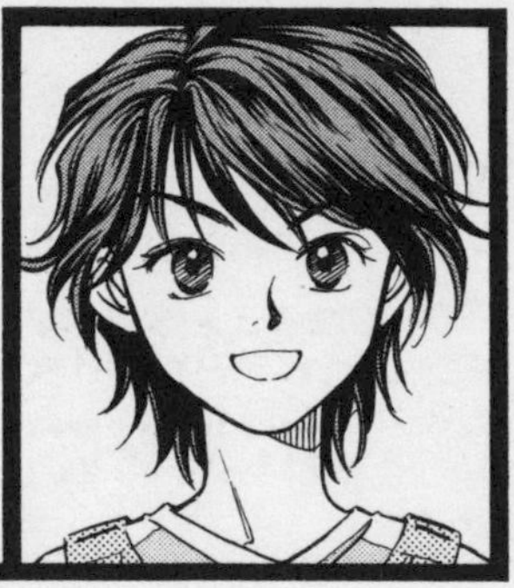

AKIRA SAIONJI

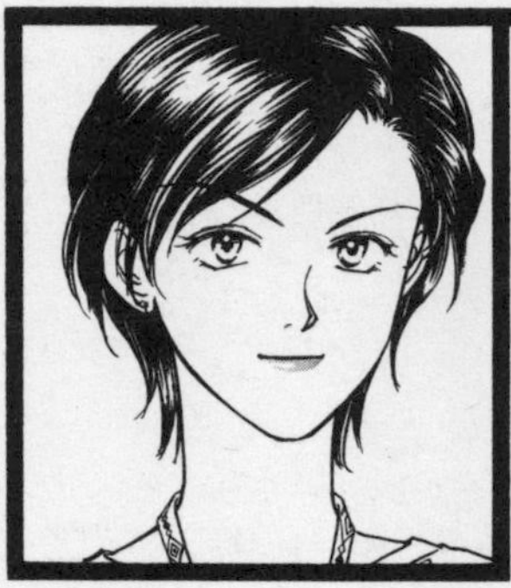

TSUBASA SHIINA

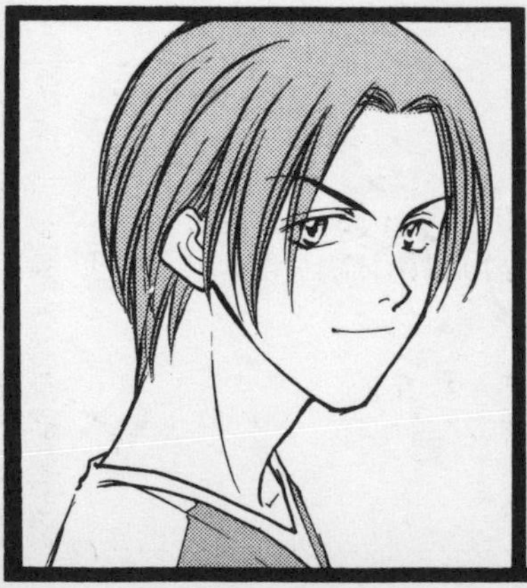

TATSUYA MIZUNO

● JOSUI JUNIOR HIGH SOCCER TEAM MIDFIELDER

TEPPEI KOIWA

EDOGAWA FIRST JUNIOR HIGH

TAKI SUGIHARA

TAKANAWA JUNIOR HIGH

DAICHI FUWA

JOSUI JUNIOR HIGH SOCCER TEAM

GOAL KEEPER

TO REALIZE HIS DREAM, SHŌ KAZAMATSURI, A BENCH WARMER AT SOCCER POWERHOUSE MUSASHINOMORI, TRANSFERRED TO JOSUI JUNIOR HIGH SO HE COULD PLAY THE GAME HE LOVES.

JOSUI'S SOCCER TEAM WAS A JOKE UNTIL SOUJŪ MATSUSHITA, A FORMER JAPAN LEAGUE PLAYER, TOOK ON THE COACHING DUTIES. UNDER MATSUSHITA'S GUIDANCE, THE TEAM HAS BECOME A FORCE TO BE RECKONED WITH. THEY BLASTED THROUGH THE DISTRICT PRIMARY TOURNAMENT, DEFEATING RAKUYŌ JUNIOR HIGH BEFORE HOLDING OFF HIBA JUNIOR HIGH TO WIN THE TOURNAMENT FINALS.

JOSUI'S SOCCER TEAM HAS HIT AN ALL-TIME HIGH. WHAT'S NEXT FOR THE TOURNAMENT CHAMPS?

STORY

WHISTLE!

Vol. 12
IN THE DISTANCE

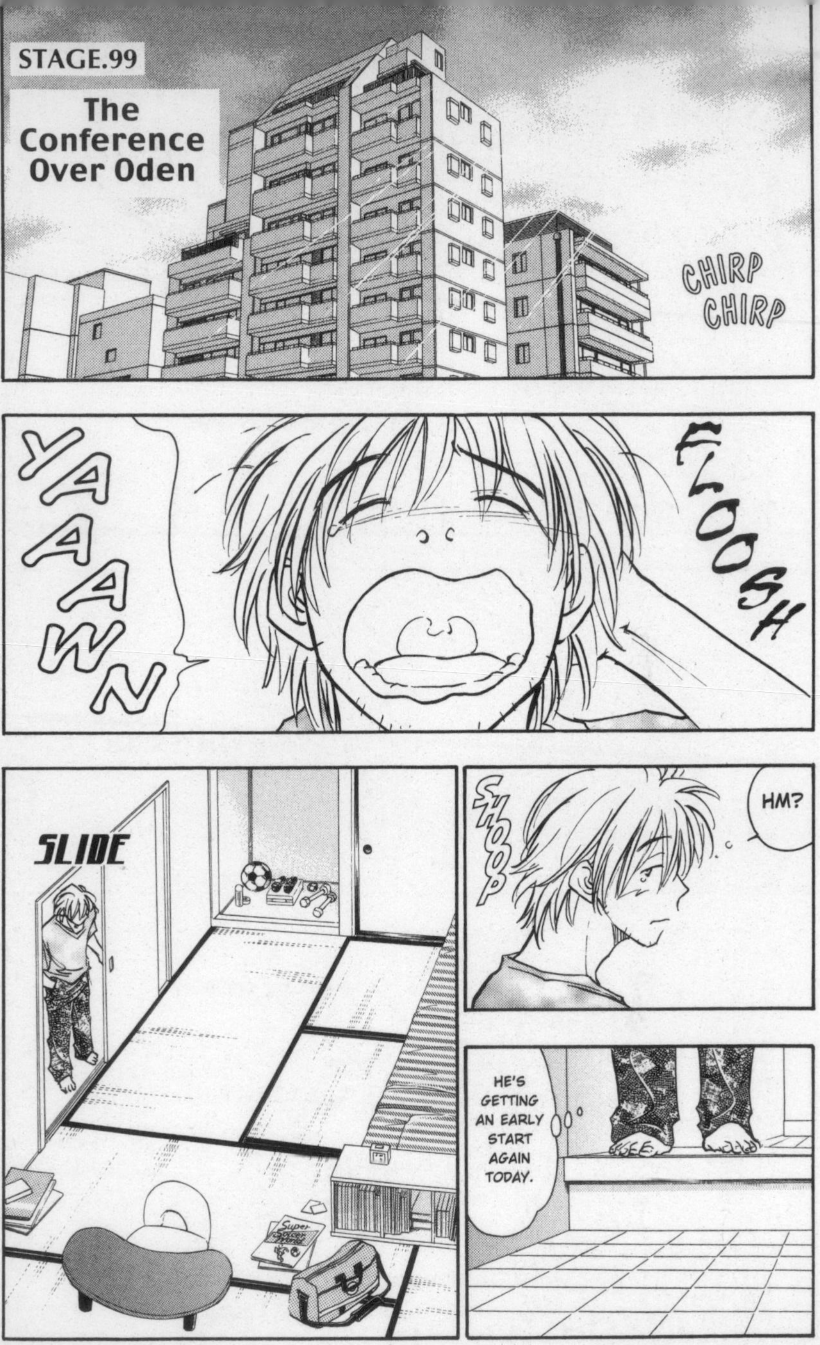
STAGE.99
The Conference Over Oden
CHIRP CHIRP
FLOOSH
YAAAWN
HM?
SHOOP
HE'S GETTING AN EARLY START AGAIN TODAY.
SLIDE

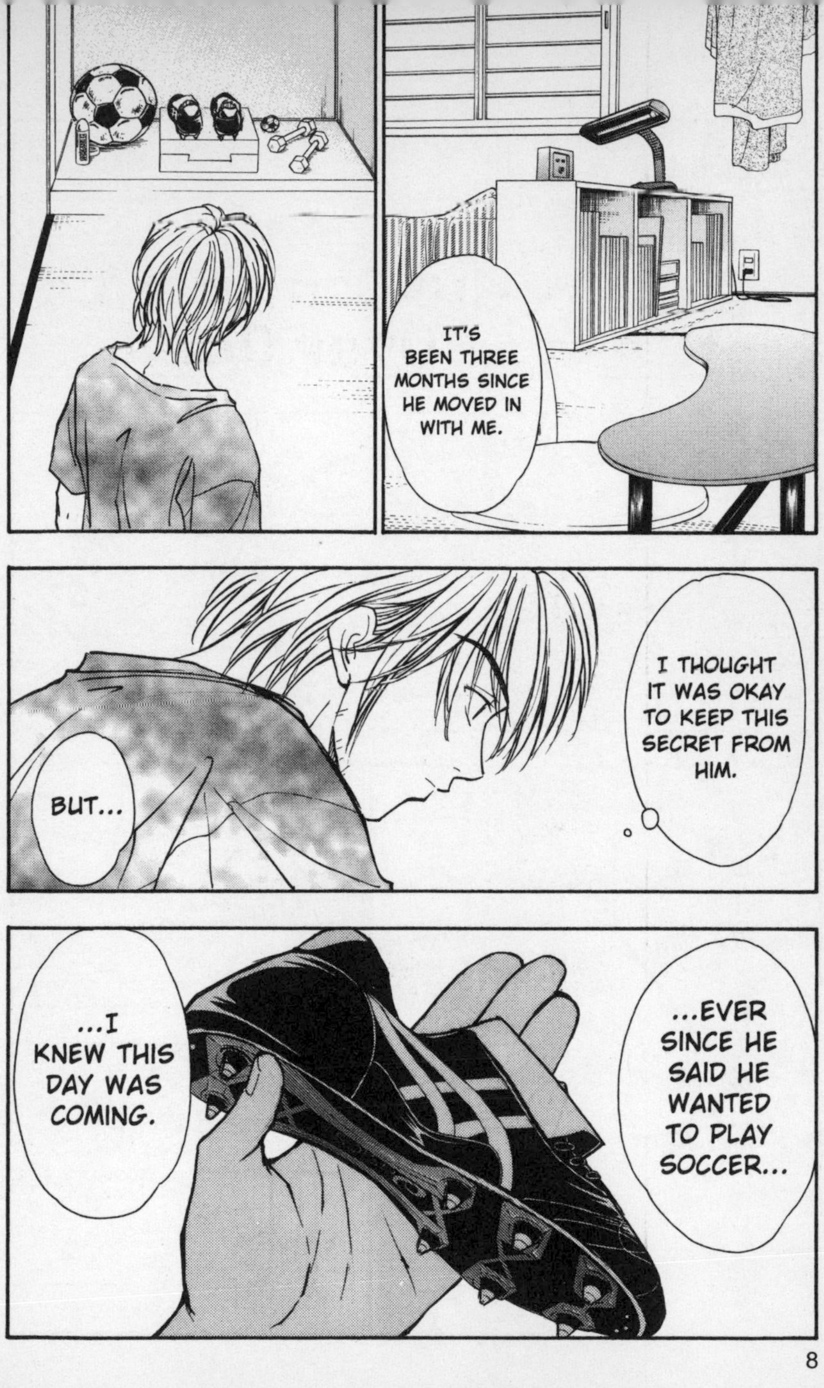
IT'S BEEN THREE MONTHS SINCE HE MOVED IN WITH ME.
I THOUGHT IT WAS OKAY TO KEEP THIS SECRET FROM HIM.
BUT...
...EVER SINCE HE SAID HE WANTED TO PLAY SOCCER...
...I KNEW THIS DAY WAS COMING.

STAGE.99 The Conference Over Oden

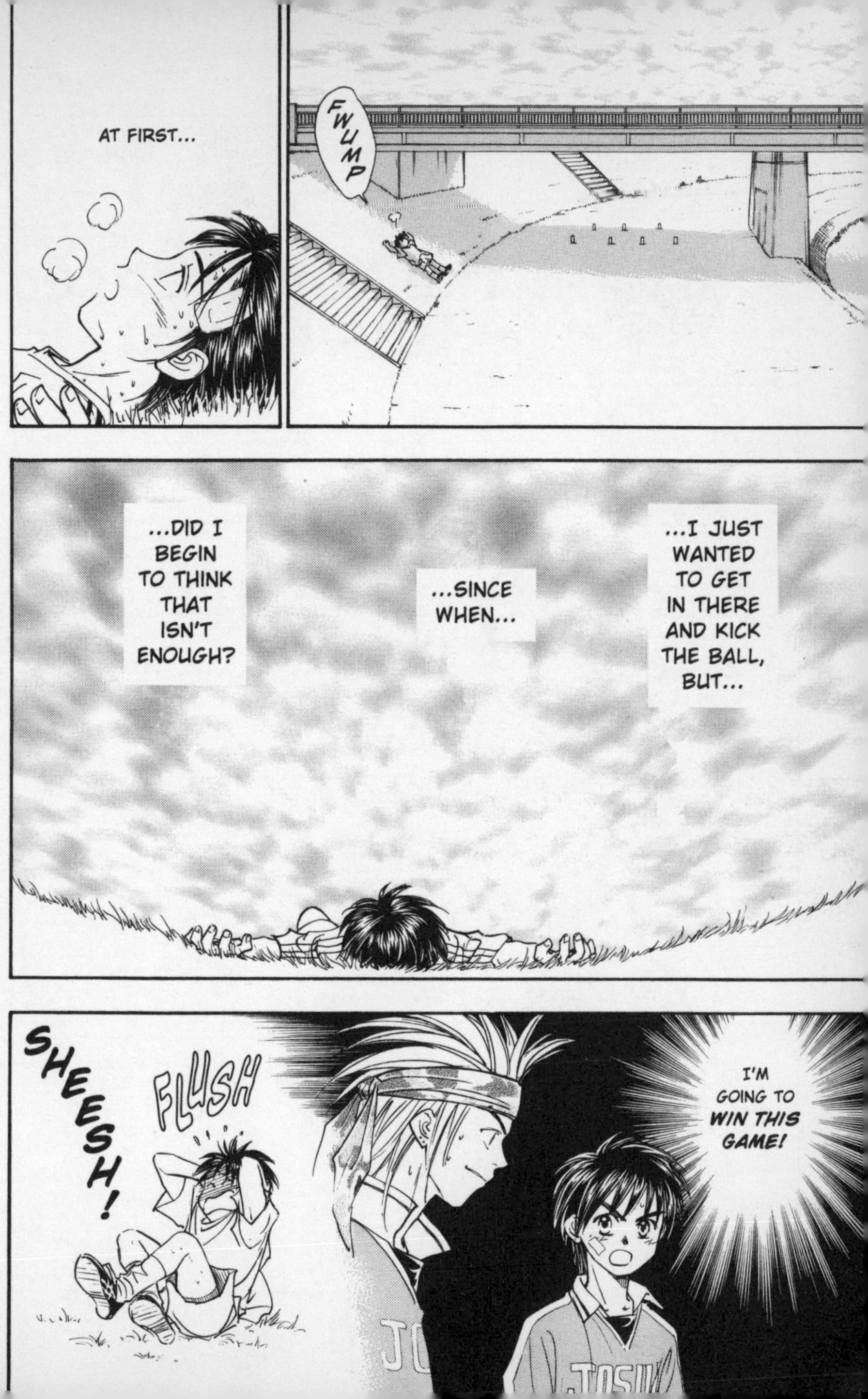
FWUMP
AT FIRST...
...I JUST WANTED TO GET IN THERE AND KICK THE BALL, BUT...
...SINCE WHEN...
...DID I BEGIN TO THINK THAT ISN'T ENOUGH?
I'M GOING TO WIN THIS GAME!
FLUSH
SHEESH!

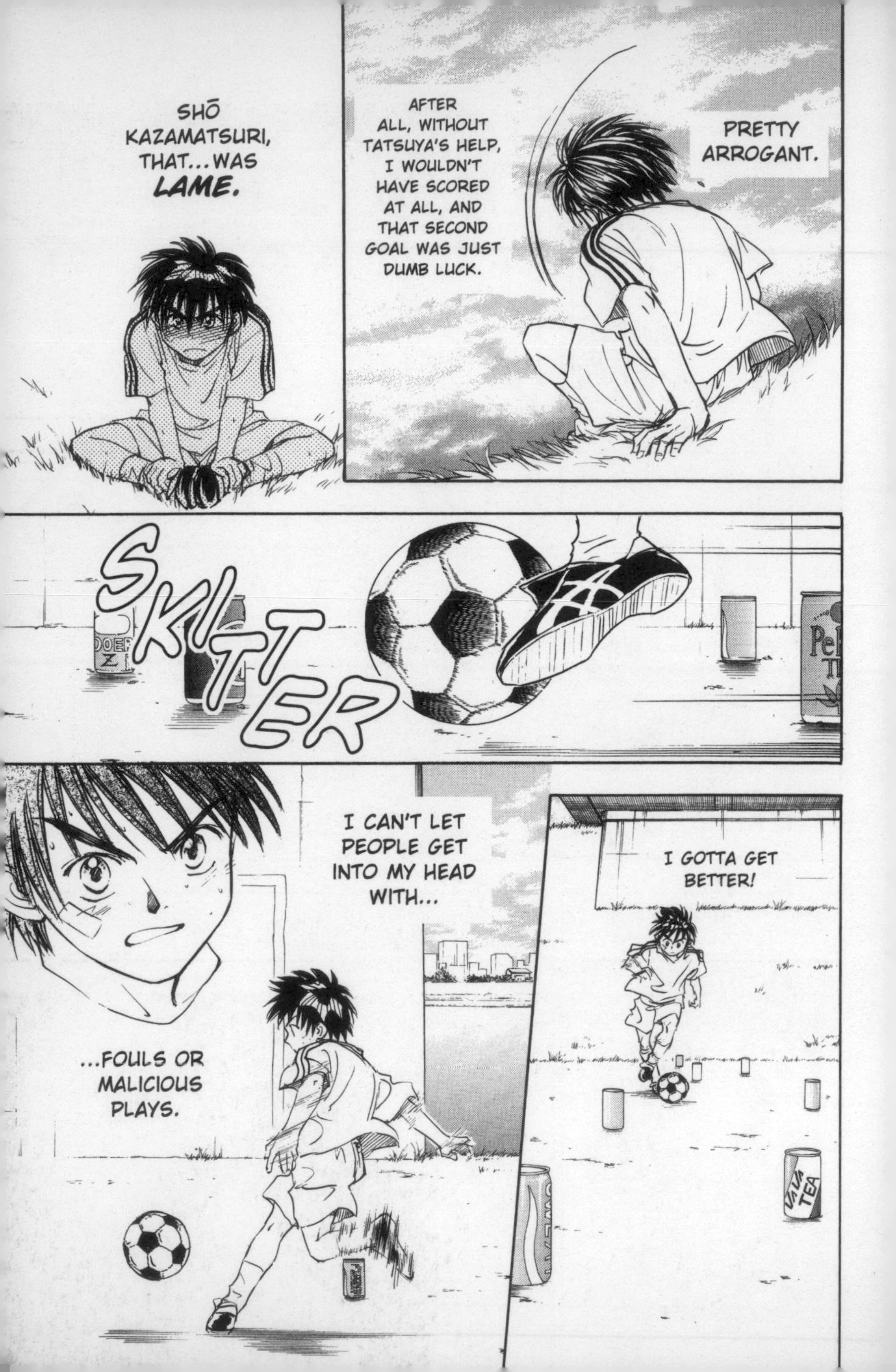
PRETTY ARROGANT.
AFTER ALL, WITHOUT TATSUYA'S HELP, I WOULDN'T HAVE SCORED AT ALL, AND THAT SECOND GOAL WAS JUST DUMB LUCK.
SHŌ KAZAMATSURI, THAT...WAS *LAME.*
SKITTER
I GOTTA GET BETTER!
VAVA TEA
I CAN'T LET PEOPLE GET INTO MY HEAD WITH...
...FOULS OR MALICIOUS PLAYS.

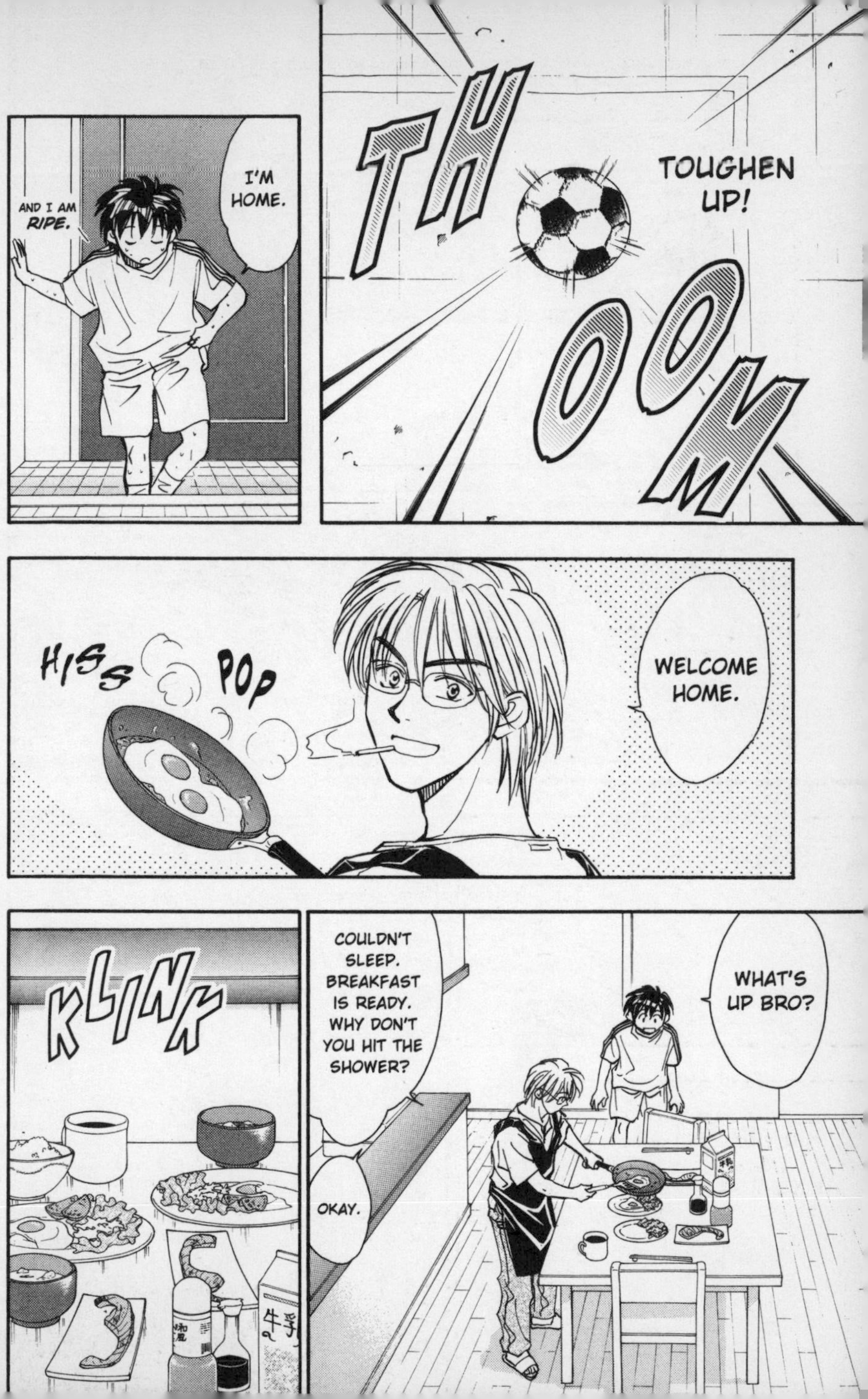
THOOM
TOUGHEN UP!
I'M HOME.
AND I AM RIPE.
HISS POP
WELCOME HOME.
WHAT'S UP BRO?
COULDN'T SLEEP. BREAKFAST IS READY. WHY DON'T YOU HIT THE SHOWER?
OKAY.
KLINK

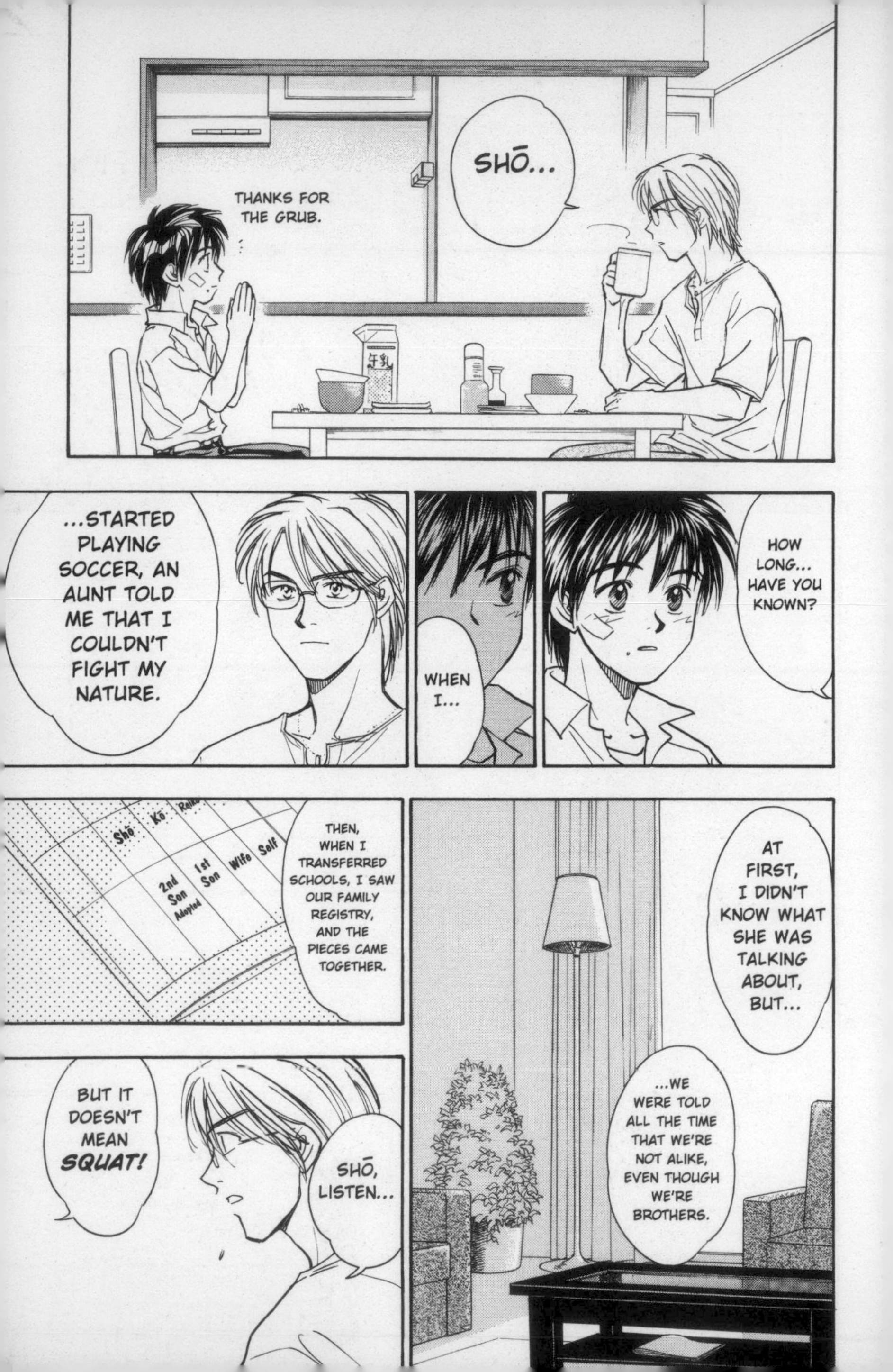
SHŌ...
THANKS FOR THE GRUB.
HOW LONG... HAVE YOU KNOWN?
WHEN I...
...STARTED PLAYING SOCCER, AN AUNT TOLD ME THAT I COULDN'T FIGHT MY NATURE.
AT FIRST, I DIDN'T KNOW WHAT SHE WAS TALKING ABOUT, BUT...
...WE WERE TOLD ALL THE TIME THAT WE'RE NOT ALIKE, EVEN THOUGH WE'RE BROTHERS.
THEN, WHEN I TRANSFERRED SCHOOLS, I SAW OUR FAMILY REGISTRY, AND THE PIECES CAME TOGETHER.
Reiko
Kō
Shō
Self
Wife
1st Son
2nd Son Adopted
SHŌ, LISTEN...
BUT IT DOESN'T MEAN **SQUAT!**

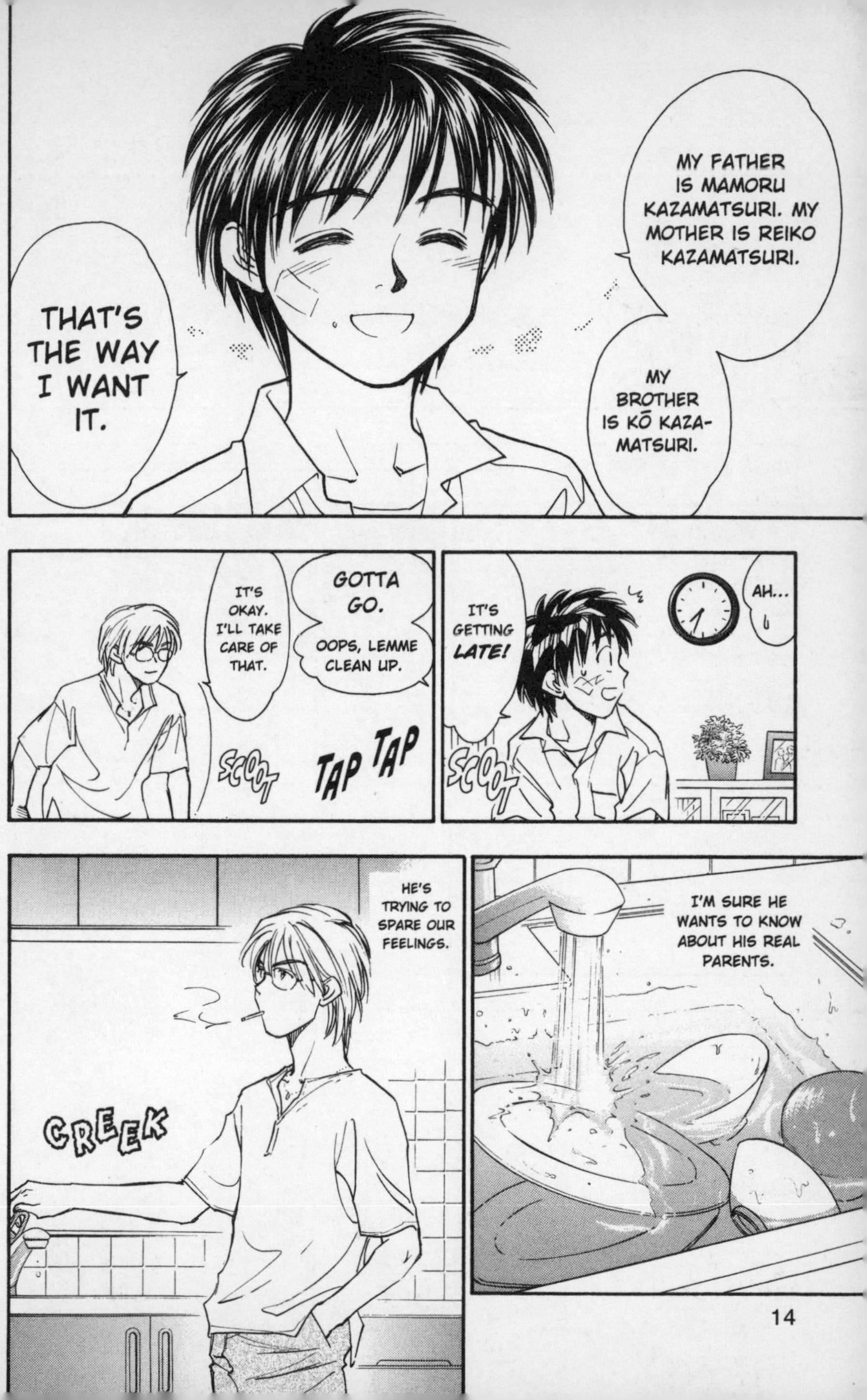
MY FATHER IS MAMORU KAZAMATSURI. MY MOTHER IS REIKO KAZAMATSURI.
MY BROTHER IS KŌ KAZA-MATSURI.
THAT'S THE WAY I WANT IT.
AH...
IT'S GETTING LATE!
SCOOT
GOTTA GO.
OOPS, LEMME CLEAN UP.
IT'S OKAY. I'LL TAKE CARE OF THAT.
TAP TAP
SCOOT
I'M SURE HE WANTS TO KNOW ABOUT HIS REAL PARENTS.
HE'S TRYING TO SPARE OUR FEELINGS.
CREEK

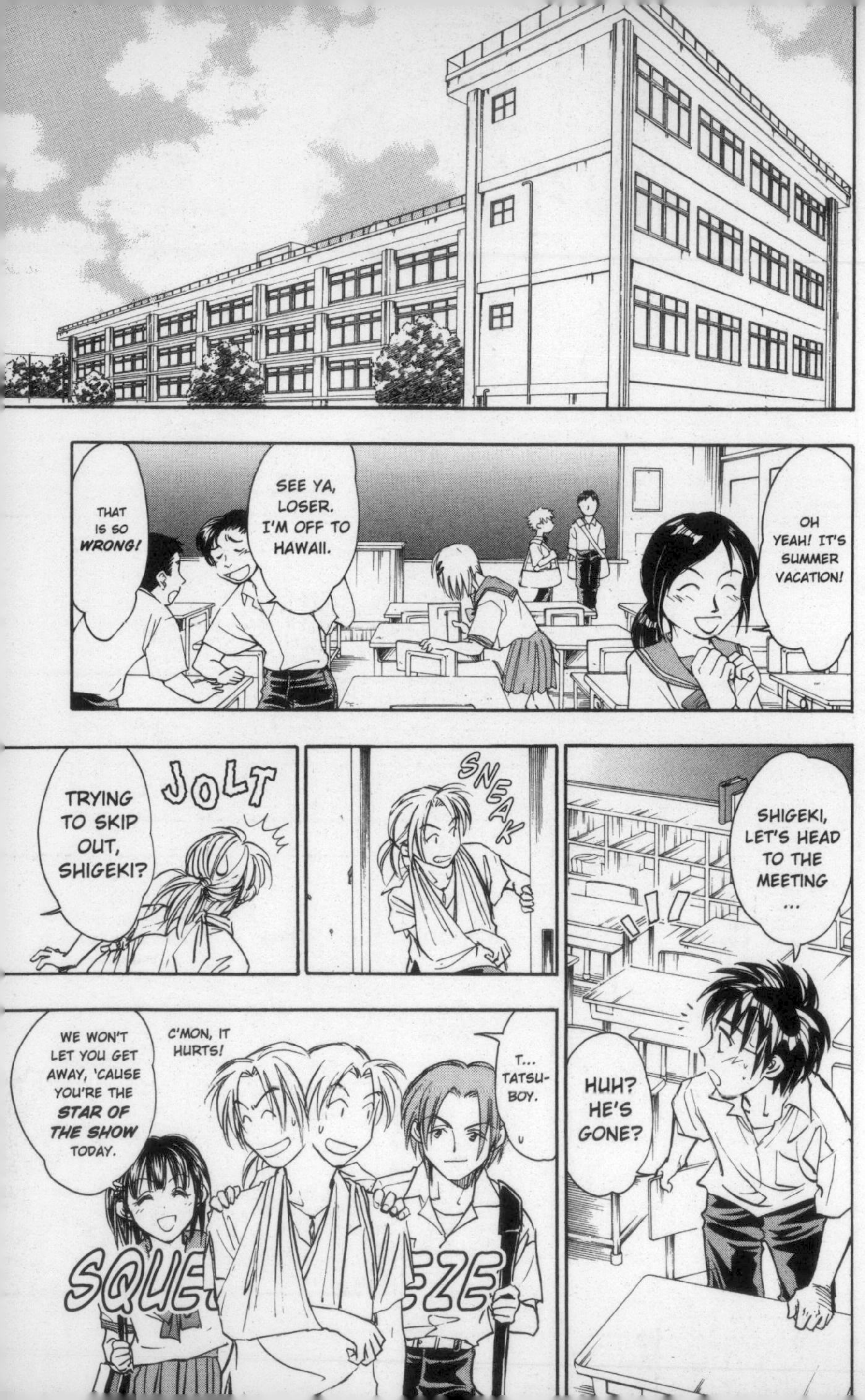
OH YEAH! IT'S SUMMER VACATION!
SEE YA, LOSER. I'M OFF TO HAWAII.
THAT IS SO WRONG!
SHIGEKI, LET'S HEAD TO THE MEETING ...
HUH? HE'S GONE?
SNEAK
JOLT
TRYING TO SKIP OUT, SHIGEKI?
T... TATSU-BOY.
C'MON, IT HURTS!
WE WON'T LET YOU GET AWAY, 'CAUSE YOU'RE THE STAR OF THE SHOW TODAY.
SQUEEZE

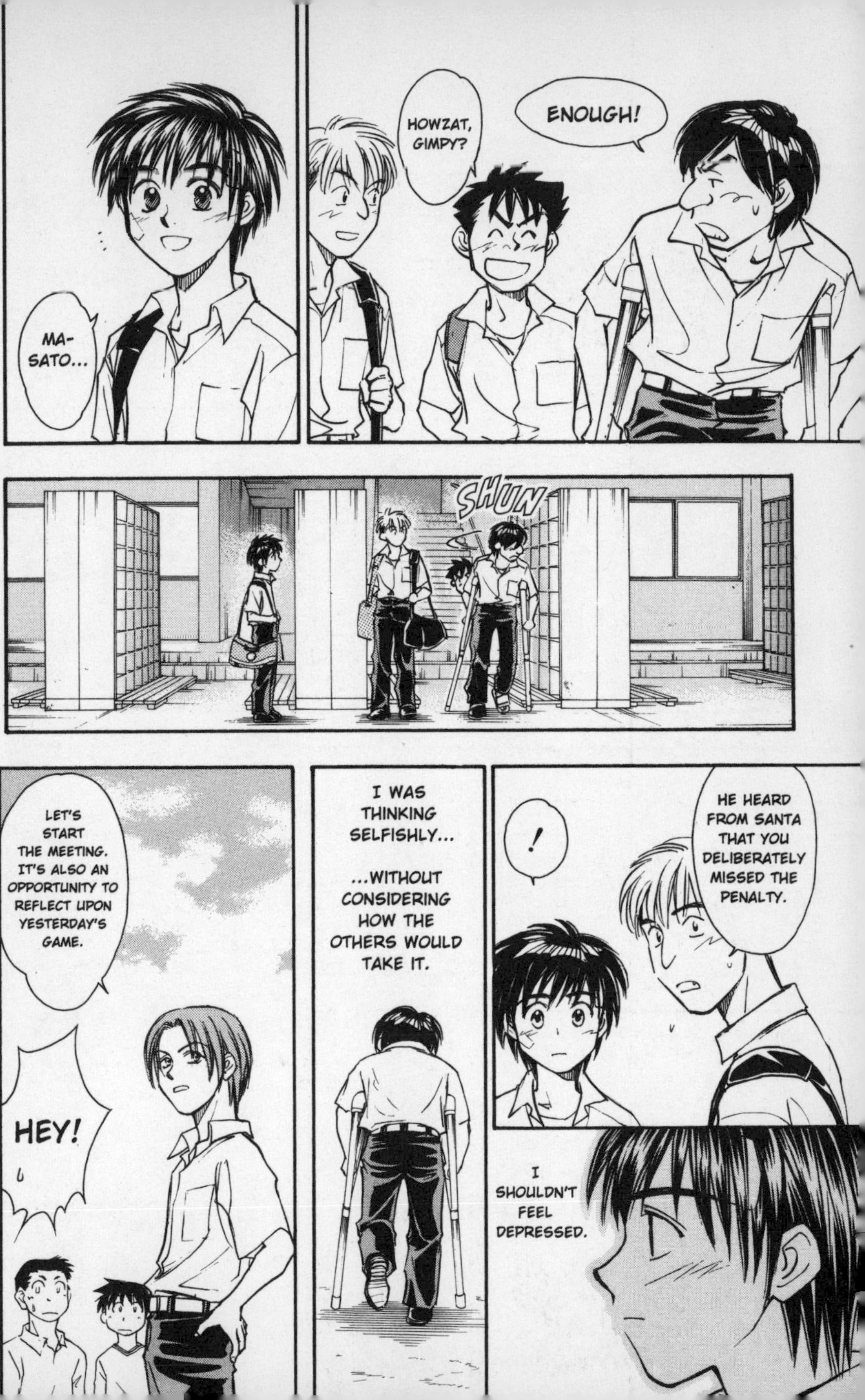
HOWZAT, GIMPY?
ENOUGH!
MA-SATO...
SHUN
HE HEARD FROM SANTA THAT YOU DELIBERATELY MISSED THE PENALTY.
!
I SHOULDN'T FEEL DEPRESSED.
I WAS THINKING SELFISHLY...
...WITHOUT CONSIDERING HOW THE OTHERS WOULD TAKE IT.
LET'S START THE MEETING. IT'S ALSO AN OPPORTUNITY TO REFLECT UPON YESTERDAY'S GAME.
HEY!

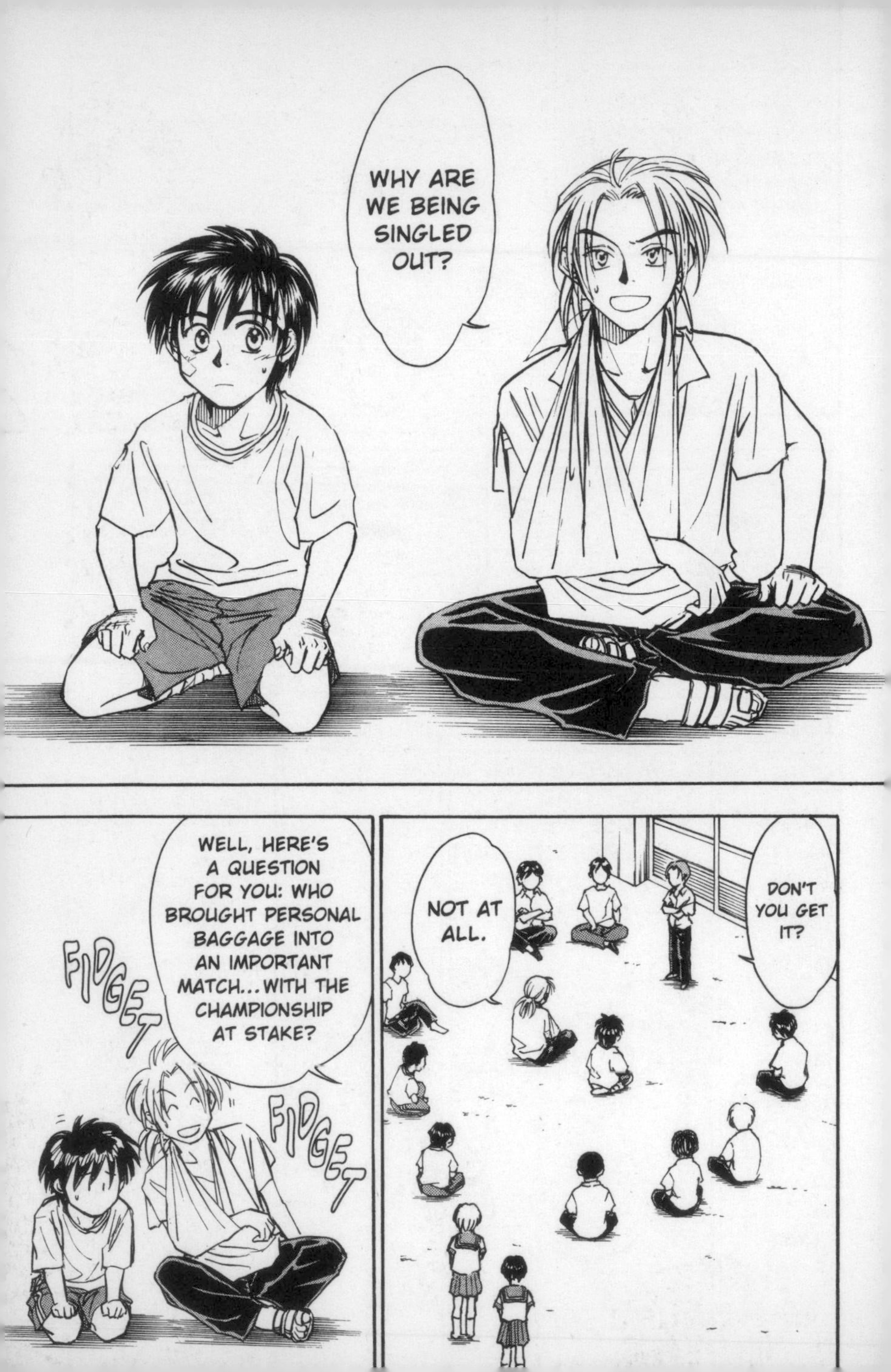
WHY ARE WE BEING SINGLED OUT?
DON'T YOU GET IT?
NOT AT ALL.
WELL, HERE'S A QUESTION FOR YOU: WHO BROUGHT PERSONAL BAGGAGE INTO AN IMPORTANT MATCH...WITH THE CHAMPIONSHIP AT STAKE?
FIDGET
FIDGET

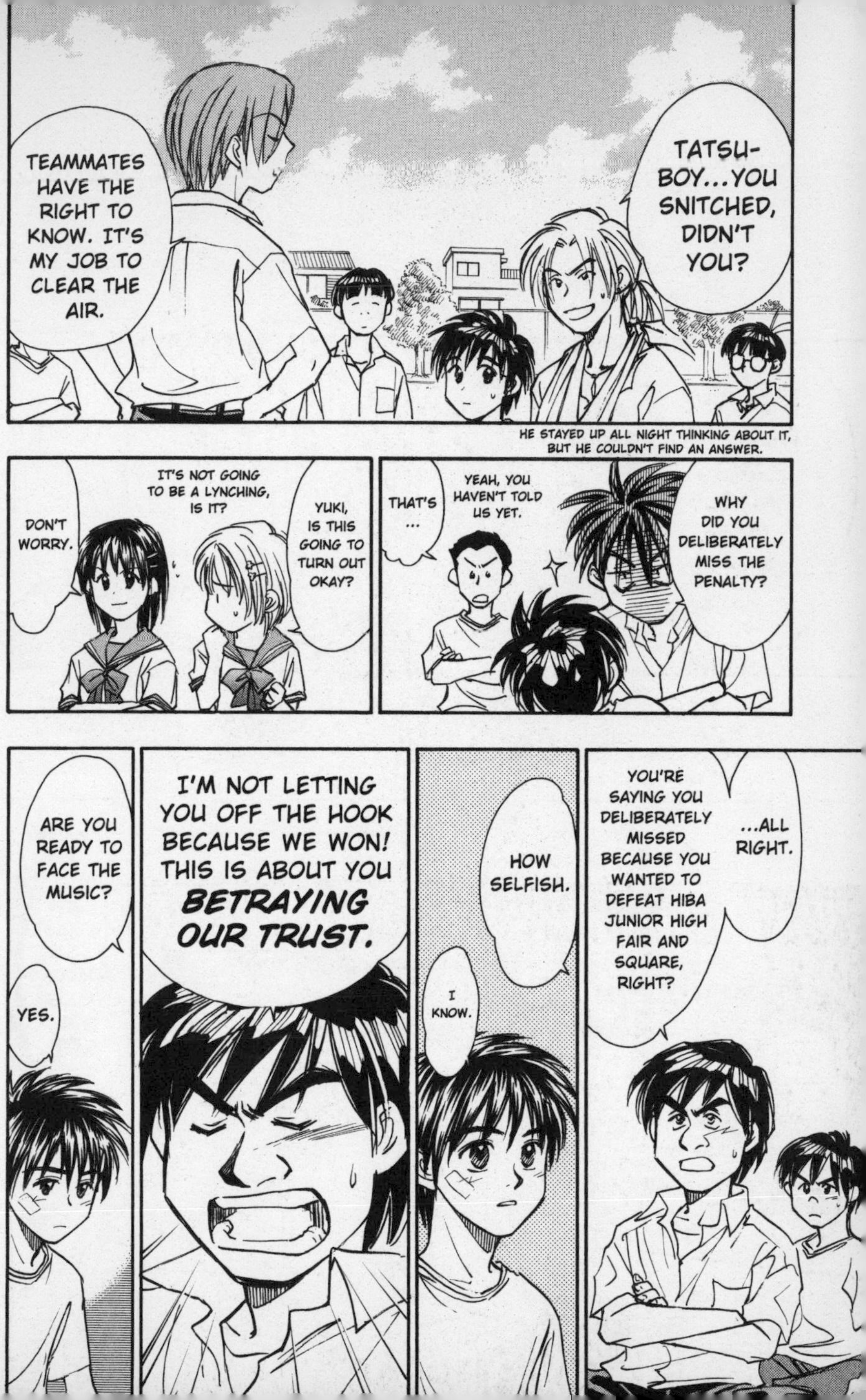
TATSU-BOY...YOU SNITCHED, DIDN'T YOU?
TEAMMATES HAVE THE RIGHT TO KNOW. IT'S MY JOB TO CLEAR THE AIR.
HE STAYED UP ALL NIGHT THINKING ABOUT IT, BUT HE COULDN'T FIND AN ANSWER.
WHY DID YOU DELIBERATELY MISS THE PENALTY?
YEAH, YOU HAVEN'T TOLD US YET.
THAT'S ...
YUKI, IS THIS GOING TO TURN OUT OKAY?
IT'S NOT GOING TO BE A LYNCHING, IS IT?
DON'T WORRY.
...ALL RIGHT.
YOU'RE SAYING YOU DELIBERATELY MISSED BECAUSE YOU WANTED TO DEFEAT HIBA JUNIOR HIGH FAIR AND SQUARE, RIGHT?
HOW SELFISH.
I KNOW.
I'M NOT LETTING YOU OFF THE HOOK BECAUSE WE WON! THIS IS ABOUT YOU BETRAYING OUR TRUST.
ARE YOU READY TO FACE THE MUSIC?
YES.

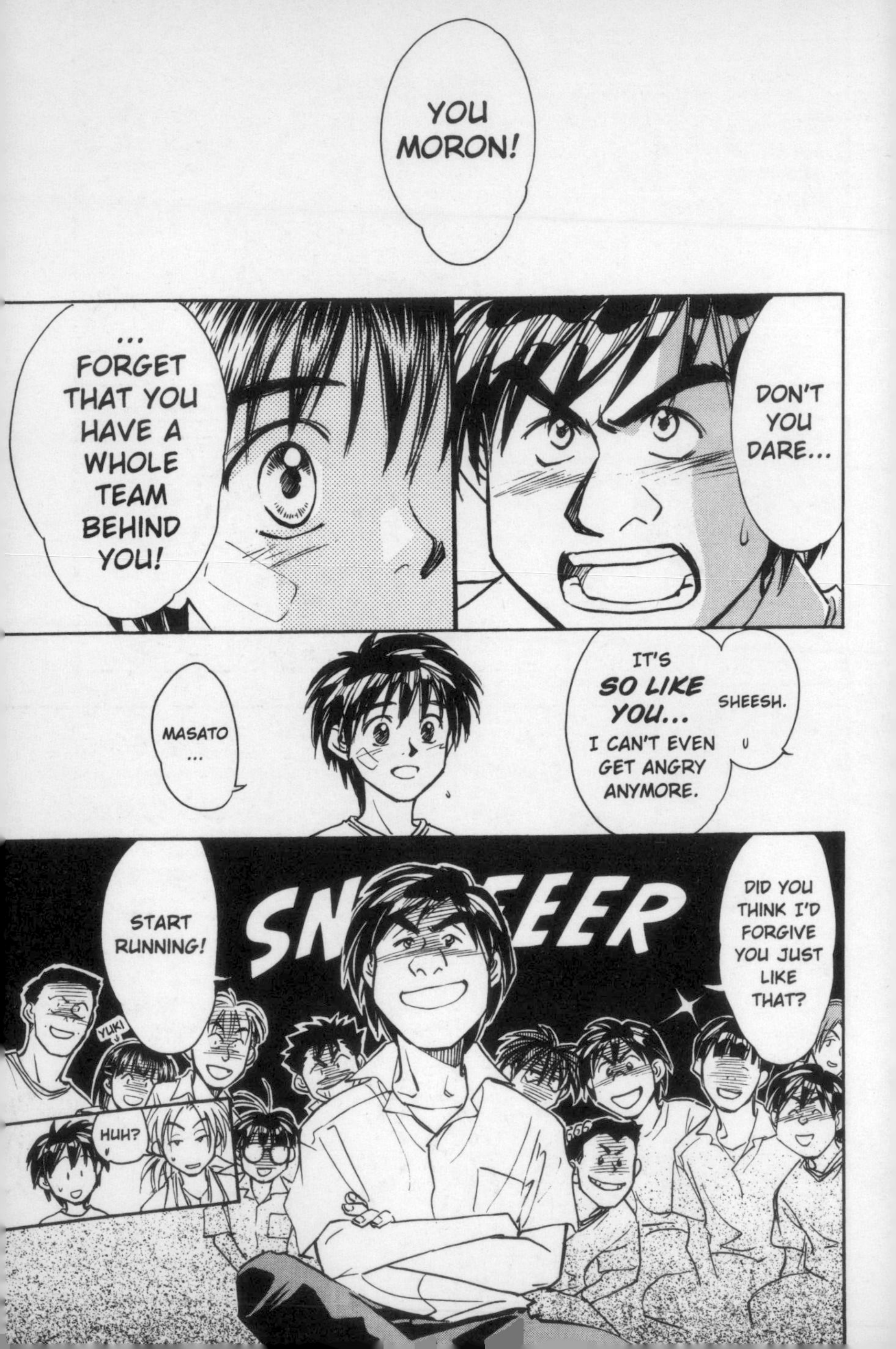
YOU MORON!
DON'T YOU DARE...
... FORGET THAT YOU HAVE A WHOLE TEAM BEHIND YOU!
IT'S SO LIKE YOU... I CAN'T EVEN GET ANGRY ANYMORE.
SHEESH.
MASATO ...
DID YOU THINK I'D FORGIVE YOU JUST LIKE THAT?
START RUNNING!
YUKI
HUH?

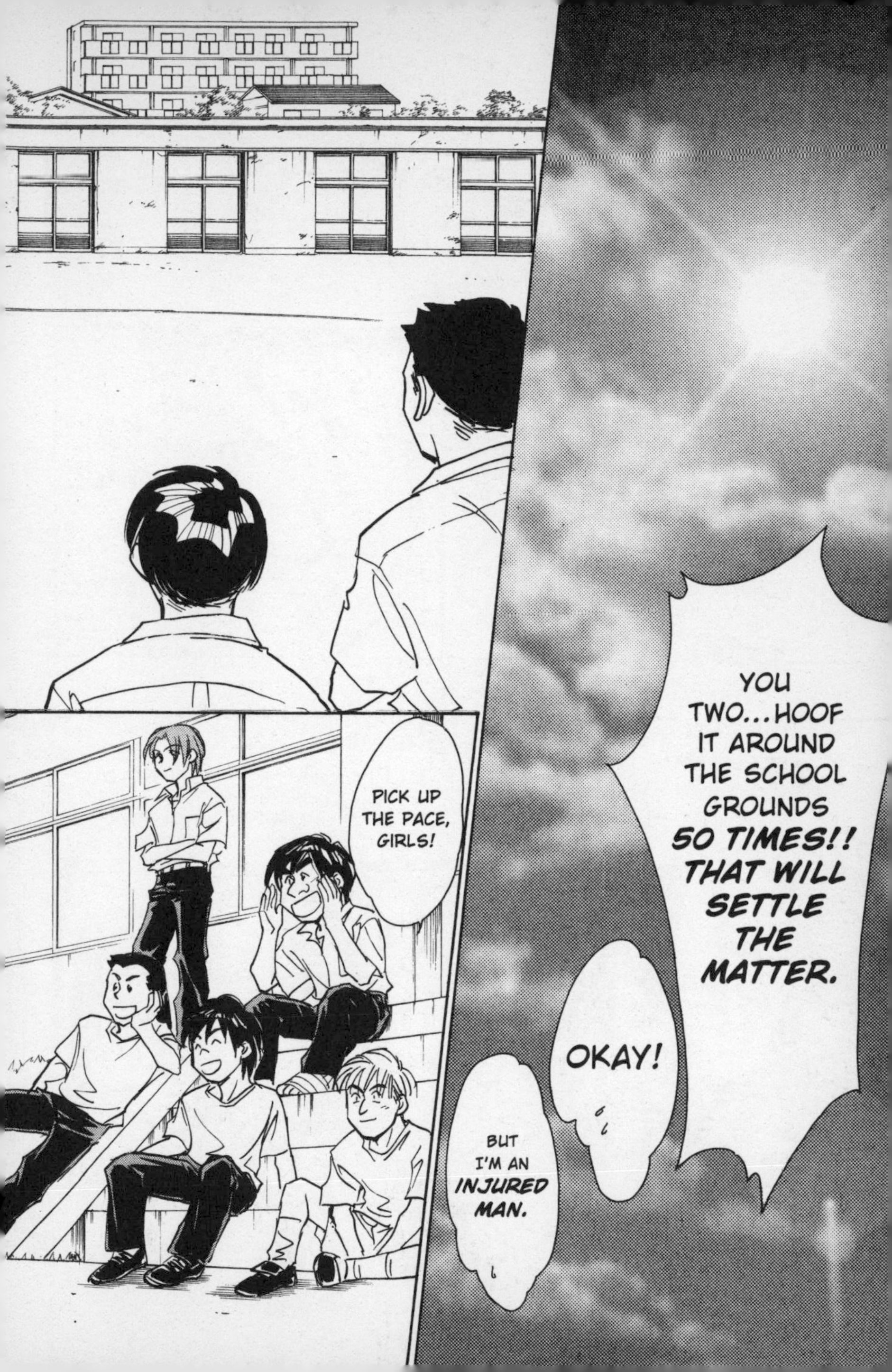
YOU TWO...HOOF IT AROUND THE SCHOOL GROUNDS 50 TIMES!! THAT WILL SETTLE THE MATTER.
OKAY!
BUT I'M AN INJURED MAN.
PICK UP THE PACE, GIRLS!

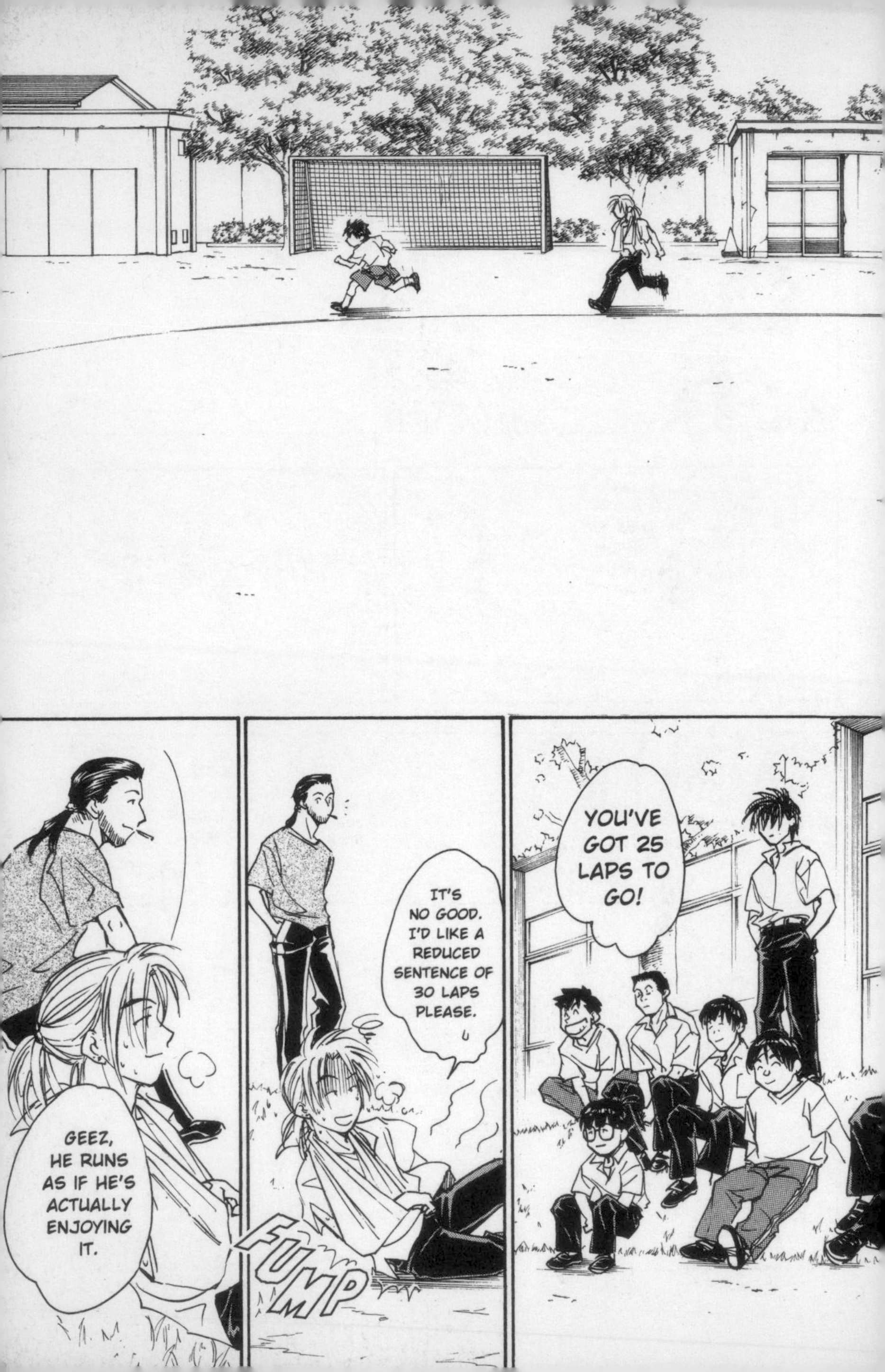
YOU'VE GOT 25 LAPS TO GO!
IT'S NO GOOD. I'D LIKE A REDUCED SENTENCE OF 30 LAPS PLEASE.
FUMP
GEEZ, HE RUNS AS IF HE'S ACTUALLY ENJOYING IT.

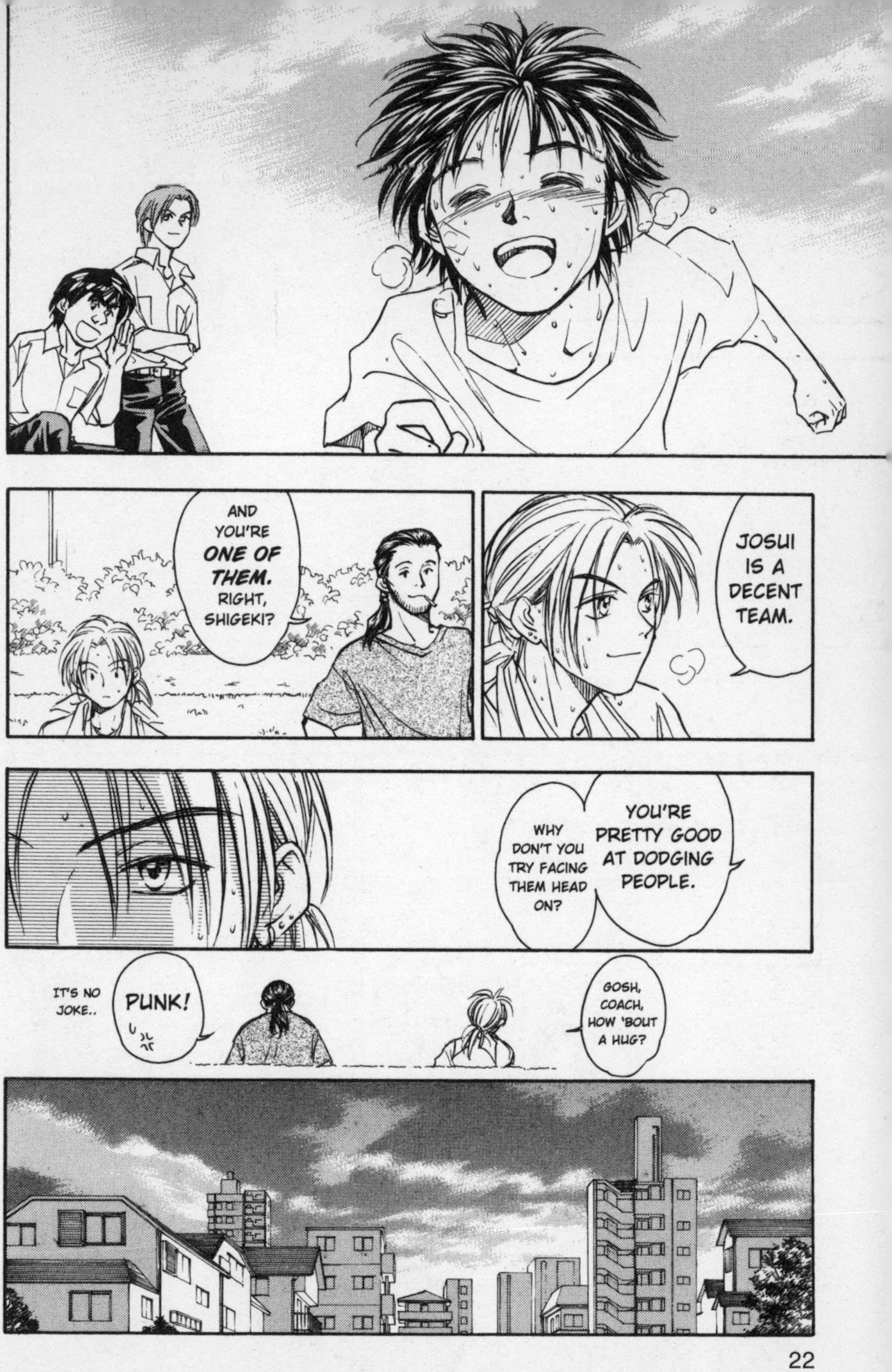
JOSUI IS A DECENT TEAM.
AND YOU'RE ONE OF THEM. RIGHT, SHIGEKI?
YOU'RE PRETTY GOOD AT DODGING PEOPLE.
WHY DON'T YOU TRY FACING THEM HEAD ON?
GOSH, COACH, HOW 'BOUT A HUG?
PUNK!
IT'S NO JOKE..

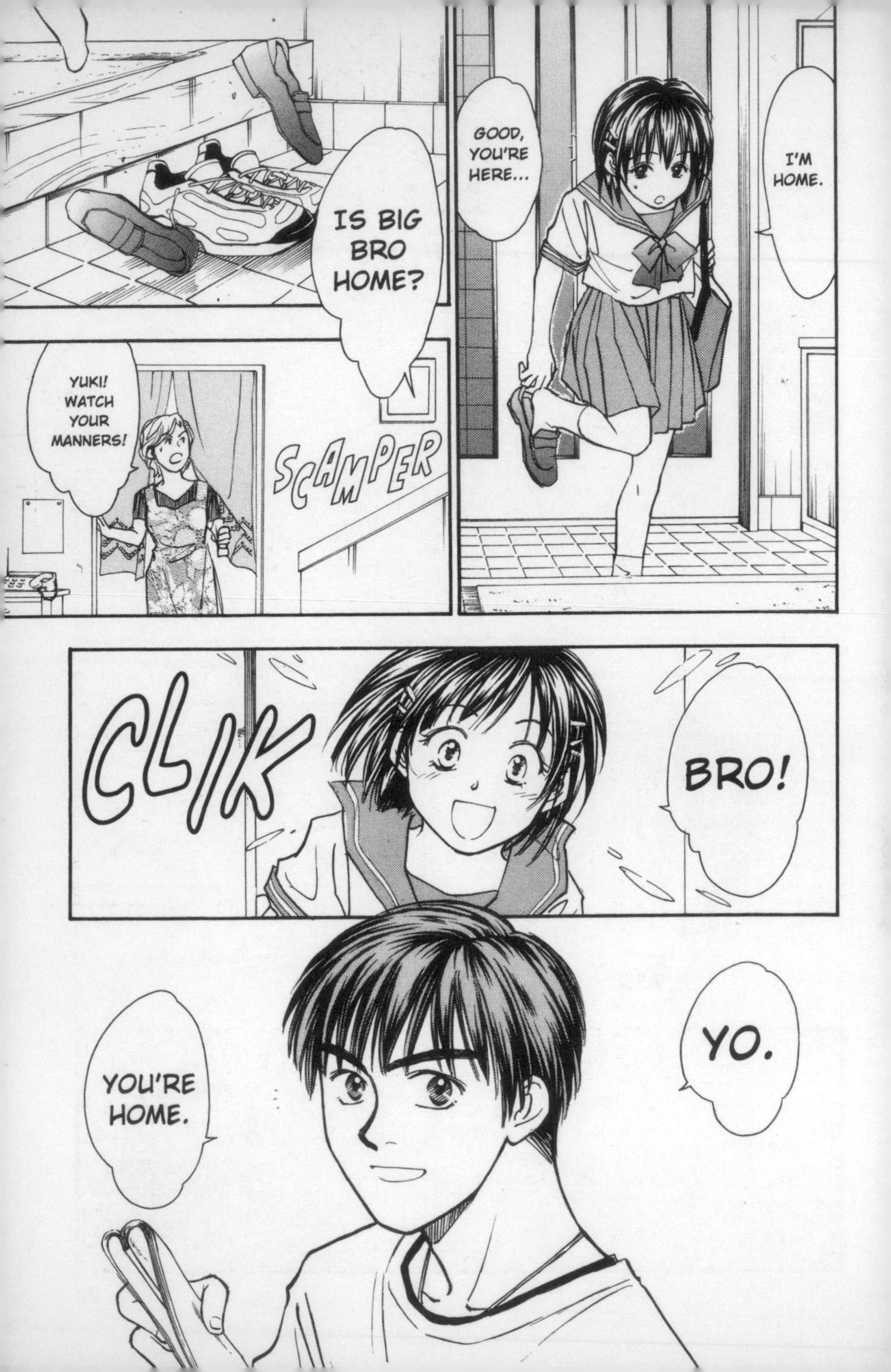
I'M HOME.
GOOD, YOU'RE HERE...
IS BIG BRO HOME?
SCAMPER
YUKI! WATCH YOUR MANNERS!
BRO!
CLIK
YO.
YOU'RE HOME.

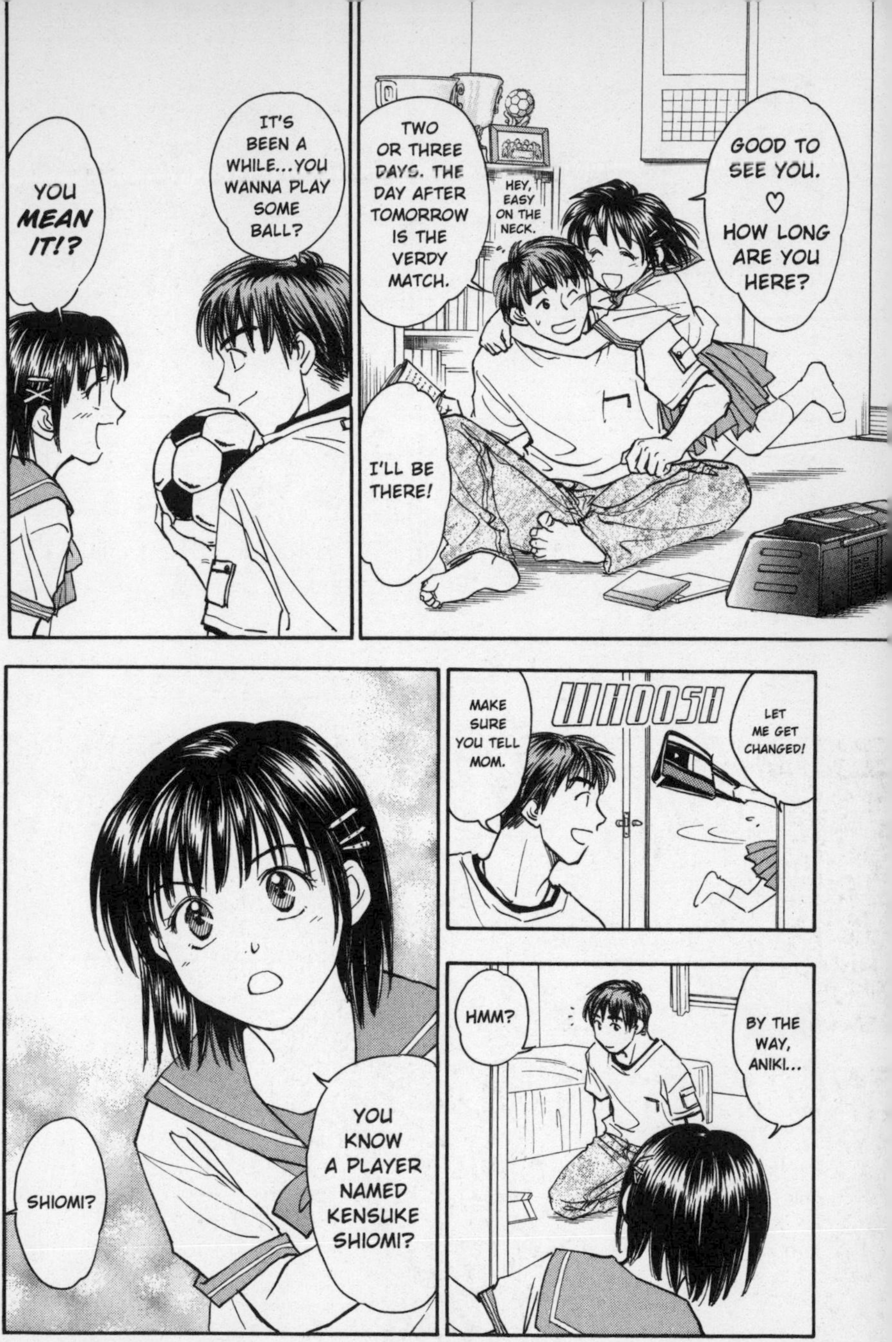
GOOD TO SEE YOU. ♡ HOW LONG ARE YOU HERE?
HEY, EASY ON THE NECK.
TWO OR THREE DAYS. THE DAY AFTER TOMORROW IS THE VERDY MATCH.
I'LL BE THERE!
IT'S BEEN A WHILE...YOU WANNA PLAY SOME BALL?
YOU *MEAN IT!?*
LET ME GET CHANGED!
WHOOSH
MAKE SURE YOU TELL MOM.
BY THE WAY, ANIKI...
HMM?
YOU KNOW A PLAYER NAMED KENSUKE SHIOMI?
SHIOMI?

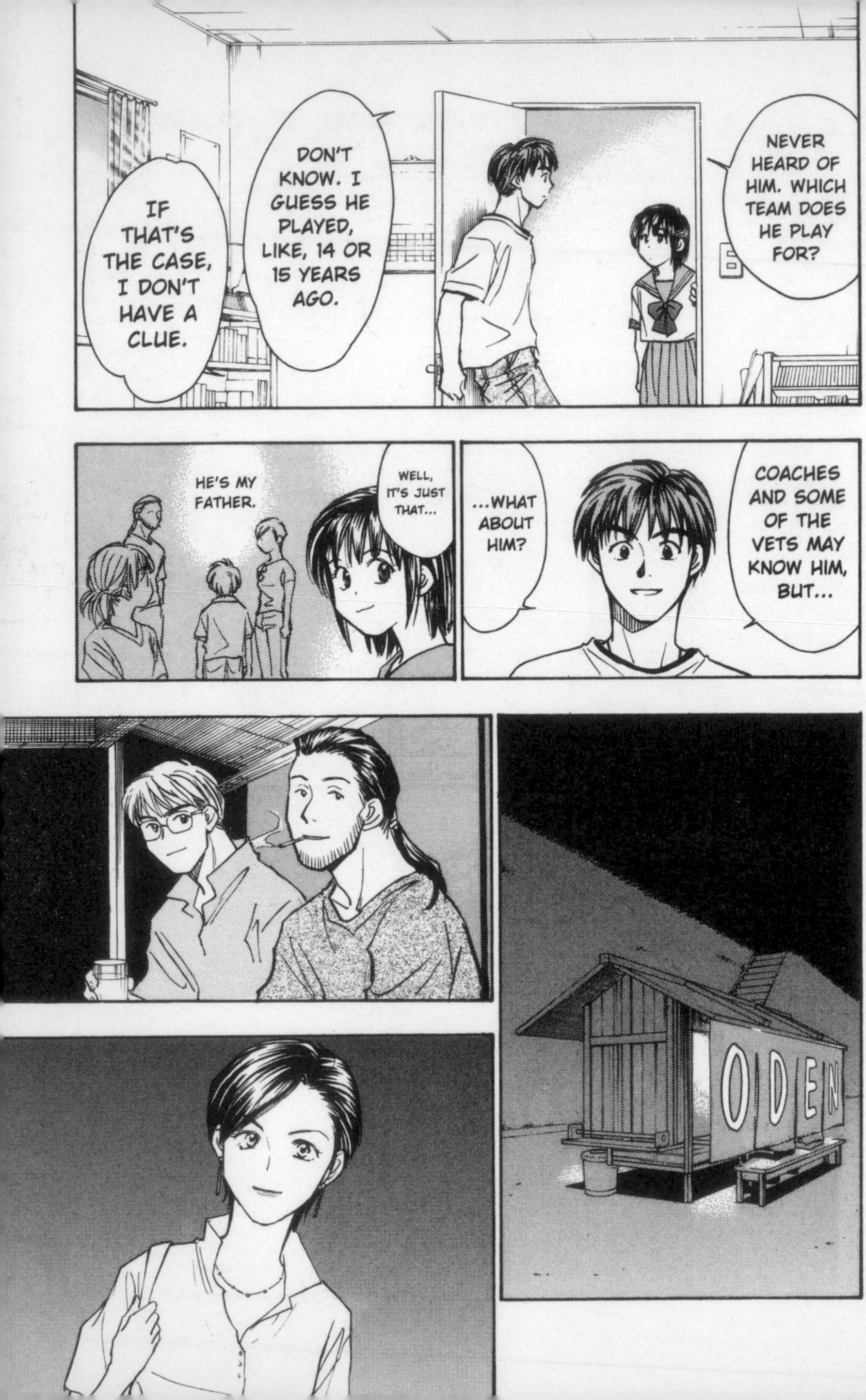
NEVER HEARD OF HIM. WHICH TEAM DOES HE PLAY FOR?
DON'T KNOW. I GUESS HE PLAYED, LIKE, 14 OR 15 YEARS AGO.
IF THAT'S THE CASE, I DON'T HAVE A CLUE.
COACHES AND SOME OF THE VETS MAY KNOW HIM, BUT...
...WHAT ABOUT HIM?
WELL, IT'S JUST THAT...
HE'S MY FATHER.
ODEN

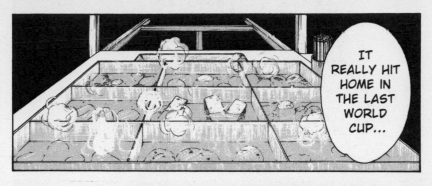

IT REALLY HIT HOME IN THE LAST WORLD CUP...

COMPARED TO THE REST OF THE WORLD, JAPANESE SOCCER HAS SUCH A SHORT HISTORY AND...

...THAT JAPAN LACKS EXPERIENCE.

PRACTICALLY SPEAKING, WHAT DO YOU HAVE IN MIND?

...THERE ARE MANY THINGS TO BE DONE, SUCH AS STRENGTHENING THE J-LEAGUE, BUT...

...THE **KEY THING** IS TO CREATE A GOOD ENVIRONMENT FOR THE SPORT AND NURTURE YOUNG PLAYERS.

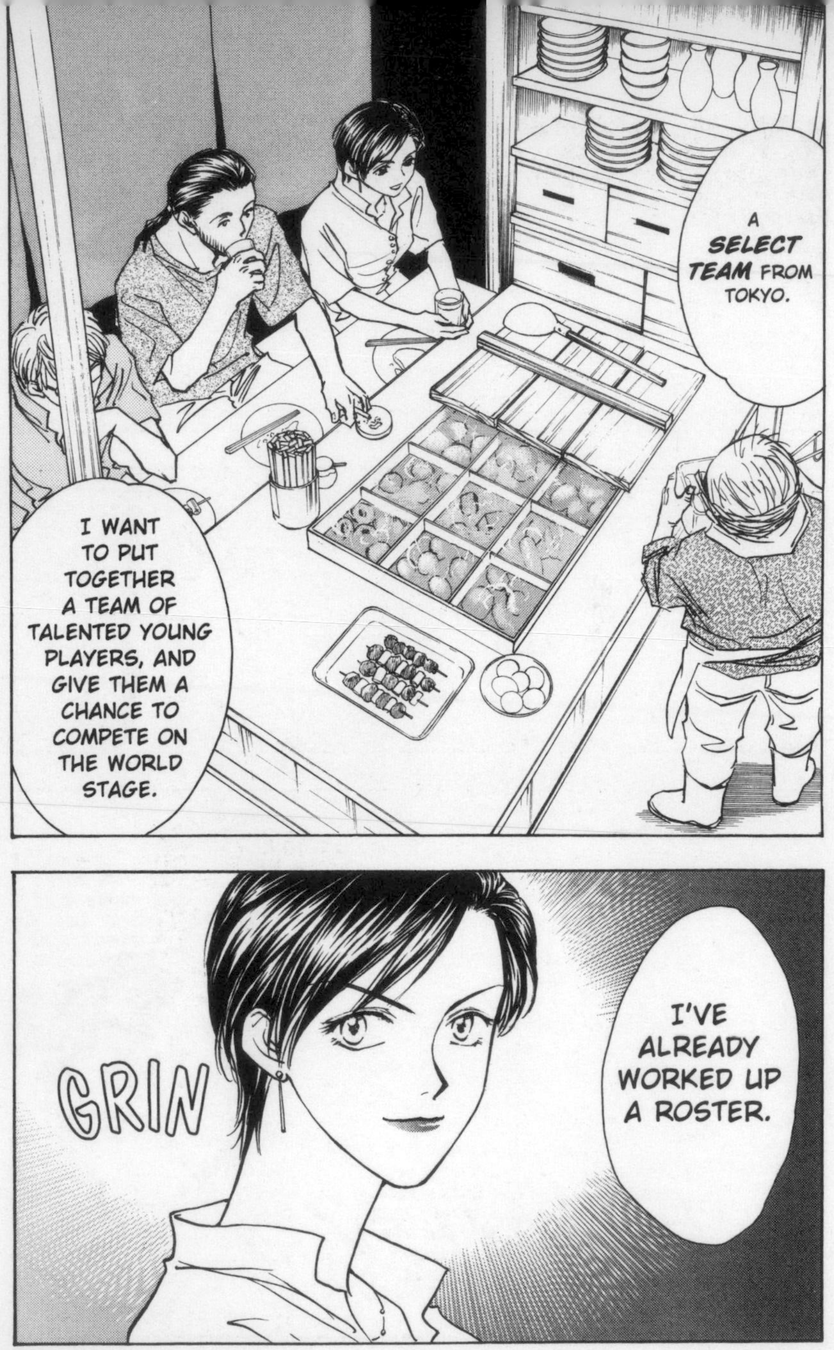
A SELECT TEAM FROM TOKYO.
I WANT TO PUT TOGETHER A TEAM OF TALENTED YOUNG PLAYERS, AND GIVE THEM A CHANCE TO COMPETE ON THE WORLD STAGE.
I'VE ALREADY WORKED UP A ROSTER.
GRIN

WHISTLE!™

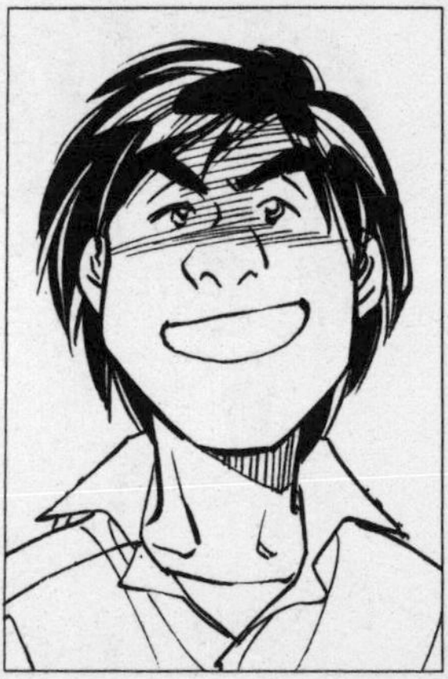

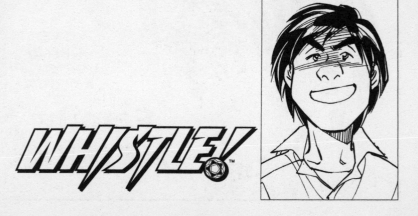

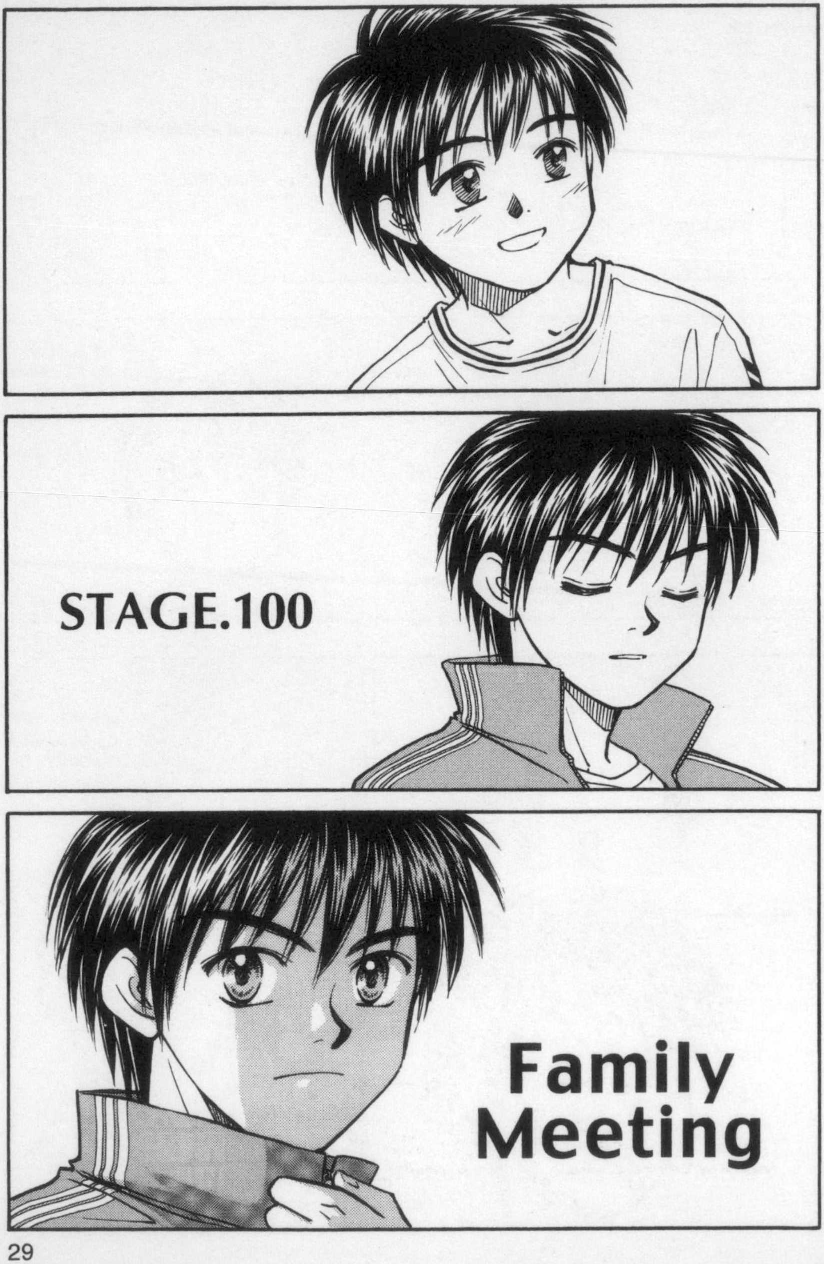
STAGE.100
Family Meeting

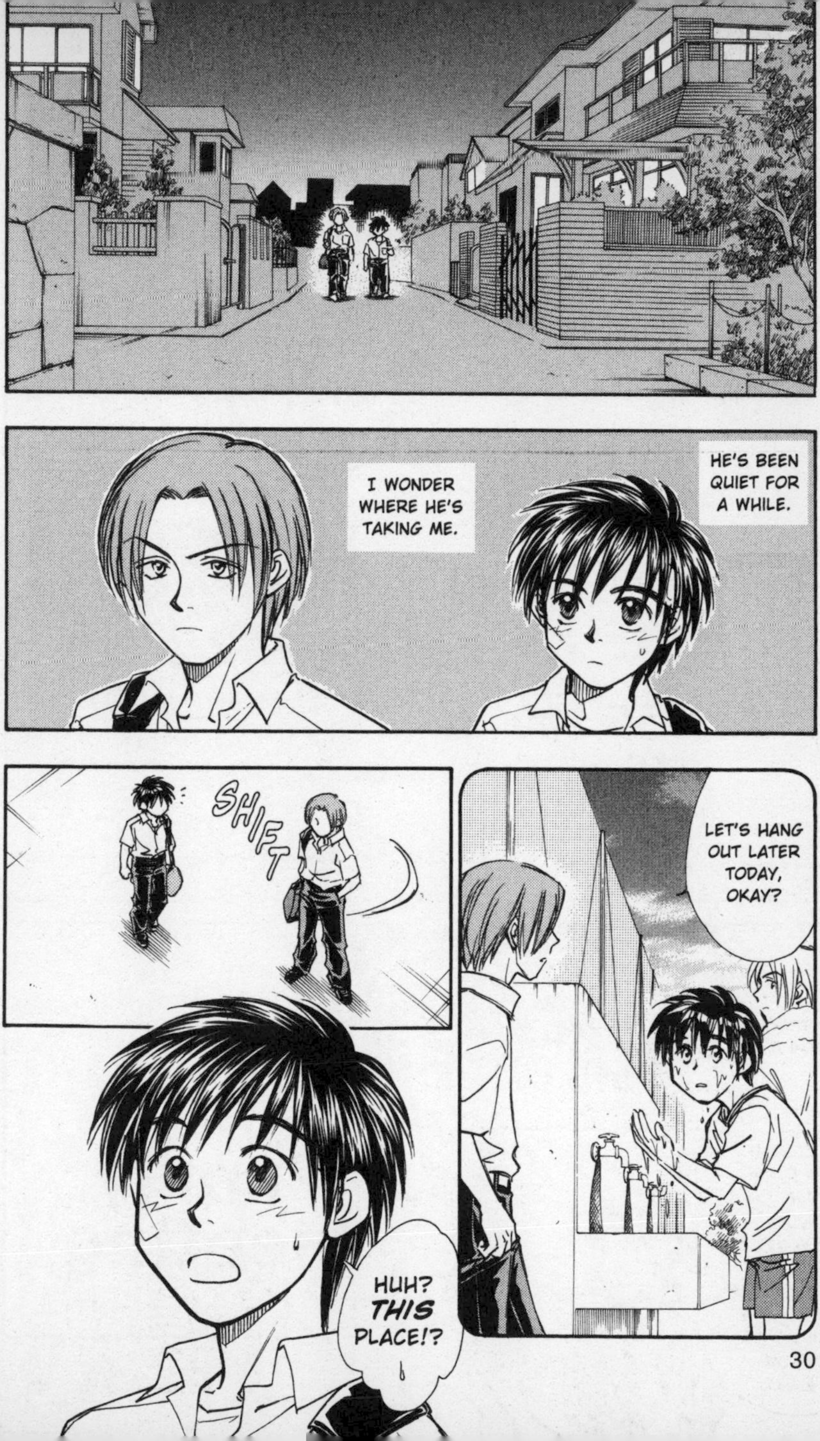
HE'S BEEN QUIET FOR A WHILE.
I WONDER WHERE HE'S TAKING ME.
LET'S HANG OUT LATER TODAY, OKAY?
SHIFT
HUH? THIS PLACE!?

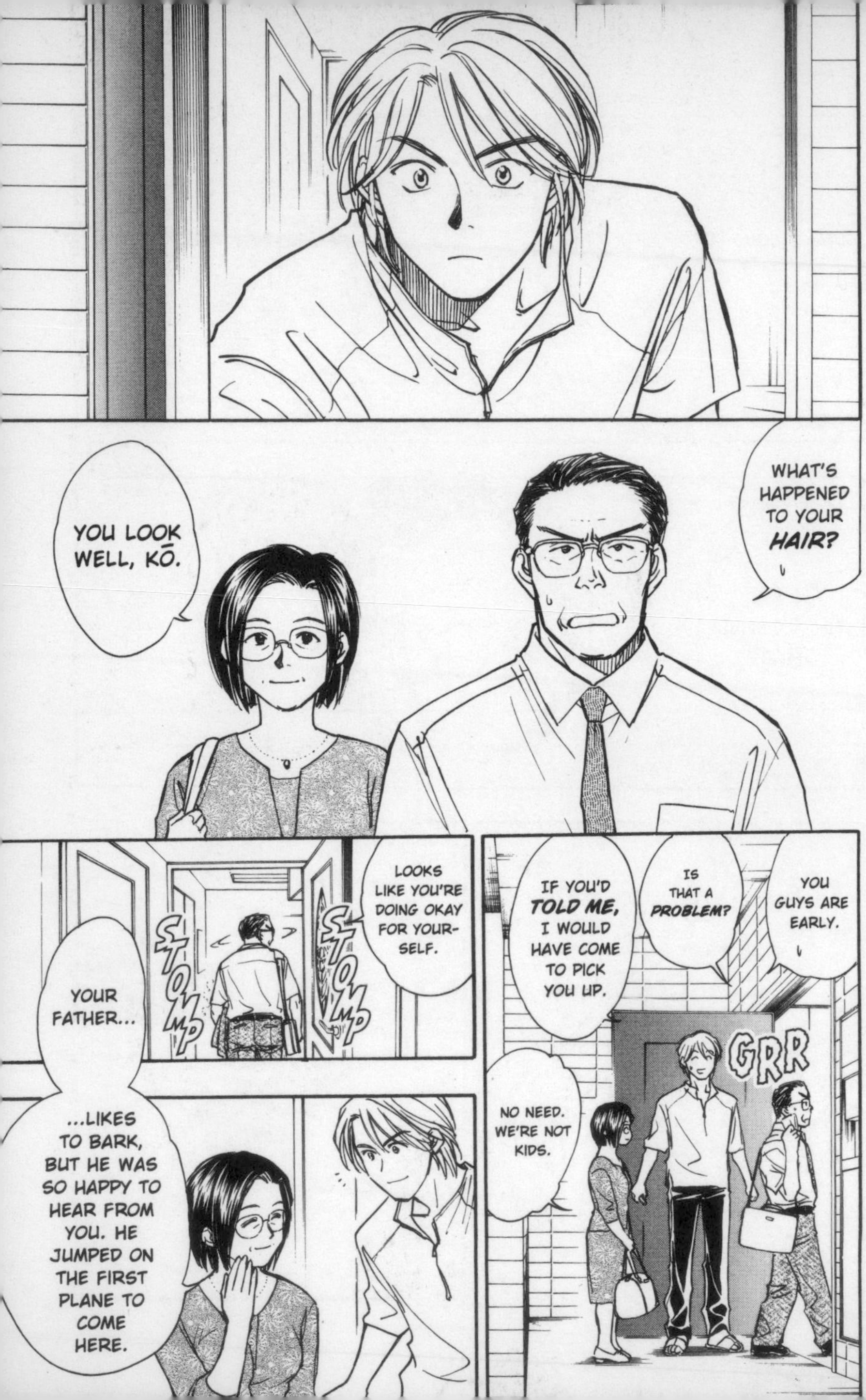
WHAT'S HAPPENED TO YOUR HAIR?
YOU LOOK WELL, KŌ.
YOU GUYS ARE EARLY.
IS THAT A PROBLEM?
IF YOU'D TOLD ME, I WOULD HAVE COME TO PICK YOU UP.
GRR
NO NEED. WE'RE NOT KIDS.
LOOKS LIKE YOU'RE DOING OKAY FOR YOUR-SELF.
STOMP
STOMP
YOUR FATHER...
...LIKES TO BARK, BUT HE WAS SO HAPPY TO HEAR FROM YOU. HE JUMPED ON THE FIRST PLANE TO COME HERE.

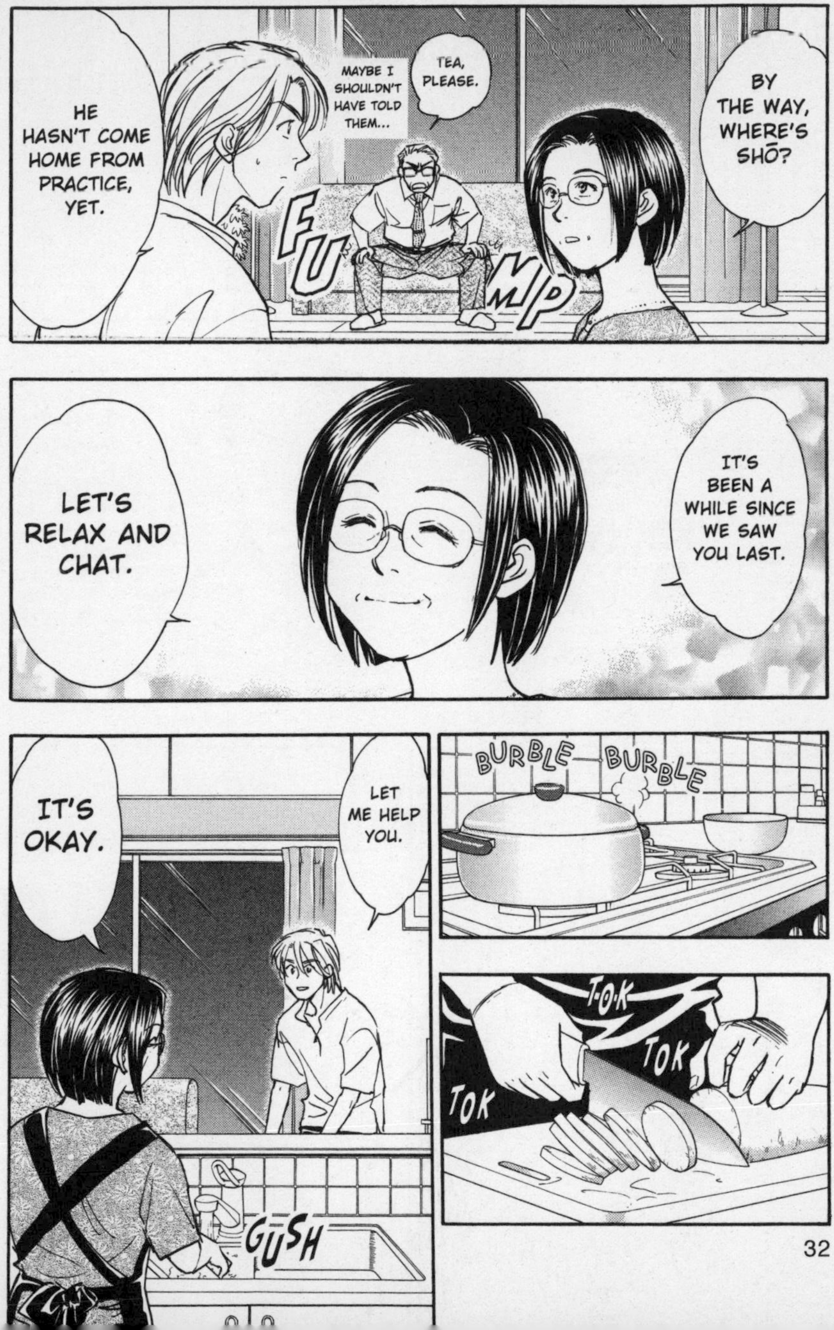
BY THE WAY, WHERE'S SHŌ?
TEA, PLEASE.
MAYBE I SHOULDN'T HAVE TOLD THEM...
FUMP
HE HASN'T COME HOME FROM PRACTICE, YET.
IT'S BEEN A WHILE SINCE WE SAW YOU LAST.
LET'S RELAX AND CHAT.
BURBLE BURBLE
T·O·K
TOK
TOK
LET ME HELP YOU.
IT'S OKAY.
GUSH

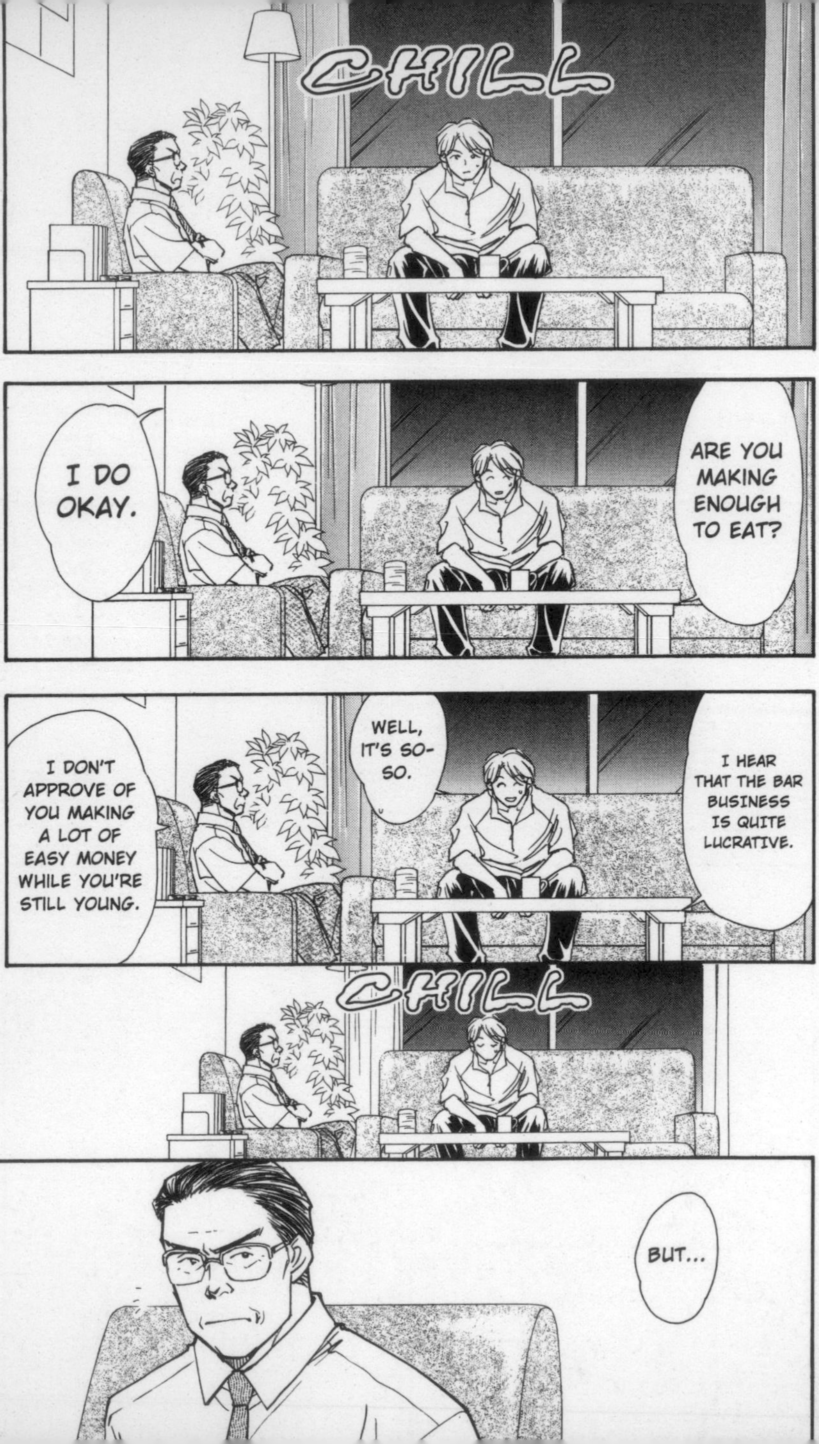
CHILL
ARE YOU MAKING ENOUGH TO EAT?
I DO OKAY.
I HEAR THAT THE BAR BUSINESS IS QUITE LUCRATIVE.
WELL, IT'S SO-SO.
I DON'T APPROVE OF YOU MAKING A LOT OF EASY MONEY WHILE YOU'RE STILL YOUNG.
CHILL
BUT...

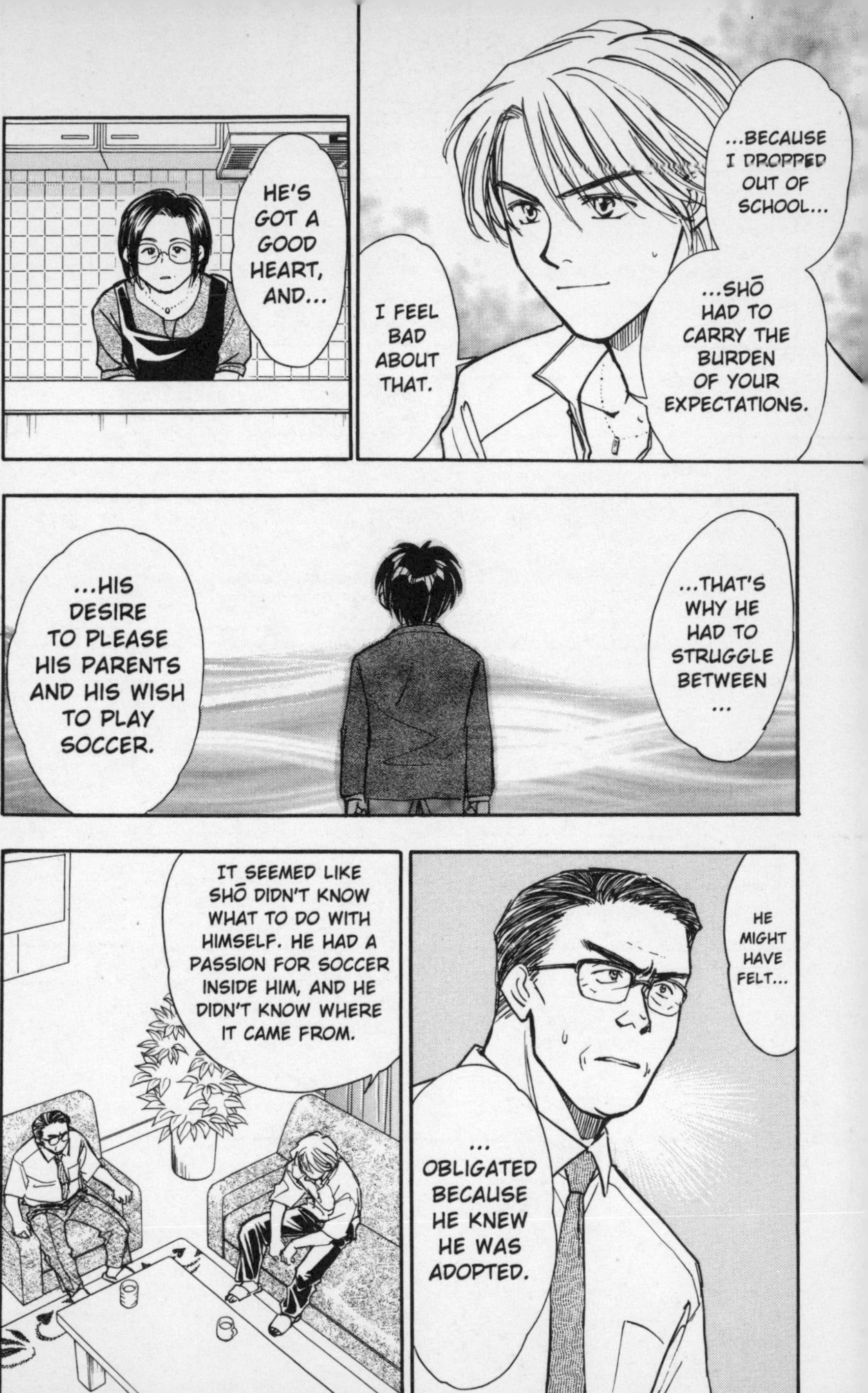
...BECAUSE I DROPPED OUT OF SCHOOL...
...SHŌ HAD TO CARRY THE BURDEN OF YOUR EXPECTATIONS.
I FEEL BAD ABOUT THAT.
HE'S GOT A GOOD HEART, AND...
...THAT'S WHY HE HAD TO STRUGGLE BETWEEN ...
...HIS DESIRE TO PLEASE HIS PARENTS AND HIS WISH TO PLAY SOCCER.
HE MIGHT HAVE FELT...
...OBLIGATED BECAUSE HE KNEW HE WAS ADOPTED.
IT SEEMED LIKE SHŌ DIDN'T KNOW WHAT TO DO WITH HIMSELF. HE HAD A PASSION FOR SOCCER INSIDE HIM, AND HE DIDN'T KNOW WHERE IT CAME FROM.

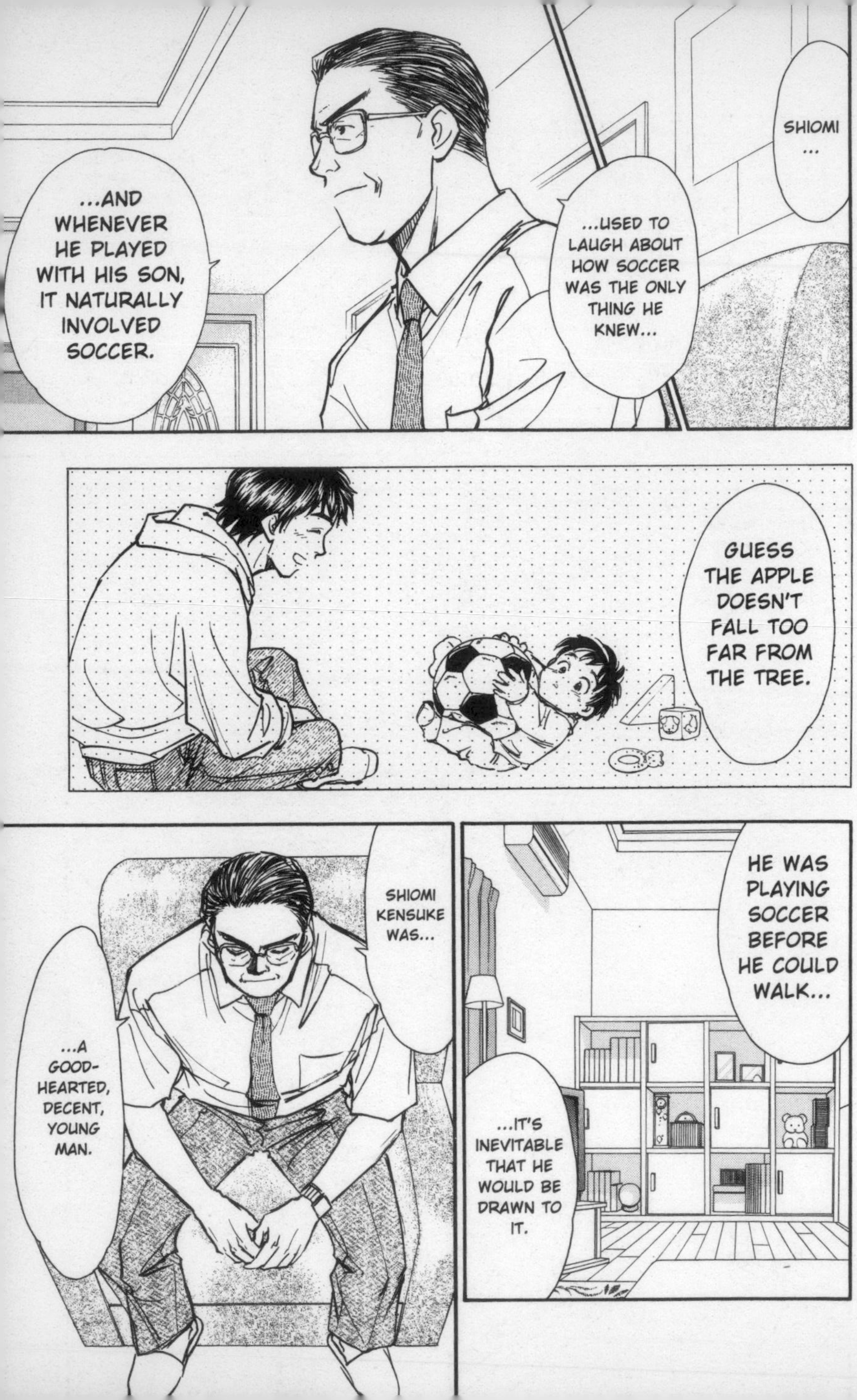
SHIOMI ...
...USED TO LAUGH ABOUT HOW SOCCER WAS THE ONLY THING HE KNEW...
...AND WHENEVER HE PLAYED WITH HIS SON, IT NATURALLY INVOLVED SOCCER.
GUESS THE APPLE DOESN'T FALL TOO FAR FROM THE TREE.
HE WAS PLAYING SOCCER BEFORE HE COULD WALK...
...IT'S INEVITABLE THAT HE WOULD BE DRAWN TO IT.
SHIOMI KENSUKE WAS...
...A GOOD-HEARTED, DECENT, YOUNG MAN.

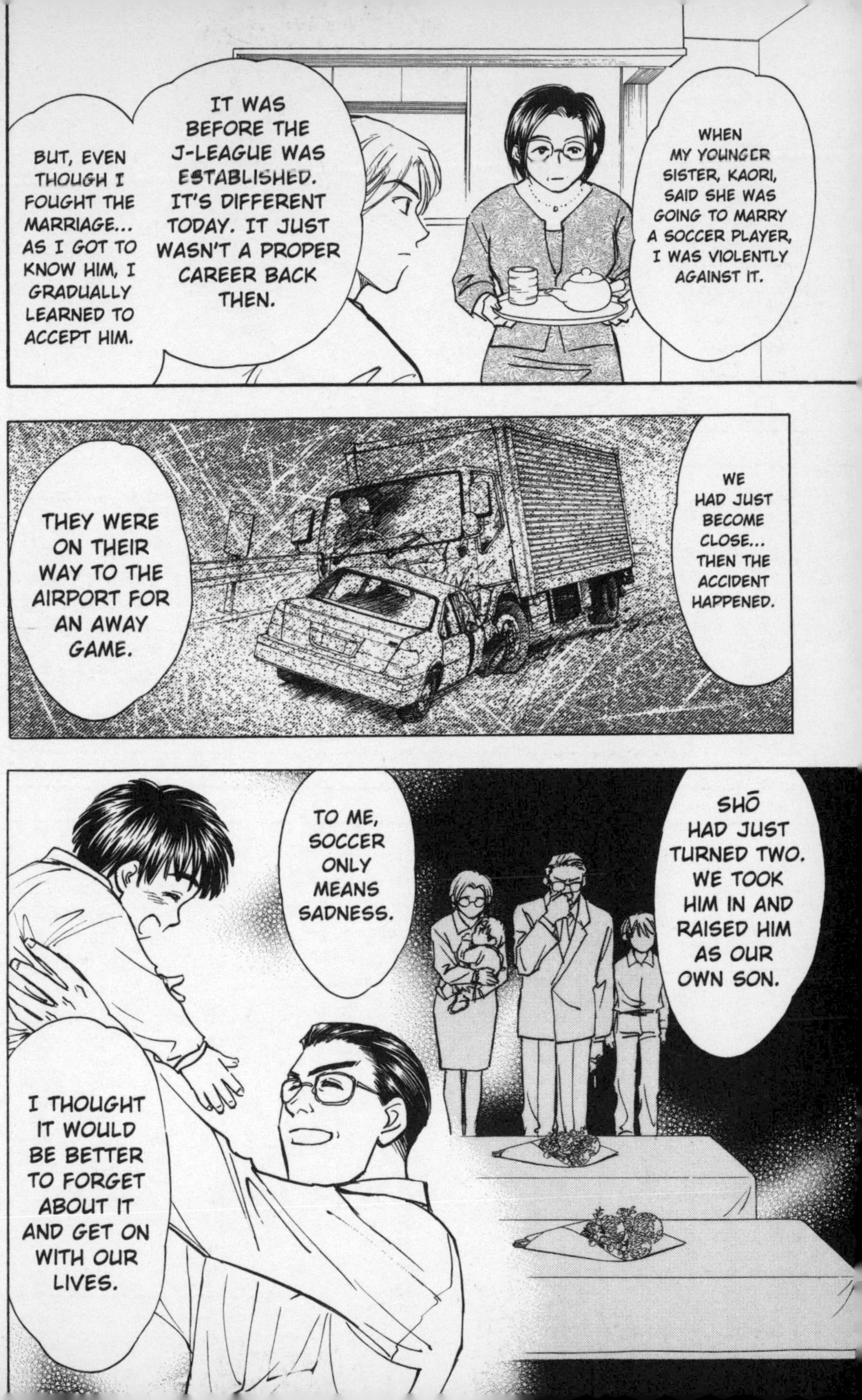
WHEN MY YOUNGER SISTER, KAORI, SAID SHE WAS GOING TO MARRY A SOCCER PLAYER, I WAS VIOLENTLY AGAINST IT.
IT WAS BEFORE THE J-LEAGUE WAS ESTABLISHED. IT'S DIFFERENT TODAY. IT JUST WASN'T A PROPER CAREER BACK THEN.
BUT, EVEN THOUGH I FOUGHT THE MARRIAGE... AS I GOT TO KNOW HIM, I GRADUALLY LEARNED TO ACCEPT HIM.
WE HAD JUST BECOME CLOSE... THEN THE ACCIDENT HAPPENED.
THEY WERE ON THEIR WAY TO THE AIRPORT FOR AN AWAY GAME.
SHŌ HAD JUST TURNED TWO. WE TOOK HIM IN AND RAISED HIM AS OUR OWN SON.
TO ME, SOCCER ONLY MEANS SADNESS.
I THOUGHT IT WOULD BE BETTER TO FORGET ABOUT IT AND GET ON WITH OUR LIVES.

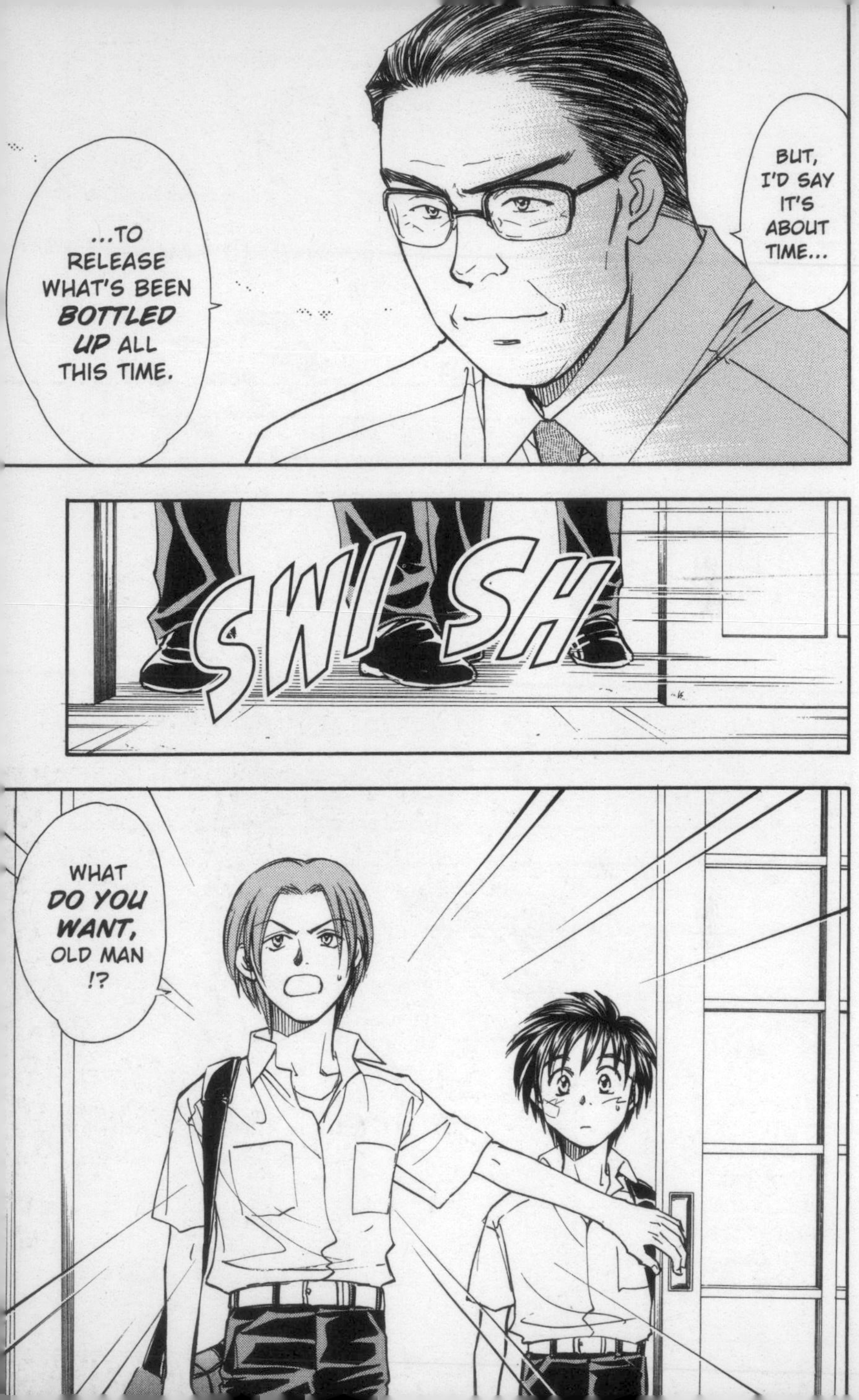
BUT, I'D SAY IT'S ABOUT TIME...
...TO RELEASE WHAT'S BEEN BOTTLED UP ALL THIS TIME.
SWISH
WHAT DO YOU WANT, OLD MAN !?

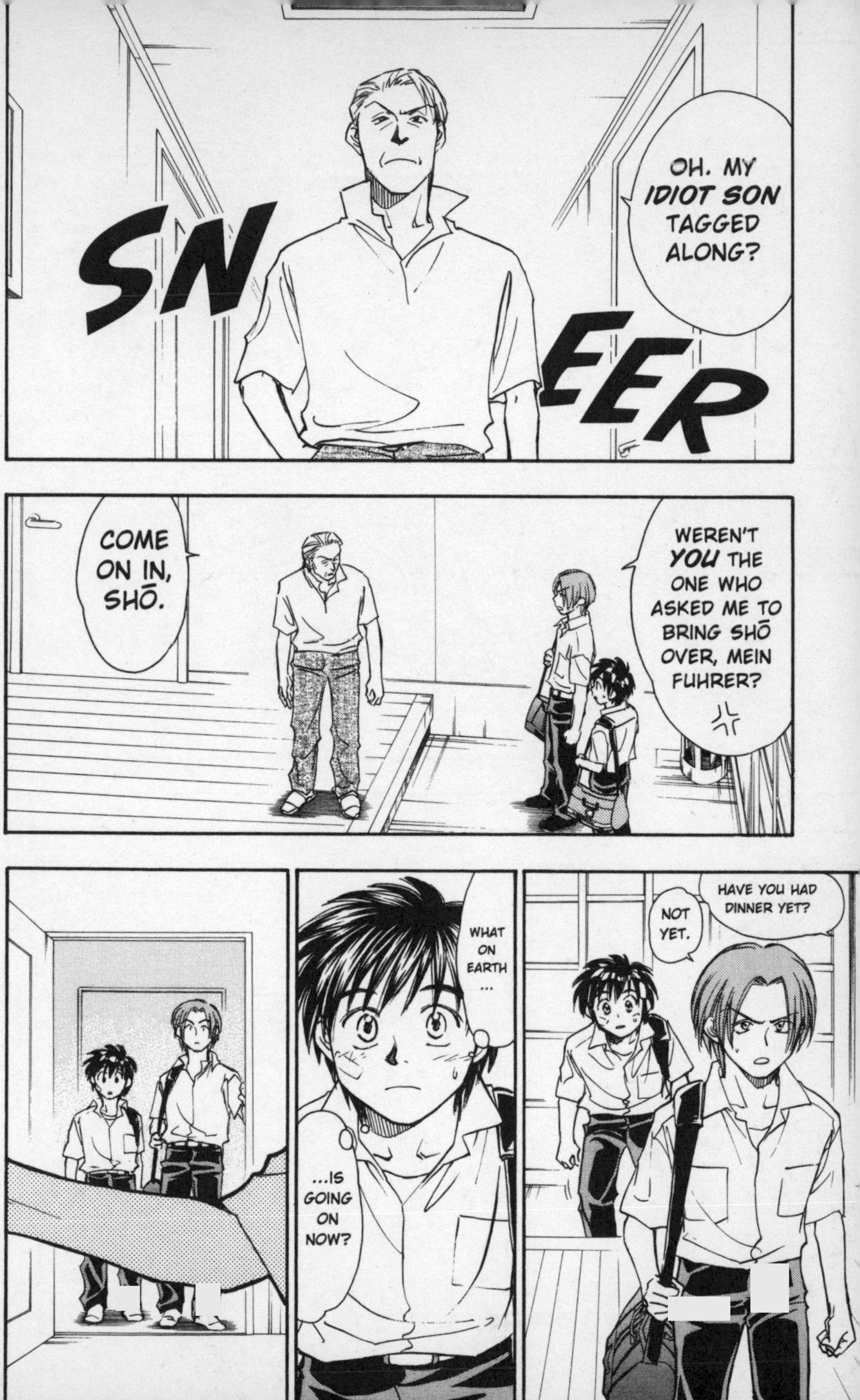
OH. MY IDIOT SON TAGGED ALONG?
SNEER
WEREN'T YOU THE ONE WHO ASKED ME TO BRING SHŌ OVER, MEIN FUHRER?
COME ON IN, SHŌ.
HAVE YOU HAD DINNER YET?
NOT YET.
WHAT ON EARTH ...
...IS GOING ON NOW?

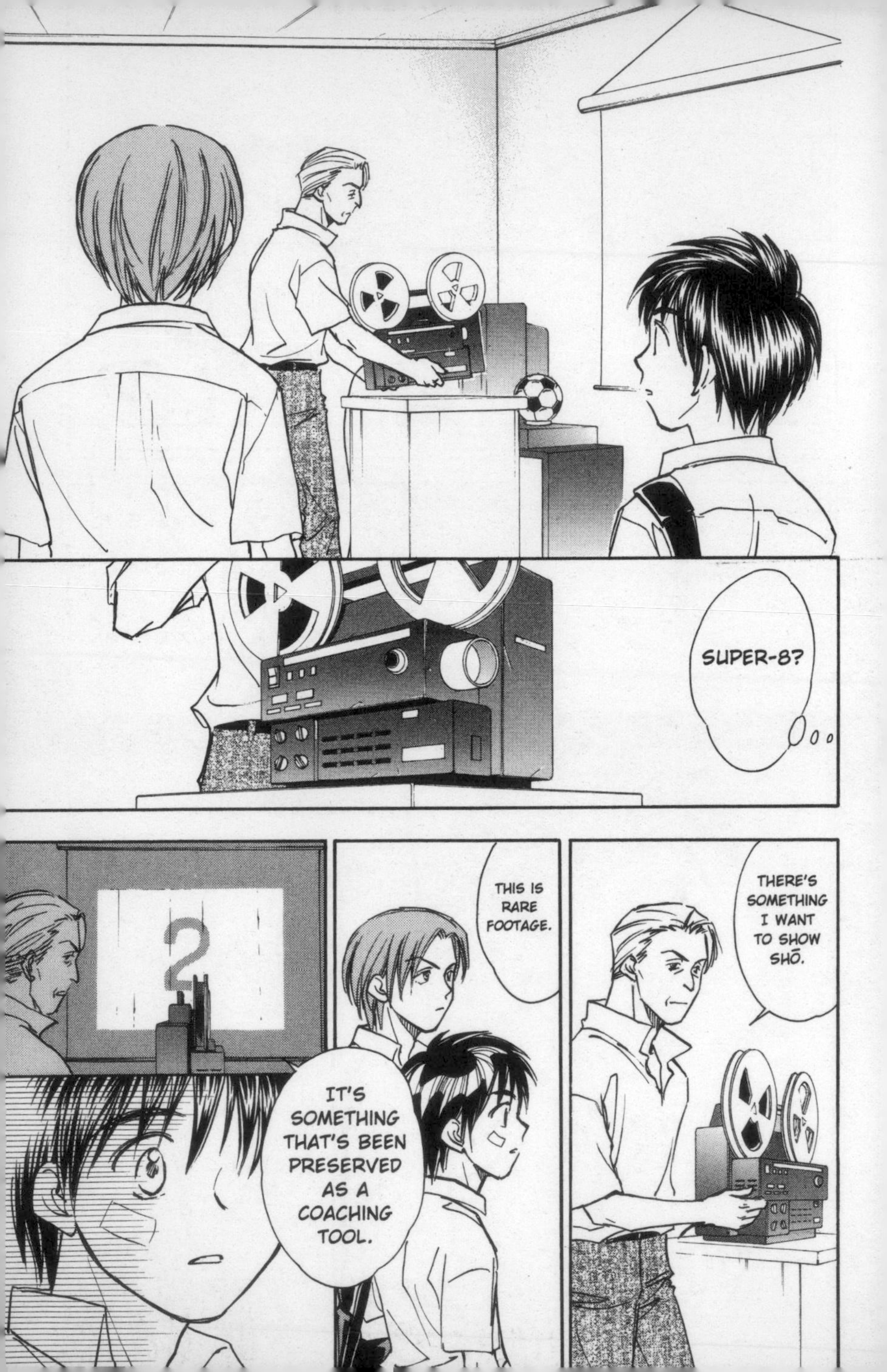
SUPER-8?
THERE'S SOMETHING I WANT TO SHOW SHŌ.
THIS IS RARE FOOTAGE.
IT'S SOMETHING THAT'S BEEN PRESERVED AS A COACHING TOOL.

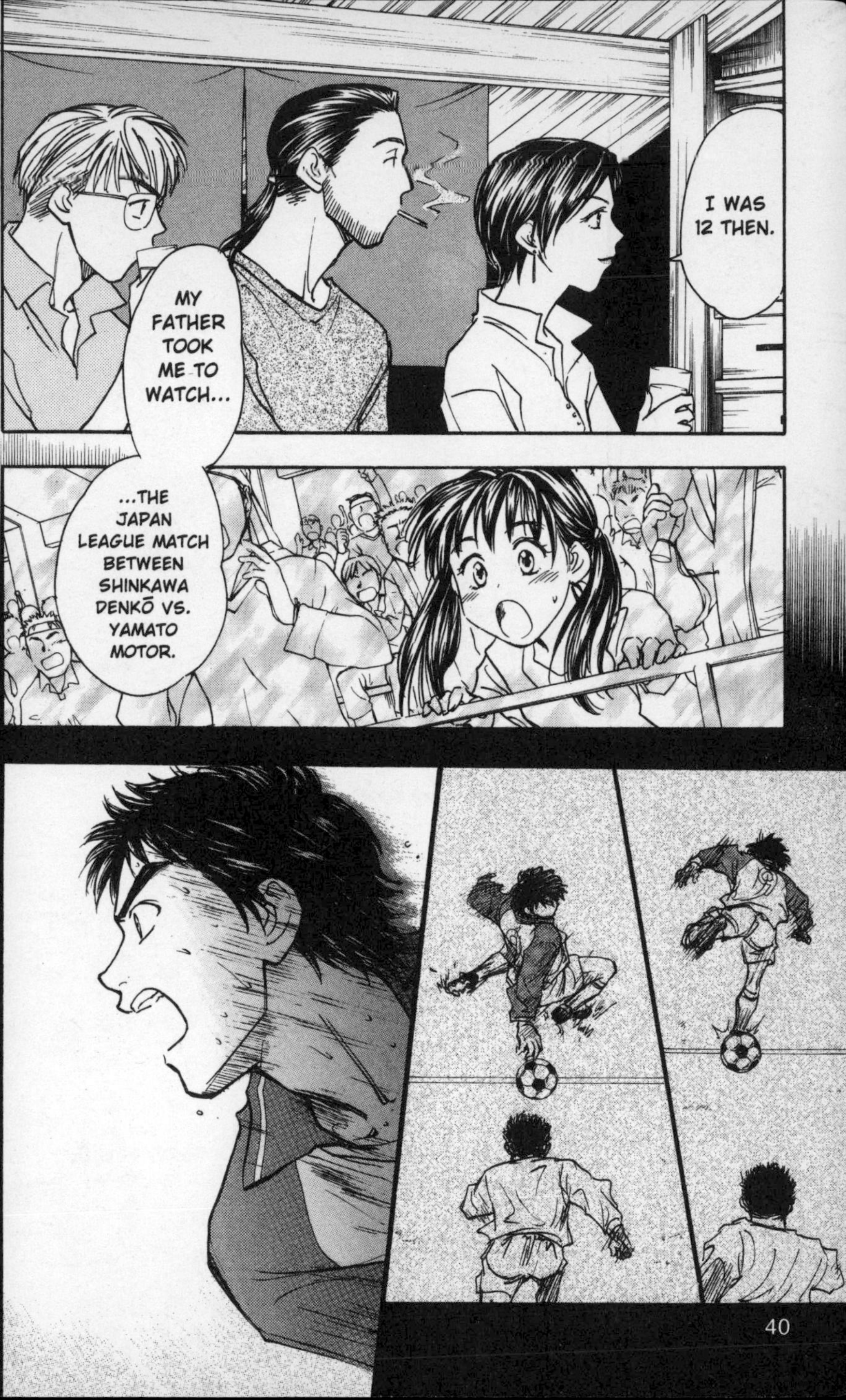
I WAS 12 THEN.
MY FATHER TOOK ME TO WATCH...
...THE JAPAN LEAGUE MATCH BETWEEN SHINKAWA DENKŌ VS. YAMATO MOTOR.

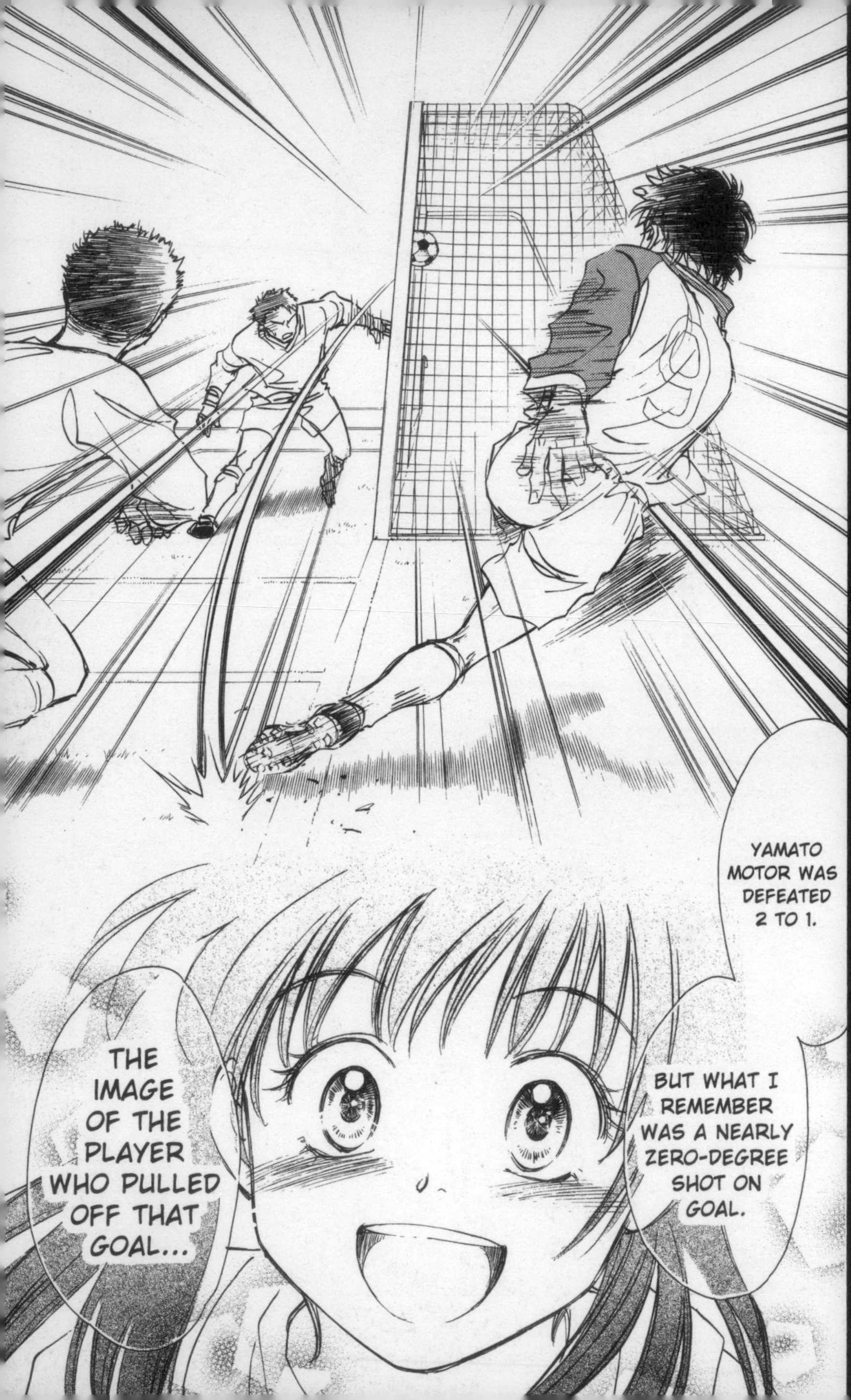
YAMATO MOTOR WAS DEFEATED 2 TO 1.
BUT WHAT I REMEMBER WAS A NEARLY ZERO-DEGREE SHOT ON GOAL.
THE IMAGE OF THE PLAYER WHO PULLED OFF THAT GOAL...

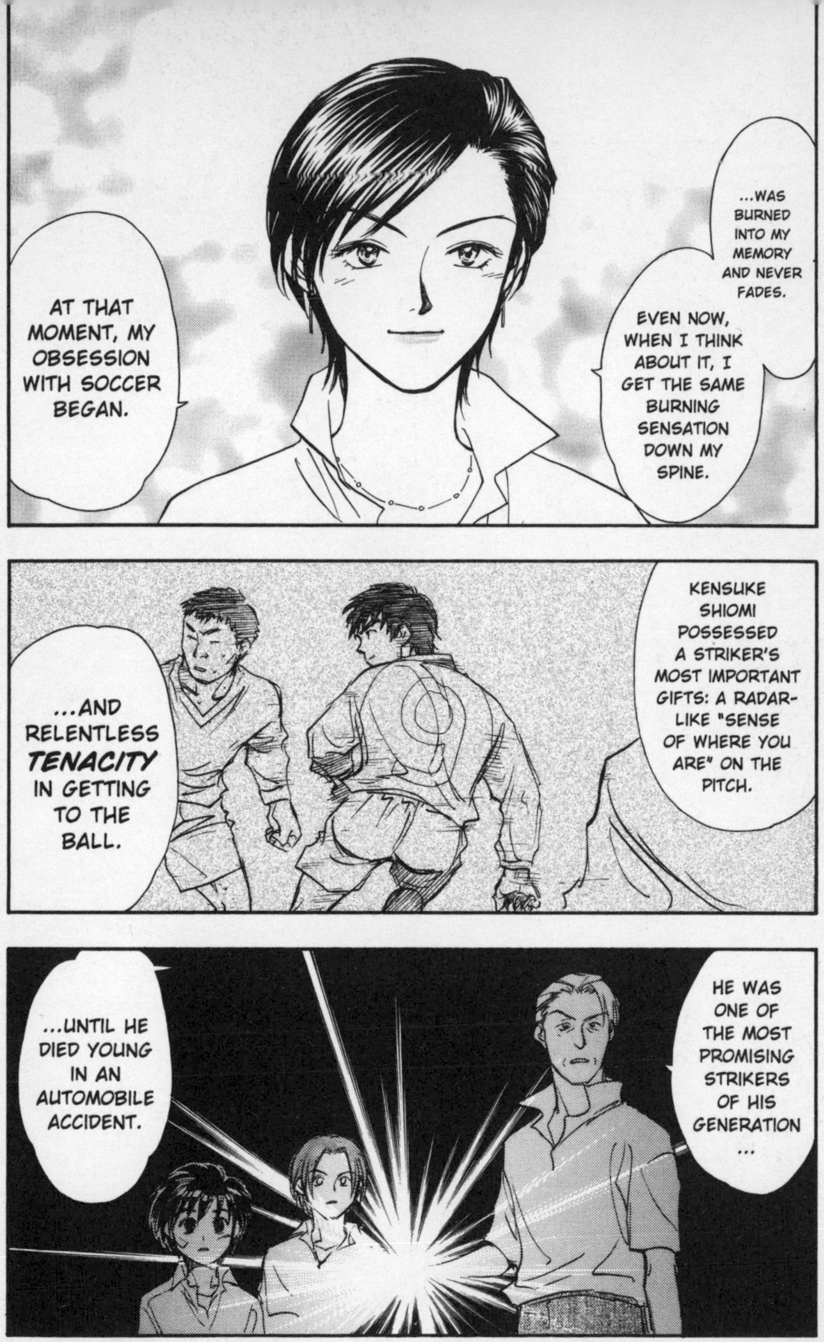
...WAS BURNED INTO MY MEMORY AND NEVER FADES.
EVEN NOW, WHEN I THINK ABOUT IT, I GET THE SAME BURNING SENSATION DOWN MY SPINE.
AT THAT MOMENT, MY OBSESSION WITH SOCCER BEGAN.
KENSUKE SHIOMI POSSESSED A STRIKER'S MOST IMPORTANT GIFTS: A RADAR-LIKE "SENSE OF WHERE YOU ARE" ON THE PITCH.
...AND RELENTLESS *TENACITY* IN GETTING TO THE BALL.
HE WAS ONE OF THE MOST PROMISING STRIKERS OF HIS GENERATION ...
...UNTIL HE DIED YOUNG IN AN AUTOMOBILE ACCIDENT.

READ THIS WAY

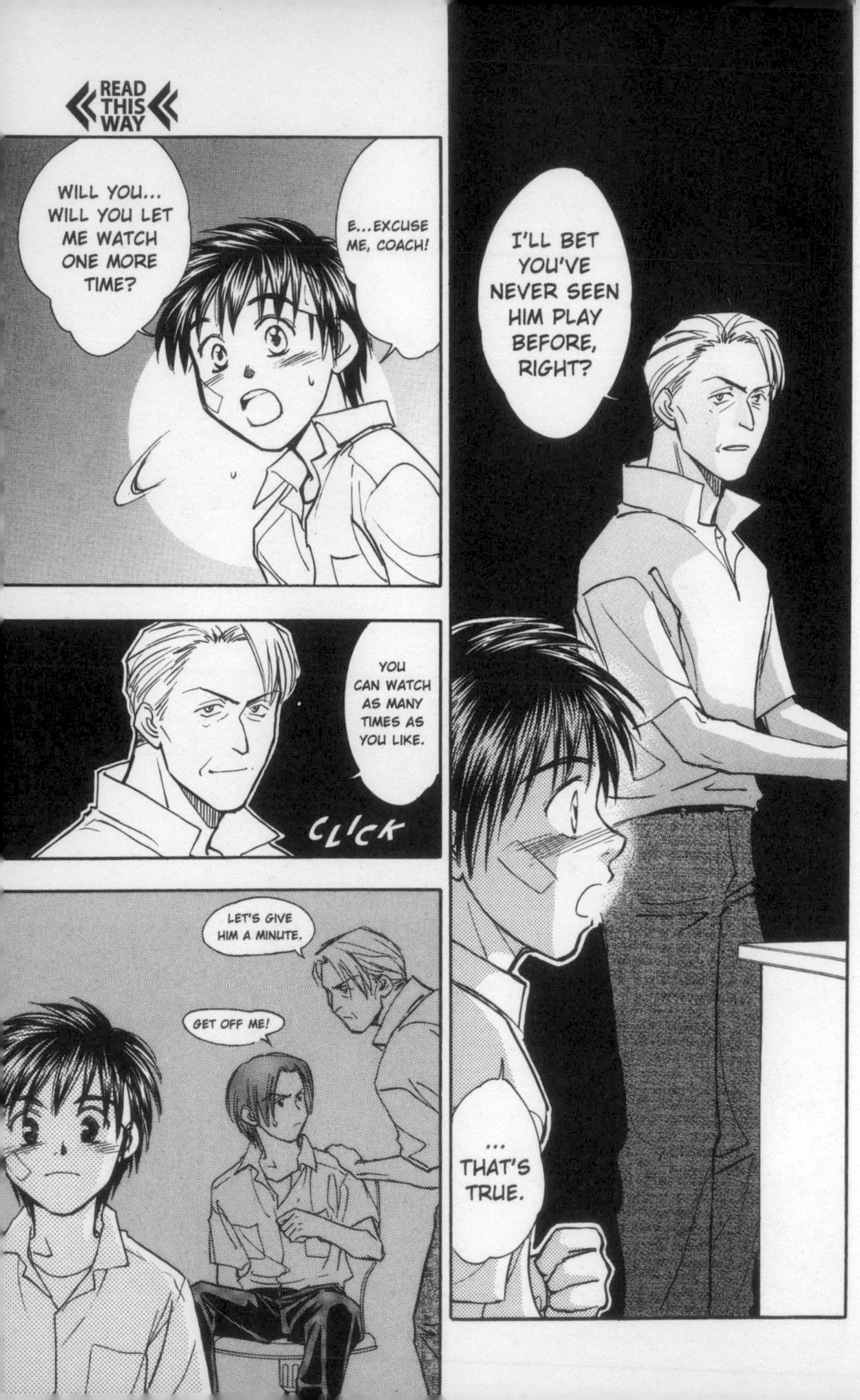
I'LL BET YOU'VE NEVER SEEN HIM PLAY BEFORE, RIGHT?
... THAT'S TRUE.
E...EXCUSE ME, COACH!
WILL YOU... WILL YOU LET ME WATCH ONE MORE TIME?
YOU CAN WATCH AS MANY TIMES AS YOU LIKE.
CLICK
LET'S GIVE HIM A MINUTE.
GET OFF ME!

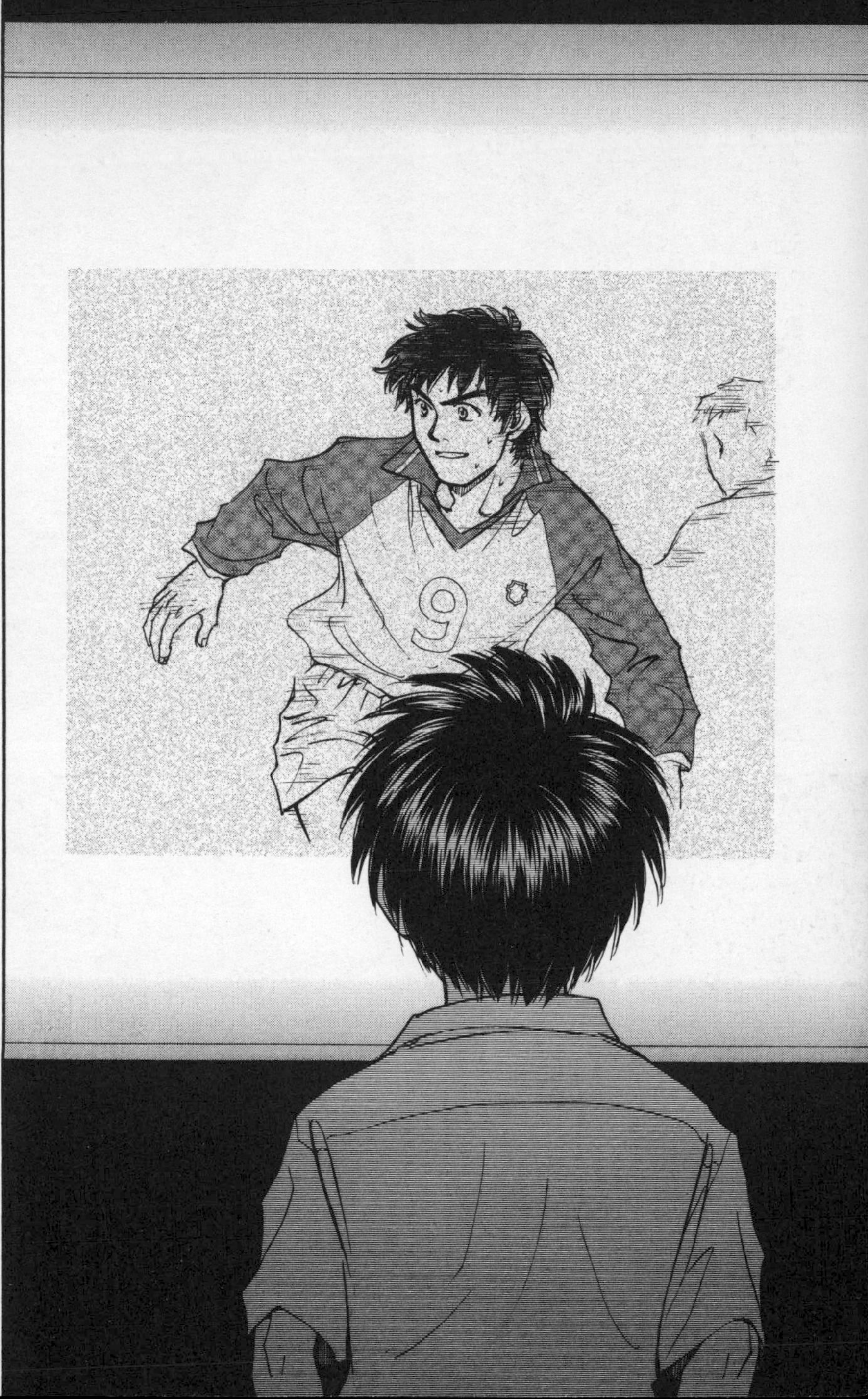

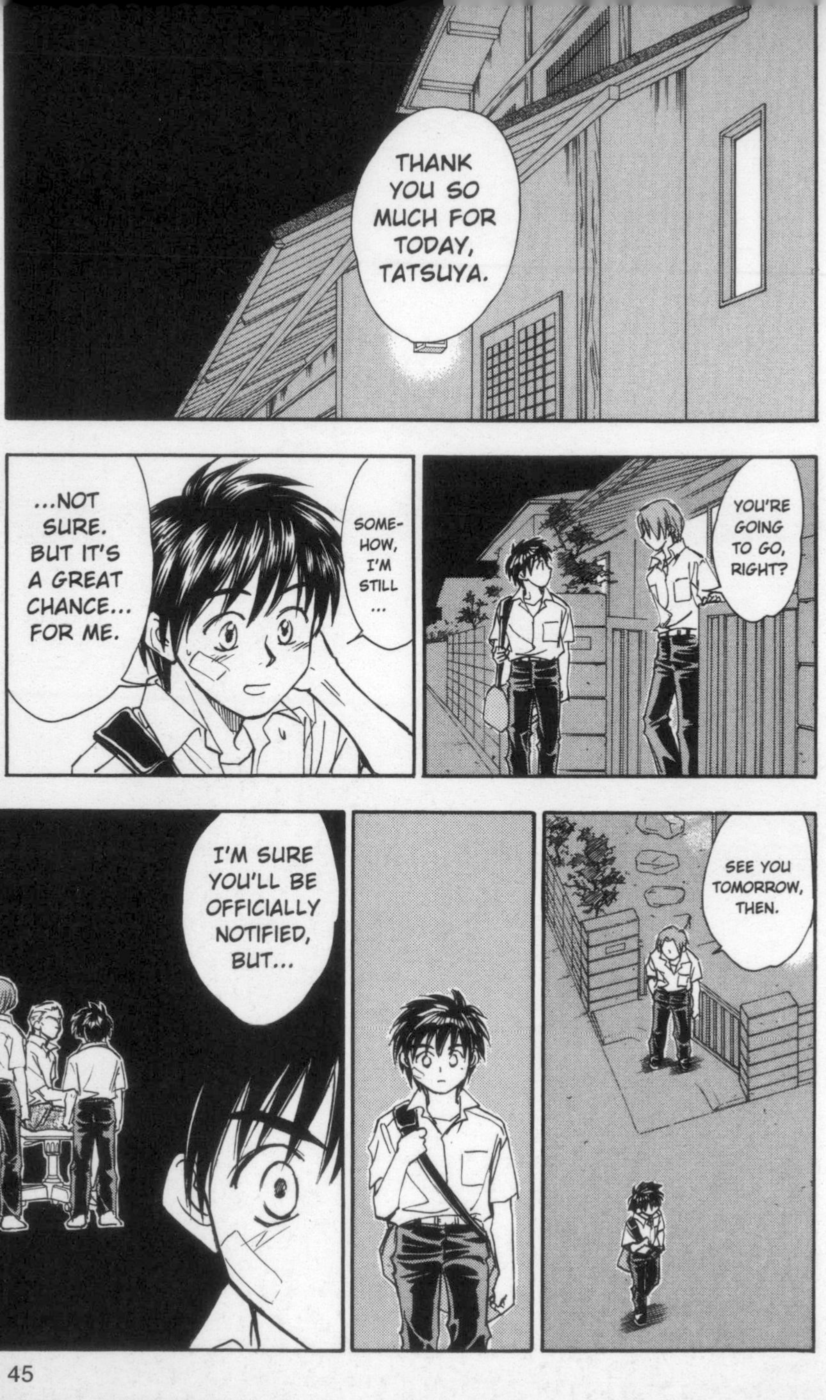
THANK YOU SO MUCH FOR TODAY, TATSUYA.
YOU'RE GOING TO GO, RIGHT?
SOME-HOW, I'M STILL ...
...NOT SURE. BUT IT'S A GREAT CHANCE... FOR ME.
SEE YOU TOMORROW, THEN.
I'M SURE YOU'LL BE OFFICIALLY NOTIFIED, BUT...

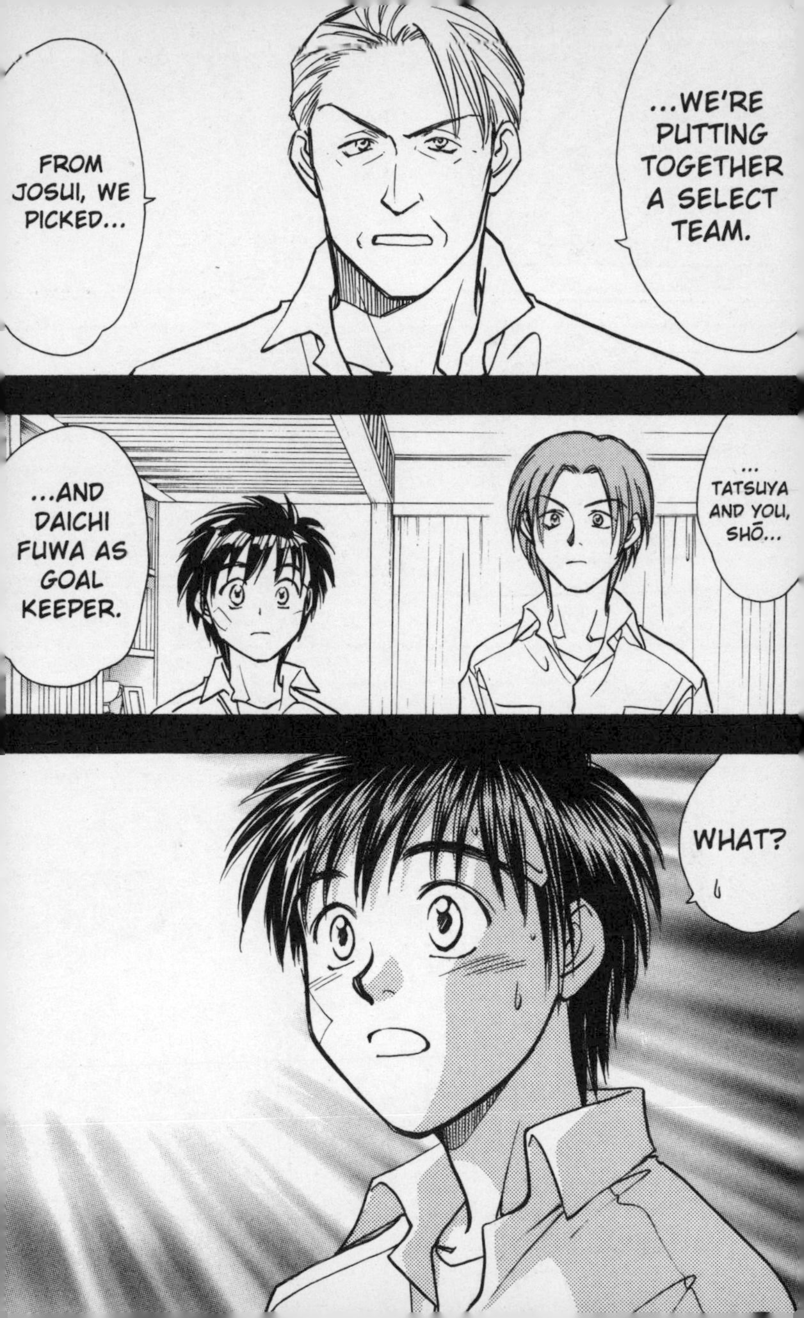
...WE'RE PUTTING TOGETHER A SELECT TEAM.
FROM JOSUI, WE PICKED...
...TATSUYA AND YOU, SHŌ...
...AND DAICHI FUWA AS GOAL KEEPER.
WHAT?

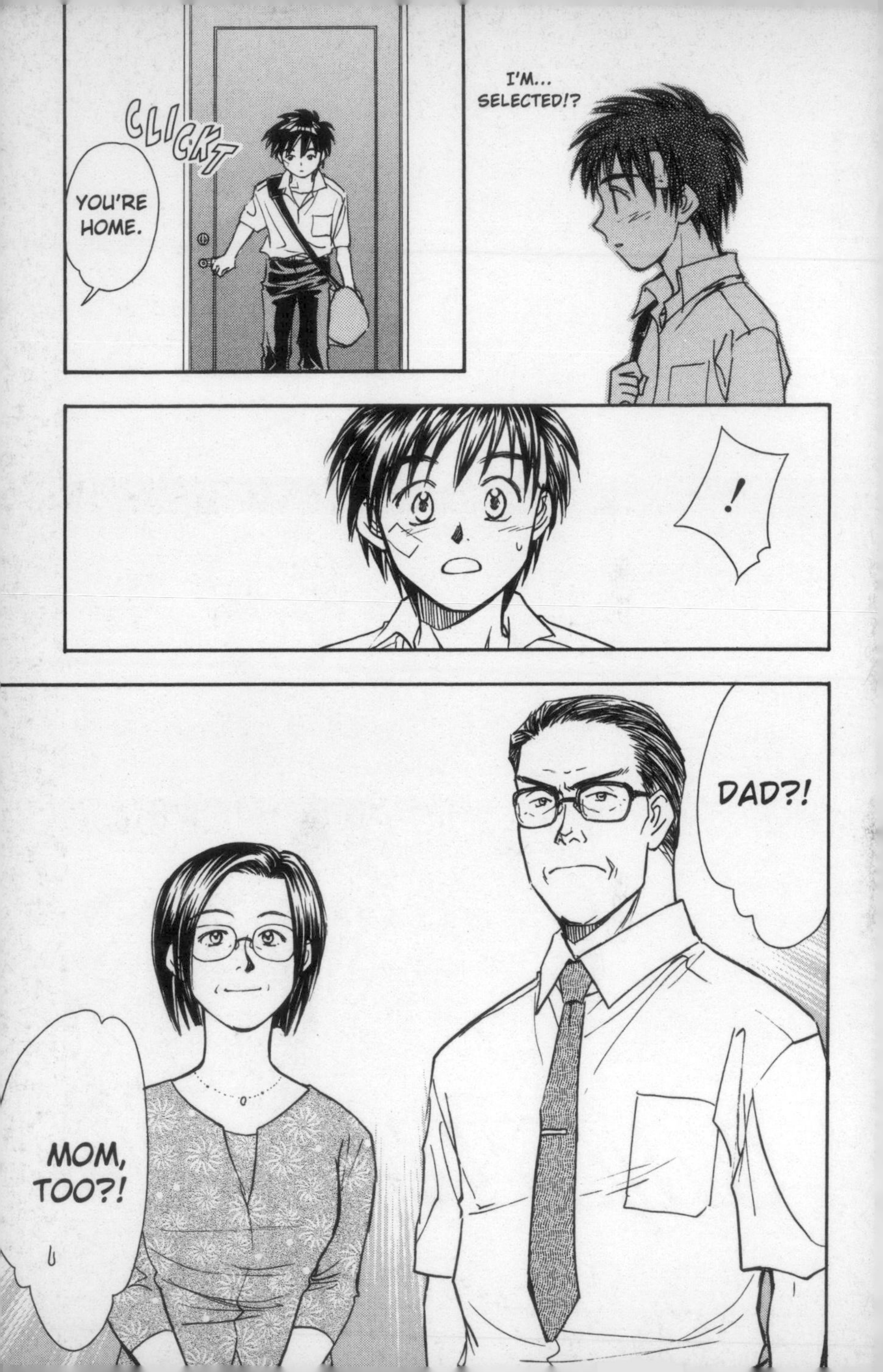
I'M... SELECTED!?
CLICK
YOU'RE HOME.
!
DAD?!
MOM, TOO?!

WHISTLE!™

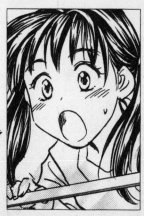

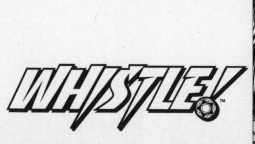

STAGE.101 Spike

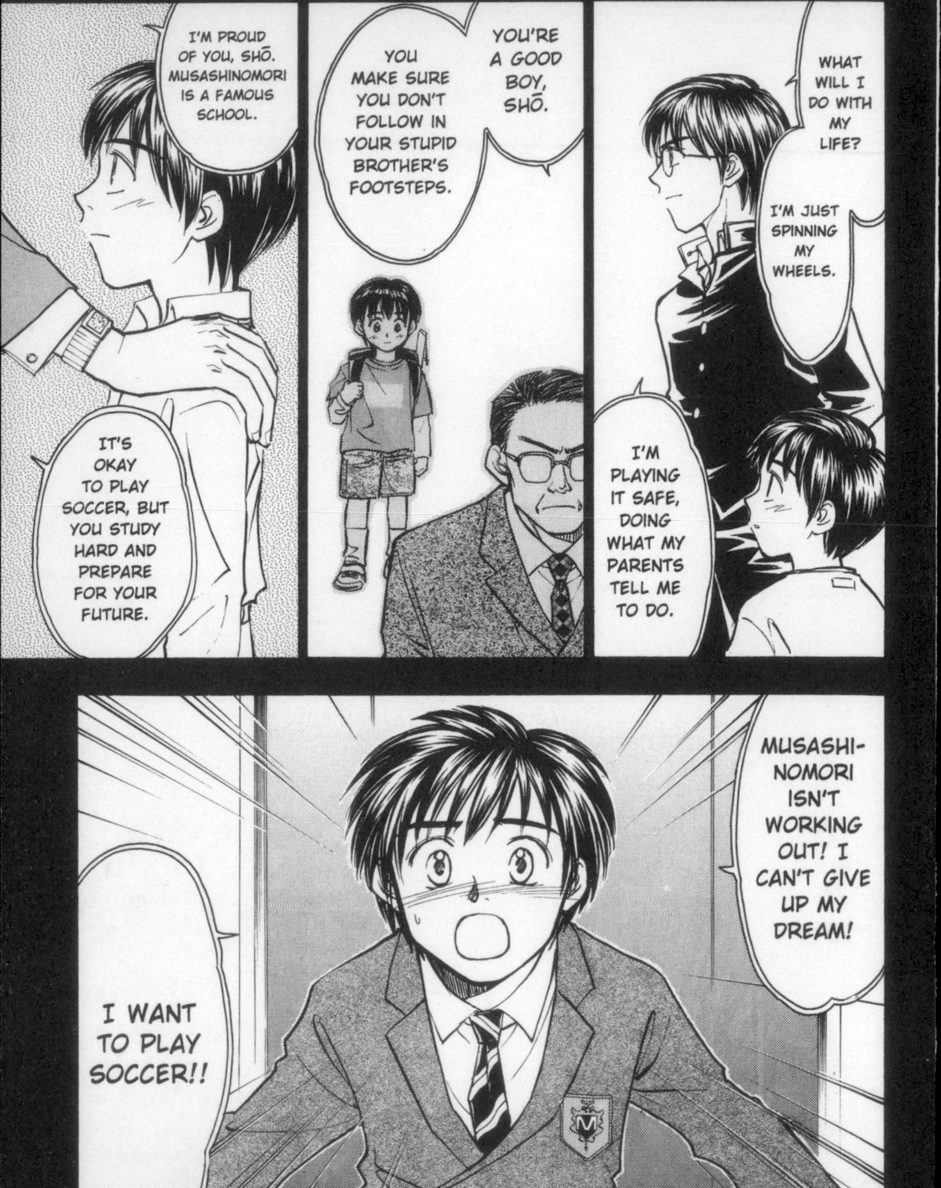
WHAT WILL I DO WITH MY LIFE?
I'M JUST SPINNING MY WHEELS.
I'M PLAYING IT SAFE, DOING WHAT MY PARENTS TELL ME TO DO.
YOU'RE A GOOD BOY, SHŌ.
YOU MAKE SURE YOU DON'T FOLLOW IN YOUR STUPID BROTHER'S FOOTSTEPS.
I'M PROUD OF YOU, SHŌ. MUSASHINOMORI IS A FAMOUS SCHOOL.
IT'S OKAY TO PLAY SOCCER, BUT YOU STUDY HARD AND PREPARE FOR YOUR FUTURE.
MUSASHI-NOMORI ISN'T WORKING OUT! I CAN'T GIVE UP MY DREAM!
I WANT TO PLAY SOCCER!!

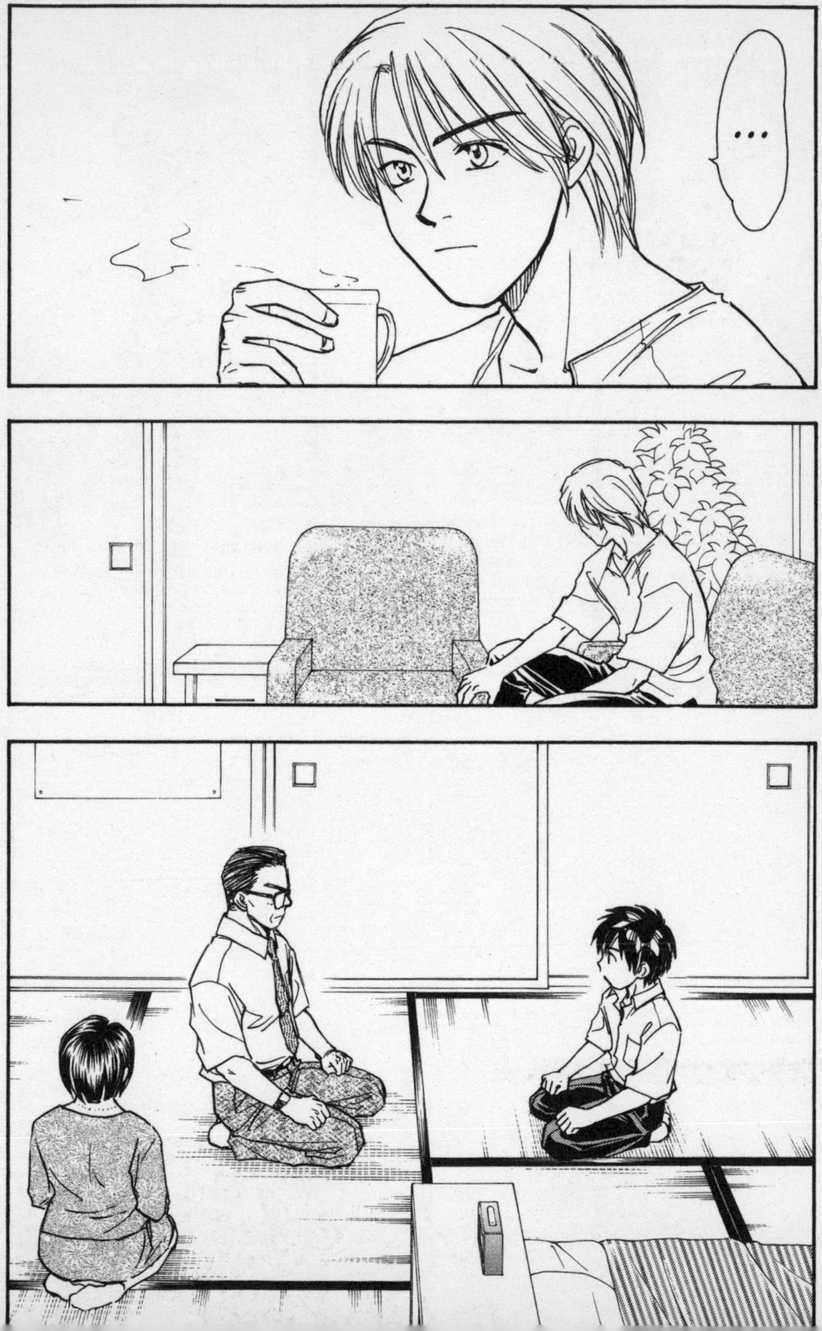
...

STAGE.101
Spike

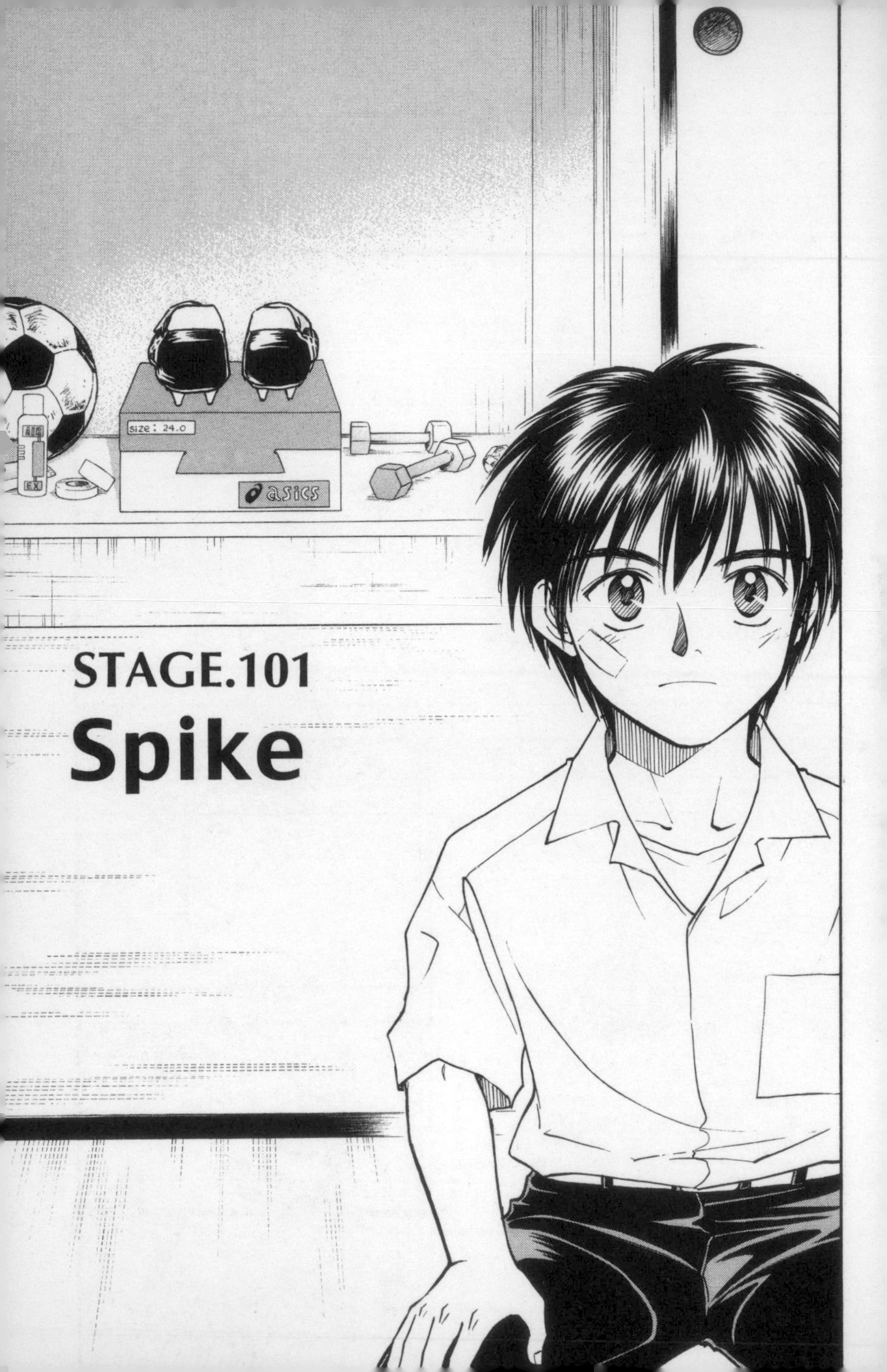
size: 24.0
asics
AIR
EX

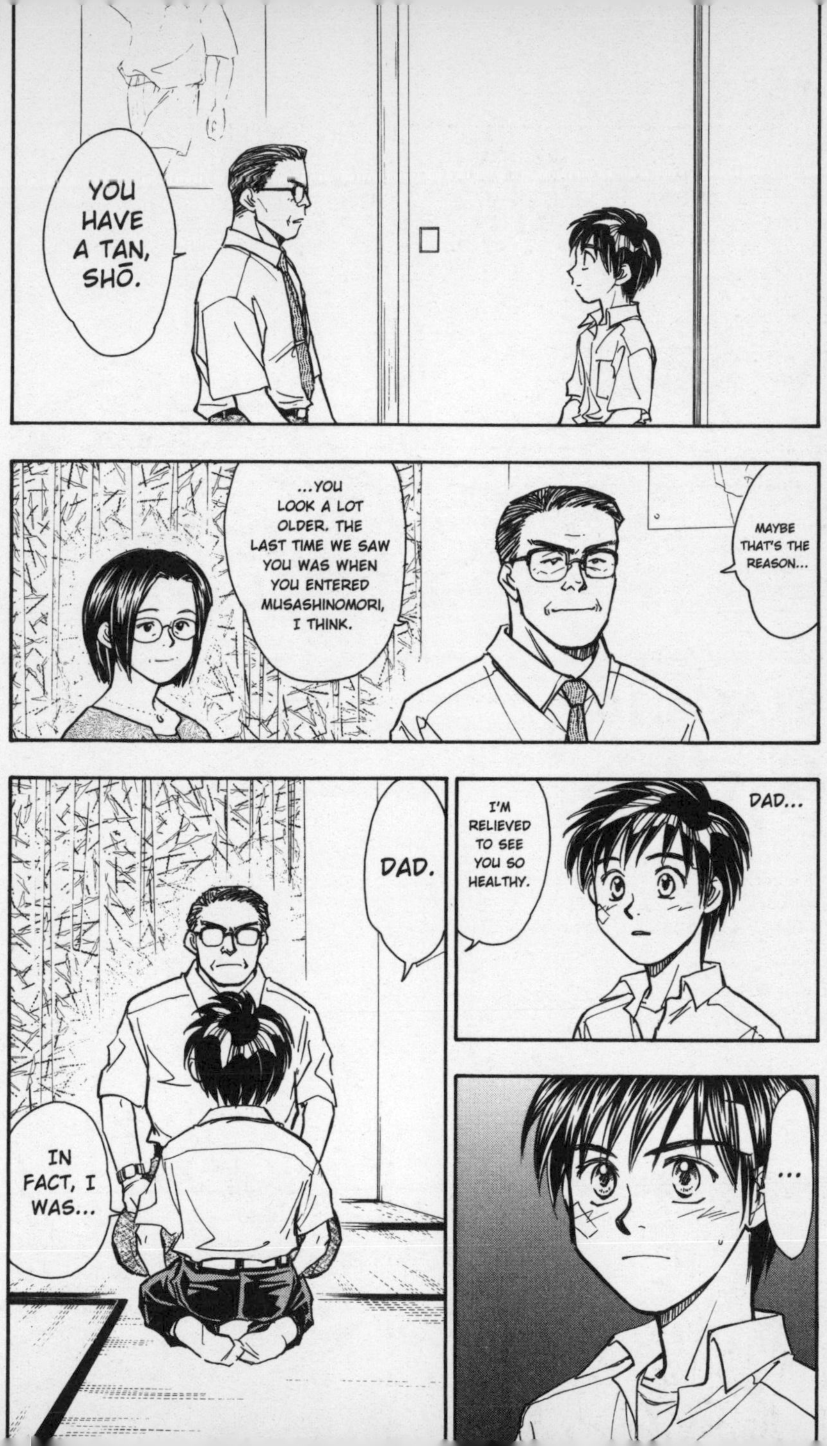
YOU HAVE A TAN, SHŌ.
MAYBE THAT'S THE REASON...
...YOU LOOK A LOT OLDER. THE LAST TIME WE SAW YOU WAS WHEN YOU ENTERED MUSASHINOMORI, I THINK.
DAD...
I'M RELIEVED TO SEE YOU SO HEALTHY.
...
DAD.
IN FACT, I WAS...

READ THIS WAY

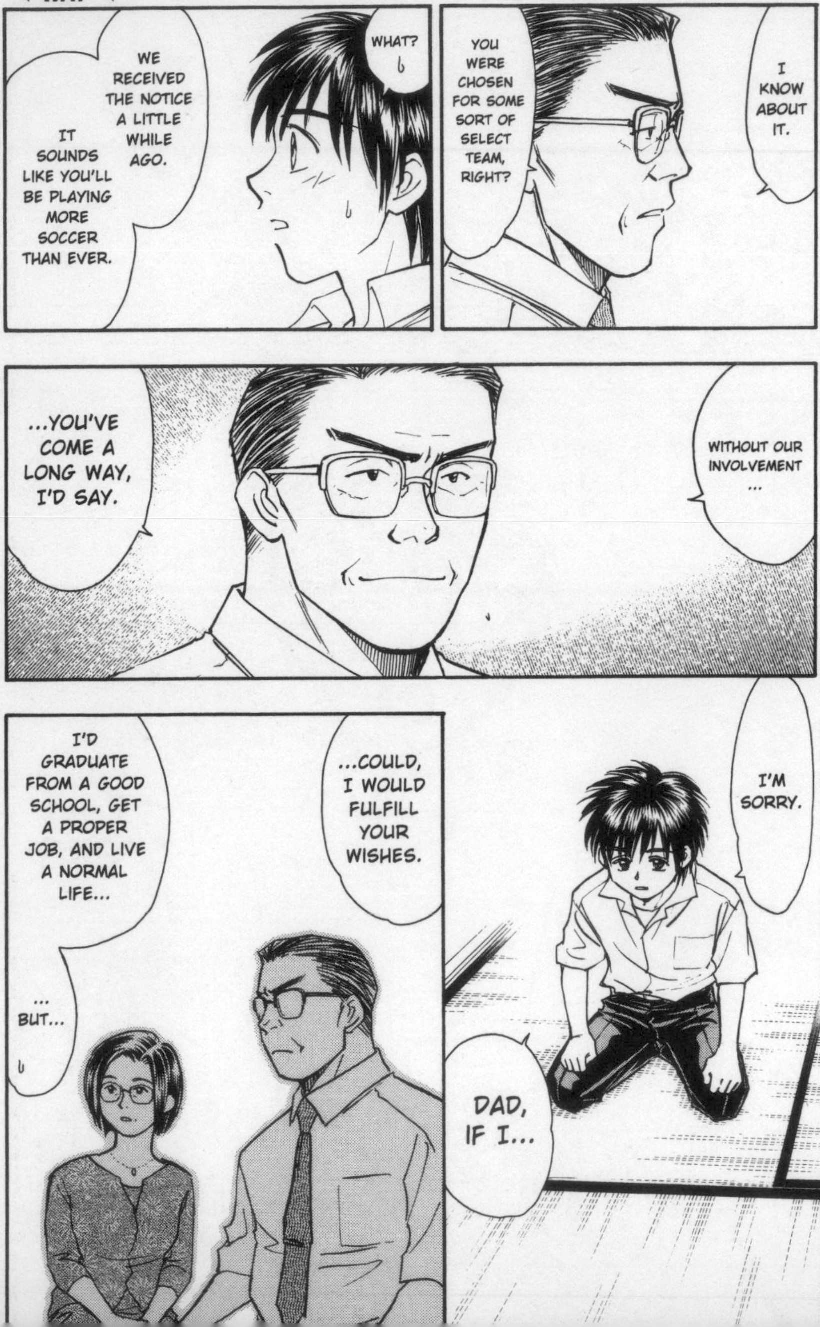
I KNOW ABOUT IT.
YOU WERE CHOSEN FOR SOME SORT OF SELECT TEAM, RIGHT?
WHAT?
WE RECEIVED THE NOTICE A LITTLE WHILE AGO.
IT SOUNDS LIKE YOU'LL BE PLAYING MORE SOCCER THAN EVER.
WITHOUT OUR INVOLVEMENT ...
...YOU'VE COME A LONG WAY, I'D SAY.
I'M SORRY.
DAD, IF I...
...COULD, I WOULD FULFILL YOUR WISHES.
I'D GRADUATE FROM A GOOD SCHOOL, GET A PROPER JOB, AND LIVE A NORMAL LIFE...
... BUT...

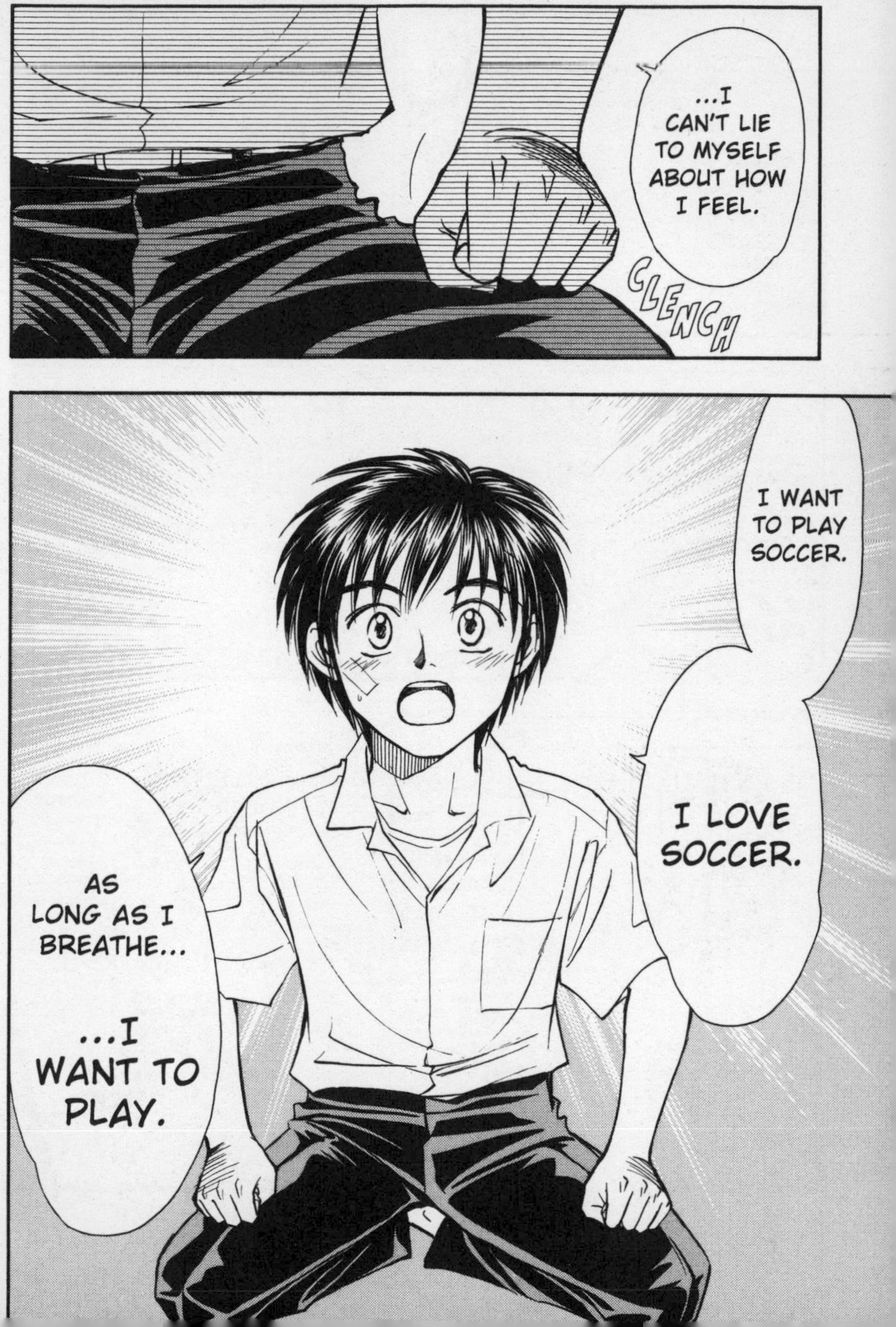
...I CAN'T LIE TO MYSELF ABOUT HOW I FEEL.
CLENCH
I WANT TO PLAY SOCCER.
I LOVE SOCCER.
AS LONG AS I BREATHE...
...I WANT TO PLAY.

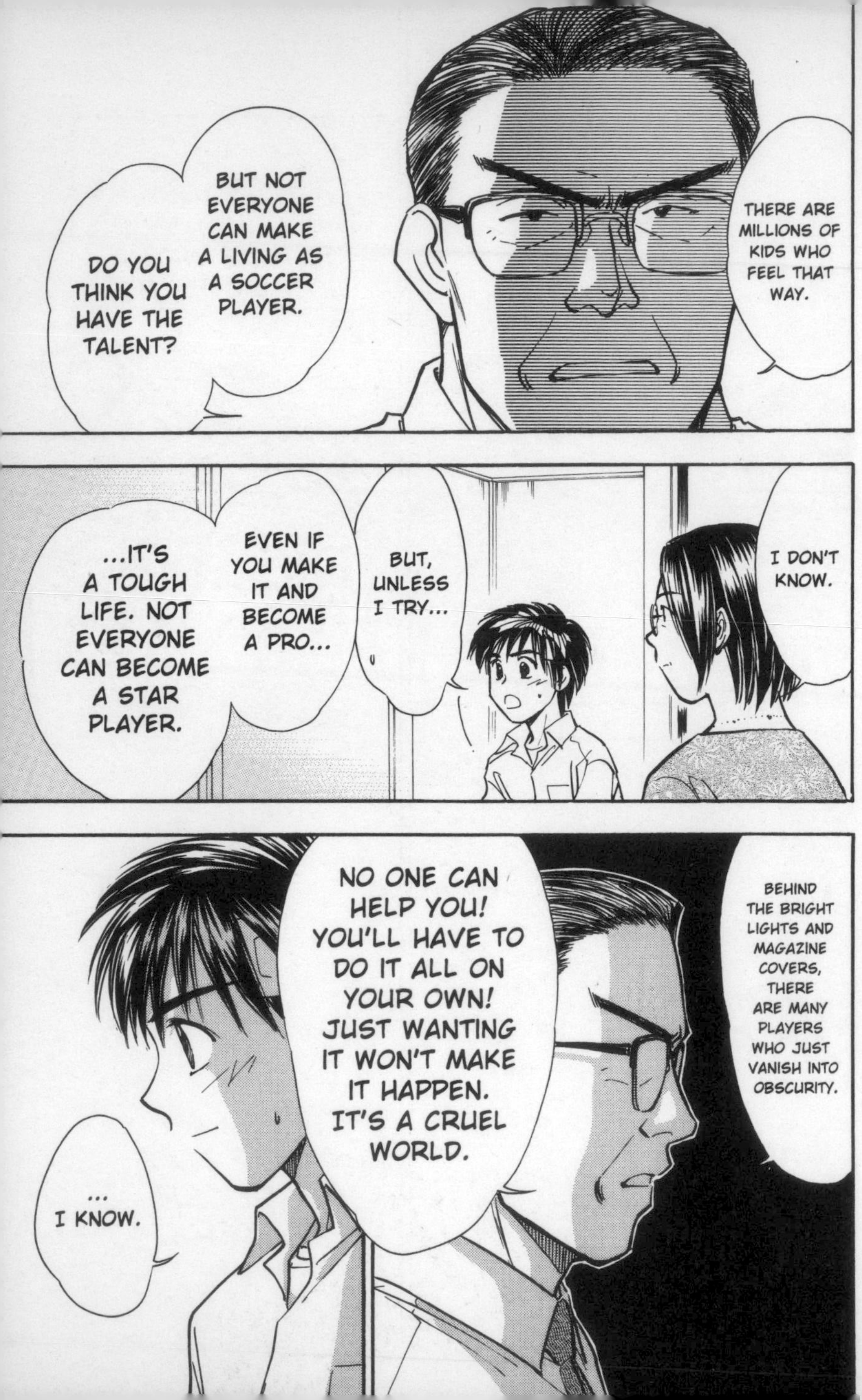
THERE ARE MILLIONS OF KIDS WHO FEEL THAT WAY.
BUT NOT EVERYONE CAN MAKE A LIVING AS A SOCCER PLAYER.
DO YOU THINK YOU HAVE THE TALENT?
I DON'T KNOW.
BUT, UNLESS I TRY...
EVEN IF YOU MAKE IT AND BECOME A PRO...
...IT'S A TOUGH LIFE. NOT EVERYONE CAN BECOME A STAR PLAYER.
BEHIND THE BRIGHT LIGHTS AND MAGAZINE COVERS, THERE ARE MANY PLAYERS WHO JUST VANISH INTO OBSCURITY.
NO ONE CAN HELP YOU! YOU'LL HAVE TO DO IT ALL ON YOUR OWN! JUST WANTING IT WON'T MAKE IT HAPPEN. IT'S A CRUEL WORLD.
... I KNOW.

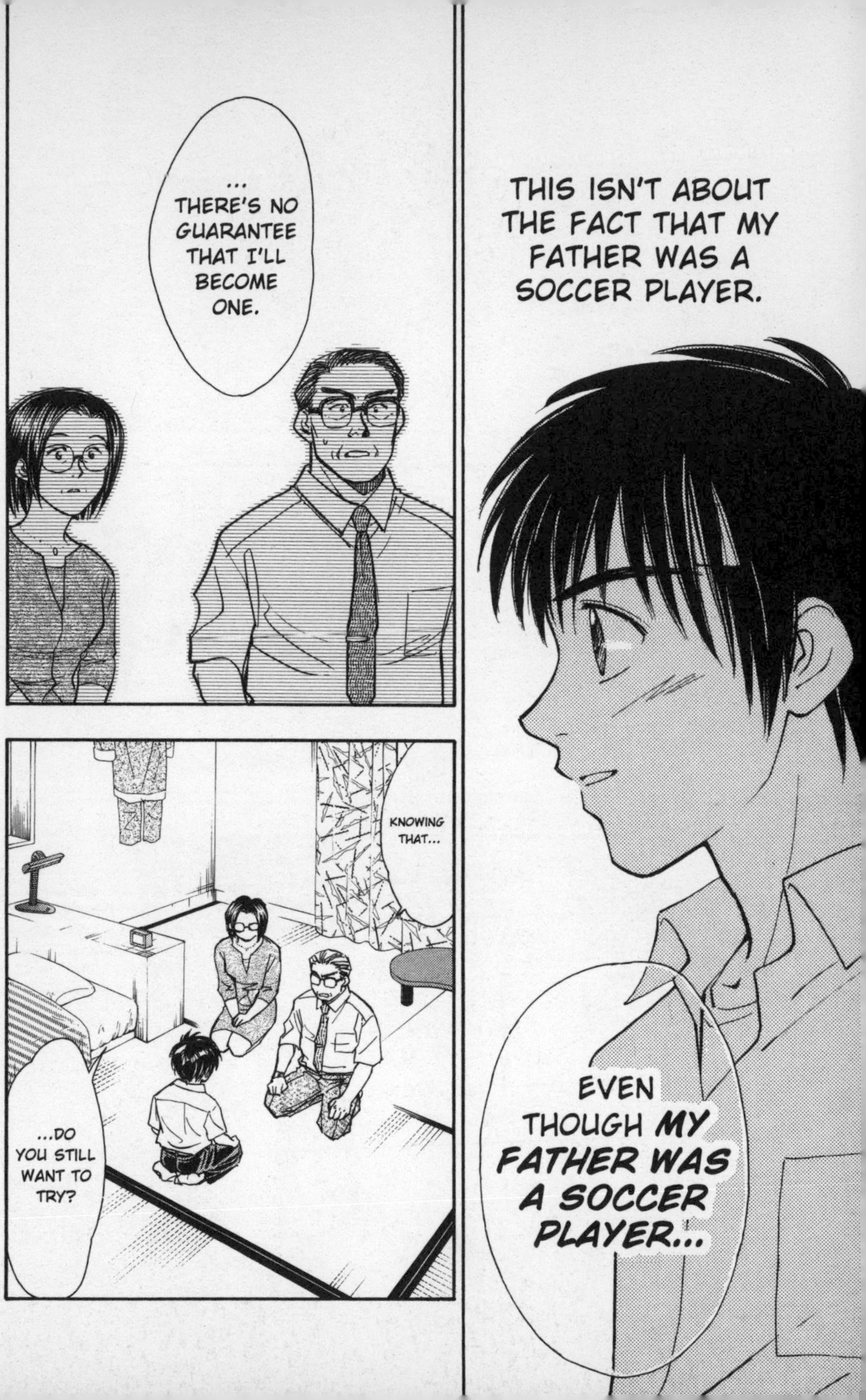
THIS ISN'T ABOUT THE FACT THAT MY FATHER WAS A SOCCER PLAYER.
EVEN THOUGH *MY FATHER WAS A SOCCER PLAYER...*
...THERE'S NO GUARANTEE THAT I'LL BECOME ONE.
KNOWING THAT...
...DO YOU STILL WANT TO TRY?

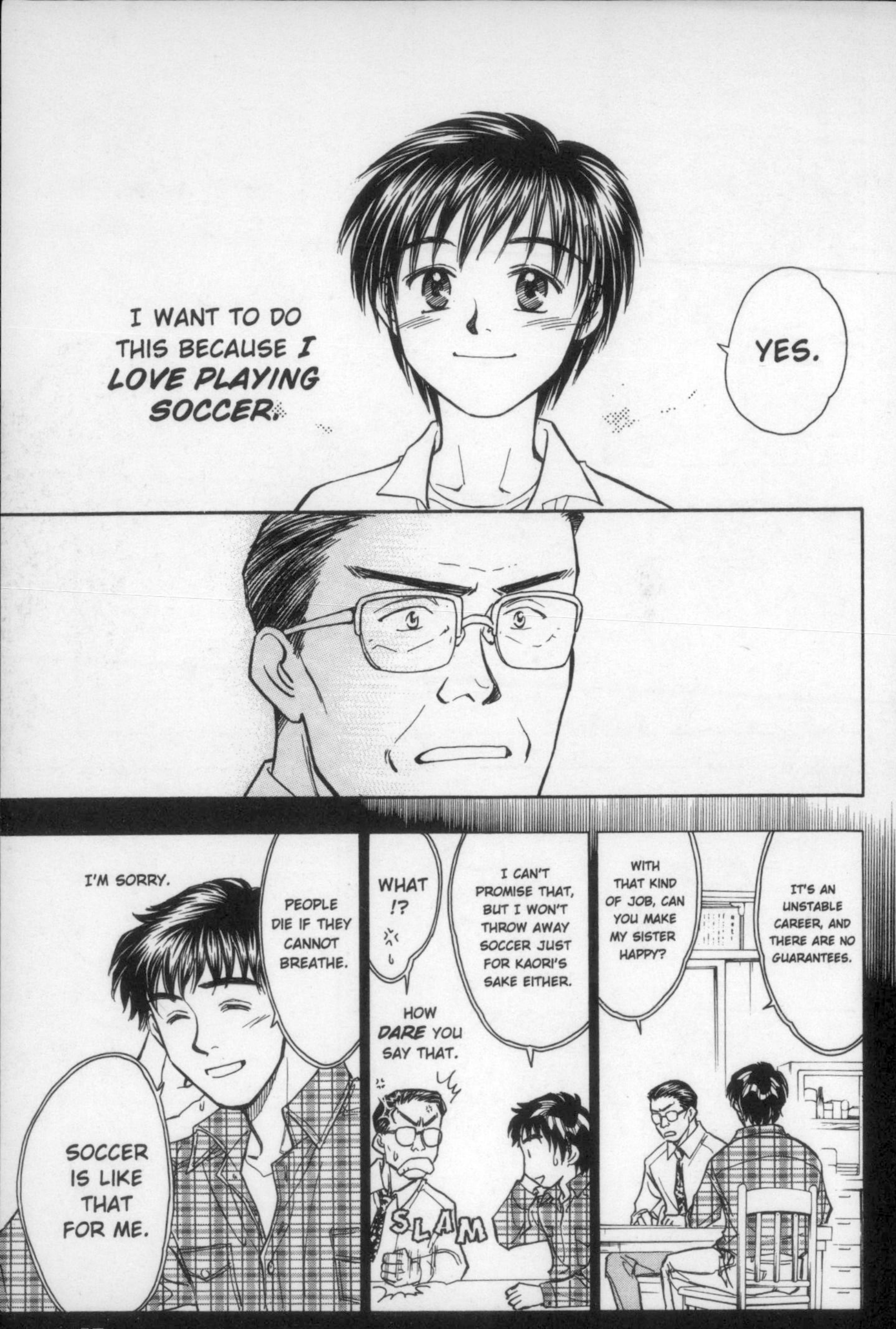
YES.
I WANT TO DO THIS BECAUSE *I LOVE PLAYING SOCCER.*
IT'S AN UNSTABLE CAREER, AND THERE ARE NO GUARANTEES.
WITH THAT KIND OF JOB, CAN YOU MAKE MY SISTER HAPPY?
I CAN'T PROMISE THAT, BUT I WON'T THROW AWAY SOCCER JUST FOR KAORI'S SAKE EITHER.
WHAT !?
HOW *DARE* YOU SAY THAT.
SLAM
I'M SORRY.
PEOPLE DIE IF THEY CANNOT BREATHE.
SOCCER IS LIKE THAT FOR ME.

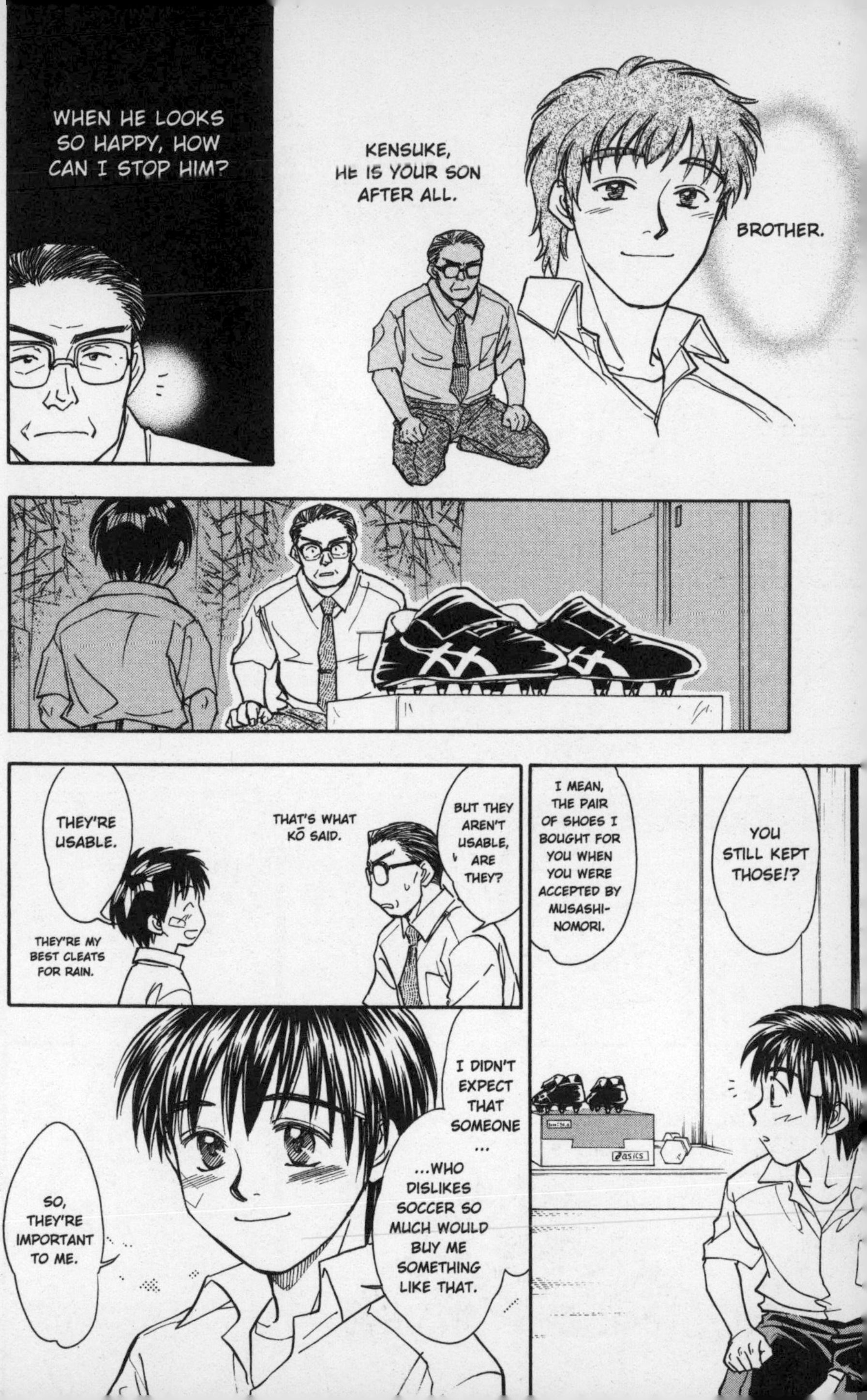

KENSUKE, HE IS YOUR SON AFTER ALL.
BROTHER.
WHEN HE LOOKS SO HAPPY, HOW CAN I STOP HIM?
YOU STILL KEPT THOSE!?
I MEAN, THE PAIR OF SHOES I BOUGHT FOR YOU WHEN YOU WERE ACCEPTED BY MUSASHI-NOMORI.
BUT THEY AREN'T USABLE, ARE THEY?
THAT'S WHAT KŌ SAID.
THEY'RE USABLE.
THEY'RE MY BEST CLEATS FOR RAIN.
I DIDN'T EXPECT THAT SOMEONE ...
...WHO DISLIKES SOCCER SO MUCH WOULD BUY ME SOMETHING LIKE THAT.
SO, THEY'RE IMPORTANT TO ME.

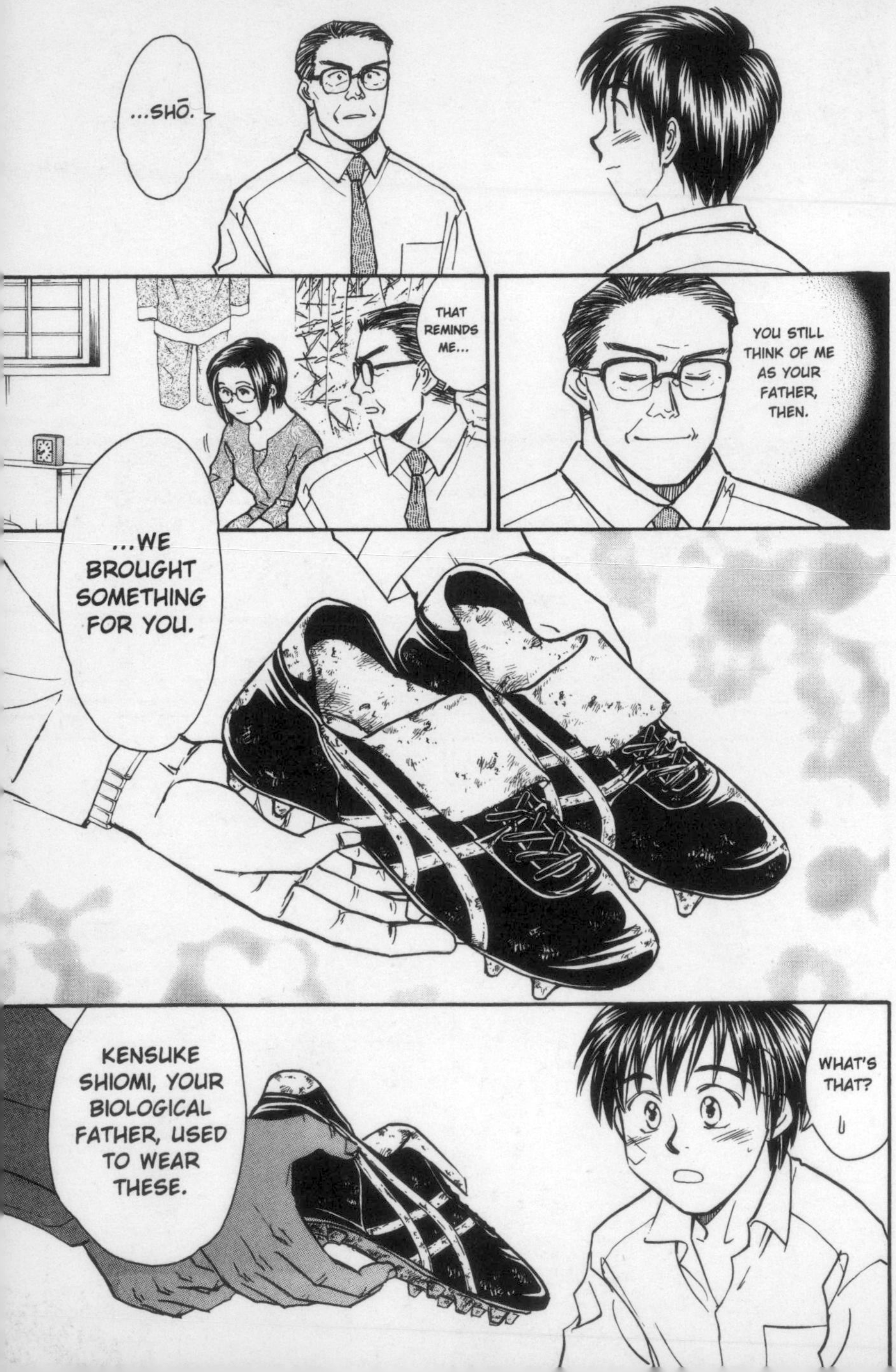
...SHŌ.
YOU STILL THINK OF ME AS YOUR FATHER, THEN.
THAT REMINDS ME...
...WE BROUGHT SOMETHING FOR YOU.
WHAT'S THAT?
KENSUKE SHIOMI, YOUR BIOLOGICAL FATHER, USED TO WEAR THESE.

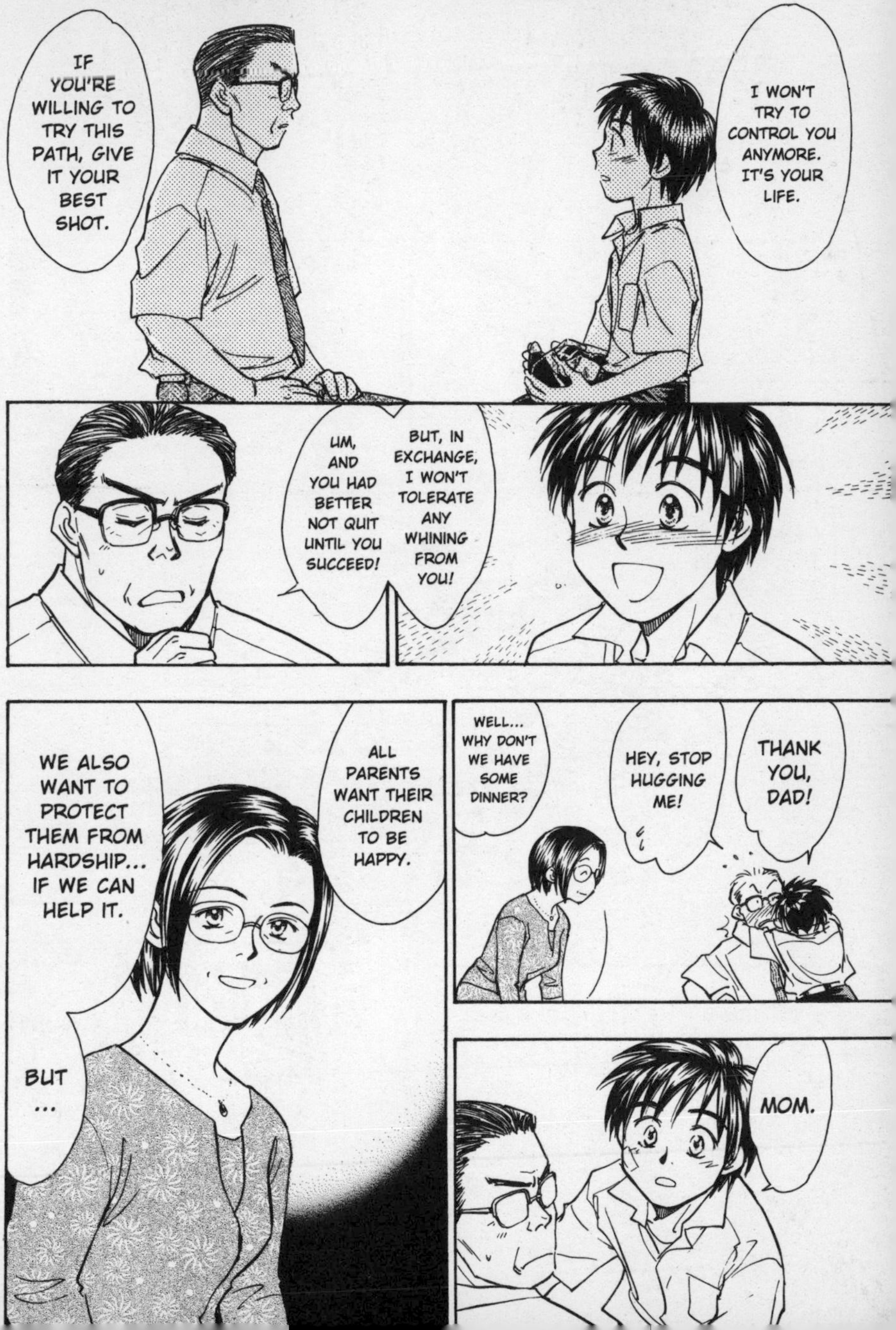
I WON'T TRY TO CONTROL YOU ANYMORE. IT'S YOUR LIFE.
IF YOU'RE WILLING TO TRY THIS PATH, GIVE IT YOUR BEST SHOT.
BUT, IN EXCHANGE, I WON'T TOLERATE ANY WHINING FROM YOU!
UM, AND YOU HAD BETTER NOT QUIT UNTIL YOU SUCCEED!
THANK YOU, DAD!
HEY, STOP HUGGING ME!
WELL... WHY DON'T WE HAVE SOME DINNER?
MOM.
ALL PARENTS WANT THEIR CHILDREN TO BE HAPPY.
WE ALSO WANT TO PROTECT THEM FROM HARDSHIP... IF WE CAN HELP IT.
BUT ...

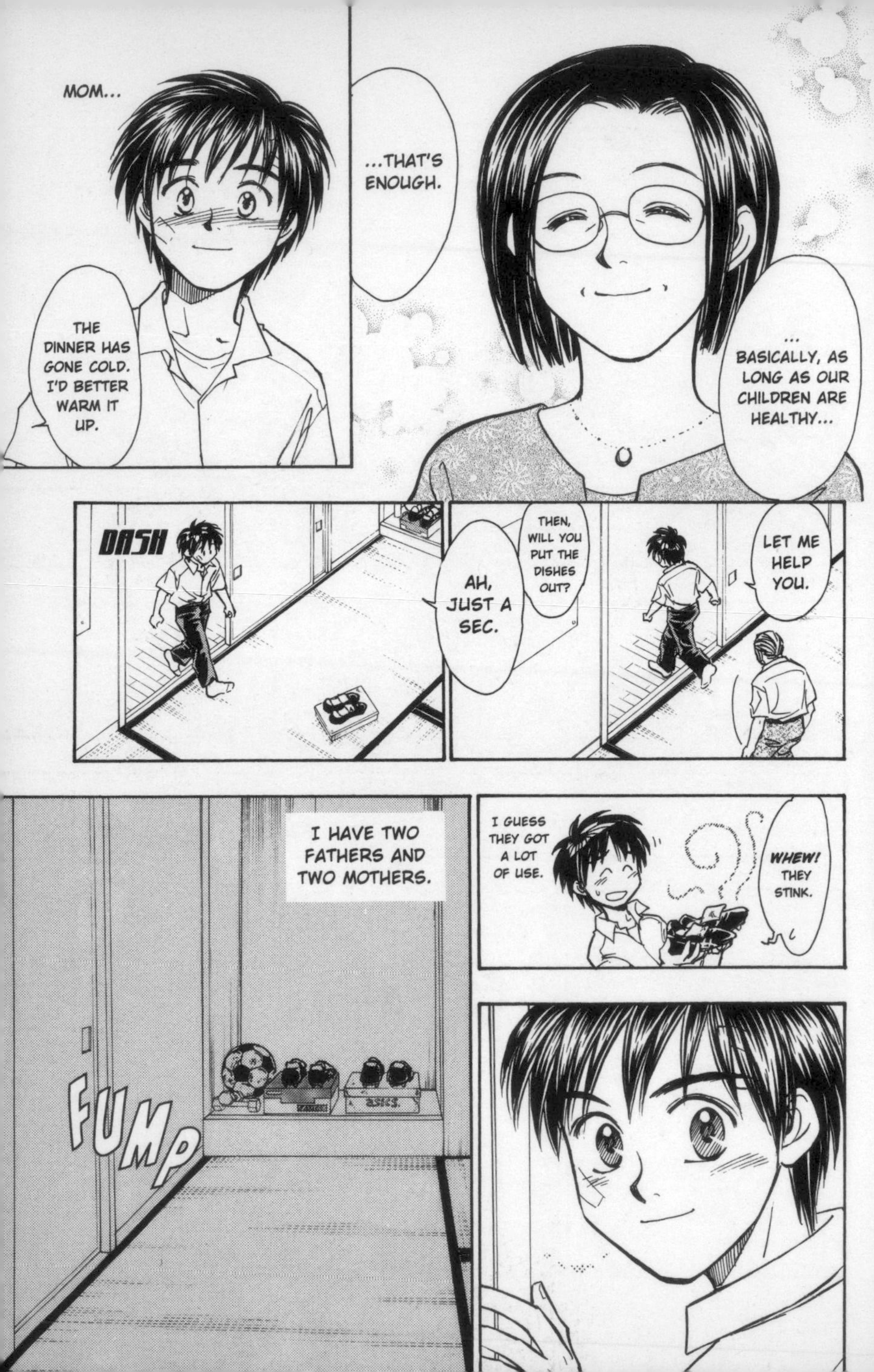
... BASICALLY, AS LONG AS OUR CHILDREN ARE HEALTHY...
...THAT'S ENOUGH.
MOM...
THE DINNER HAS GONE COLD. I'D BETTER WARM IT UP.
LET ME HELP YOU.
THEN, WILL YOU PUT THE DISHES OUT?
AH, JUST A SEC.
DASH
WHEW! THEY STINK.
I GUESS THEY GOT A LOT OF USE.
I HAVE TWO FATHERS AND TWO MOTHERS.
FUMP

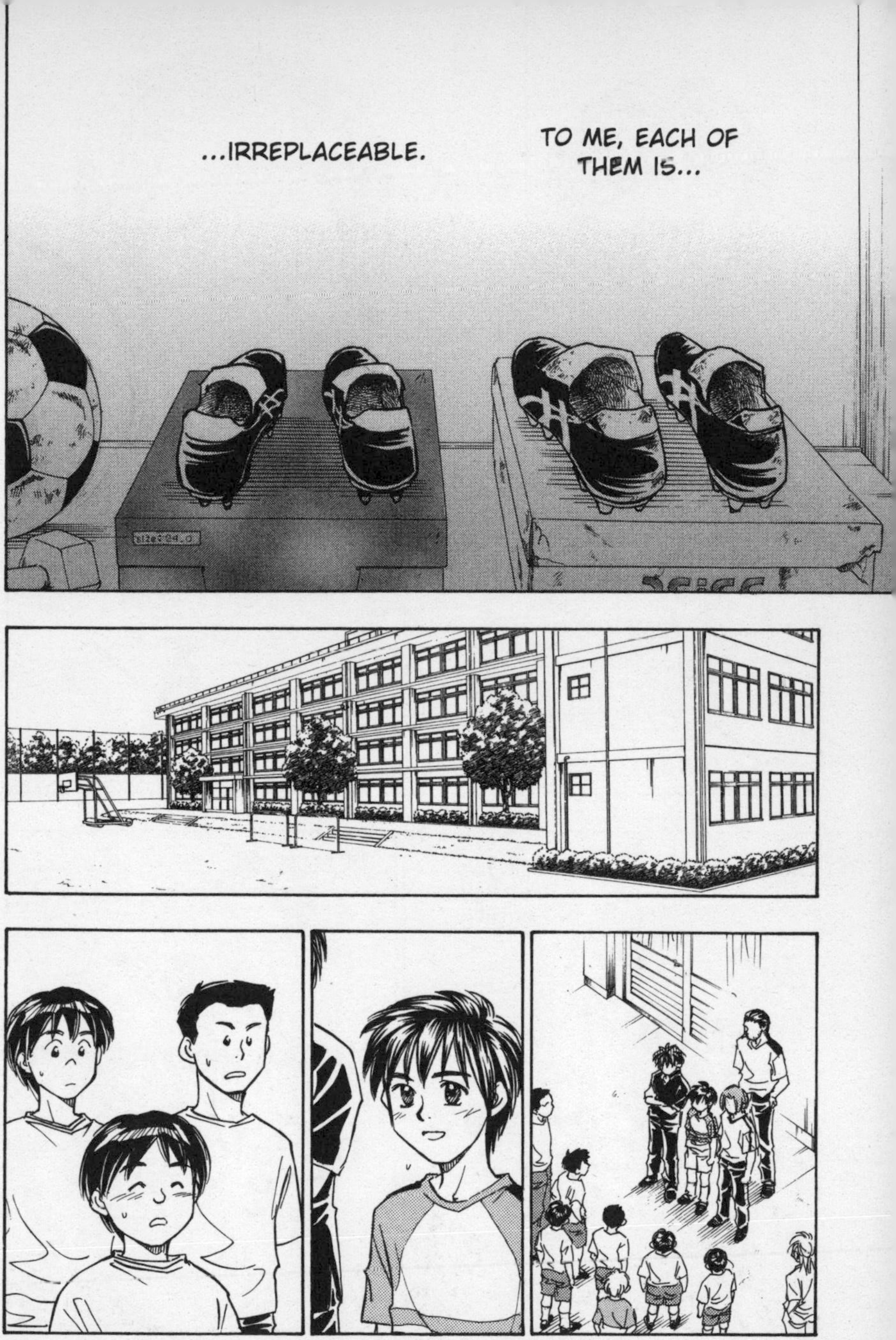
TO ME, EACH OF THEM IS...
...IRREPLACEABLE.

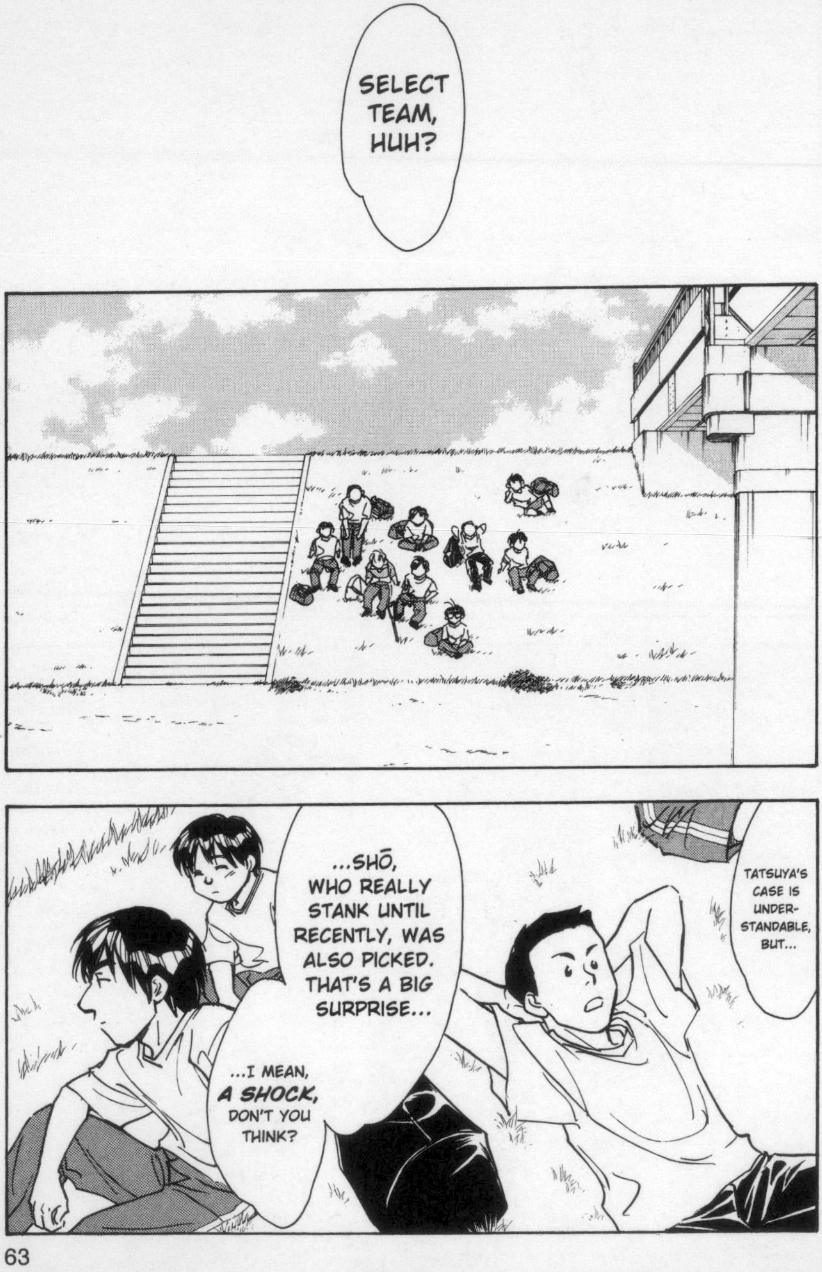
SELECT TEAM, HUH?
TATSUYA'S CASE IS UNDER-STANDABLE, BUT...
...SHŌ, WHO REALLY STANK UNTIL RECENTLY, WAS ALSO PICKED. THAT'S A BIG SURPRISE...
...I MEAN, A SHOCK, DON'T YOU THINK?

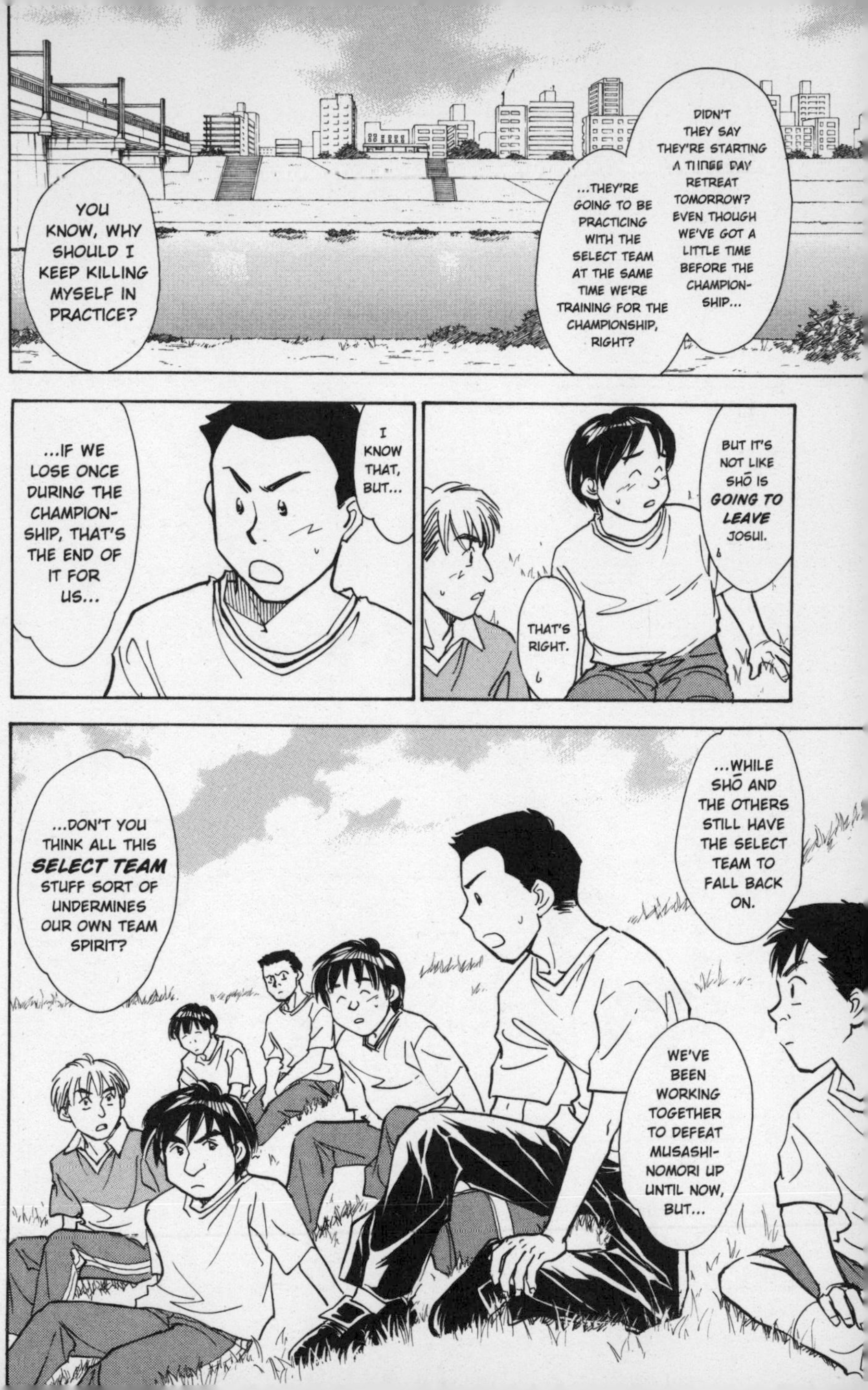
DIDN'T THEY SAY THEY'RE STARTING A THREE DAY RETREAT TOMORROW? EVEN THOUGH WE'VE GOT A LITTLE TIME BEFORE THE CHAMPIONSHIP...
...THEY'RE GOING TO BE PRACTICING WITH THE SELECT TEAM AT THE SAME TIME WE'RE TRAINING FOR THE CHAMPIONSHIP, RIGHT?
YOU KNOW, WHY SHOULD I KEEP KILLING MYSELF IN PRACTICE?
BUT IT'S NOT LIKE SHŌ IS GOING TO LEAVE JOSUI.
THAT'S RIGHT.
I KNOW THAT, BUT...
...IF WE LOSE ONCE DURING THE CHAMPIONSHIP, THAT'S THE END OF IT FOR US...
...WHILE SHŌ AND THE OTHERS STILL HAVE THE SELECT TEAM TO FALL BACK ON.
WE'VE BEEN WORKING TOGETHER TO DEFEAT MUSASHINOMORI UP UNTIL NOW, BUT...
...DON'T YOU THINK ALL THIS SELECT TEAM STUFF SORT OF UNDERMINES OUR OWN TEAM SPIRIT?

READ THIS WAY

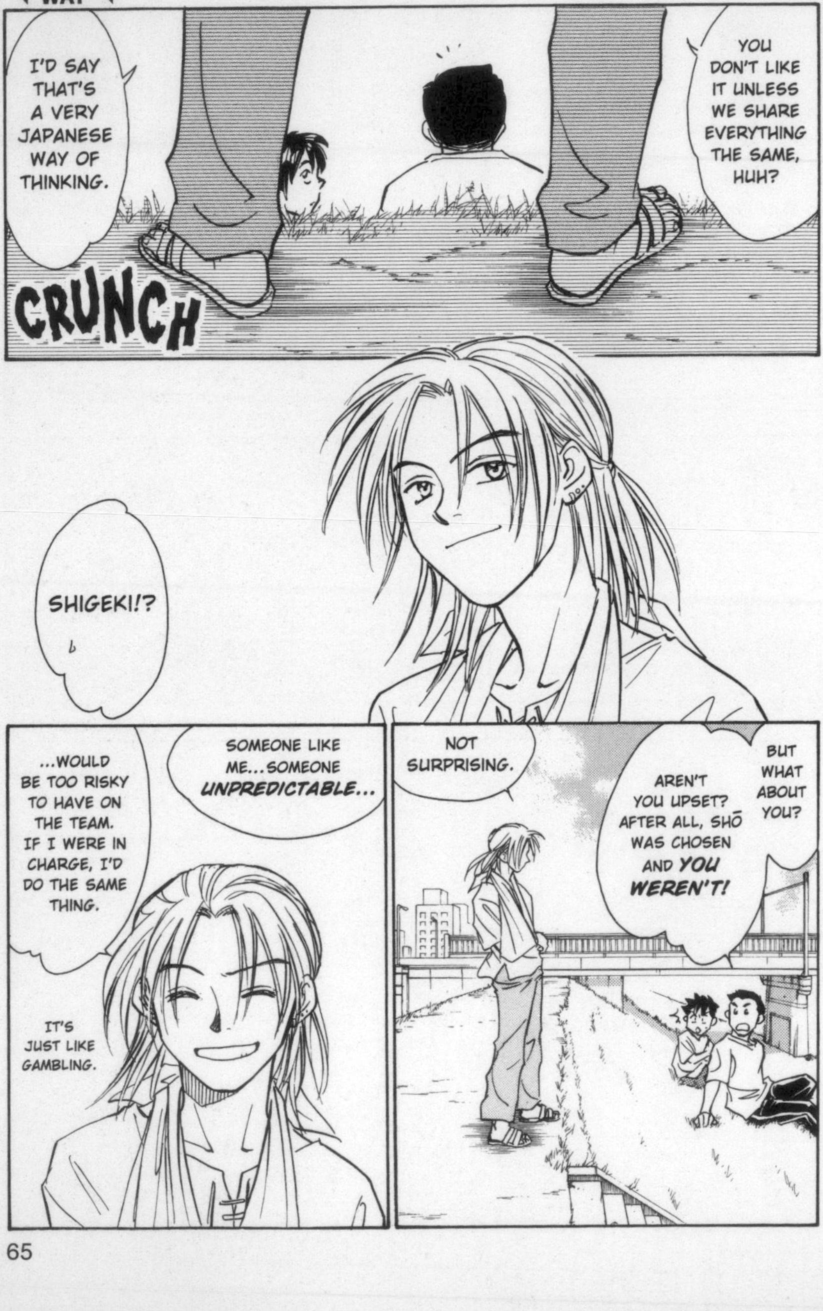

YOU DON'T LIKE IT UNLESS WE SHARE EVERYTHING THE SAME, HUH?
I'D SAY THAT'S A VERY JAPANESE WAY OF THINKING.
CRUNCH
SHIGEKI!?
BUT WHAT ABOUT YOU?
AREN'T YOU UPSET? AFTER ALL, SHŌ WAS CHOSEN AND *YOU WEREN'T!*
NOT SURPRISING.
SOMEONE LIKE ME...SOMEONE *UNPREDICTABLE...*
...WOULD BE TOO RISKY TO HAVE ON THE TEAM. IF I WERE IN CHARGE, I'D DO THE SAME THING.
IT'S JUST LIKE GAMBLING.

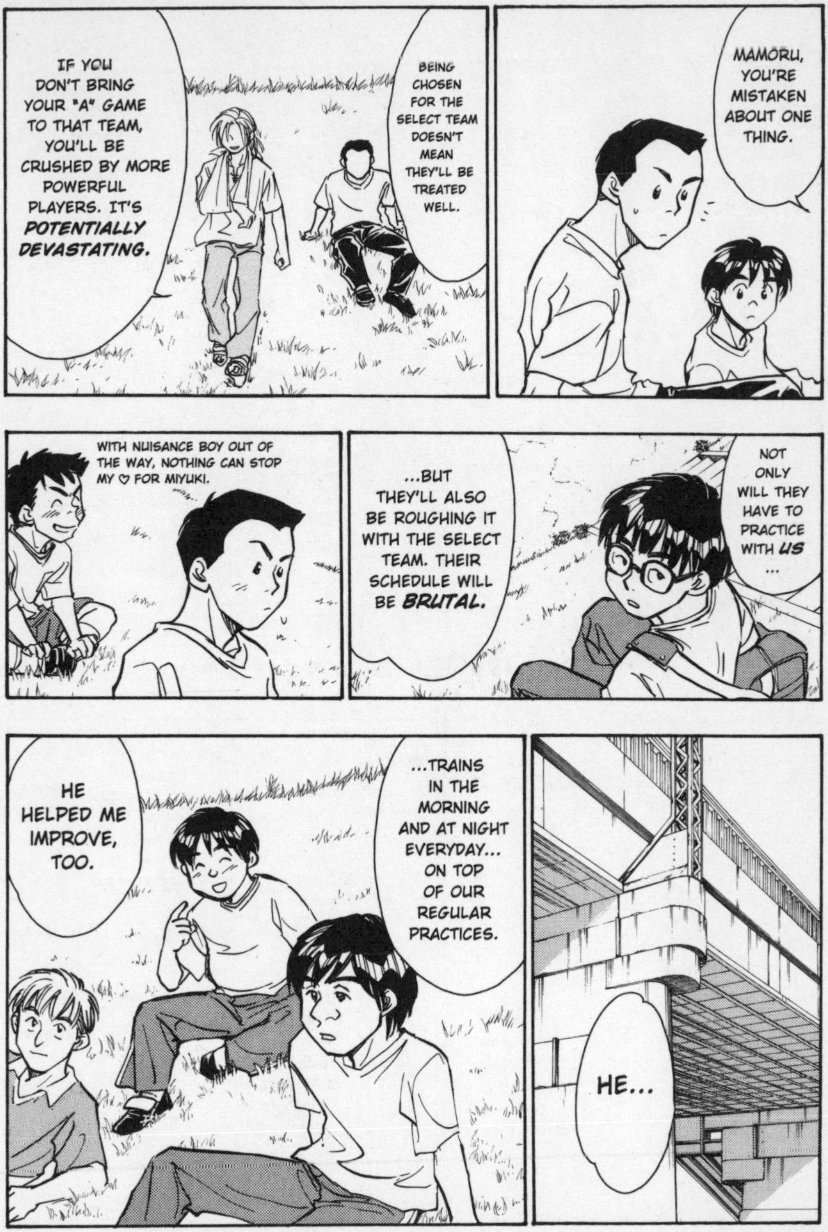
MAMORU, YOU'RE MISTAKEN ABOUT ONE THING.
BEING CHOSEN FOR THE SELECT TEAM DOESN'T MEAN THEY'LL BE TREATED WELL.
IF YOU DON'T BRING YOUR "A" GAME TO THAT TEAM, YOU'LL BE CRUSHED BY MORE POWERFUL PLAYERS. IT'S POTENTIALLY DEVASTATING.
NOT ONLY WILL THEY HAVE TO PRACTICE WITH US ...
...BUT THEY'LL ALSO BE ROUGHING IT WITH THE SELECT TEAM. THEIR SCHEDULE WILL BE BRUTAL.
WITH NUISANCE BOY OUT OF THE WAY, NOTHING CAN STOP MY ♡ FOR MIYUKI.
HE...
...TRAINS IN THE MORNING AND AT NIGHT EVERYDAY... ON TOP OF OUR REGULAR PRACTICES.
HE HELPED ME IMPROVE, TOO.

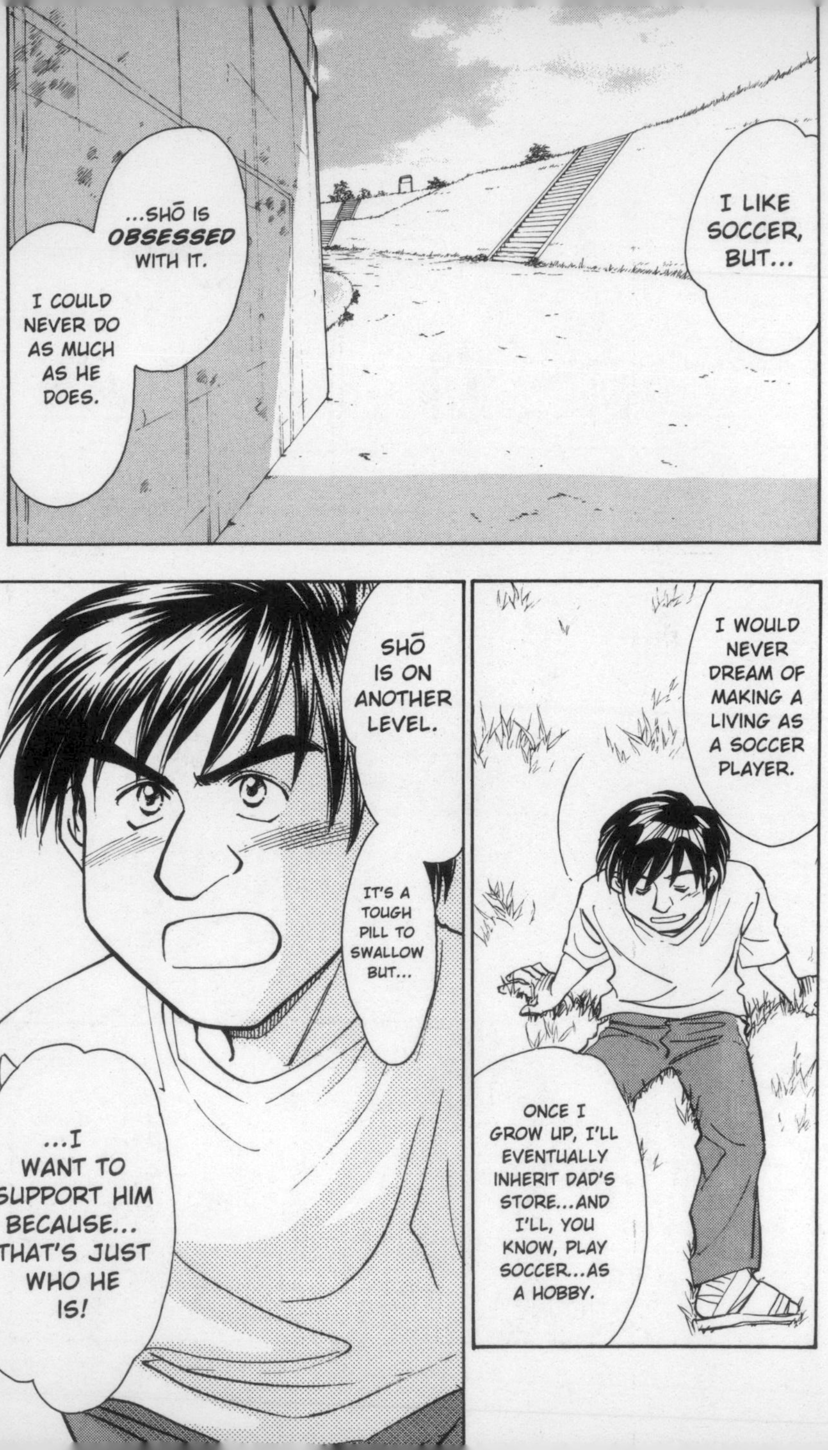
I LIKE SOCCER, BUT...
...SHŌ IS **OBSESSED** WITH IT.
I COULD NEVER DO AS MUCH AS HE DOES.
I WOULD NEVER DREAM OF MAKING A LIVING AS A SOCCER PLAYER.
ONCE I GROW UP, I'LL EVENTUALLY INHERIT DAD'S STORE...AND I'LL, YOU KNOW, PLAY SOCCER...AS A HOBBY.
SHŌ IS ON ANOTHER LEVEL.
IT'S A TOUGH PILL TO SWALLOW BUT...
...I WANT TO SUPPORT HIM BECAUSE... THAT'S JUST WHO HE IS!

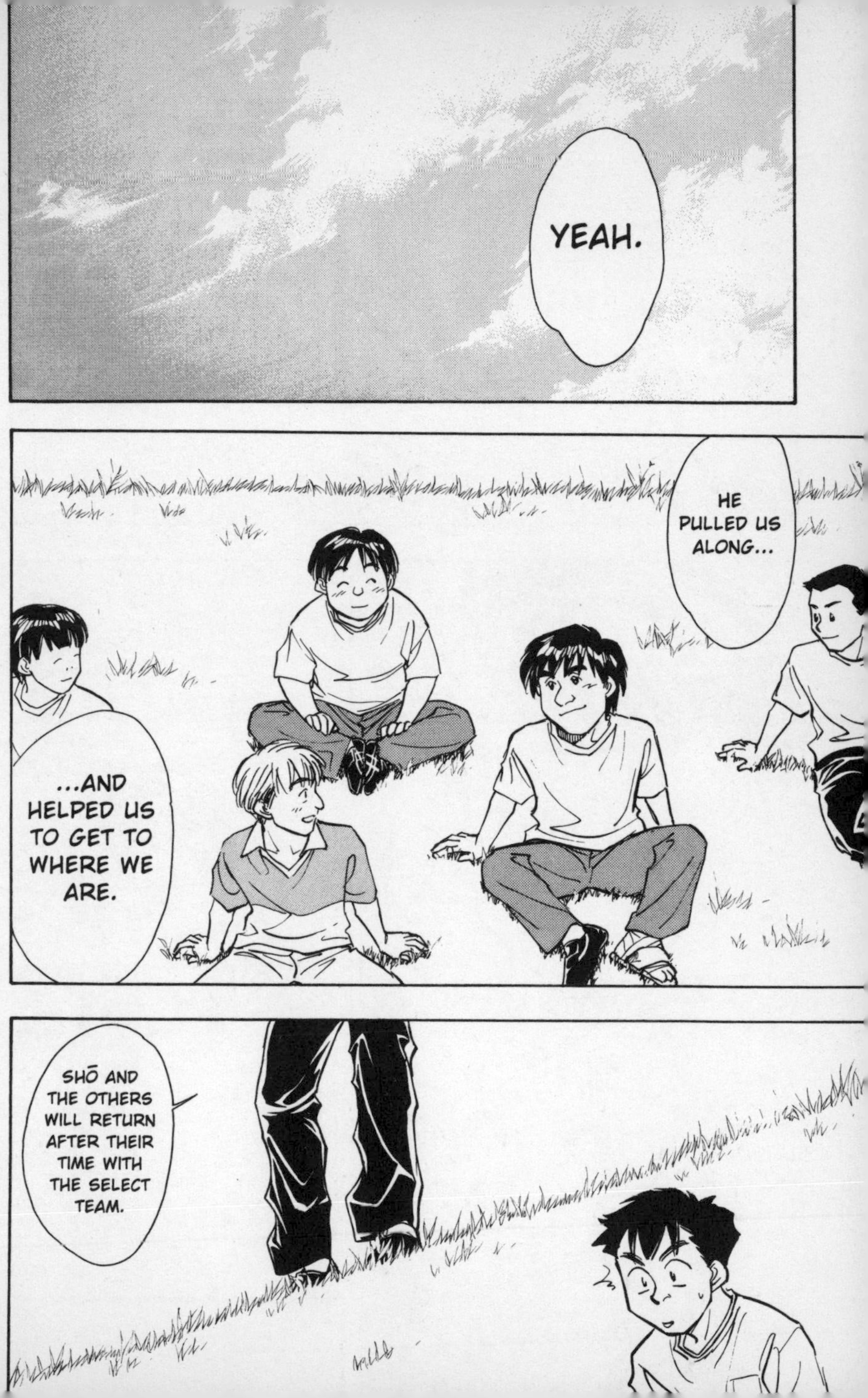
YEAH.
HE PULLED US ALONG...
...AND HELPED US TO GET TO WHERE WE ARE.
SHŌ AND THE OTHERS WILL RETURN AFTER THEIR TIME WITH THE SELECT TEAM.

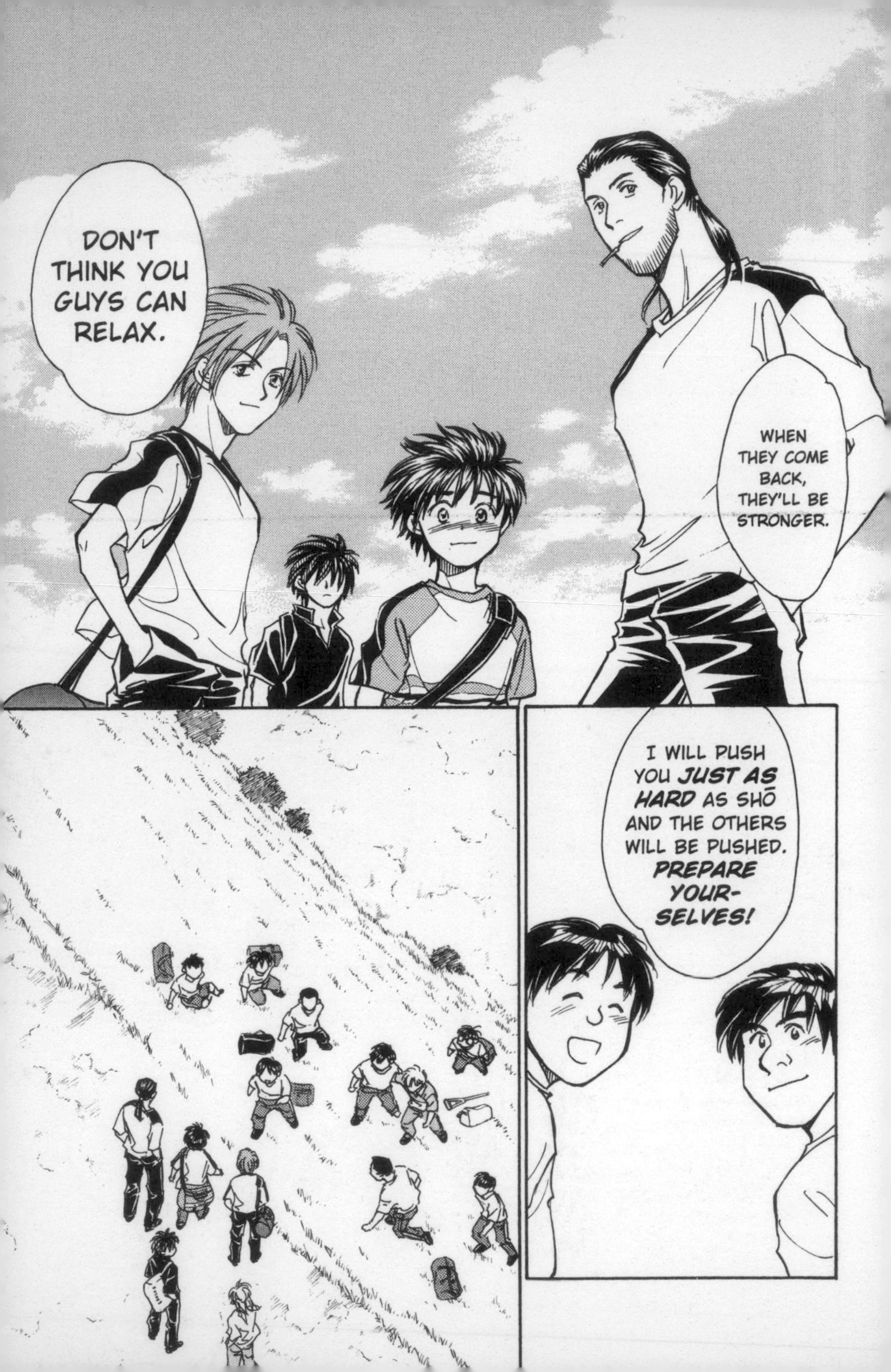
WHEN THEY COME BACK, THEY'LL BE STRONGER.
DON'T THINK YOU GUYS CAN RELAX.
I WILL PUSH YOU ***JUST AS HARD*** AS SHŌ AND THE OTHERS WILL BE PUSHED. ***PREPARE YOURSELVES!***

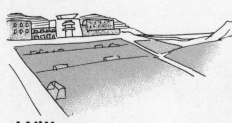

FOR THE SELECT TEAM RETREAT EPISODE, I VISITED AND RESEARCHED J VILLAGE IN FUKUSHIMA, WHICH IS A FAMOUS RETREAT FOR THE JAPAN REPRESENTATIVE TEAM.

I APPRECIATED THEIR HOSPITALITY.

J Village

IT'S A NATIONAL TRAINING CENTER FOR SOCCER: A WELL-EQUIPPED FACILITY THAT INCLUDES A STADIUM WITH NATURAL GRASS, A HUGE TRAINING GROUND AND LODGING FACILITIES.

THE NATURAL GRASS FELT VERY NICE! EVERYONE SHOULD GO VISIT!

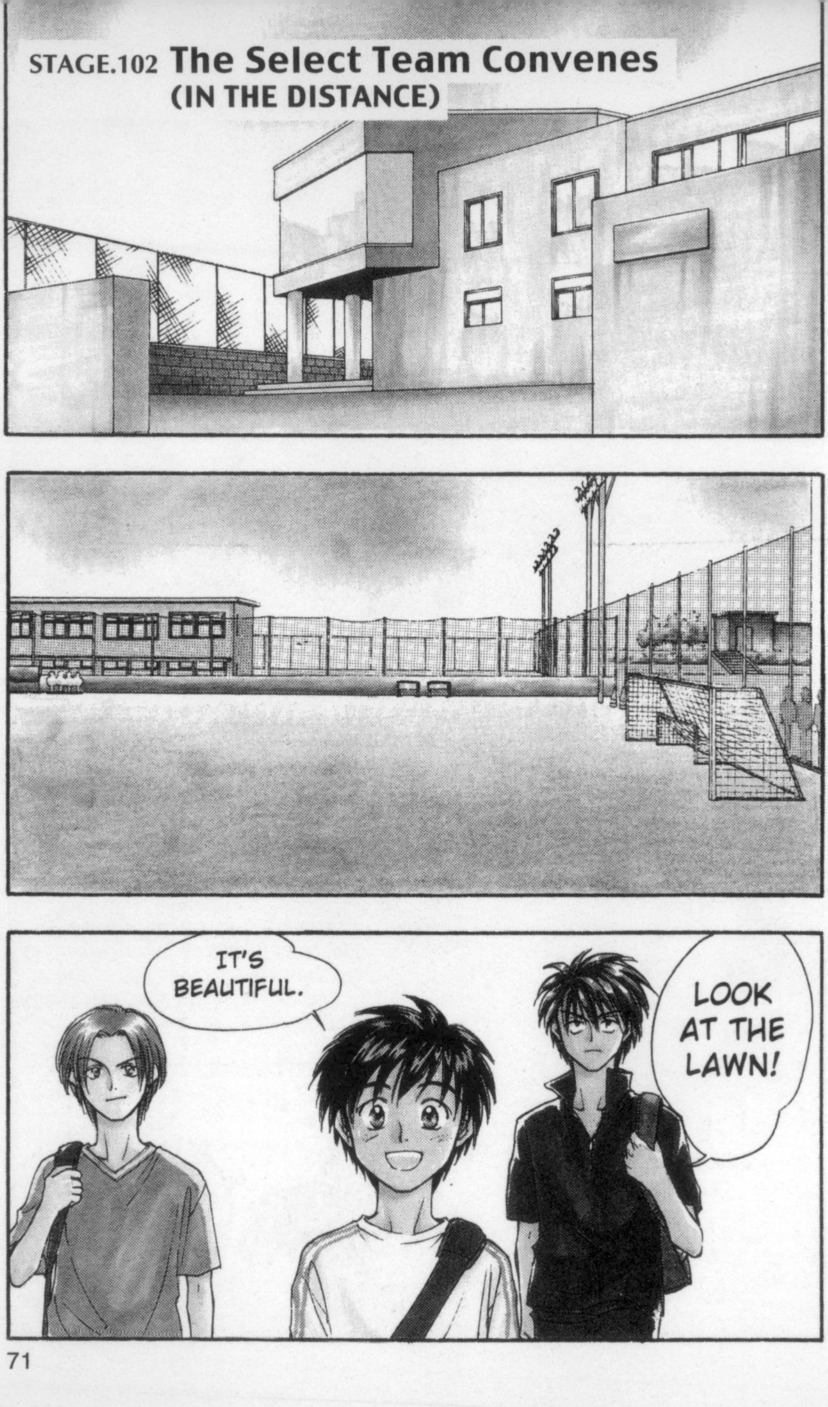
STAGE.102 The Select Team Convenes
(IN THE DISTANCE)
LOOK AT THE LAWN!
IT'S BEAUTIFUL.

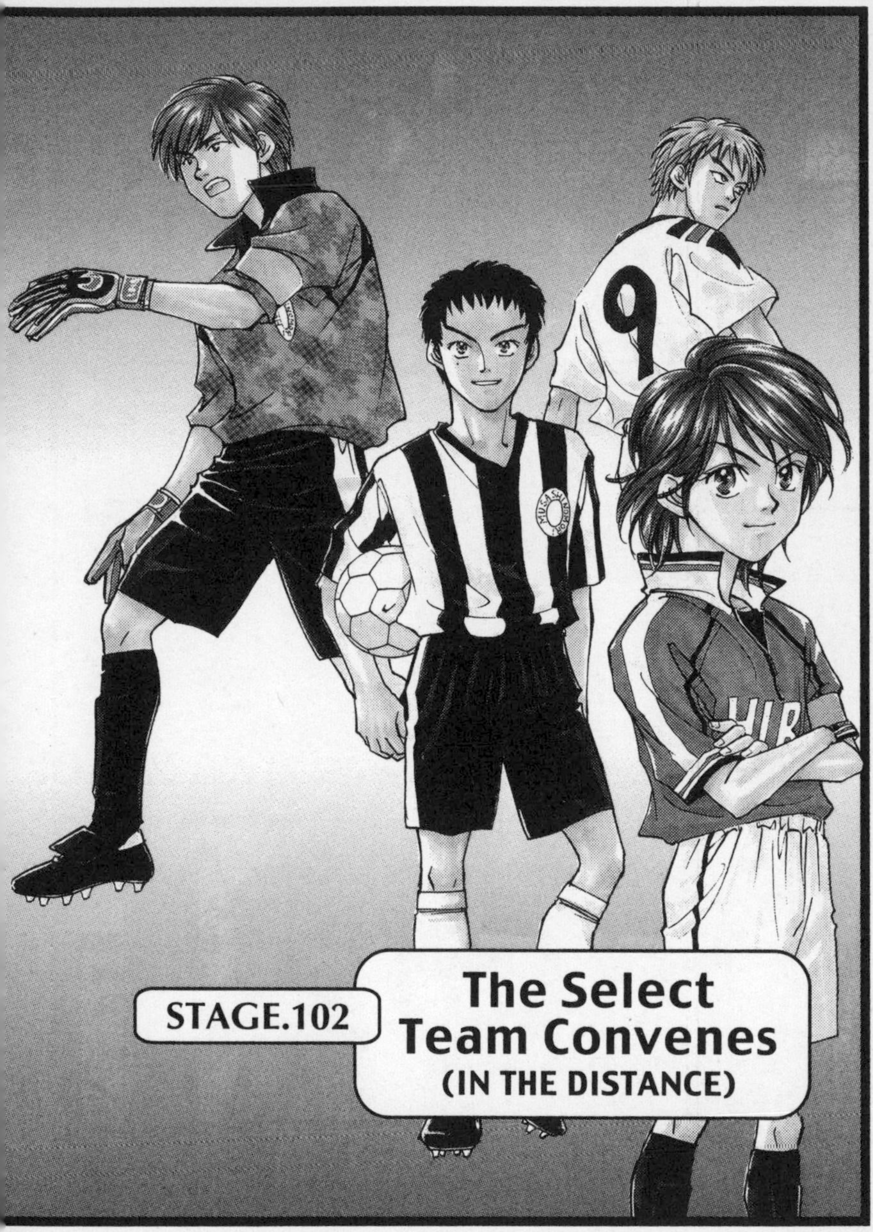
STAGE.102
The Select Team Convenes
(IN THE DISTANCE)

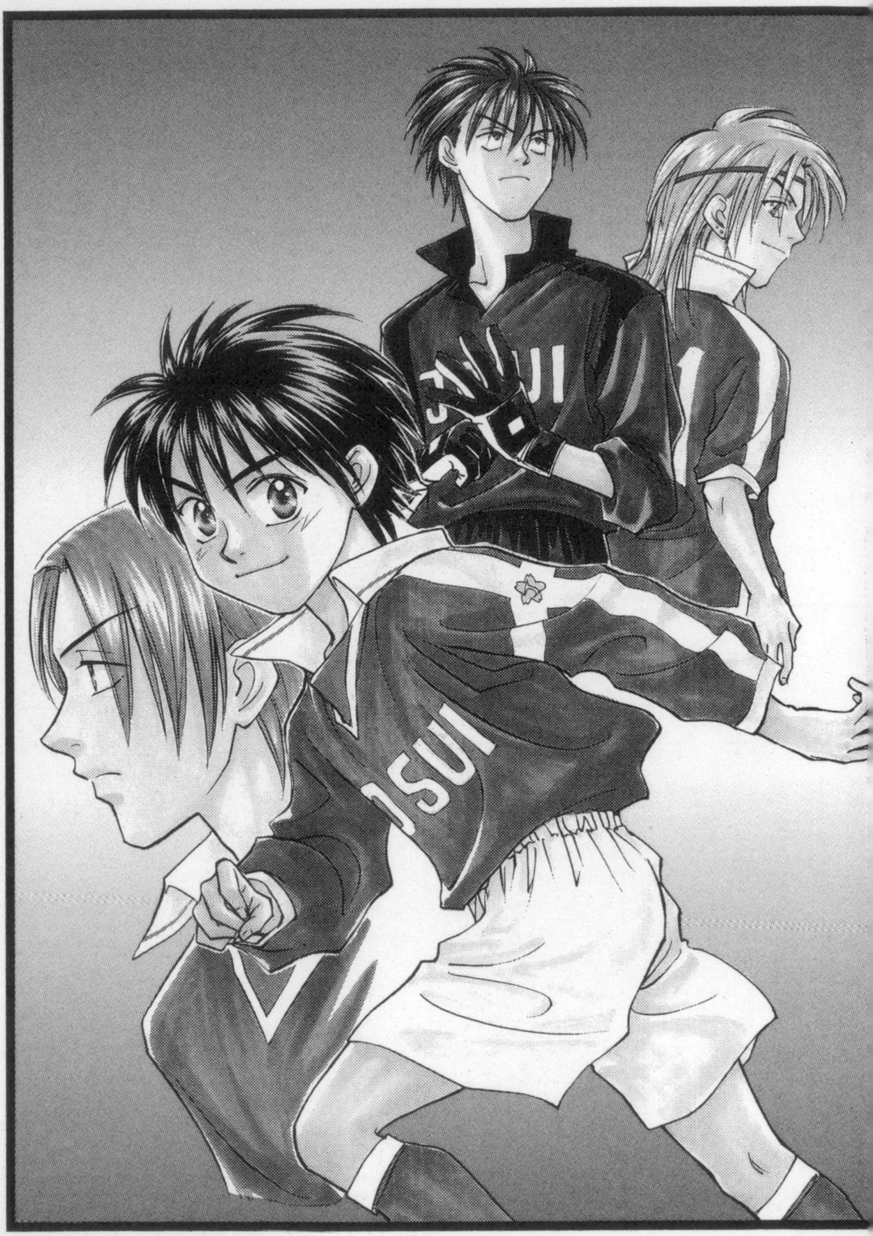

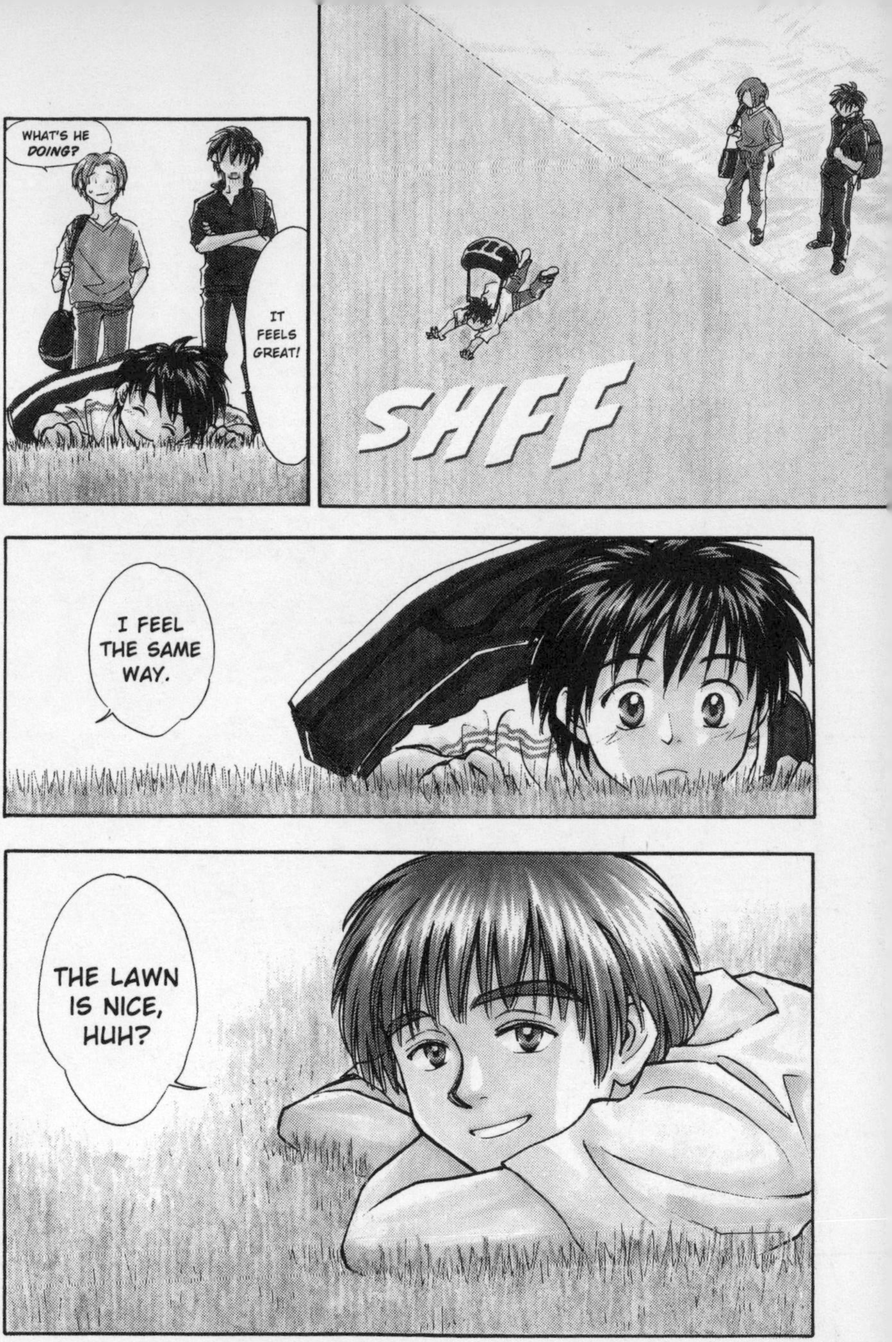
SHFF
WHAT'S HE DOING?
IT FEELS GREAT!
I FEEL THE SAME WAY.
THE LAWN IS NICE, HUH?

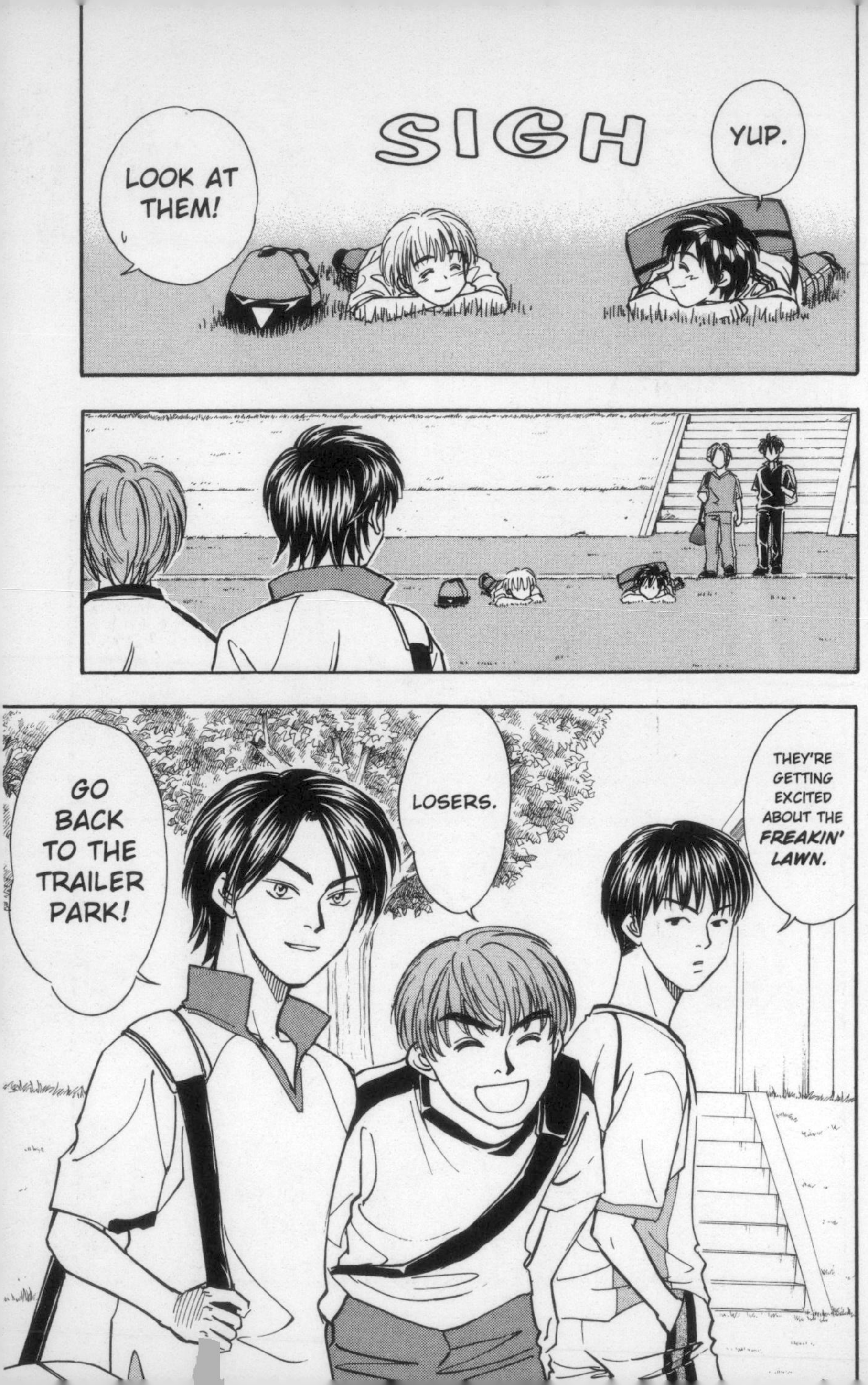
YUP.
SIGH
LOOK AT THEM!
THEY'RE GETTING EXCITED ABOUT THE FREAKIN' LAWN.
LOSERS.
GO BACK TO THE TRAILER PARK!

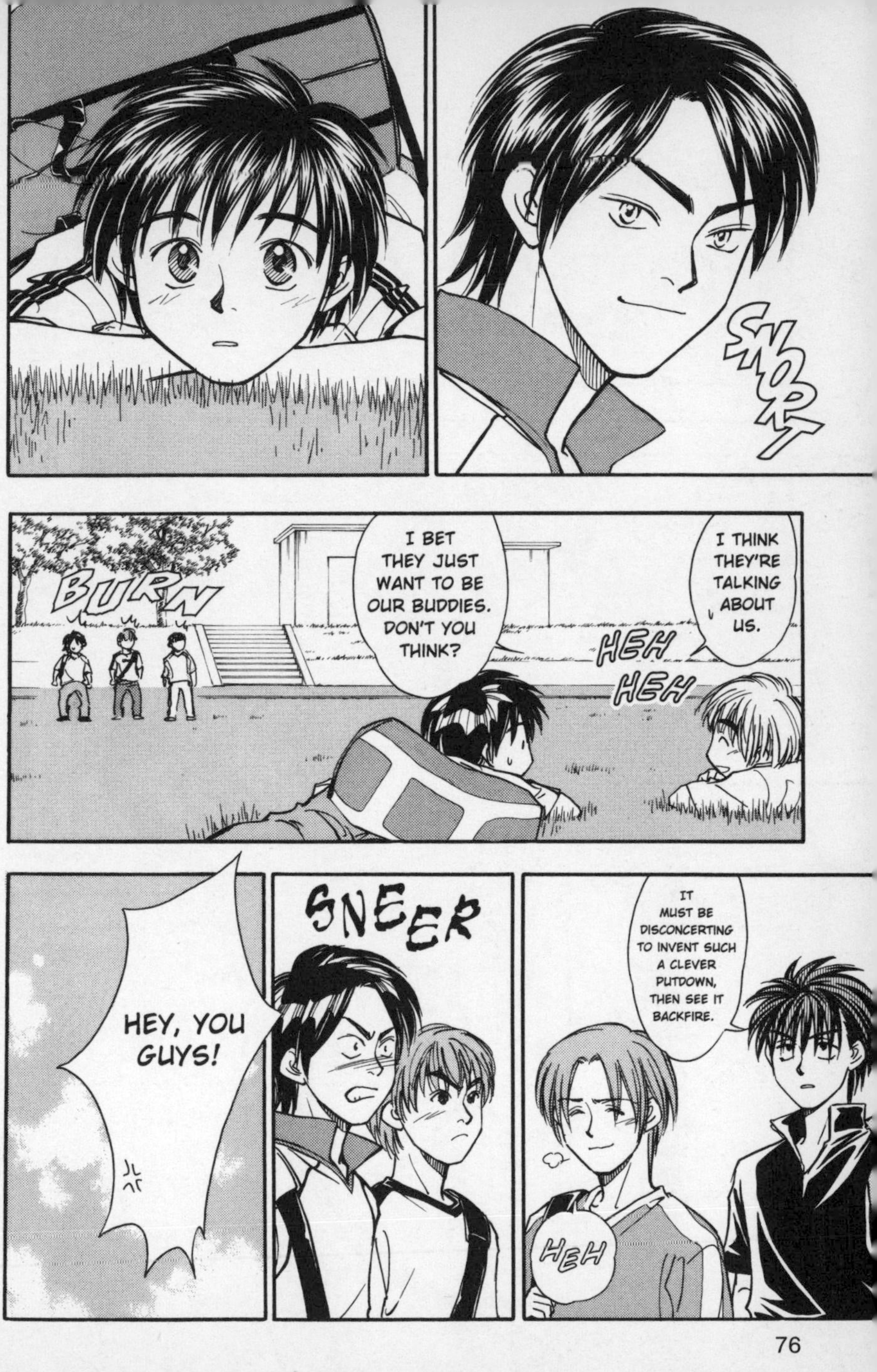
SNORT
I THINK THEY'RE TALKING ABOUT US.
HEH HEH
I BET THEY JUST WANT TO BE OUR BUDDIES. DON'T YOU THINK?
BURN
IT MUST BE DISCONCERTING TO INVENT SUCH A CLEVER PUTDOWN, THEN SEE IT BACKFIRE.
HEH
SNEER
HEY, YOU GUYS!

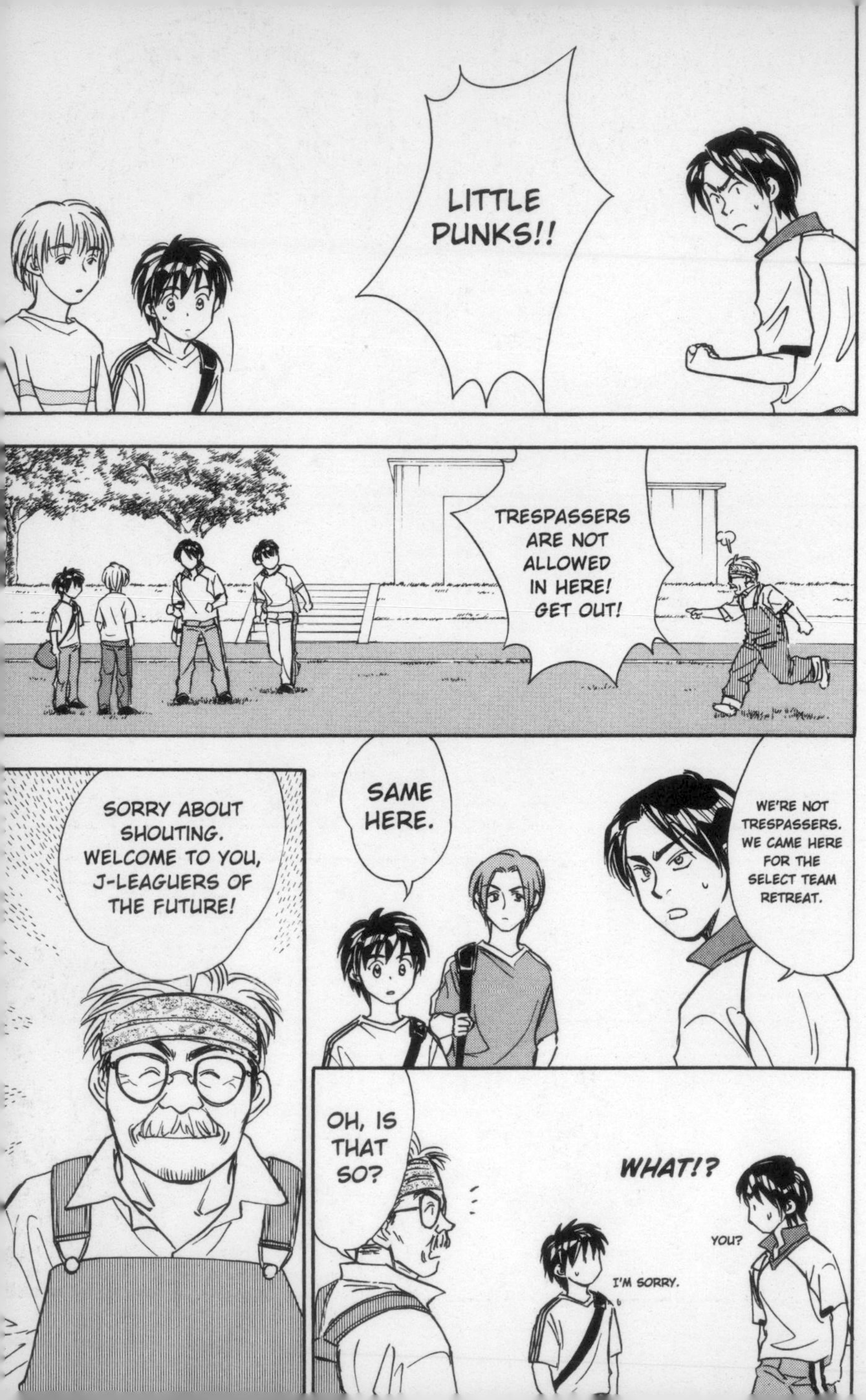
LITTLE PUNKS!!
TRESPASSERS ARE NOT ALLOWED IN HERE! GET OUT!
WE'RE NOT TRESPASSERS. WE CAME HERE FOR THE SELECT TEAM RETREAT.
SAME HERE.
OH, IS THAT SO?
WHAT!?
YOU?
I'M SORRY.
SORRY ABOUT SHOUTING. WELCOME TO YOU, J-LEAGUERS OF THE FUTURE!

AH...

AND NICE.

IT'S BIG.

HERE'S OUR ROOM.

205

SHŌ KAZAMATSURI
TEPPEI KOIWA
TAKI SUGIHARA
DAICHI FUWA

SHŌ KAZAMATSURI

TEPPEI KOIWA

TAKI SUGIHARA

DAICHI FUWA

OKAY.

SEE YOU LATER.

I'M IN ANOTHER ROOM.

205

SHŌ KAZAMATSURI
TEPPEI KOIWA
TAKI SUGIHARA
DAICHI FUWA

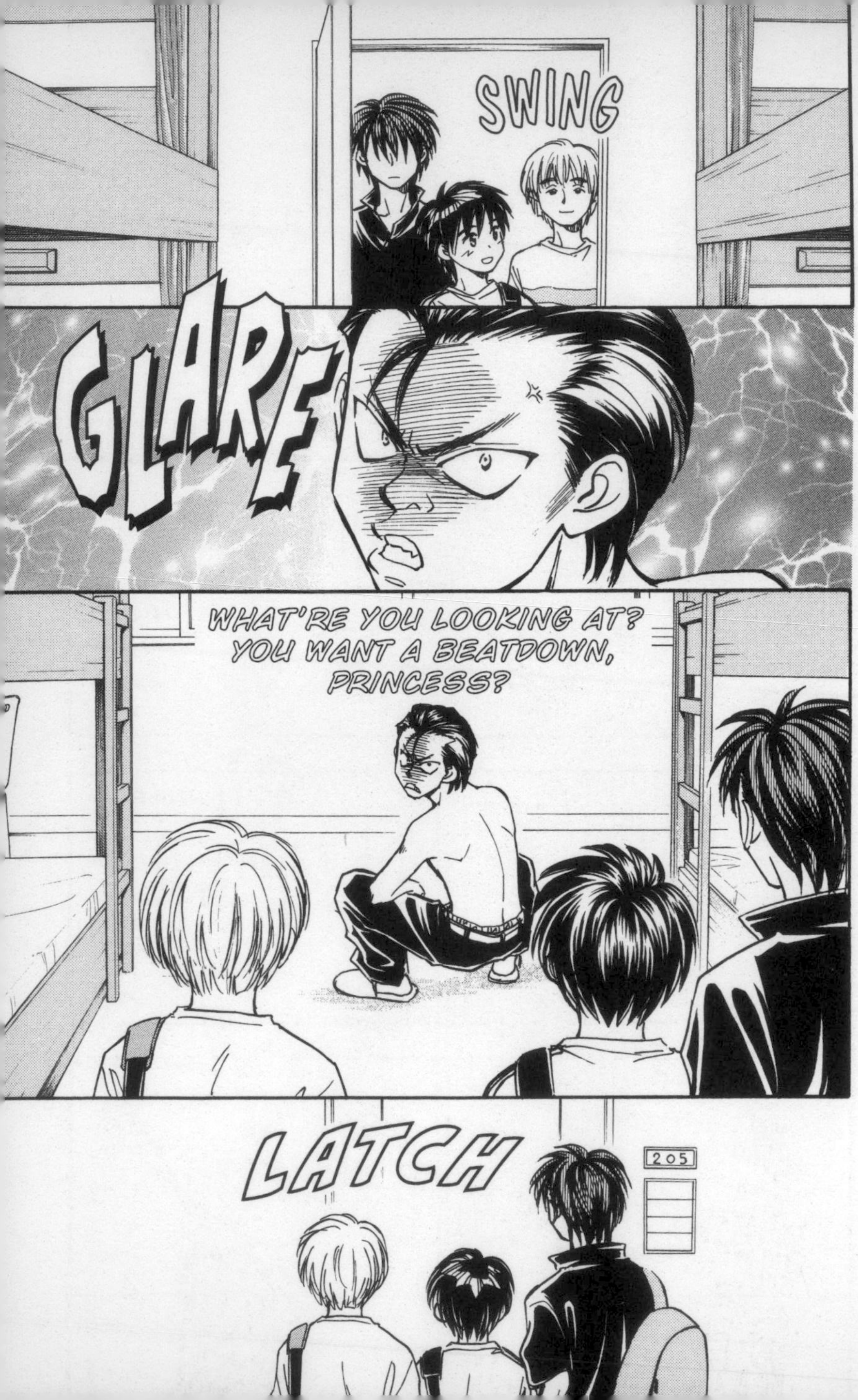
SWING
GLARE
WHAT'RE YOU LOOKING AT? YOU WANT A BEATDOWN, PRINCESS?
205
LATCH

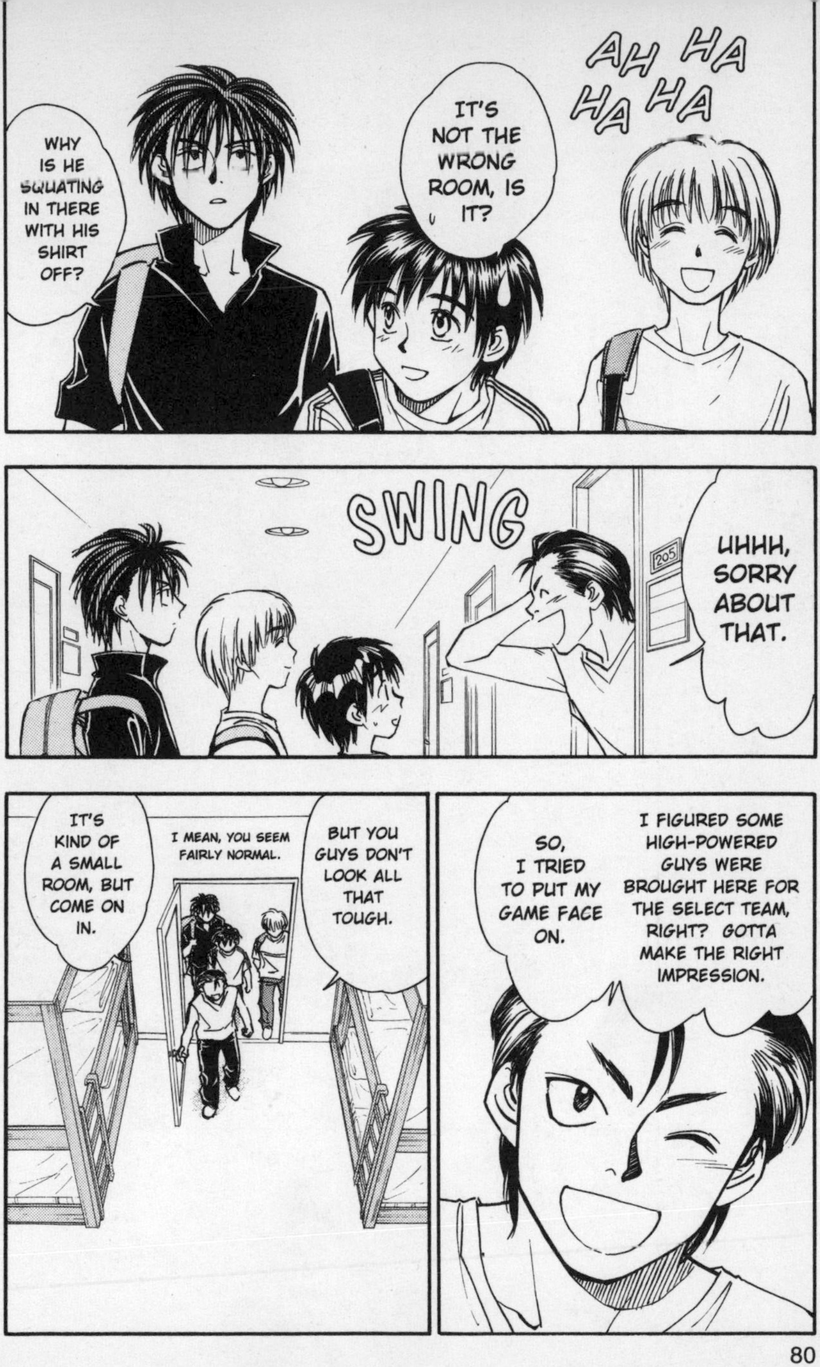
AH HA HA HA
IT'S NOT THE WRONG ROOM, IS IT?
WHY IS HE SQUATING IN THERE WITH HIS SHIRT OFF?
UHHH, SORRY ABOUT THAT.
SWING
I FIGURED SOME HIGH-POWERED GUYS WERE BROUGHT HERE FOR THE SELECT TEAM, RIGHT? GOTTA MAKE THE RIGHT IMPRESSION.
SO, I TRIED TO PUT MY GAME FACE ON.
BUT YOU GUYS DON'T LOOK ALL THAT TOUGH.
I MEAN, YOU SEEM FAIRLY NORMAL.
IT'S KIND OF A SMALL ROOM, BUT COME ON IN.

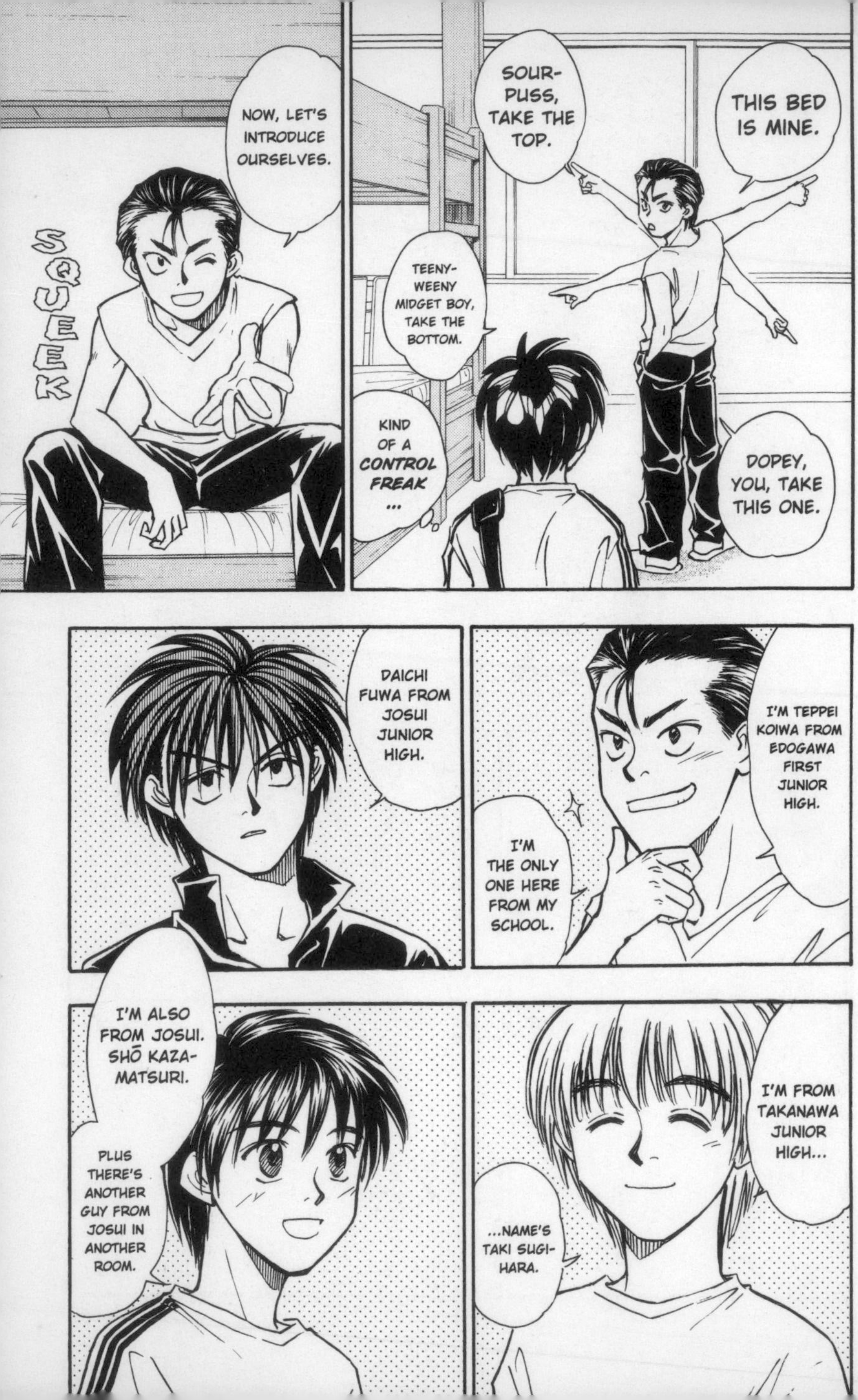
THIS BED IS MINE.
SOUR-PUSS, TAKE THE TOP.
DOPEY, YOU, TAKE THIS ONE.
TEENY-WEENY MIDGET BOY, TAKE THE BOTTOM.
KIND OF A CONTROL FREAK...
NOW, LET'S INTRODUCE OURSELVES.
SQUEEK
I'M TEPPEI KOIWA FROM EDOGAWA FIRST JUNIOR HIGH.
I'M THE ONLY ONE HERE FROM MY SCHOOL.
DAICHI FUWA FROM JOSUI JUNIOR HIGH.
I'M FROM TAKANAWA JUNIOR HIGH...
...NAME'S TAKI SUGI-HARA.
I'M ALSO FROM JOSUI. SHŌ KAZA-MATSURI.
PLUS THERE'S ANOTHER GUY FROM JOSUI IN ANOTHER ROOM.

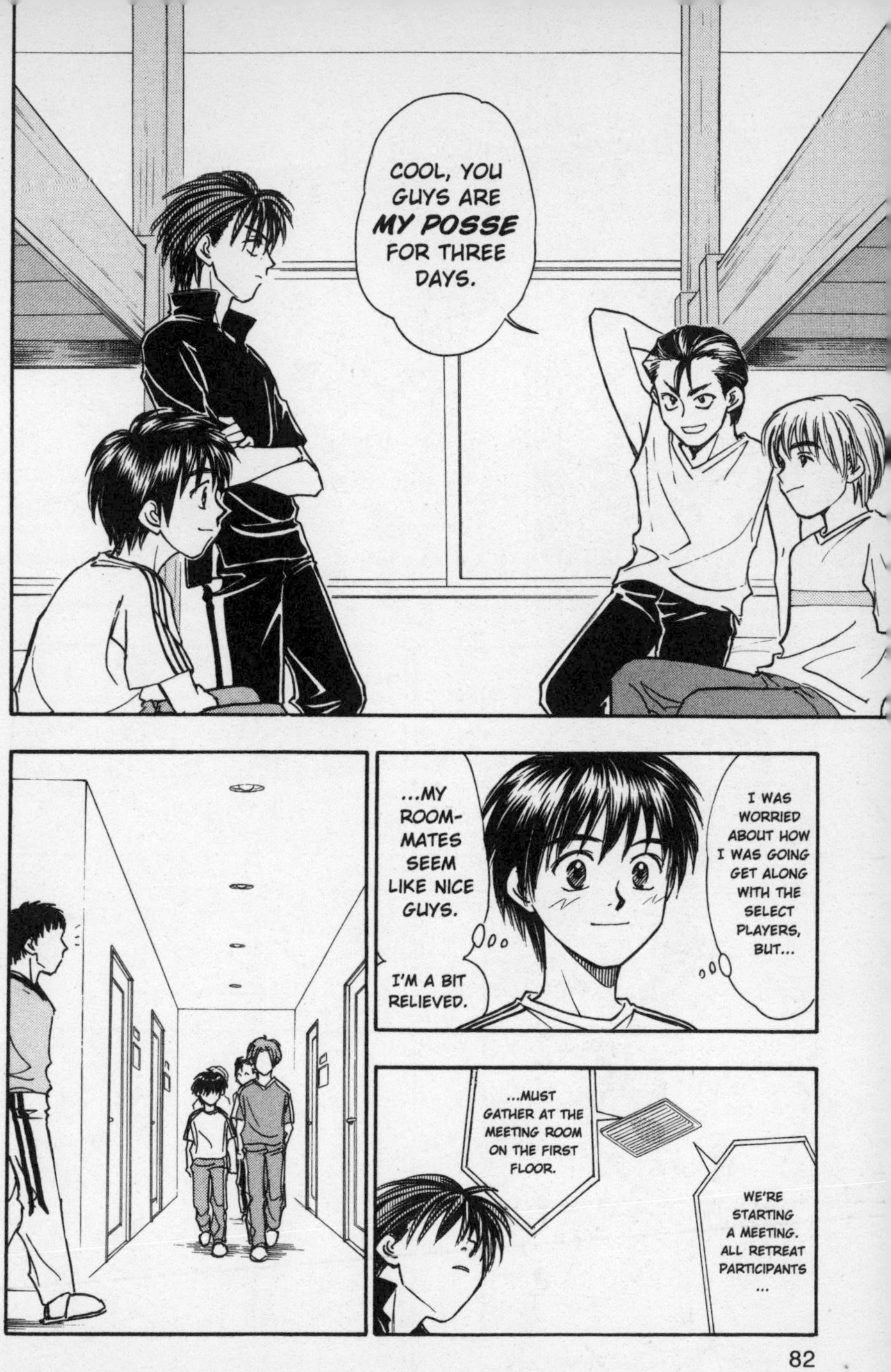
COOL, YOU GUYS ARE **MY POSSE** FOR THREE DAYS.
I WAS WORRIED ABOUT HOW I WAS GOING GET ALONG WITH THE SELECT PLAYERS, BUT...
...MY ROOM-MATES SEEM LIKE NICE GUYS.
I'M A BIT RELIEVED.
WE'RE STARTING A MEETING. ALL RETREAT PARTICIPANTS ...
...MUST GATHER AT THE MEETING ROOM ON THE FIRST FLOOR.

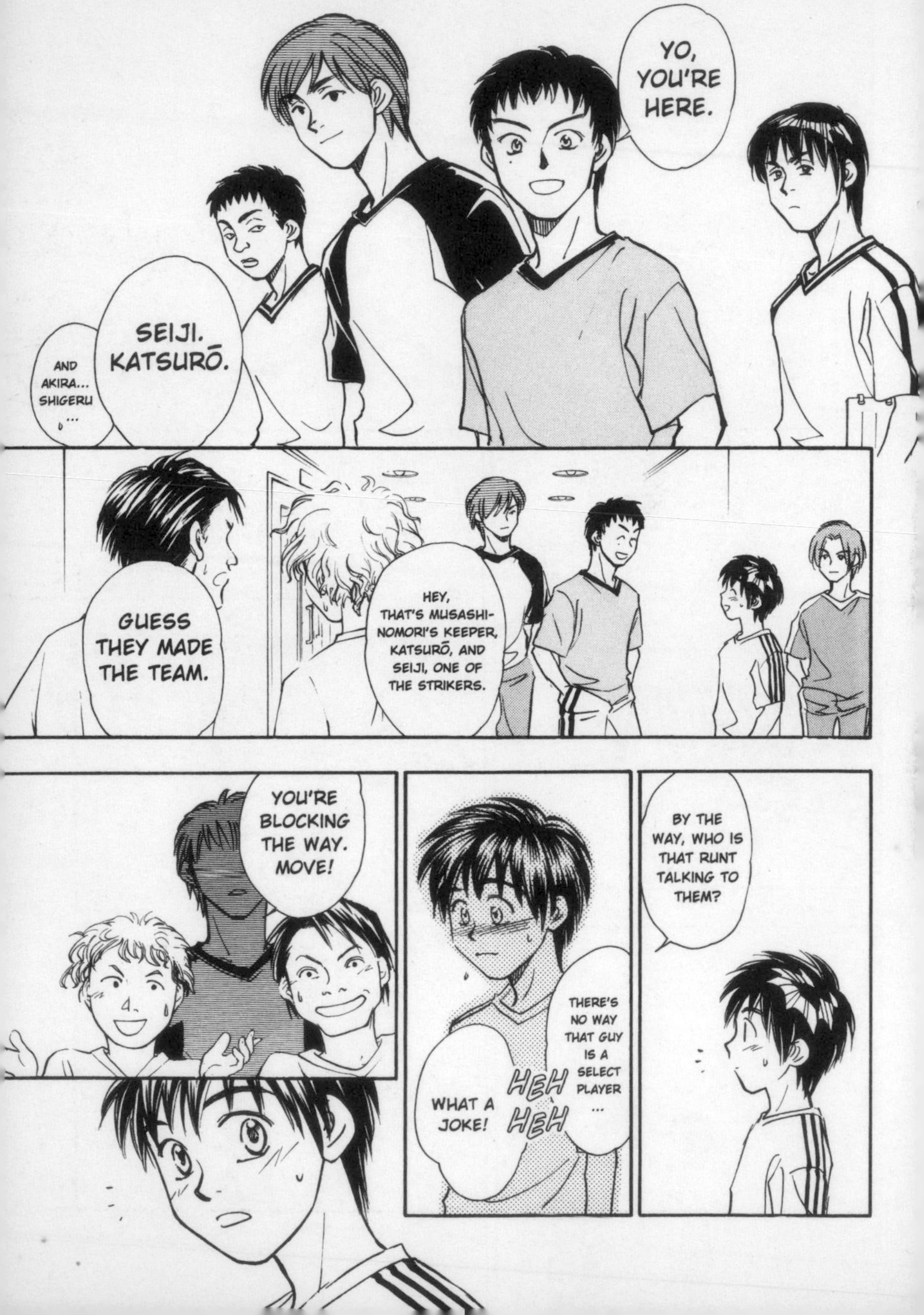
YO, YOU'RE HERE.
SEIJI. KATSURŌ.
AND AKIRA... SHIGERU...
HEY, THAT'S MUSASHI-NOMORI'S KEEPER, KATSURŌ, AND SEIJI, ONE OF THE STRIKERS.
GUESS THEY MADE THE TEAM.
BY THE WAY, WHO IS THAT RUNT TALKING TO THEM?
THERE'S NO WAY THAT GUY IS A SELECT PLAYER...
HEH HEH
WHAT A JOKE!
YOU'RE BLOCKING THE WAY. MOVE!

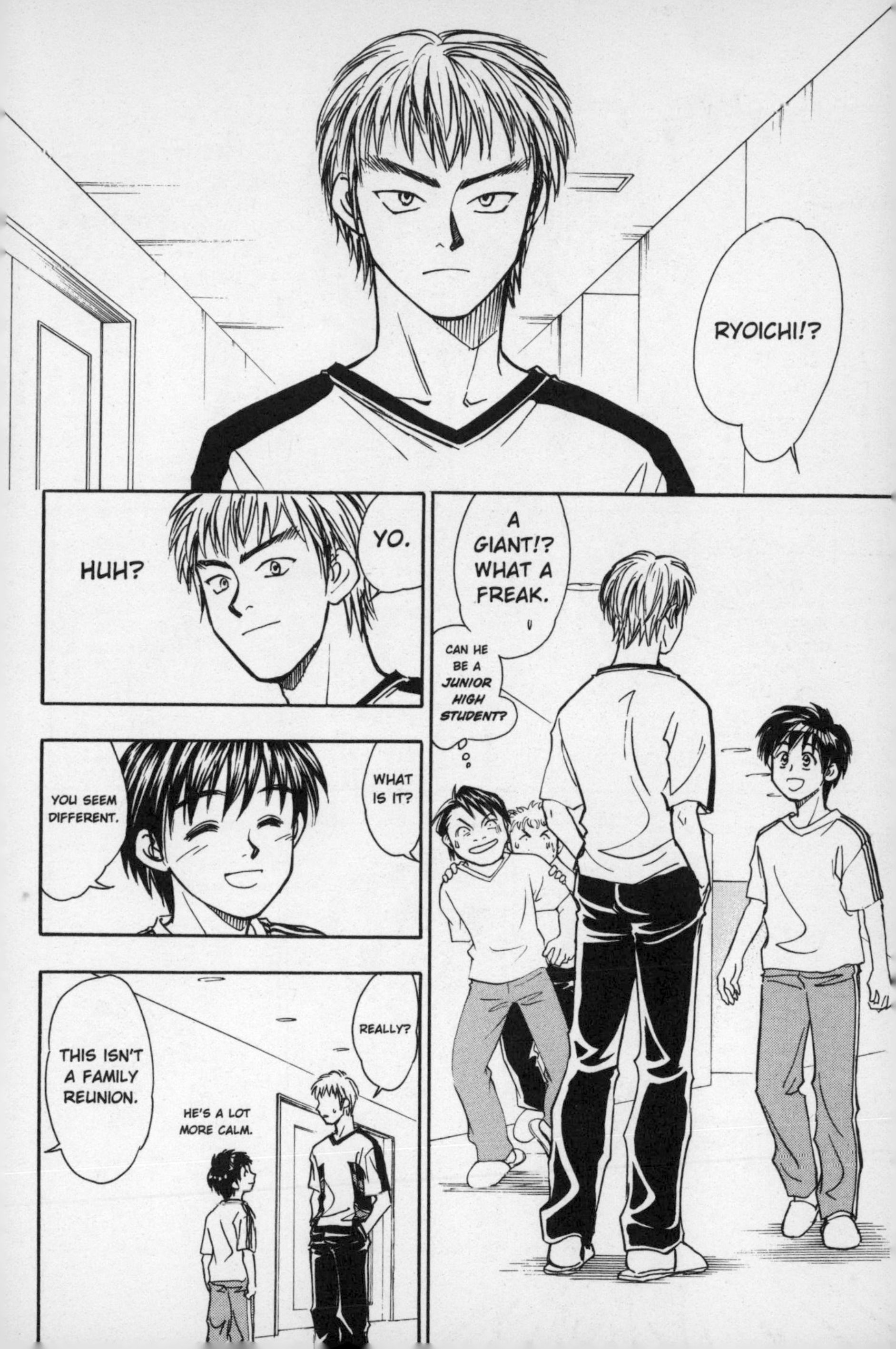
RYOICHI!?
A GIANT!? WHAT A FREAK.
CAN HE BE A JUNIOR HIGH STUDENT?
YO.
HUH?
WHAT IS IT?
YOU SEEM DIFFERENT.
REALLY?
THIS ISN'T A FAMILY REUNION.
HE'S A LOT MORE CALM.

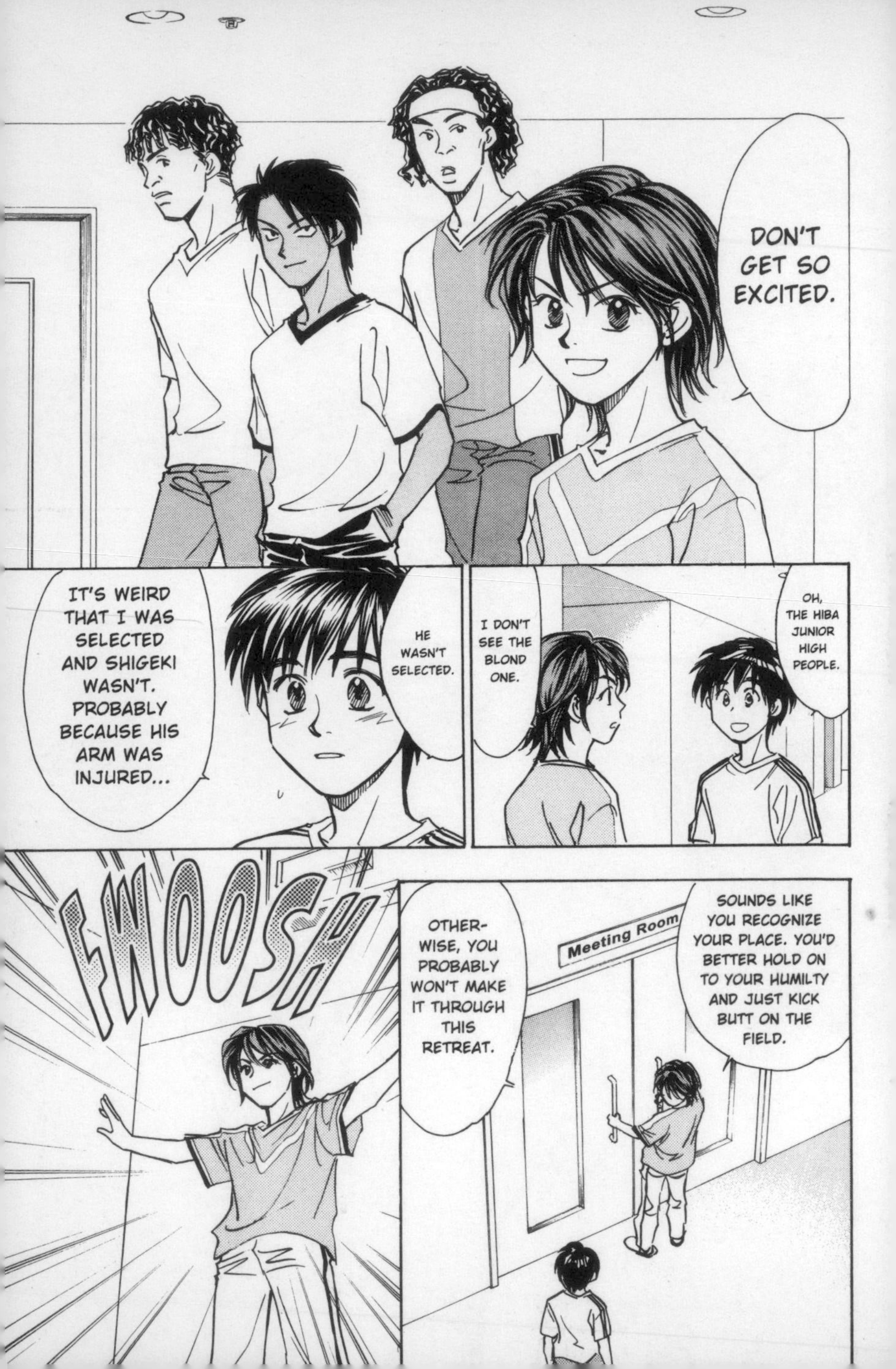
DON'T GET SO EXCITED.
OH, THE HIBA JUNIOR HIGH PEOPLE.
I DON'T SEE THE BLOND ONE.
HE WASN'T SELECTED.
IT'S WEIRD THAT I WAS SELECTED AND SHIGEKI WASN'T. PROBABLY BECAUSE HIS ARM WAS INJURED...
SOUNDS LIKE YOU RECOGNIZE YOUR PLACE. YOU'D BETTER HOLD ON TO YOUR HUMILTY AND JUST KICK BUTT ON THE FIELD.
OTHER-WISE, YOU PROBABLY WON'T MAKE IT THROUGH THIS RETREAT.
Meeting Room
FWOOSH

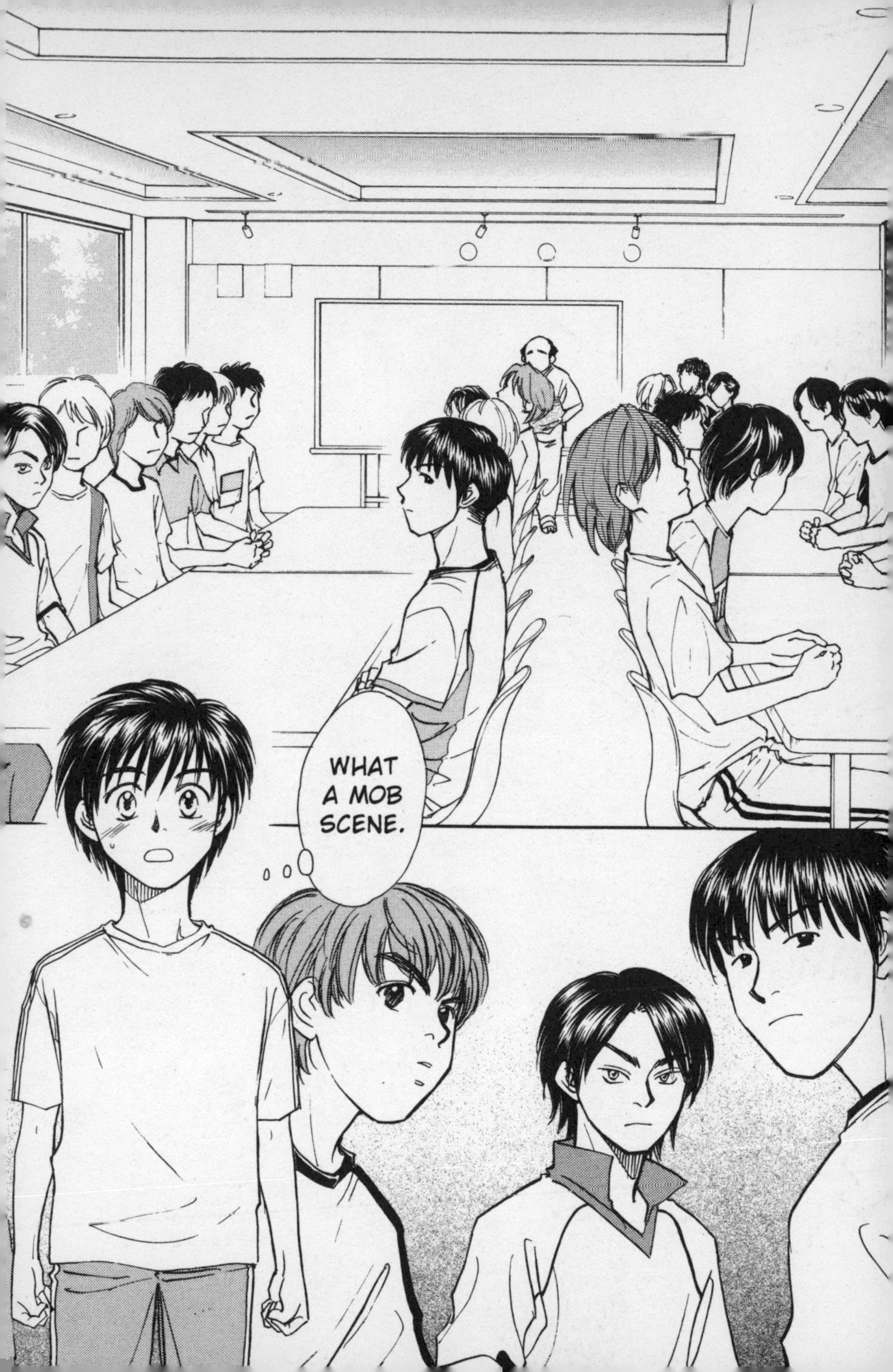
WHAT A MOB SCENE.

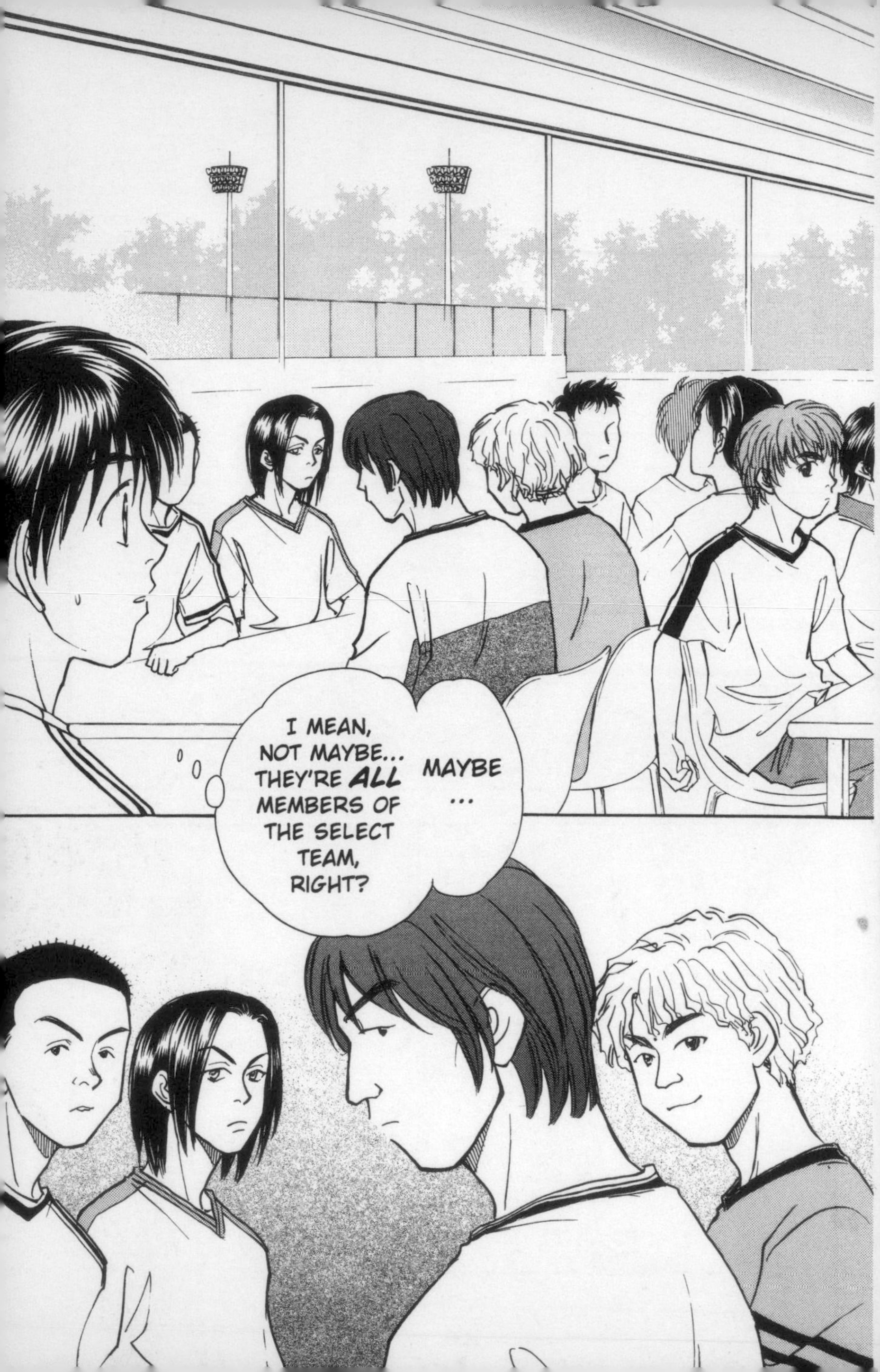
MAYBE ...
I MEAN, NOT MAYBE... THEY'RE ALL MEMBERS OF THE SELECT TEAM, RIGHT?

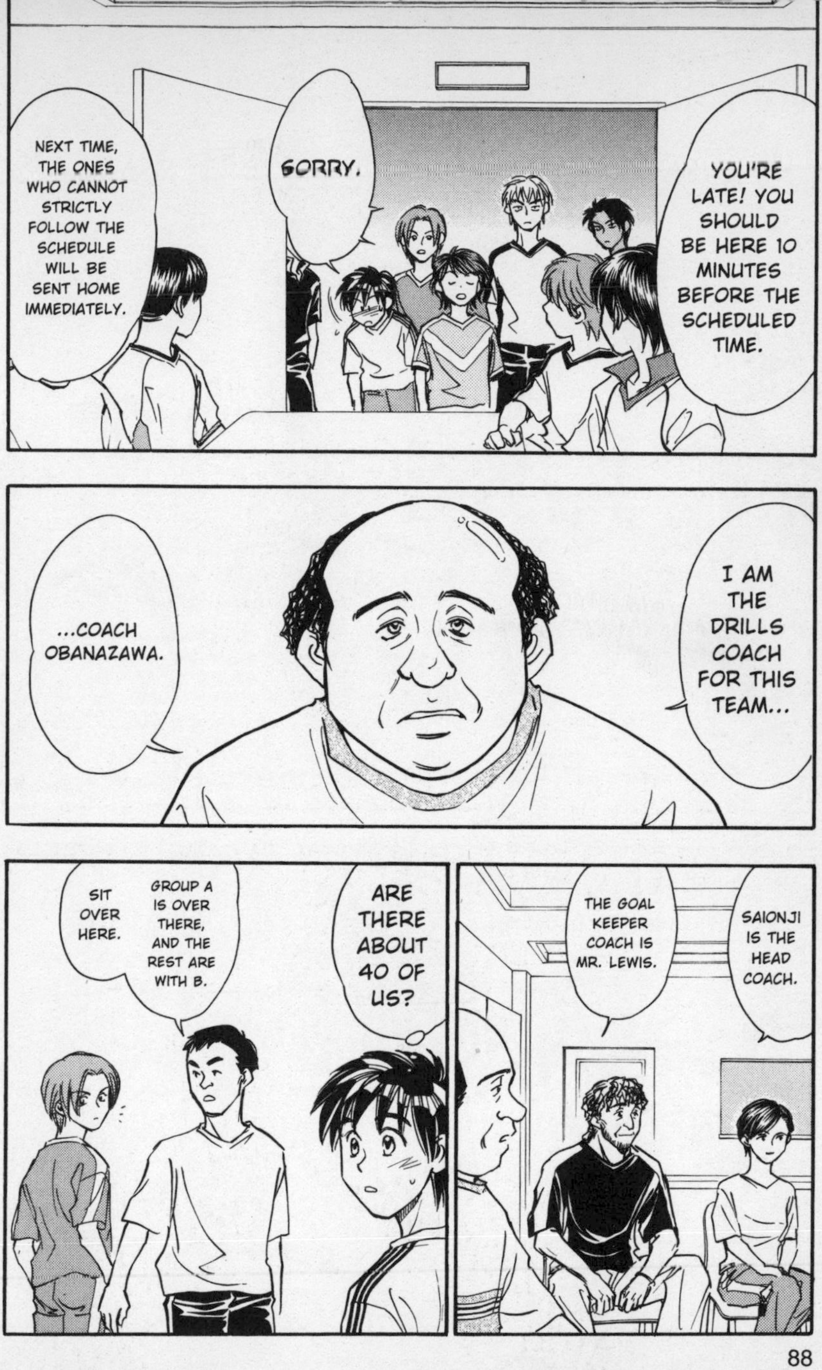
YOU'RE LATE! YOU SHOULD BE HERE 10 MINUTES BEFORE THE SCHEDULED TIME.
SORRY.
NEXT TIME, THE ONES WHO CANNOT STRICTLY FOLLOW THE SCHEDULE WILL BE SENT HOME IMMEDIATELY.
I AM THE DRILLS COACH FOR THIS TEAM...
...COACH OBANAZAWA.
SAIONJI IS THE HEAD COACH.
THE GOAL KEEPER COACH IS MR. LEWIS.
ARE THERE ABOUT 40 OF US?
GROUP A IS OVER THERE, AND THE REST ARE WITH B.
SIT OVER HERE.

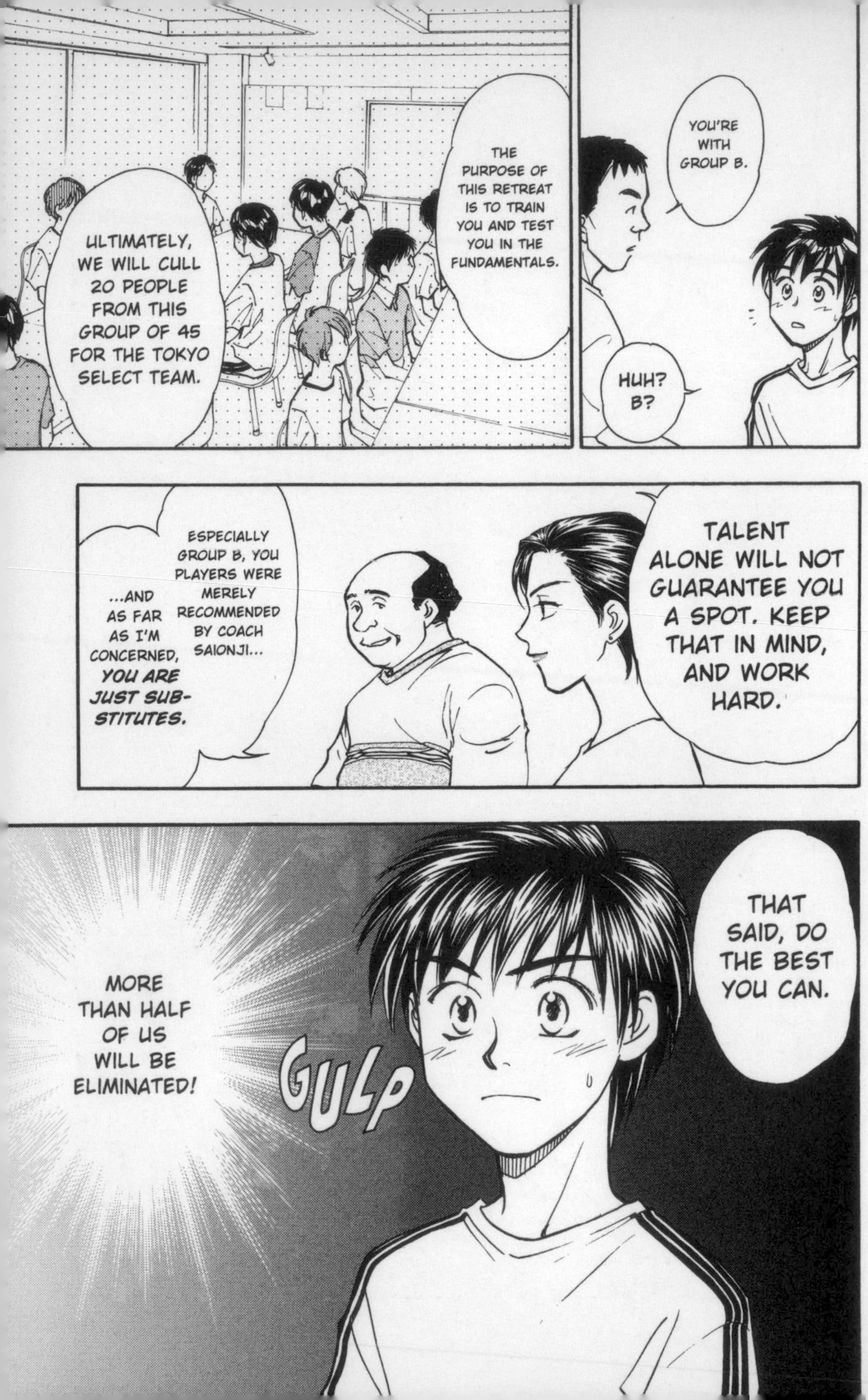
YOU'RE WITH GROUP B.
HUH? B?
THE PURPOSE OF THIS RETREAT IS TO TRAIN YOU AND TEST YOU IN THE FUNDAMENTALS.
ULTIMATELY, WE WILL CULL 20 PEOPLE FROM THIS GROUP OF 45 FOR THE TOKYO SELECT TEAM.
TALENT ALONE WILL NOT GUARANTEE YOU A SPOT. KEEP THAT IN MIND, AND WORK HARD.
ESPECIALLY GROUP B, YOU PLAYERS WERE MERELY RECOMMENDED BY COACH SAIONJI...
...AND AS FAR AS I'M CONCERNED, *YOU ARE JUST SUBSTITUTES.*
THAT SAID, DO THE BEST YOU CAN.
GULP
MORE THAN HALF OF US WILL BE ELIMINATED!

WHISTLE!™

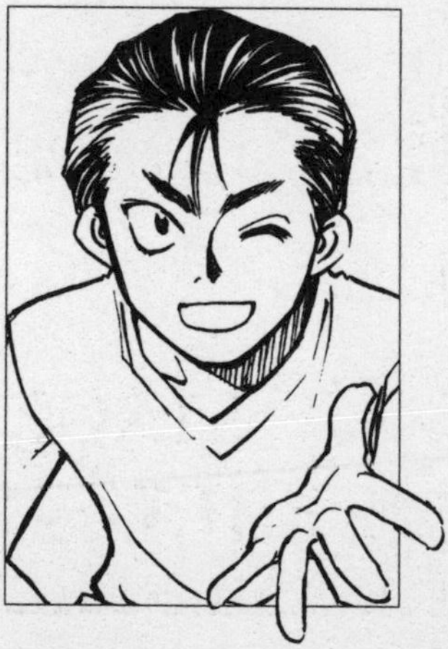

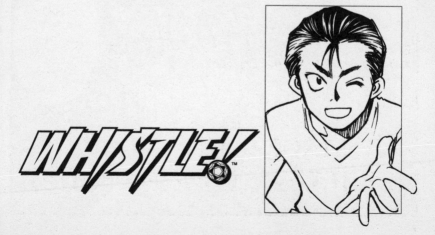

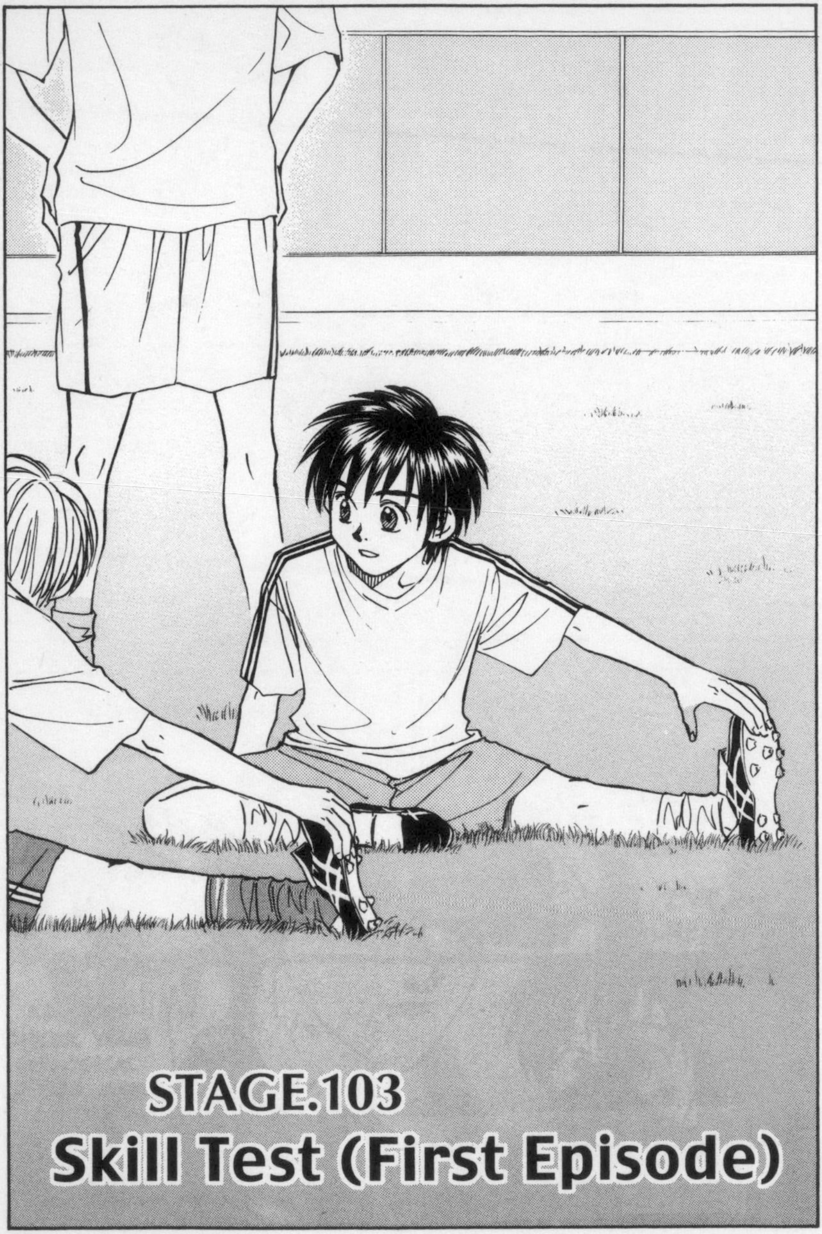
STAGE.103
Skill Test (First Episode)

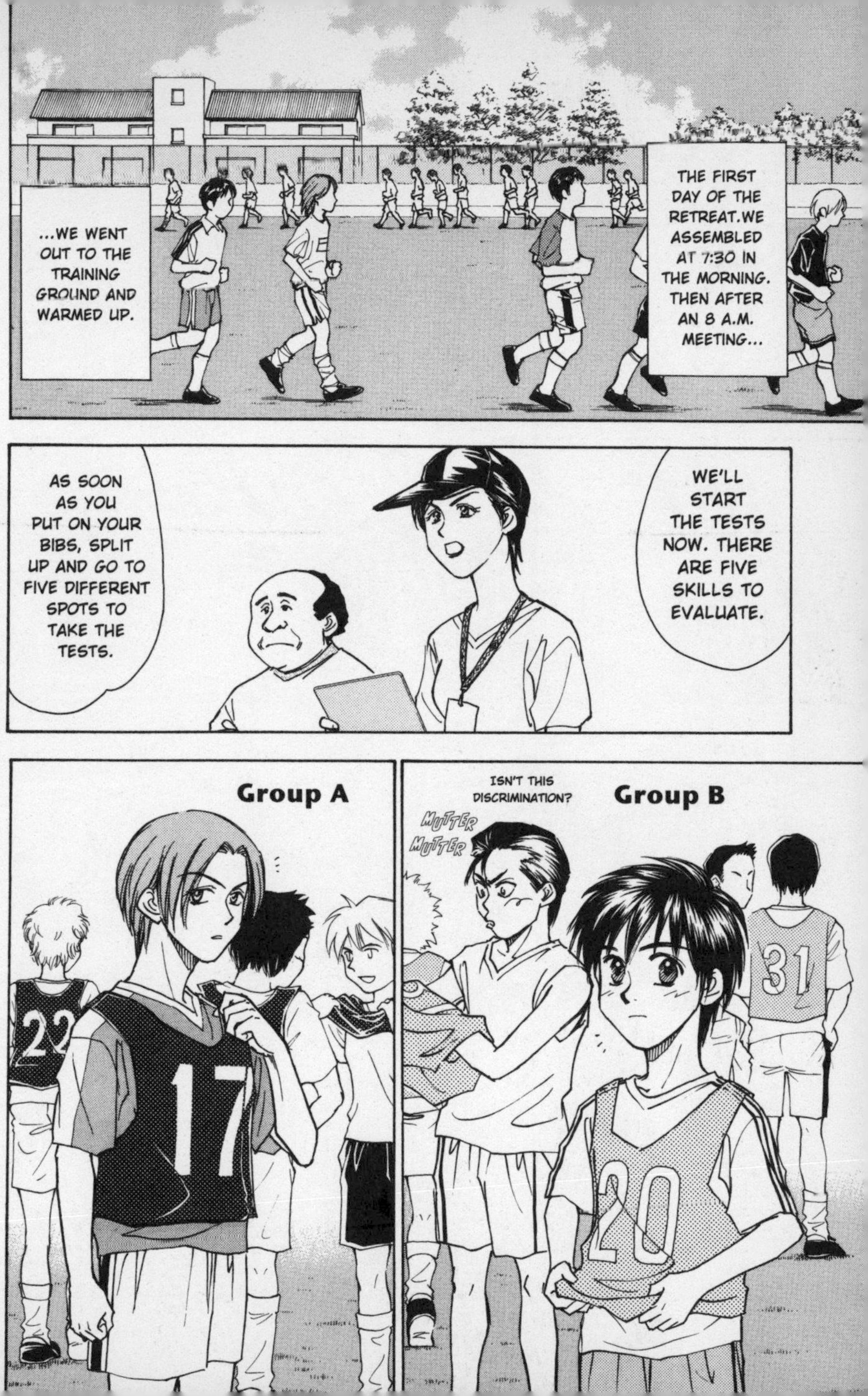
THE FIRST DAY OF THE RETREAT. WE ASSEMBLED AT 7:30 IN THE MORNING. THEN AFTER AN 8 A.M. MEETING...
...WE WENT OUT TO THE TRAINING GROUND AND WARMED UP.
WE'LL START THE TESTS NOW. THERE ARE FIVE SKILLS TO EVALUATE.
AS SOON AS YOU PUT ON YOUR BIBS, SPLIT UP AND GO TO FIVE DIFFERENT SPOTS TO TAKE THE TESTS.
Group B
ISN'T THIS DISCRIMINATION?
MUTTER MUTTER
Group A

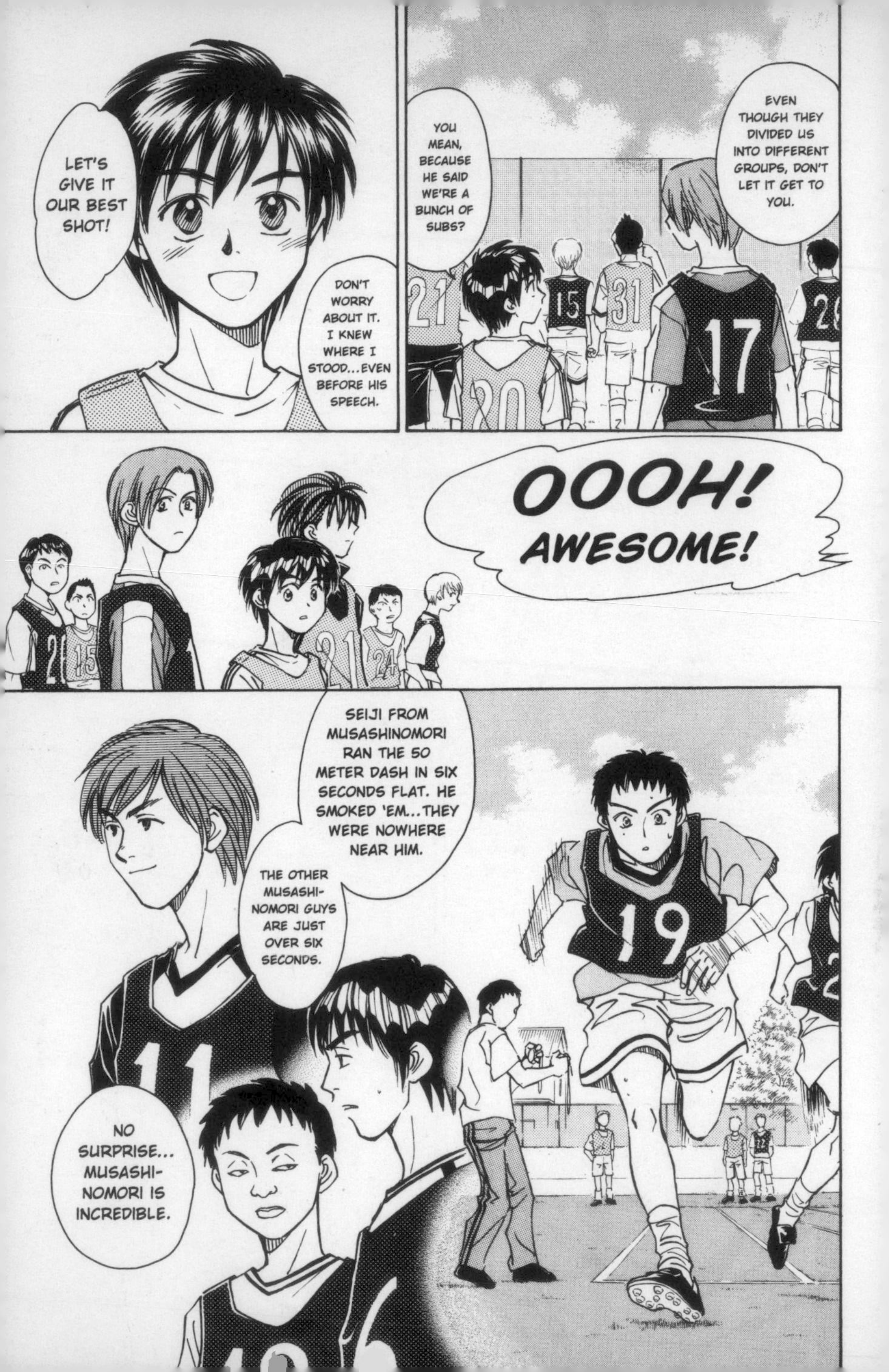
EVEN THOUGH THEY DIVIDED US INTO DIFFERENT GROUPS, DON'T LET IT GET TO YOU.
YOU MEAN, BECAUSE HE SAID WE'RE A BUNCH OF SUBS?
DON'T WORRY ABOUT IT. I KNEW WHERE I STOOD...EVEN BEFORE HIS SPEECH.
LET'S GIVE IT OUR BEST SHOT!
OOOH! AWESOME!
SEIJI FROM MUSASHINOMORI RAN THE 50 METER DASH IN SIX SECONDS FLAT. HE SMOKED 'EM...THEY WERE NOWHERE NEAR HIM.
THE OTHER MUSASHI-NOMORI GUYS ARE JUST OVER SIX SECONDS.
NO SURPRISE... MUSASHI-NOMORI IS INCREDIBLE.

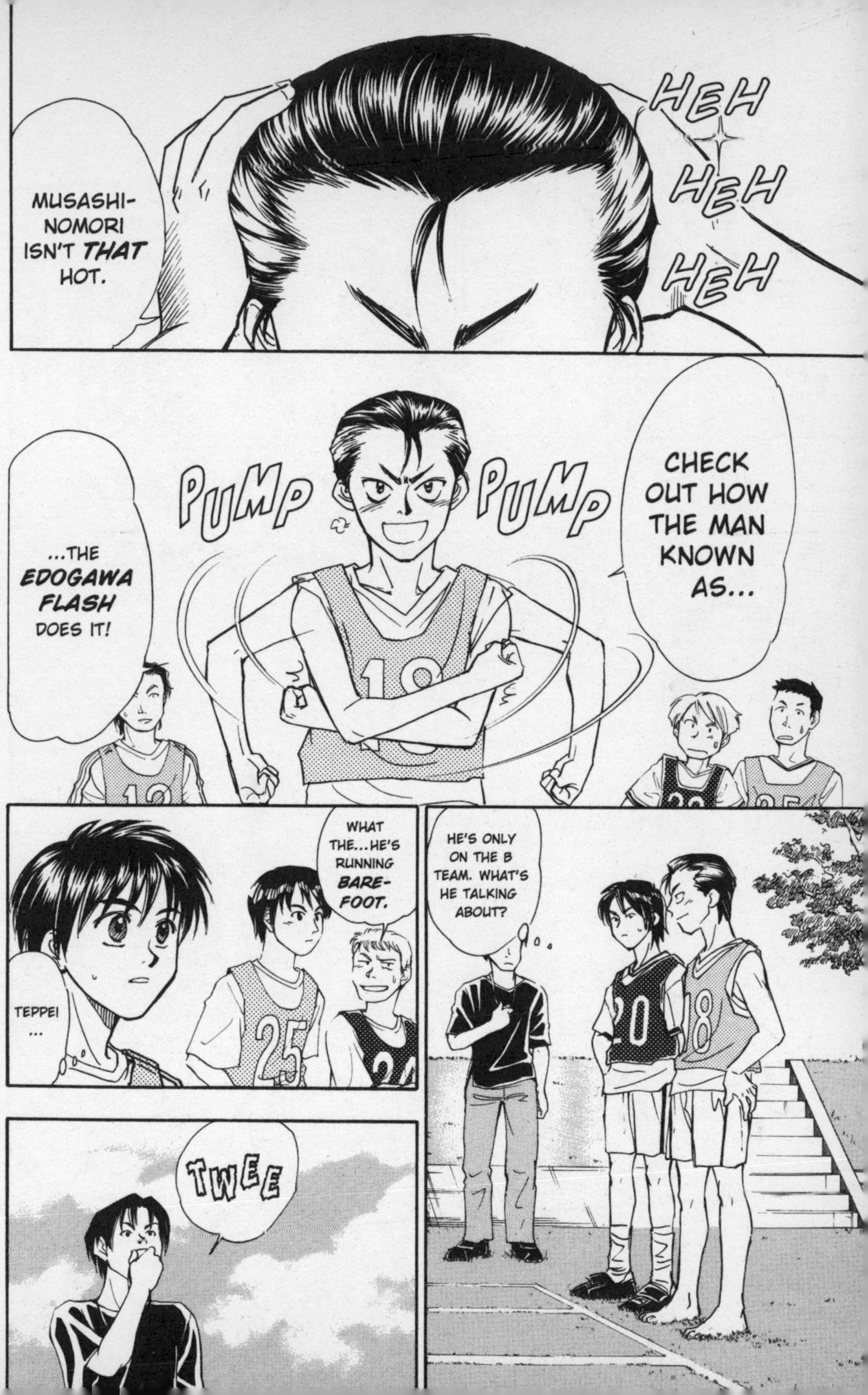
HEH HEH HEH
MUSASHI-NOMORI ISN'T *THAT* HOT.
CHECK OUT HOW THE MAN KNOWN AS...
PUMP PUMP
...THE *EDOGAWA FLASH* DOES IT!
HE'S ONLY ON THE B TEAM. WHAT'S HE TALKING ABOUT?
WHAT THE...HE'S RUNNING *BARE-FOOT.*
TEPPEI ...
TWEE

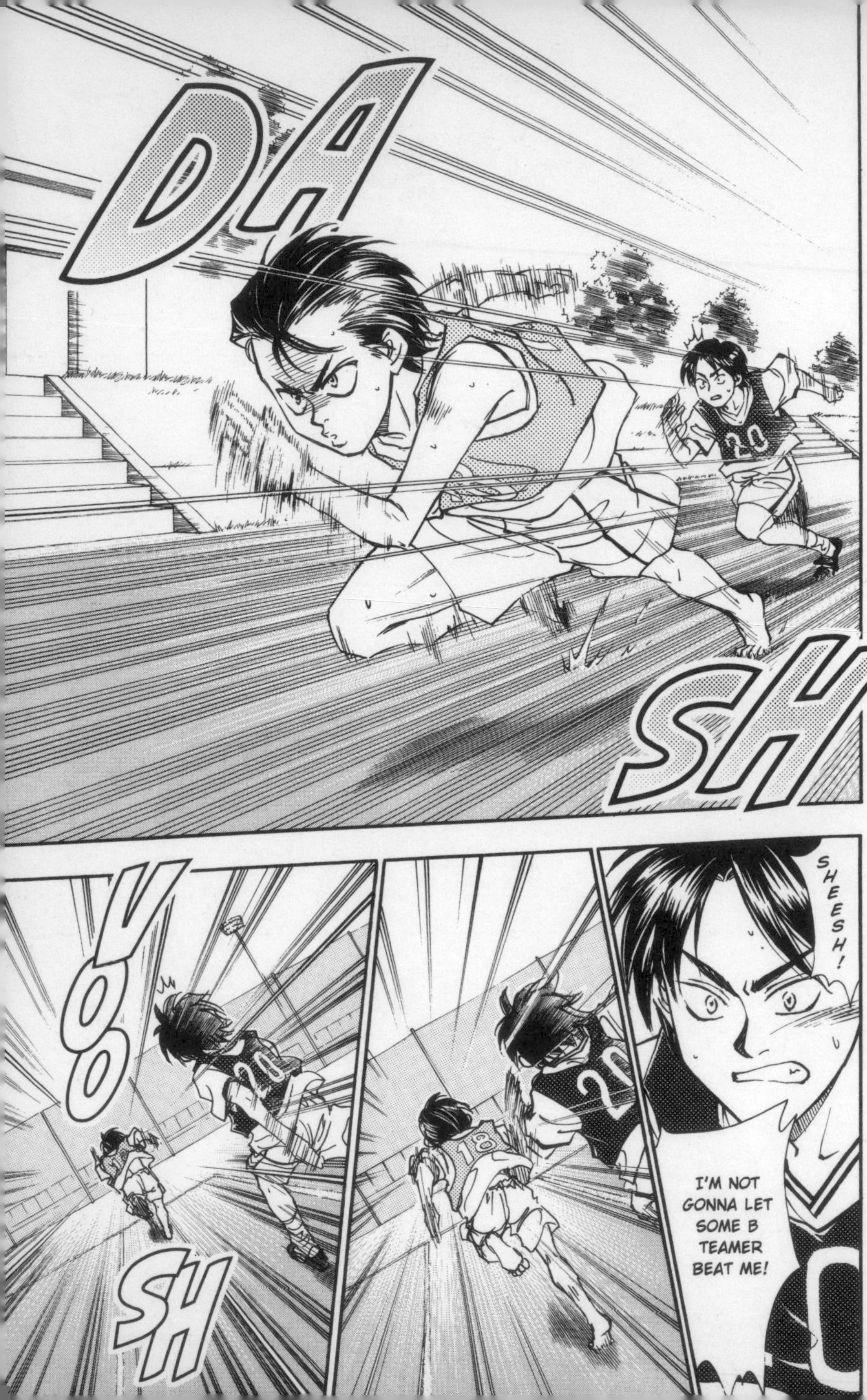
DA
SH
SHEESH!
I'M NOT GONNA LET SOME B TEAMER BEAT ME!
VOOO
SH

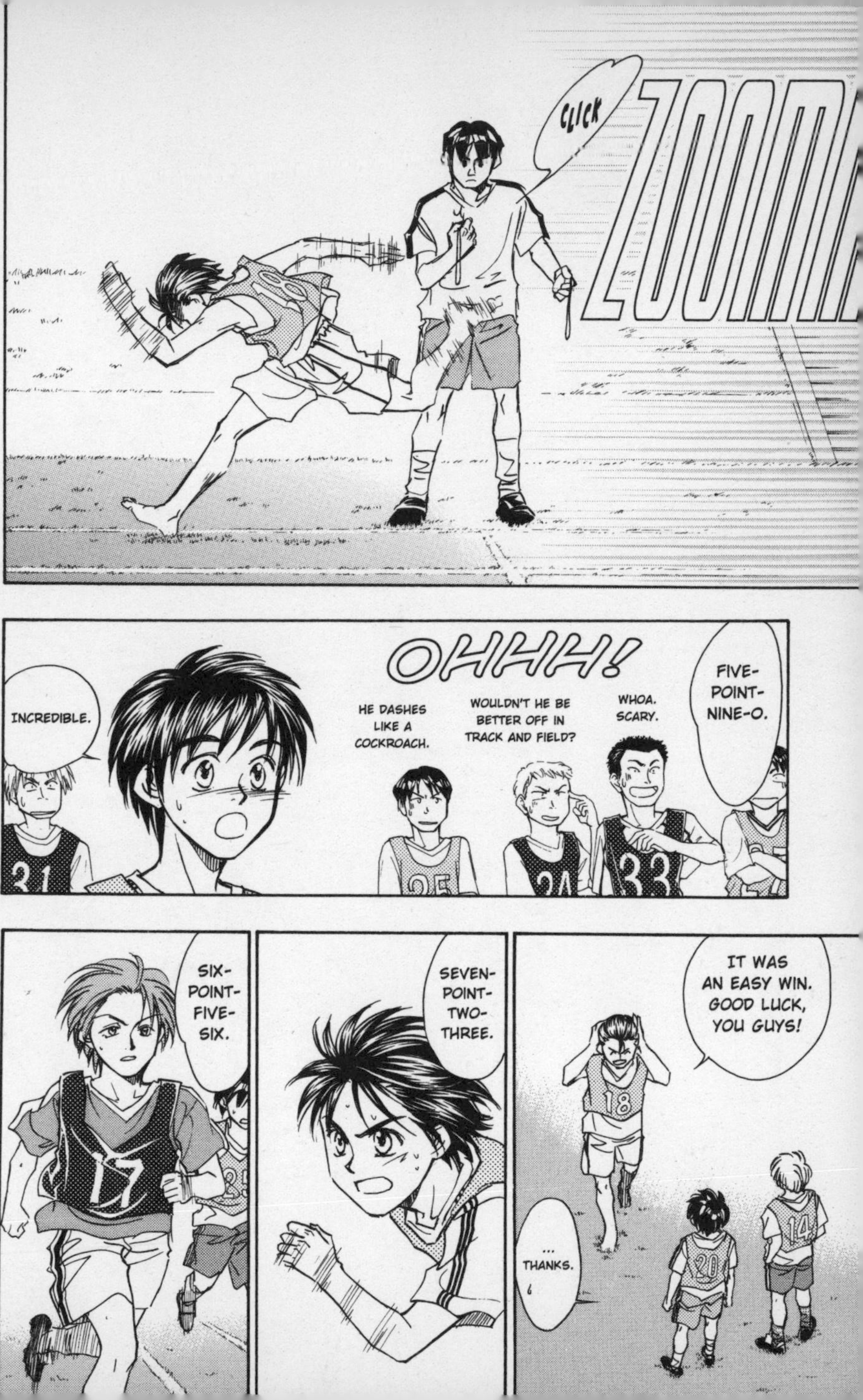
CLICK
ZOOM
FIVE-POINT-NINE-O.
OHHH!
WHOA. SCARY.
WOULDN'T HE BE BETTER OFF IN TRACK AND FIELD?
HE DASHES LIKE A COCKROACH.
INCREDIBLE.
IT WAS AN EASY WIN. GOOD LUCK, YOU GUYS!
... THANKS.
SEVEN-POINT-TWO-THREE.
SIX-POINT-FIVE-SIX.

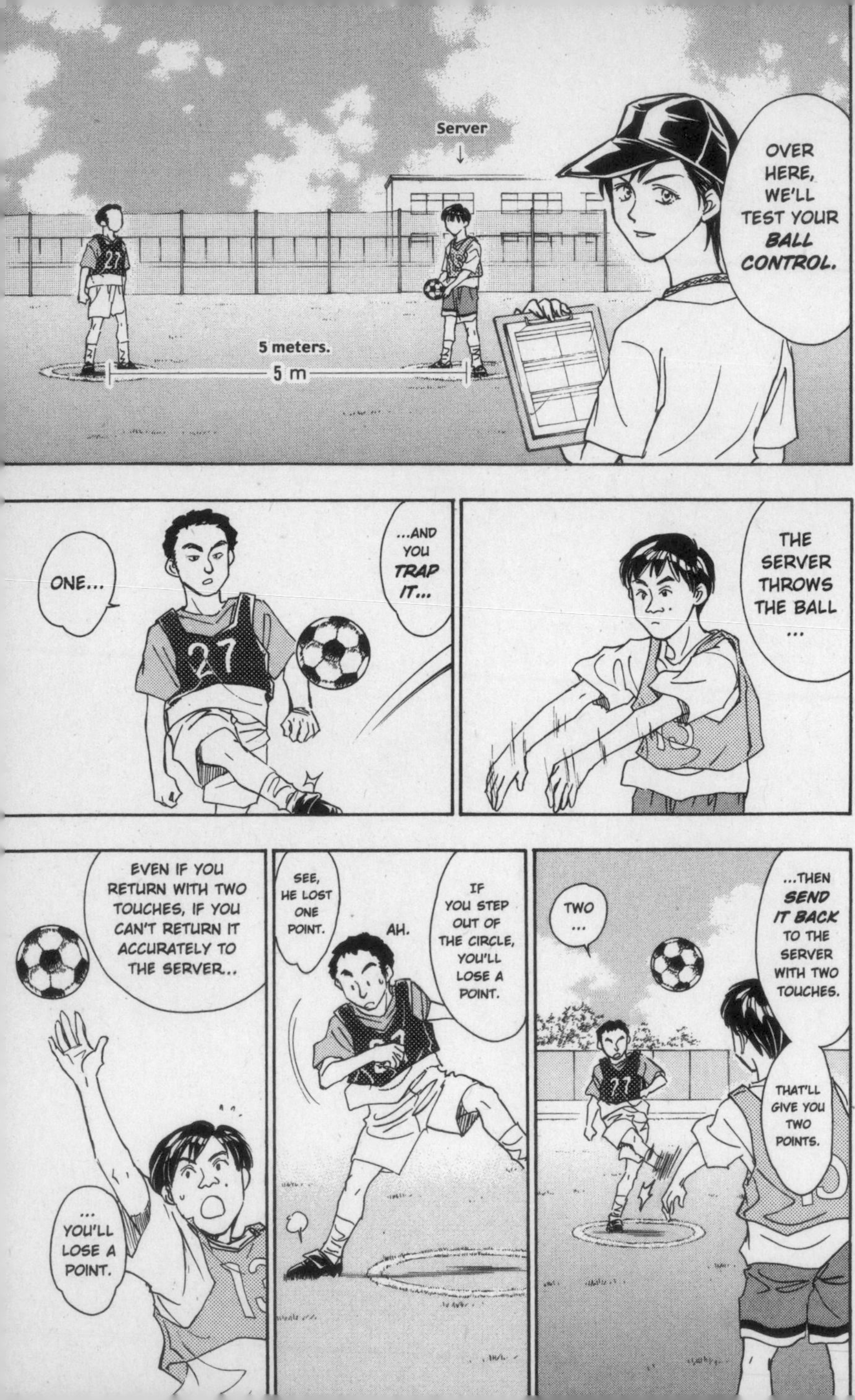
OVER HERE, WE'LL TEST YOUR **BALL CONTROL.**
Server
5 meters.
5 m
THE SERVER THROWS THE BALL...
...AND YOU **TRAP IT...**
ONE...
...THEN **SEND IT BACK** TO THE SERVER WITH TWO TOUCHES.
TWO...
THAT'LL GIVE YOU TWO POINTS.
IF YOU STEP OUT OF THE CIRCLE, YOU'LL LOSE A POINT.
SEE, HE LOST ONE POINT.
AH.
EVEN IF YOU RETURN WITH TWO TOUCHES, IF YOU CAN'T RETURN IT ACCURATELY TO THE SERVER...
...YOU'LL LOSE A POINT.

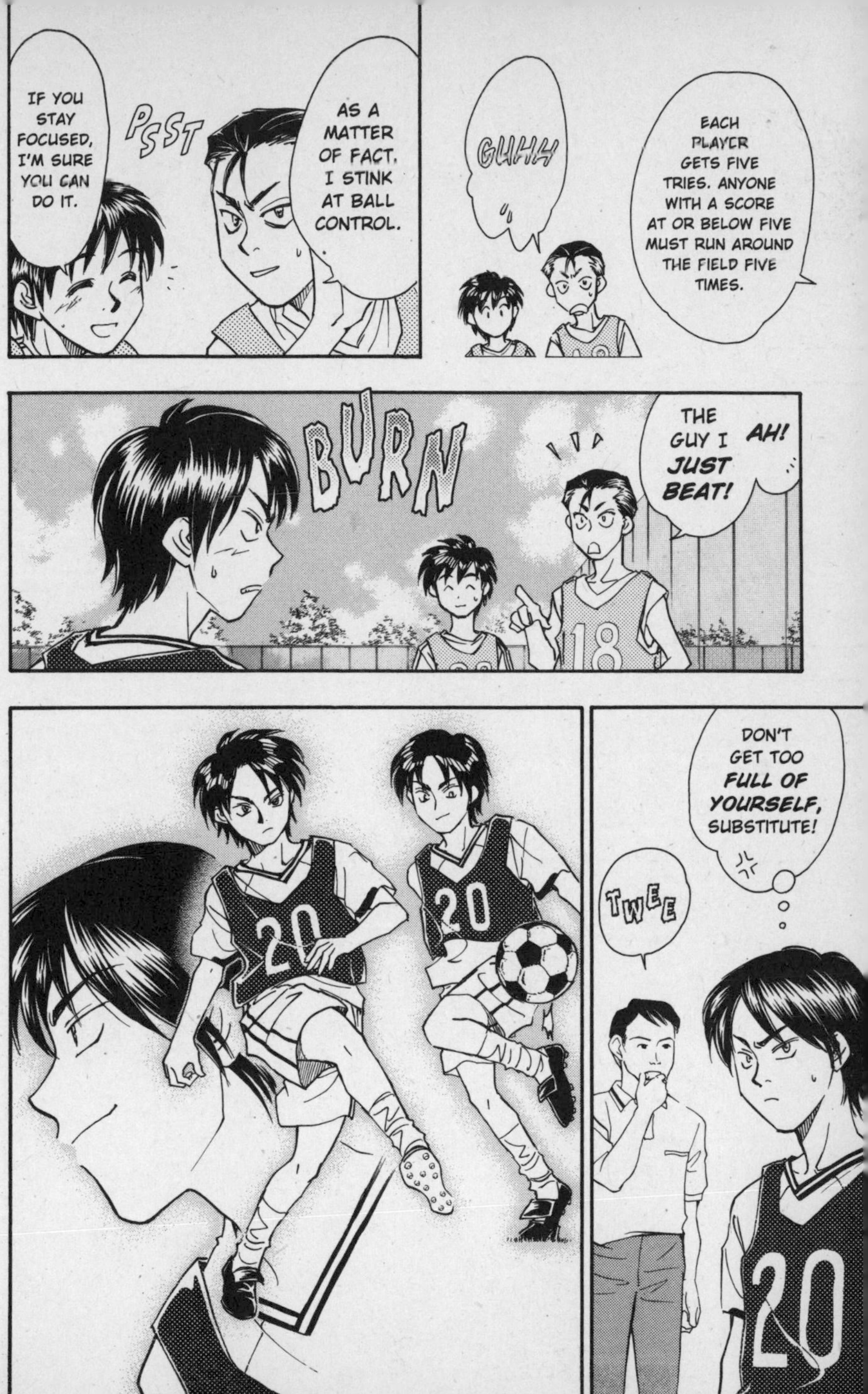
EACH PLAYER GETS FIVE TRIES. ANYONE WITH A SCORE AT OR BELOW FIVE MUST RUN AROUND THE FIELD FIVE TIMES.
GUHH
AS A MATTER OF FACT, I STINK AT BALL CONTROL.
PSST
IF YOU STAY FOCUSED, I'M SURE YOU CAN DO IT.
AH!
THE GUY I JUST BEAT!
BURN
DON'T GET TOO FULL OF YOURSELF, SUBSTITUTE!
TWEE

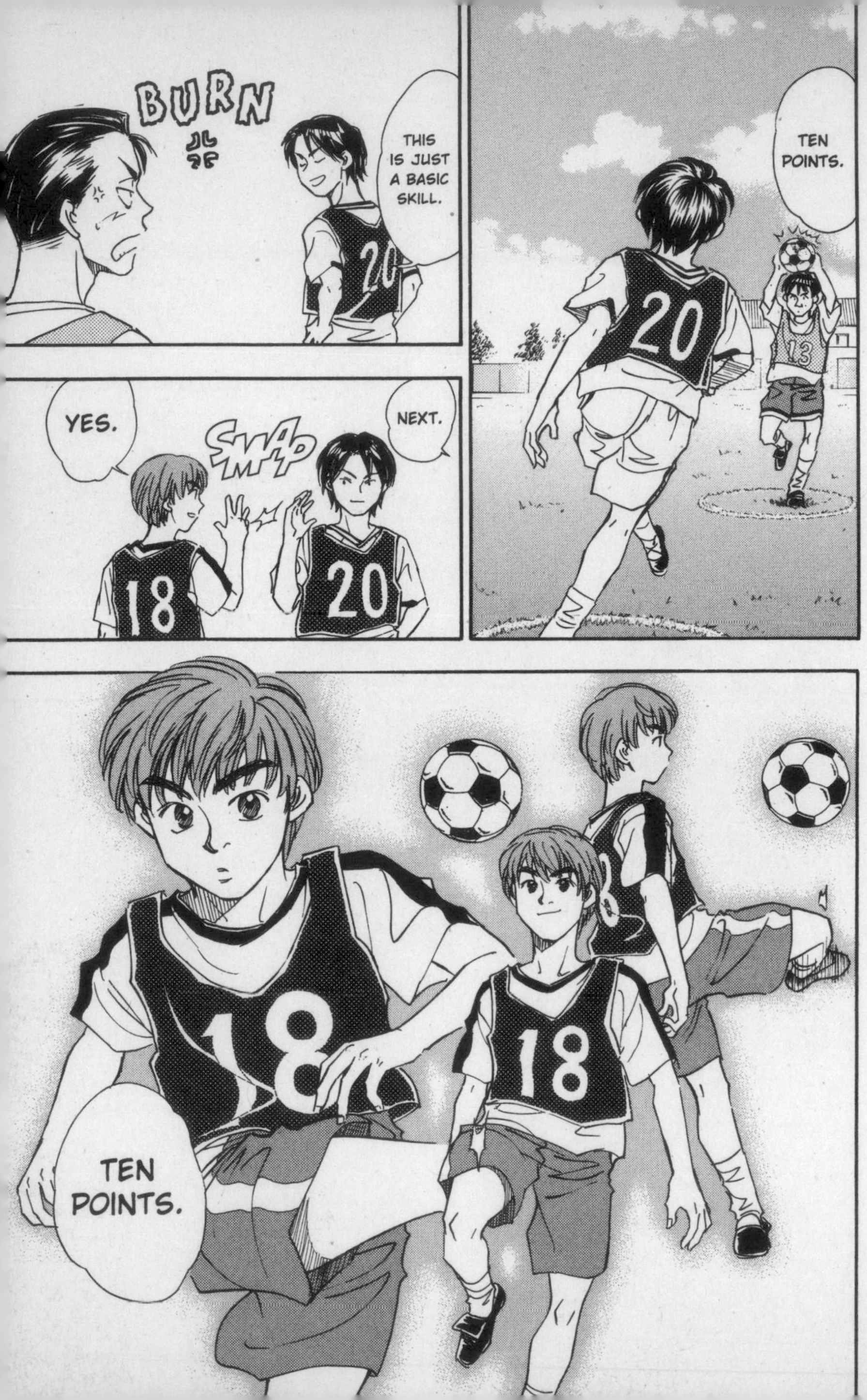
TEN POINTS.
THIS IS JUST A BASIC SKILL.
BURN
NEXT.
SMAP
YES.
TEN POINTS.

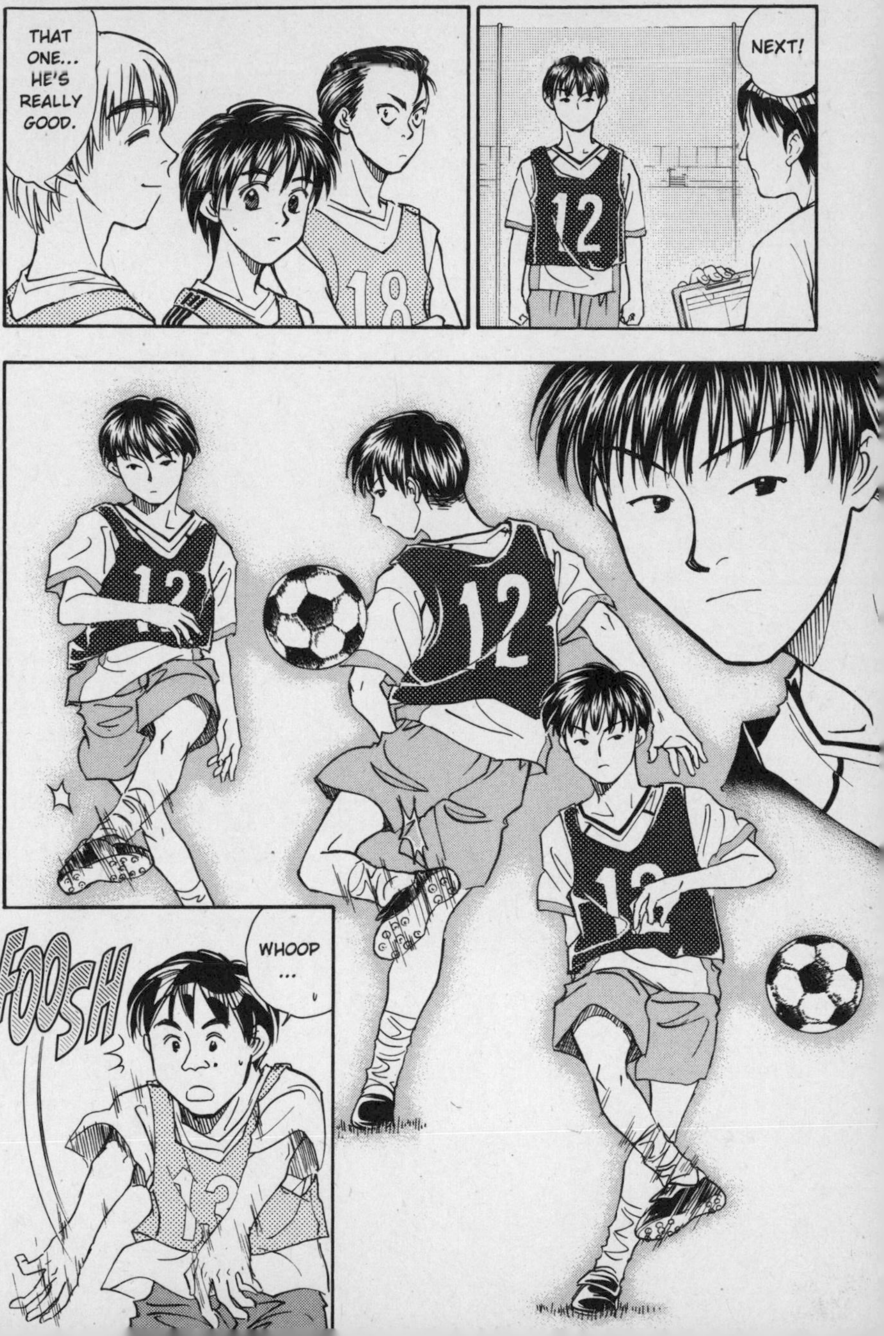
NEXT!
THAT ONE... HE'S REALLY GOOD.
WHOOP ...
FOOSH

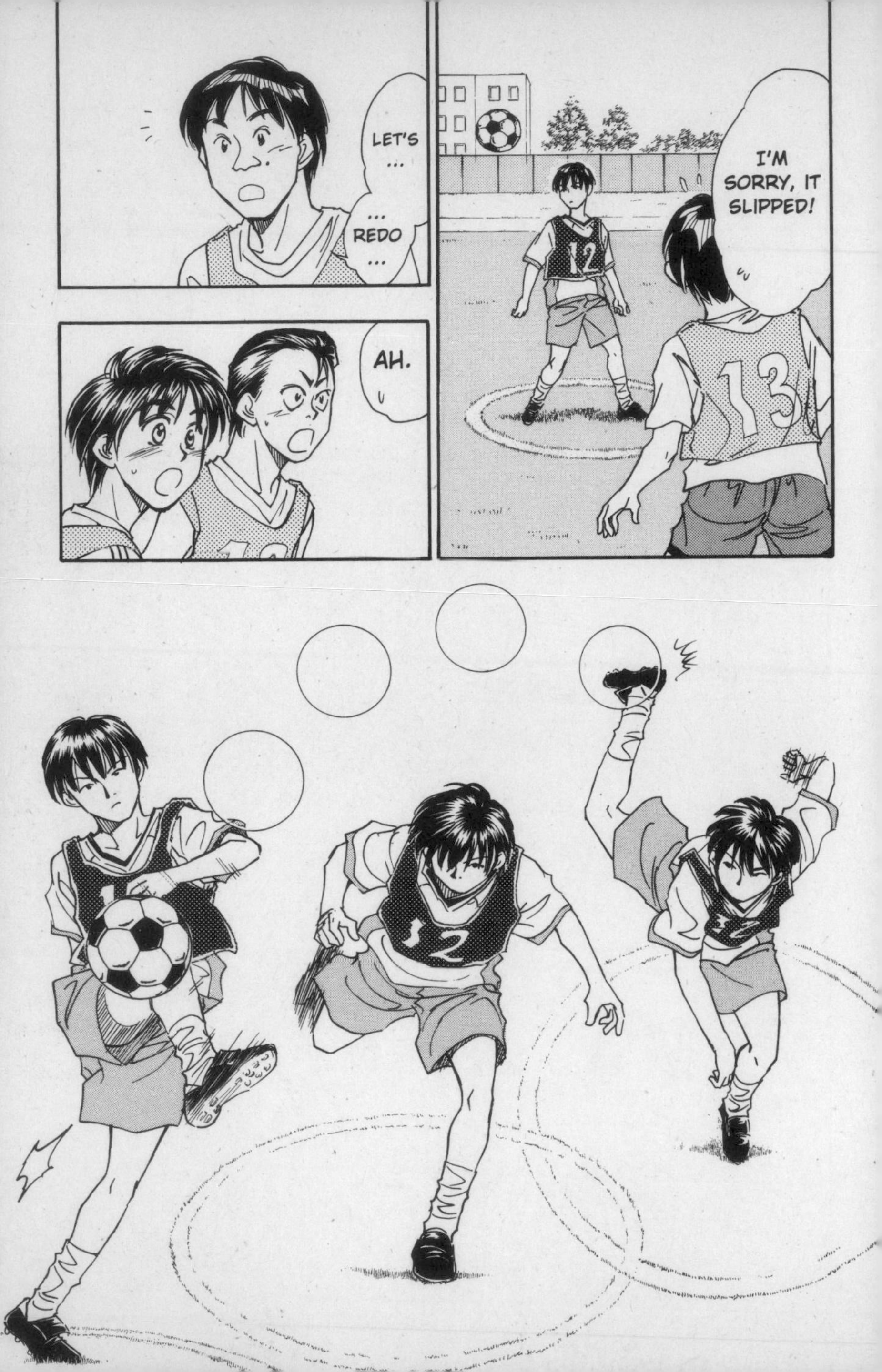
I'M SORRY, IT SLIPPED!
LET'S ...
... REDO ...
AH.

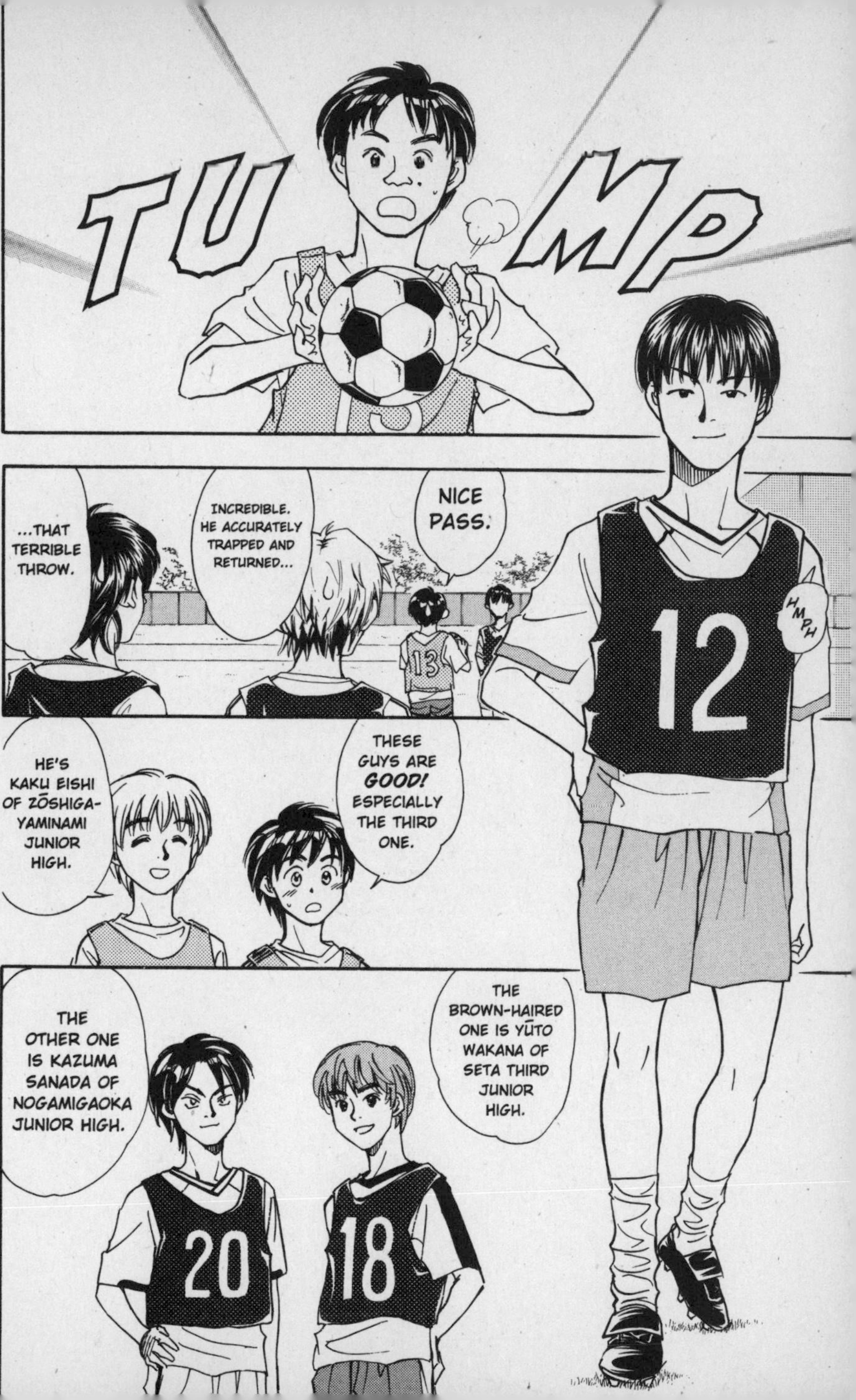
TUMP
HMPH
NICE PASS.
INCREDIBLE. HE ACCURATELY TRAPPED AND RETURNED...
...THAT TERRIBLE THROW.
THESE GUYS ARE *GOOD!* ESPECIALLY THE THIRD ONE.
HE'S KAKU EISHI OF ZŌSHIGAYAMINAMI JUNIOR HIGH.
THE BROWN-HAIRED ONE IS YŪTO WAKANA OF SETA THIRD JUNIOR HIGH.
THE OTHER ONE IS KAZUMA SANADA OF NOGAMIGAOKA JUNIOR HIGH.

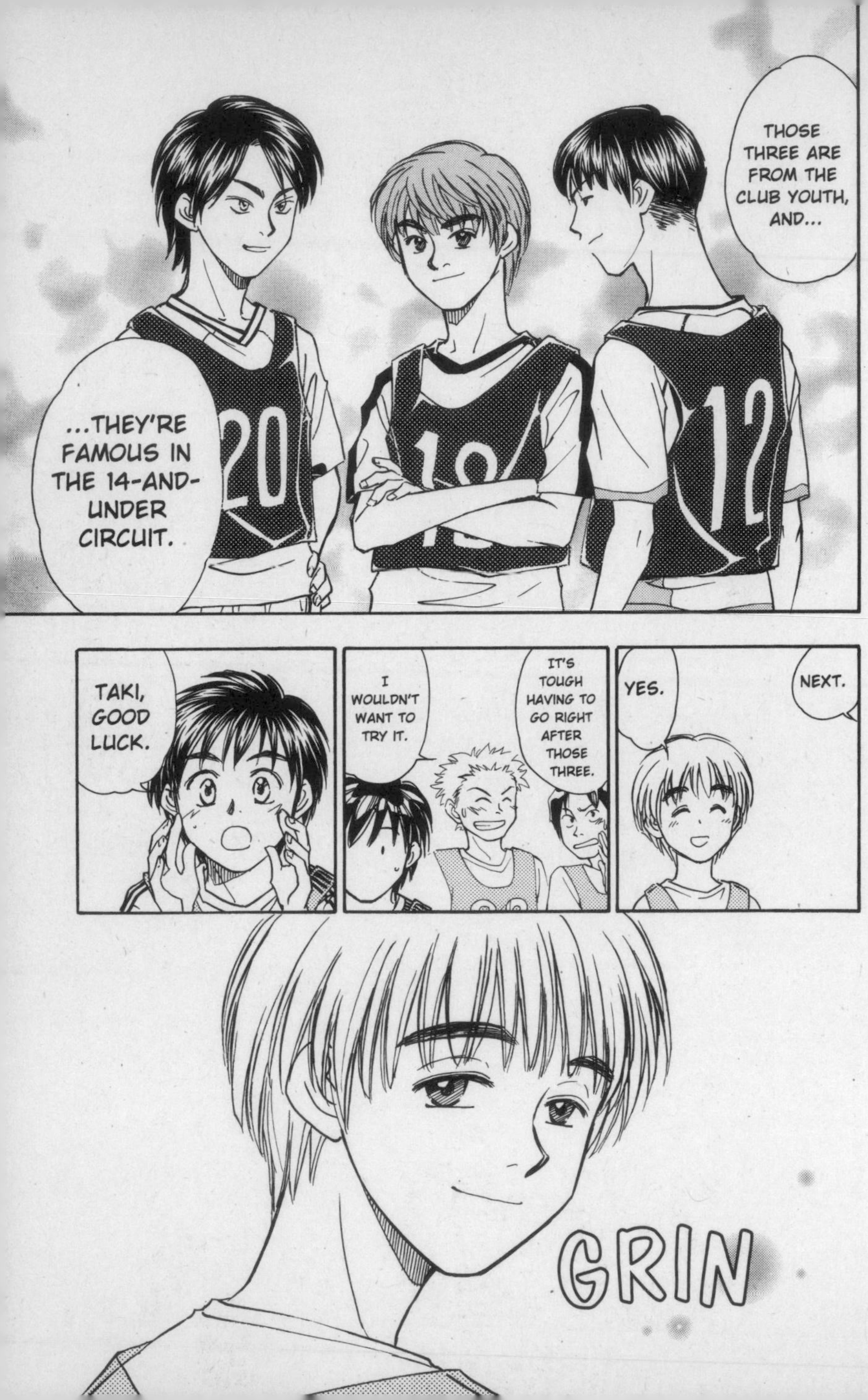
THOSE THREE ARE FROM THE CLUB YOUTH, AND...
...THEY'RE FAMOUS IN THE 14-AND-UNDER CIRCUIT.
NEXT.
YES.
IT'S TOUGH HAVING TO GO RIGHT AFTER THOSE THREE.
I WOULDN'T WANT TO TRY IT.
TAKI, GOOD LUCK.
GRIN

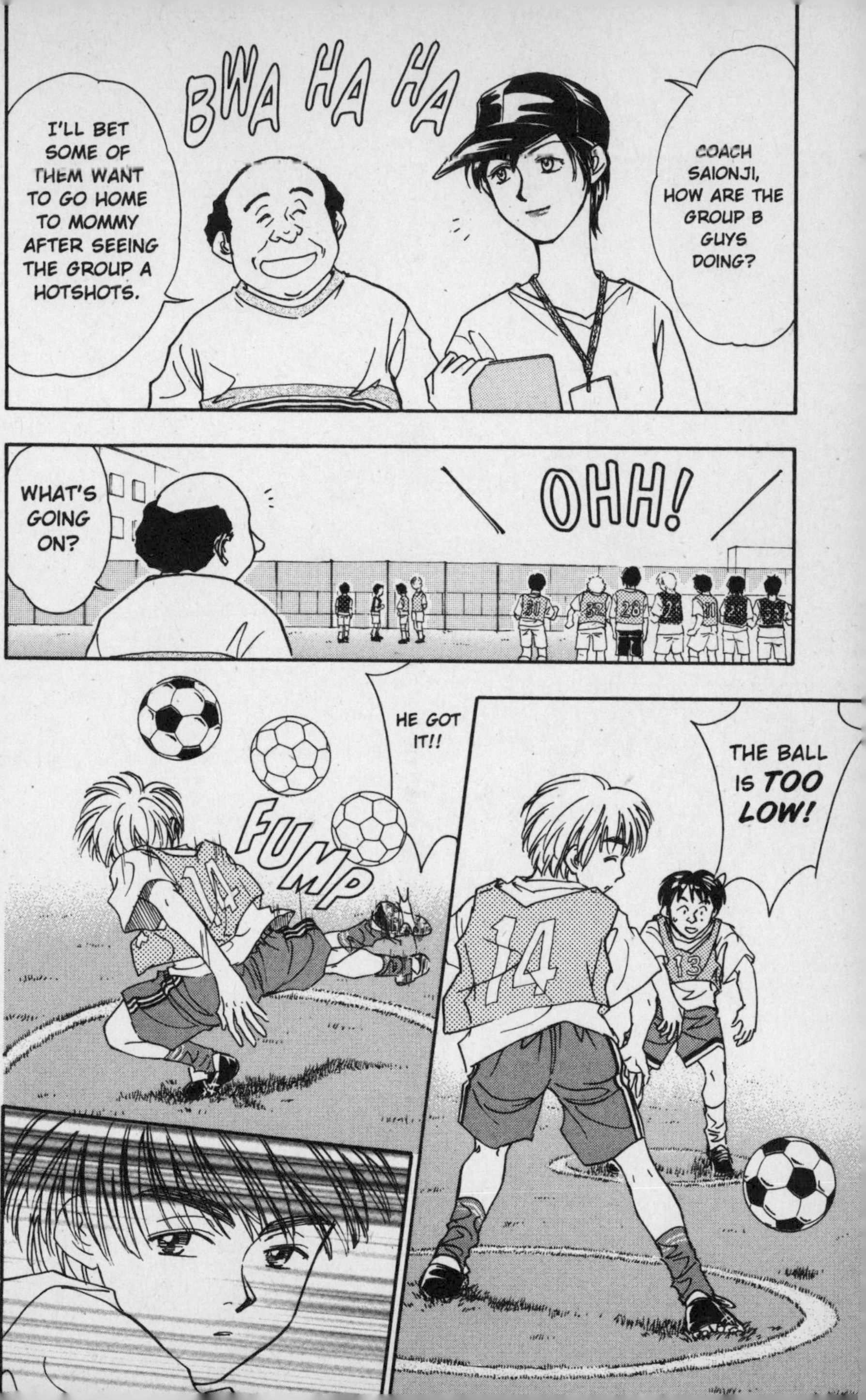
COACH SAIONJI, HOW ARE THE GROUP B GUYS DOING?
I'LL BET SOME OF THEM WANT TO GO HOME TO MOMMY AFTER SEEING THE GROUP A HOTSHOTS.
BWA HA HA
OHH!
WHAT'S GOING ON?
THE BALL IS TOO LOW!
HE GOT IT!!
FUMP

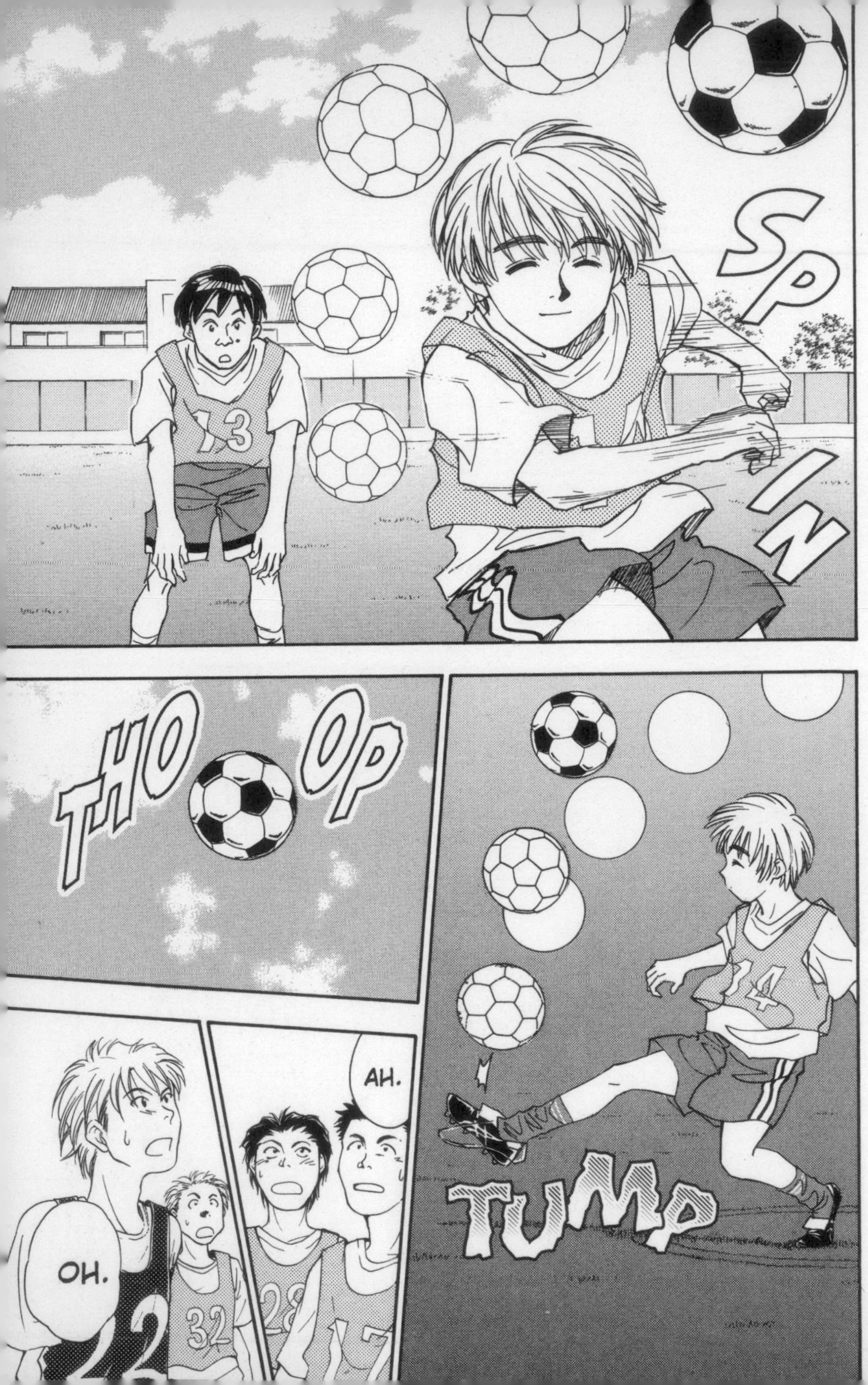
SPIN
TUMP
THOOP
AH.
OH.

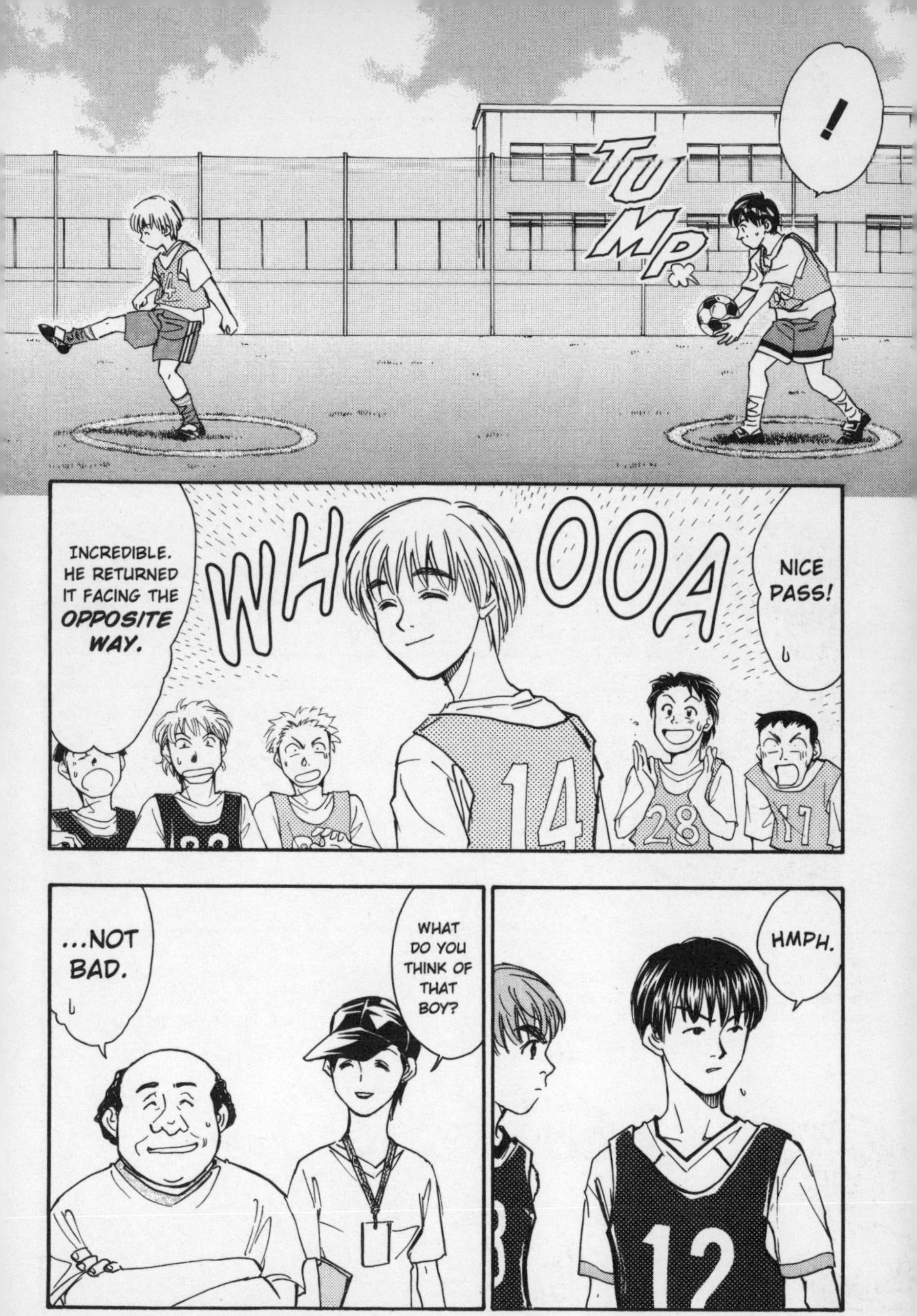
!
TUMP
NICE PASS!
WHOOA
INCREDIBLE. HE RETURNED IT FACING THE OPPOSITE WAY.
HMPH.
WHAT DO YOU THINK OF THAT BOY?
...NOT BAD.

READ THIS WAY

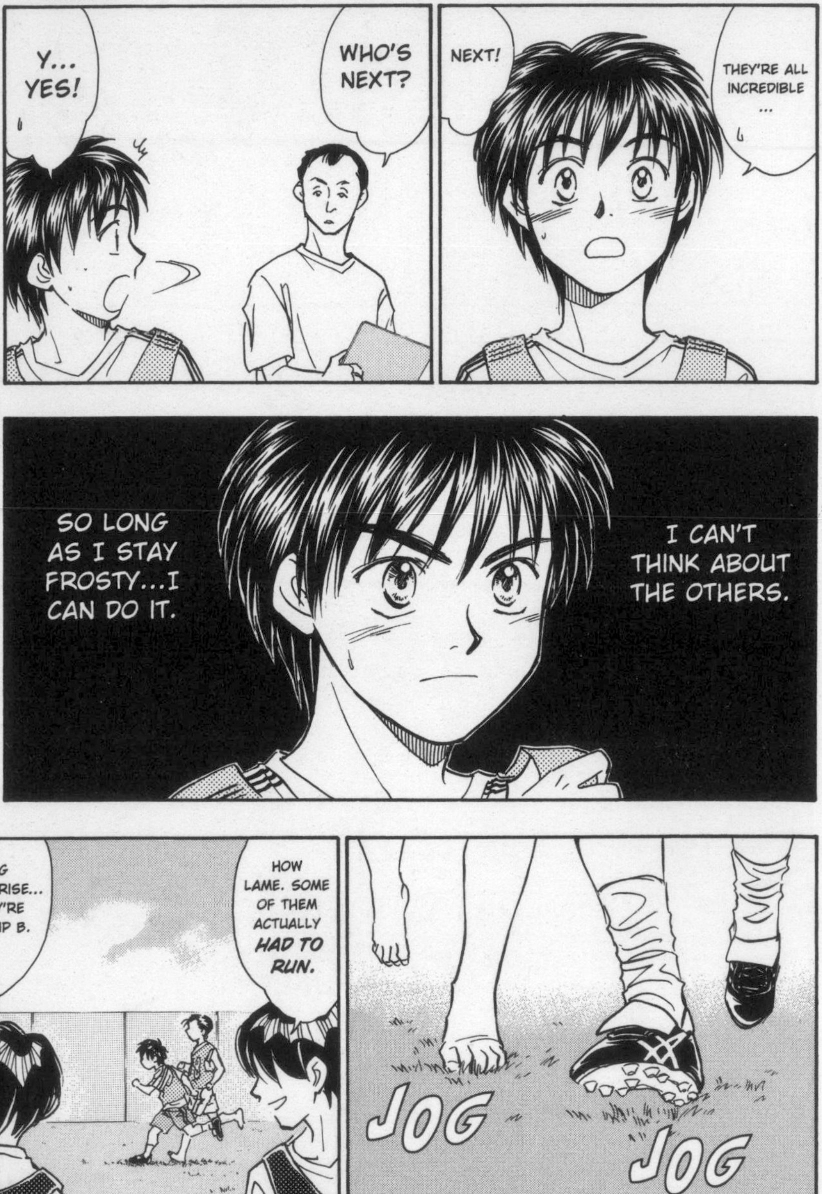

THEY'RE ALL INCREDIBLE ...
NEXT!
WHO'S NEXT?
Y... YES!
I CAN'T THINK ABOUT THE OTHERS.
SO LONG AS I STAY FROSTY...I CAN DO IT.
JOG
JOG
HOW LAME. SOME OF THEM ACTUALLY HAD TO RUN.
BIG SURPRISE... THEY'RE GROUP B.

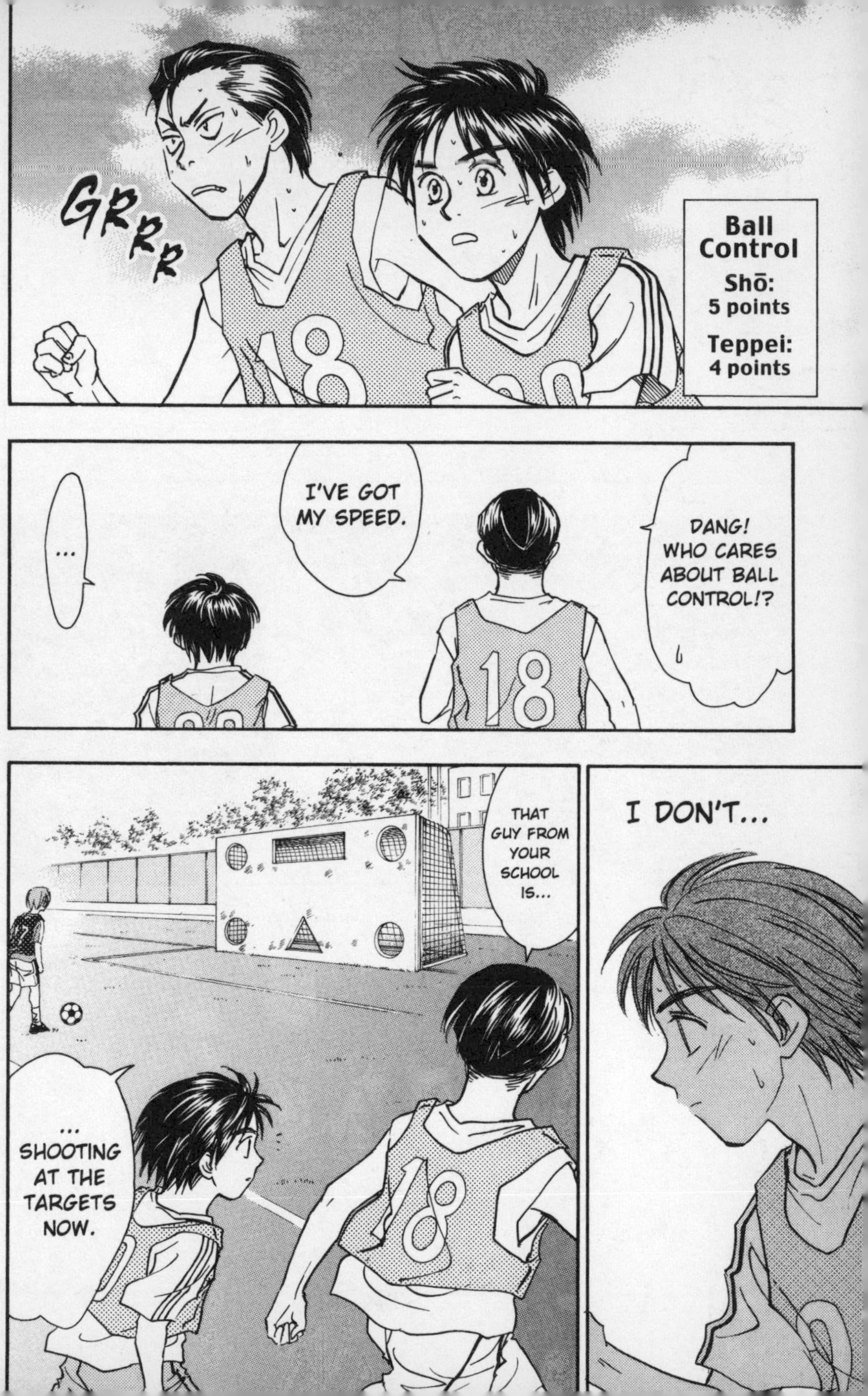
Ball Control
Shō: 5 points
Teppei: 4 points
GRRR
DANG! WHO CARES ABOUT BALL CONTROL!?
I'VE GOT MY SPEED.
...
I DON'T...
THAT GUY FROM YOUR SCHOOL IS...
... SHOOTING AT THE TARGETS NOW.

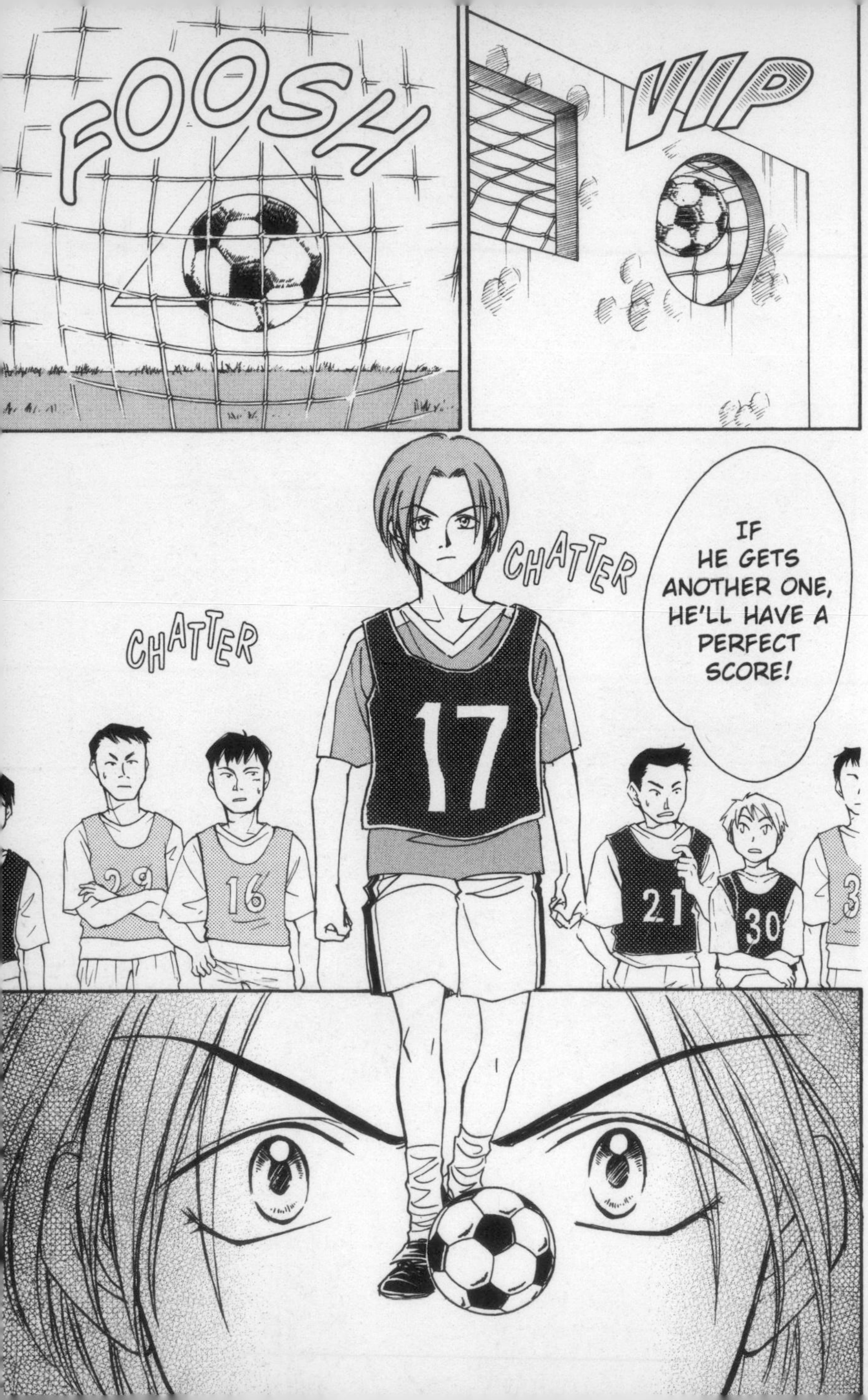
VIIP
FOOSH
IF HE GETS ANOTHER ONE, HE'LL HAVE A PERFECT SCORE!
CHATTER
CHATTER

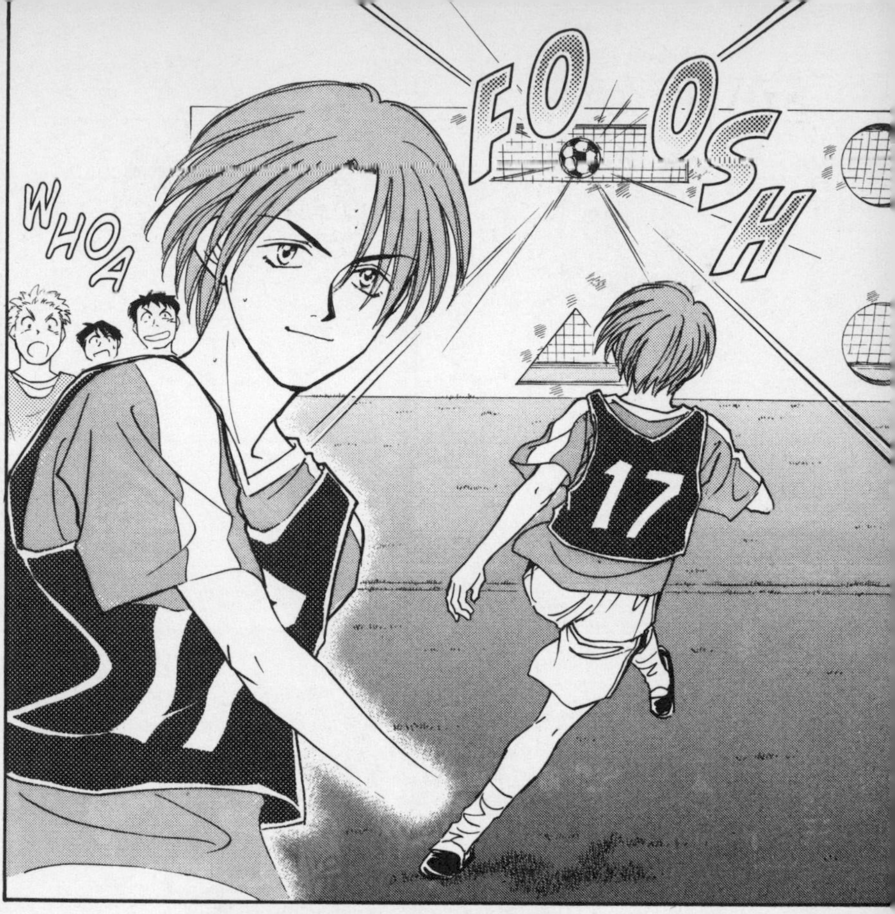
FOOSH
WHOA
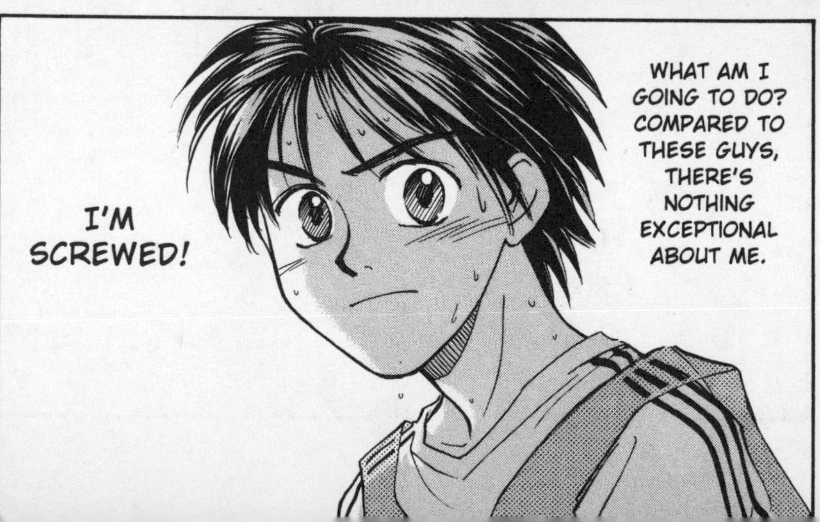
WHAT AM I GOING TO DO? COMPARED TO THESE GUYS, THERE'S NOTHING EXCEPTIONAL ABOUT ME.
I'M SCREWED!

STAGE.104

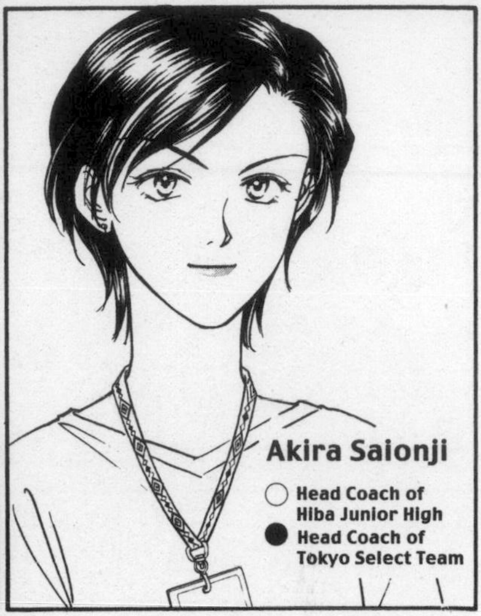
Akira Saionji
Head Coach of Hiba Junior High
Head Coach of Tokyo Select Team

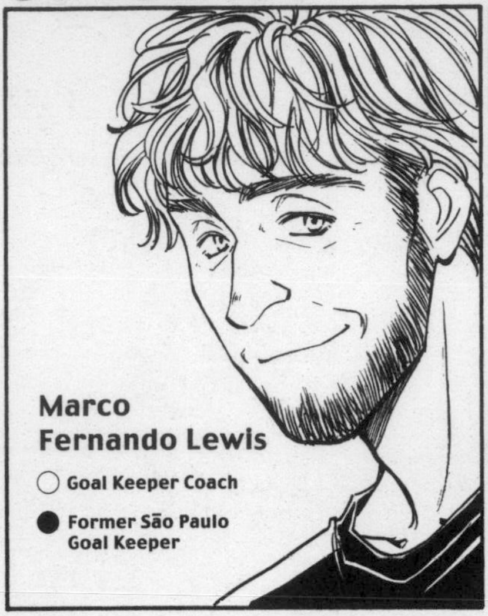
Marco Fernando Lewis
Goal Keeper Coach
Former São Paulo Goal Keeper

Skill Test (Second Episode)

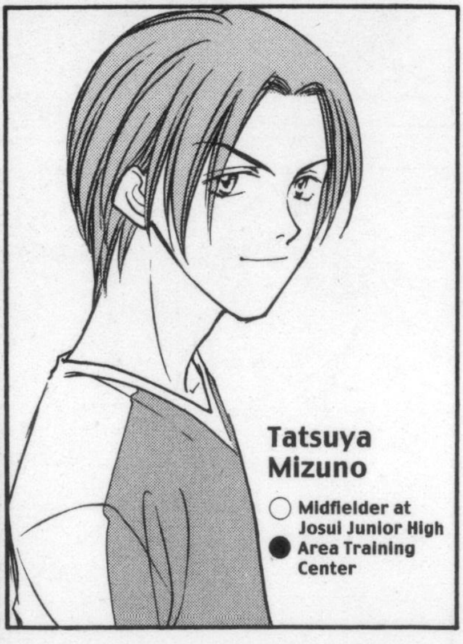
Tatsuya Mizuno
Midfielder at Josui Junior High
Area Training Center

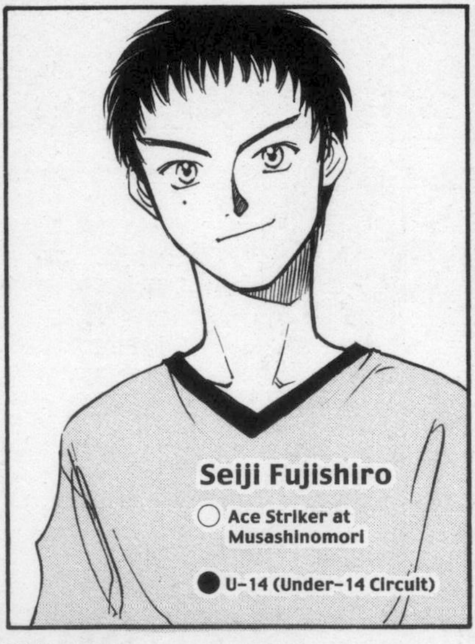
Seiji Fujishiro
Ace Striker at Musashinomori
U-14 (Under-14 Circuit)

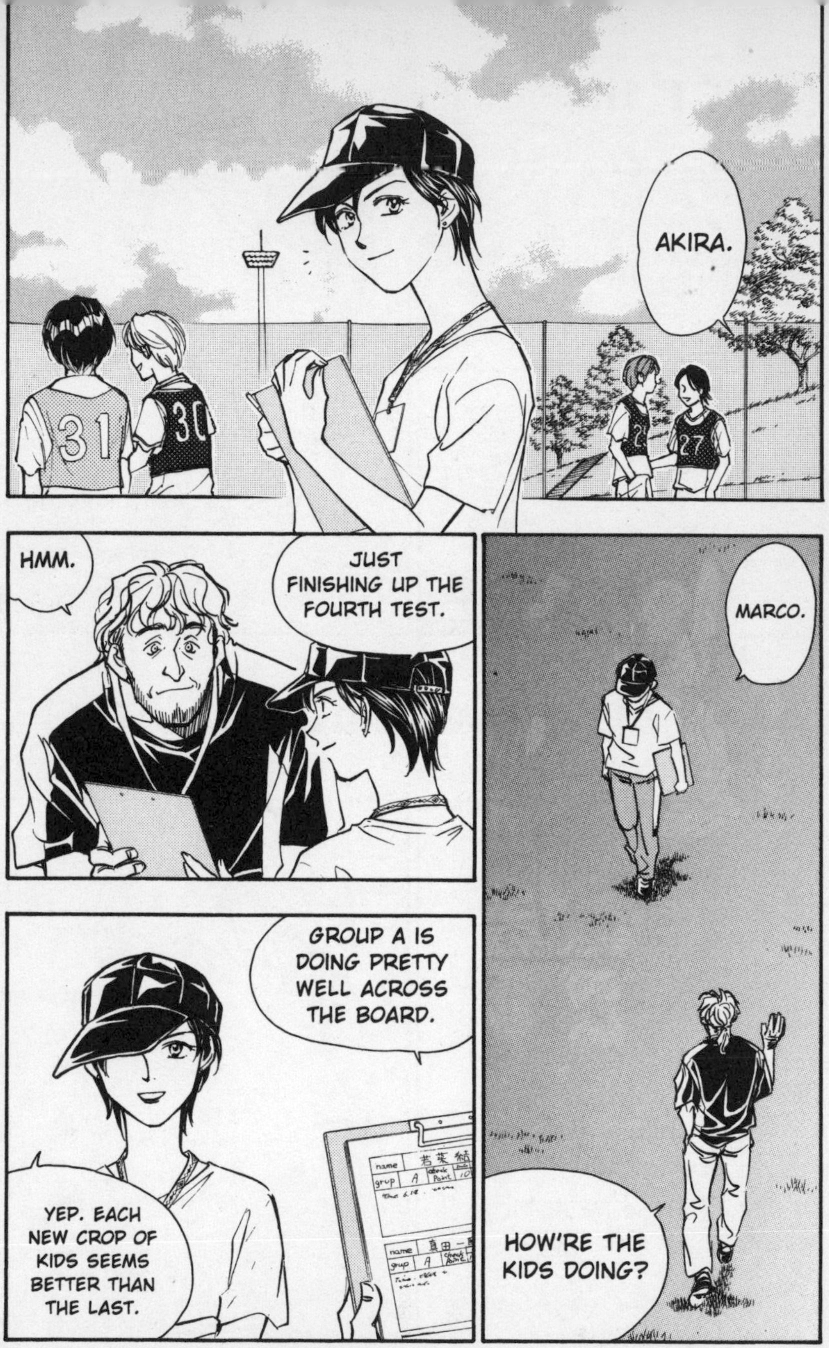
AKIRA.
MARCO.
HOW'RE THE KIDS DOING?
JUST FINISHING UP THE FOURTH TEST.
HMM.
GROUP A IS DOING PRETTY WELL ACROSS THE BOARD.
YEP. EACH NEW CROP OF KIDS SEEMS BETTER THAN THE LAST.

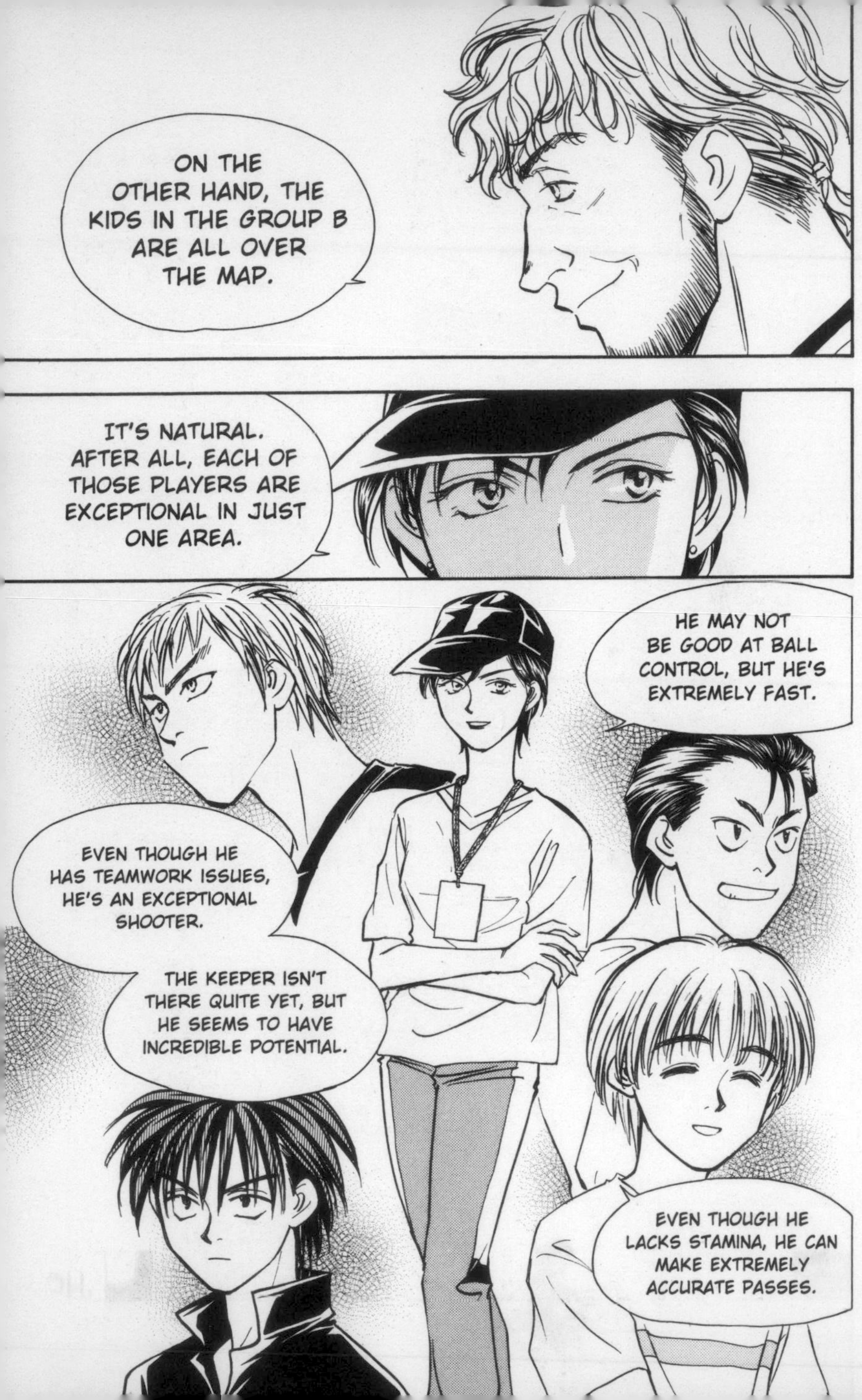
ON THE OTHER HAND, THE KIDS IN THE GROUP B ARE ALL OVER THE MAP.
IT'S NATURAL. AFTER ALL, EACH OF THOSE PLAYERS ARE EXCEPTIONAL IN JUST ONE AREA.
HE MAY NOT BE GOOD AT BALL CONTROL, BUT HE'S EXTREMELY FAST.
EVEN THOUGH HE HAS TEAMWORK ISSUES, HE'S AN EXCEPTIONAL SHOOTER.
THE KEEPER ISN'T THERE QUITE YET, BUT HE SEEMS TO HAVE INCREDIBLE POTENTIAL.
EVEN THOUGH HE LACKS STAMINA, HE CAN MAKE EXTREMELY ACCURATE PASSES.

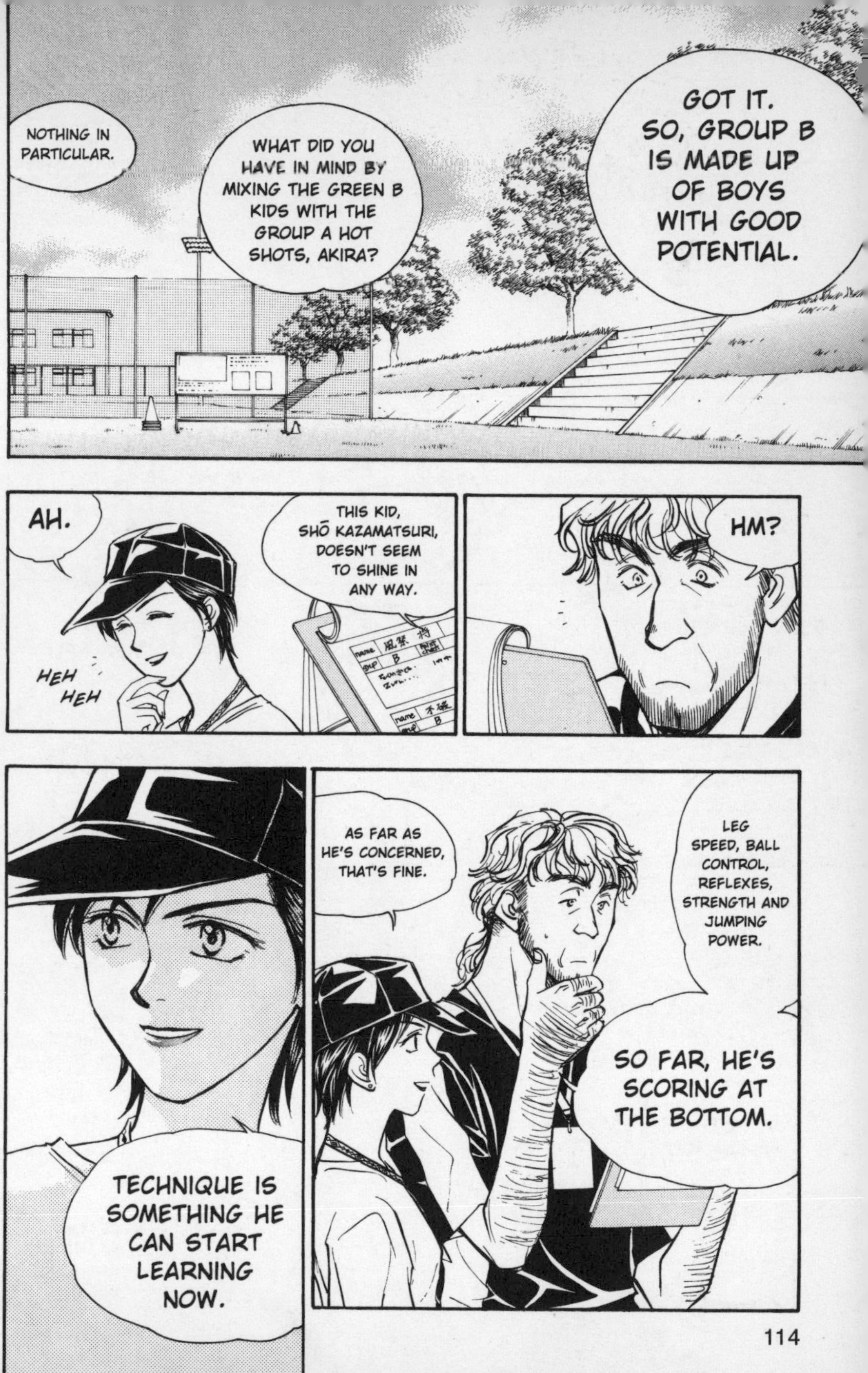
GOT IT. SO, GROUP B IS MADE UP OF BOYS WITH GOOD POTENTIAL.
WHAT DID YOU HAVE IN MIND BY MIXING THE GREEN B KIDS WITH THE GROUP A HOT SHOTS, AKIRA?
NOTHING IN PARTICULAR.
HM?
AH.
THIS KID, SHŌ KAZAMATSURI, DOESN'T SEEM TO SHINE IN ANY WAY.
HEH HEH
LEG SPEED, BALL CONTROL, REFLEXES, STRENGTH AND JUMPING POWER.
SO FAR, HE'S SCORING AT THE BOTTOM.
AS FAR AS HE'S CONCERNED, THAT'S FINE.
TECHNIQUE IS SOMETHING HE CAN START LEARNING NOW.

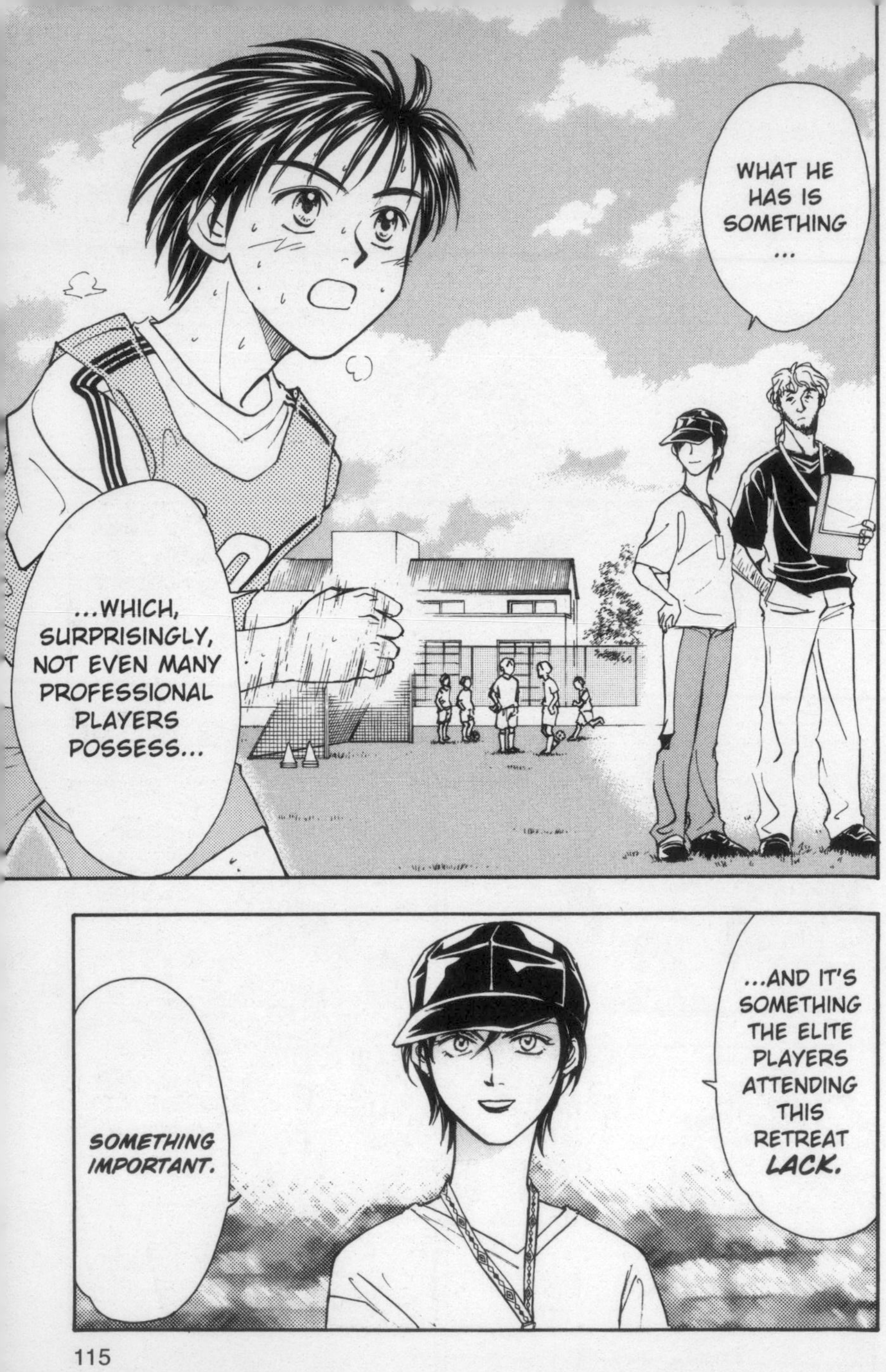
WHAT HE HAS IS SOMETHING ...
...WHICH, SURPRISINGLY, NOT EVEN MANY PROFESSIONAL PLAYERS POSSESS...
...AND IT'S SOMETHING THE ELITE PLAYERS ATTENDING THIS RETREAT *LACK.*
SOMETHING IMPORTANT.

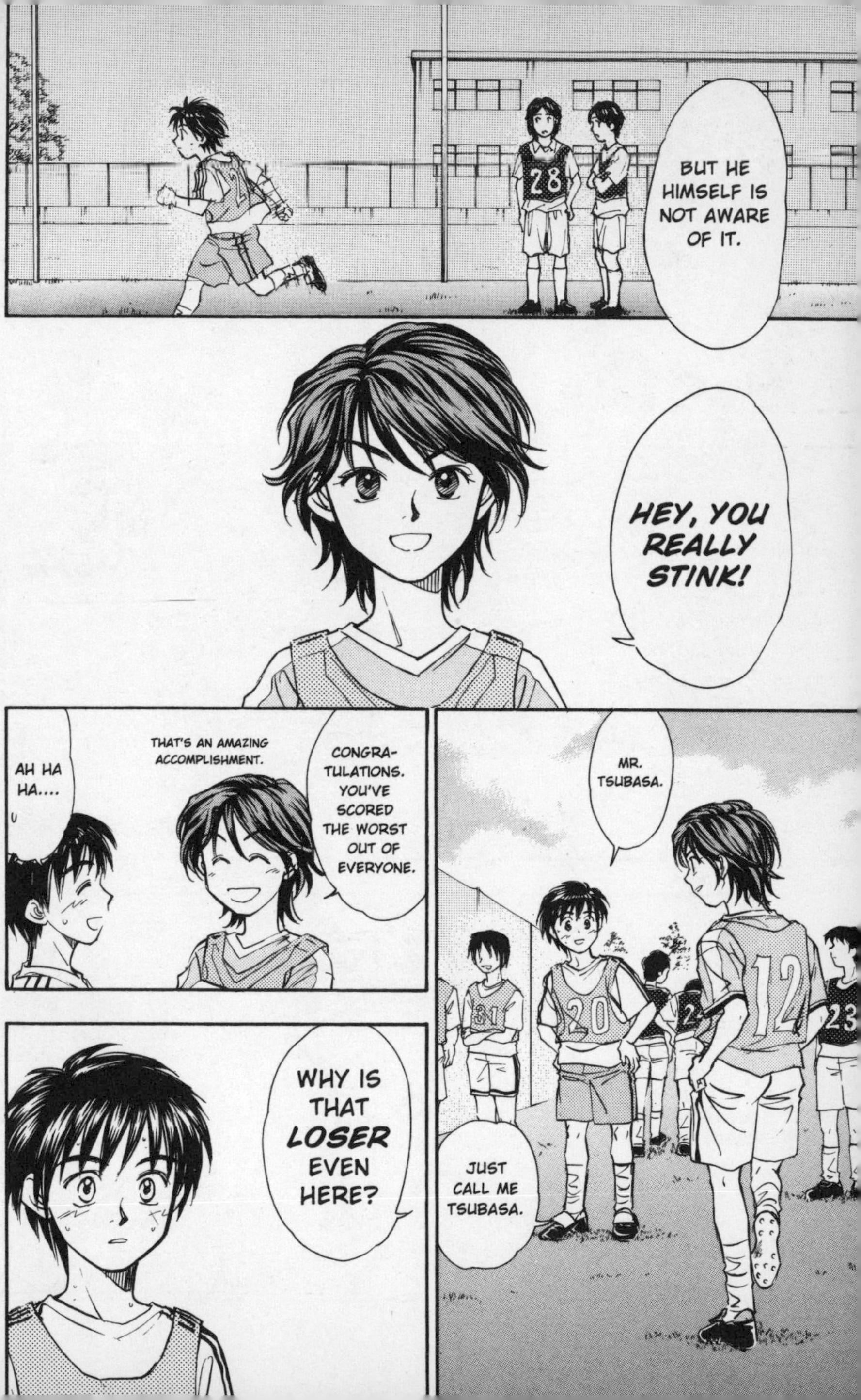
BUT HE HIMSELF IS NOT AWARE OF IT.
HEY, YOU REALLY STINK!
MR. TSUBASA.
JUST CALL ME TSUBASA.
CONGRATULATIONS. YOU'VE SCORED THE WORST OUT OF EVERYONE.
THAT'S AN AMAZING ACCOMPLISHMENT.
AH HA HA....
WHY IS THAT LOSER EVEN HERE?

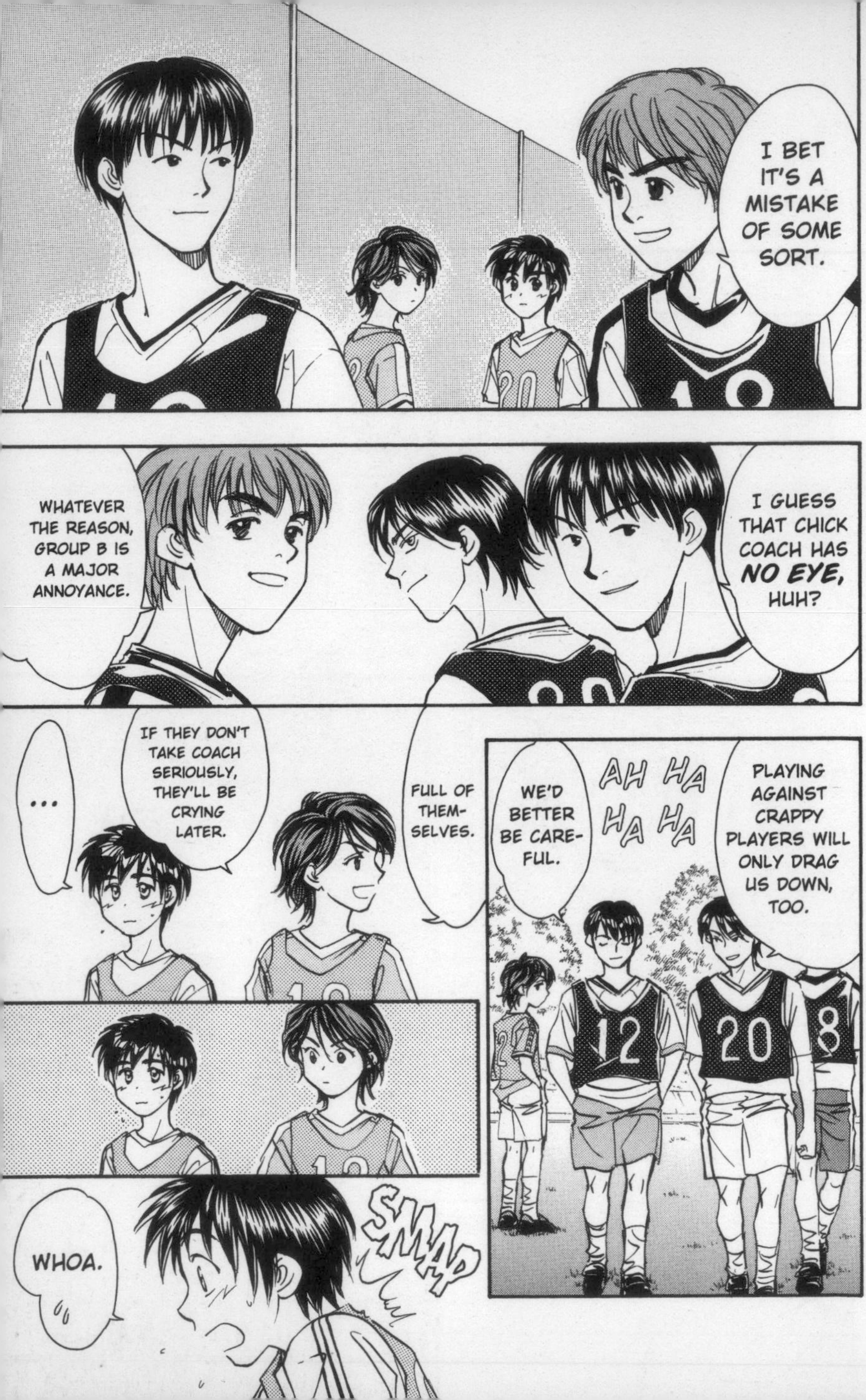
I BET IT'S A MISTAKE OF SOME SORT.
I GUESS THAT CHICK COACH HAS **NO EYE,** HUH?
WHATEVER THE REASON, GROUP B IS A MAJOR ANNOYANCE.
PLAYING AGAINST CRAPPY PLAYERS WILL ONLY DRAG US DOWN, TOO.
AH HA HA HA
WE'D BETTER BE CARE-FUL.
FULL OF THEM-SELVES.
IF THEY DON'T TAKE COACH SERIOUSLY, THEY'LL BE CRYING LATER.
...
SNAP
WHOA.

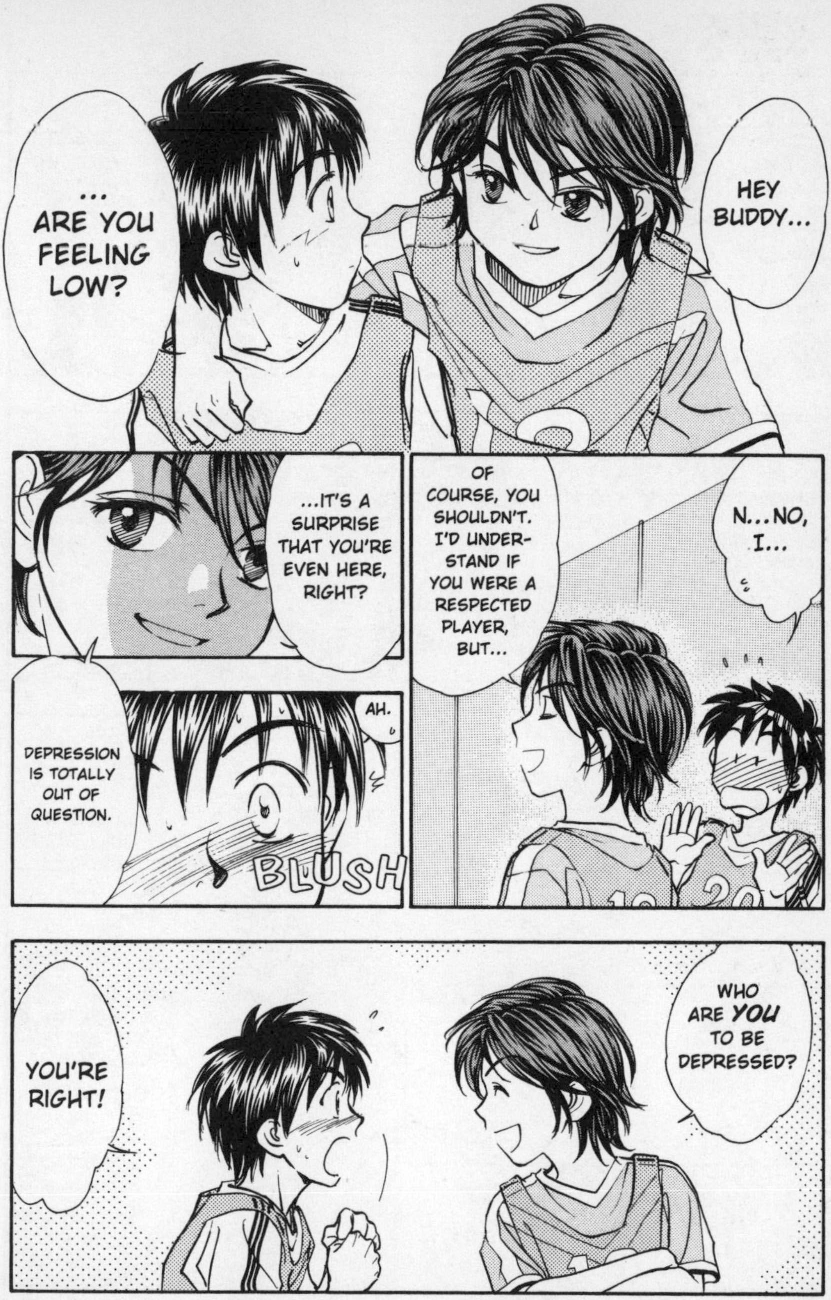
HEY BUDDY...
... ARE YOU FEELING LOW?
N...NO, I...
OF COURSE, YOU SHOULDN'T. I'D UNDERSTAND IF YOU WERE A RESPECTED PLAYER, BUT...
...IT'S A SURPRISE THAT YOU'RE EVEN HERE, RIGHT?
AH.
DEPRESSION IS TOTALLY OUT OF QUESTION.
BLUSH
WHO ARE *YOU* TO BE DEPRESSED?
YOU'RE RIGHT!

READ THIS WAY

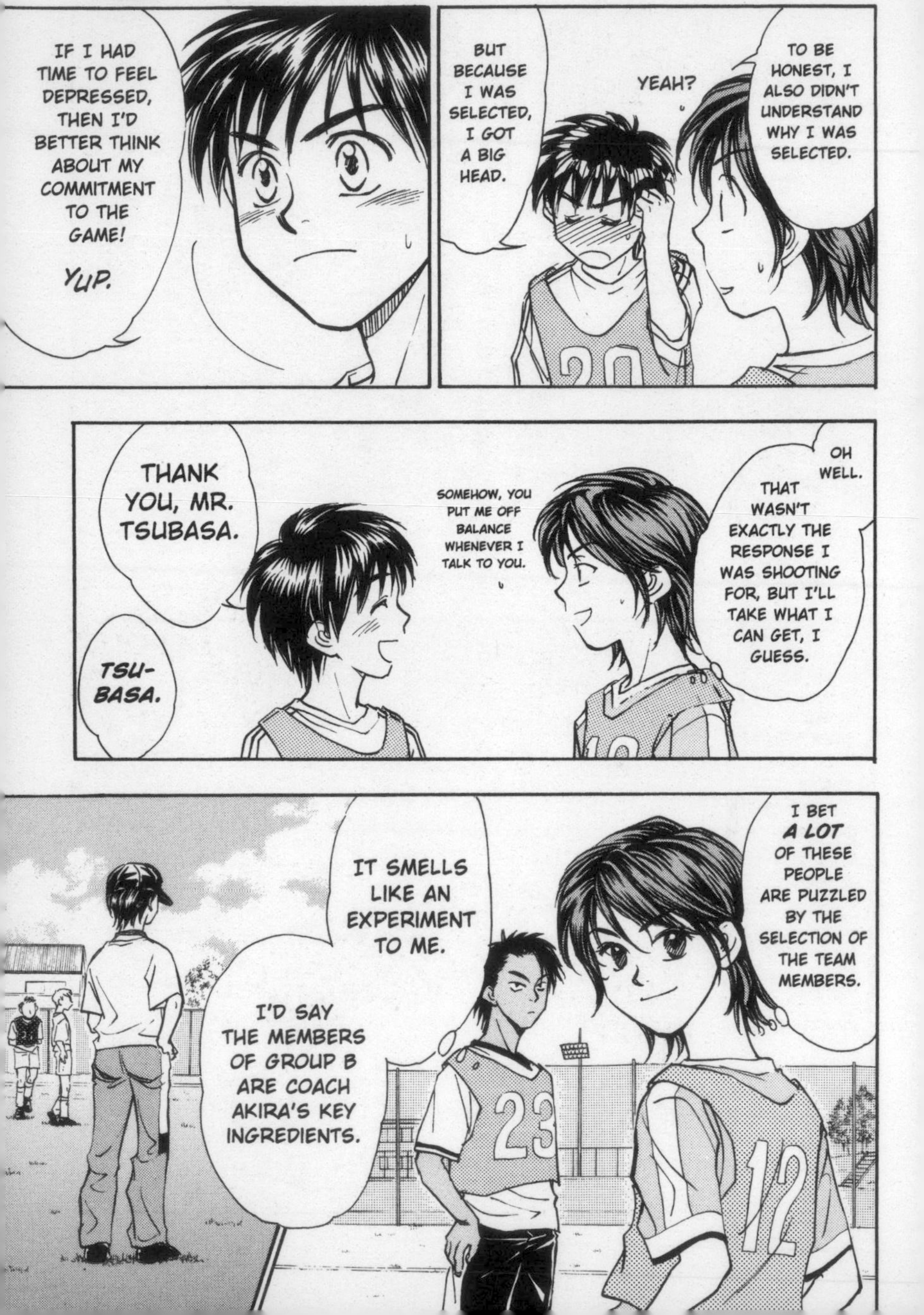
TO BE HONEST, I ALSO DIDN'T UNDERSTAND WHY I WAS SELECTED.
YEAH?
BUT BECAUSE I WAS SELECTED, I GOT A BIG HEAD.
IF I HAD TIME TO FEEL DEPRESSED, THEN I'D BETTER THINK ABOUT MY COMMITMENT TO THE GAME!
YUP.
OH WELL.
THAT WASN'T EXACTLY THE RESPONSE I WAS SHOOTING FOR, BUT I'LL TAKE WHAT I CAN GET, I GUESS.
SOMEHOW, YOU PUT ME OFF BALANCE WHENEVER I TALK TO YOU.
THANK YOU, MR. TSUBASA.
TSU-BASA.
I BET A LOT OF THESE PEOPLE ARE PUZZLED BY THE SELECTION OF THE TEAM MEMBERS.
IT SMELLS LIKE AN EXPERIMENT TO ME.
I'D SAY THE MEMBERS OF GROUP B ARE COACH AKIRA'S KEY INGREDIENTS.

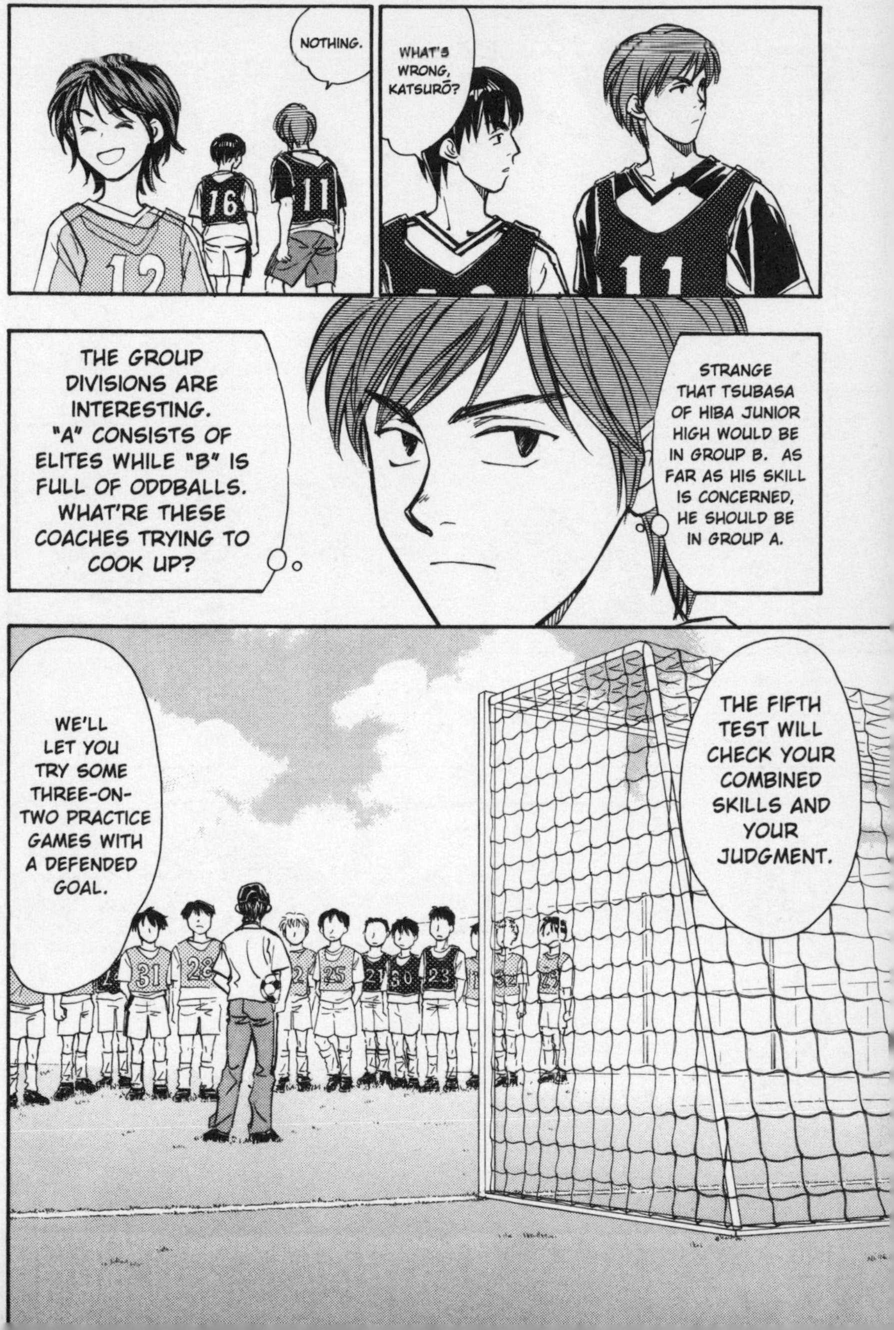
WHAT'S WRONG, KATSURŌ?
NOTHING.
STRANGE THAT TSUBASA OF HIBA JUNIOR HIGH WOULD BE IN GROUP B. AS FAR AS HIS SKILL IS CONCERNED, HE SHOULD BE IN GROUP A.
THE GROUP DIVISIONS ARE INTERESTING. "A" CONSISTS OF ELITES WHILE "B" IS FULL OF ODDBALLS. WHAT'RE THESE COACHES TRYING TO COOK UP?
THE FIFTH TEST WILL CHECK YOUR COMBINED SKILLS AND YOUR JUDGMENT.
WE'LL LET YOU TRY SOME THREE-ON-TWO PRACTICE GAMES WITH A DEFENDED GOAL.

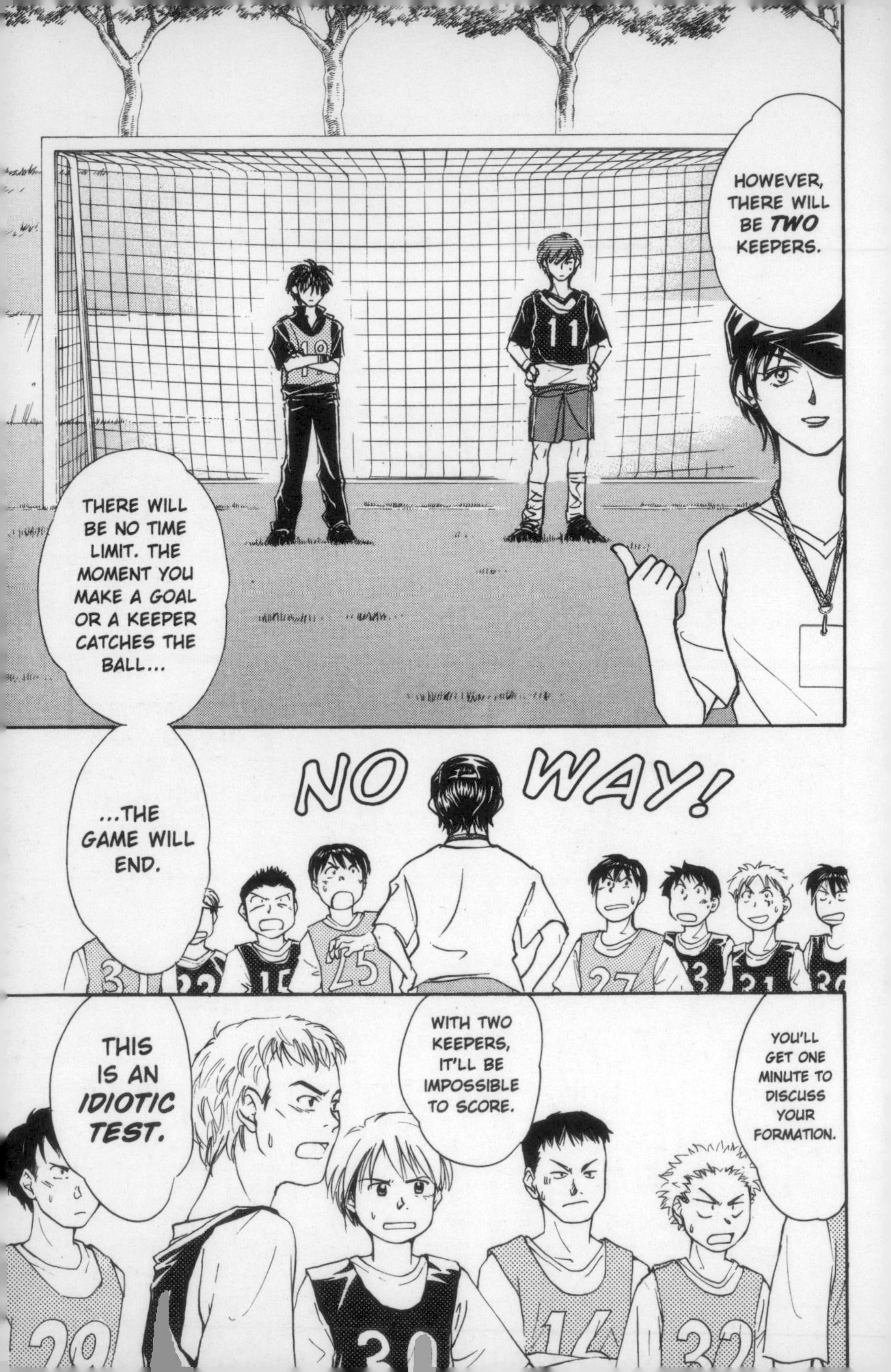
HOWEVER, THERE WILL BE *TWO* KEEPERS.
THERE WILL BE NO TIME LIMIT. THE MOMENT YOU MAKE A GOAL OR A KEEPER CATCHES THE BALL...
...THE GAME WILL END.
NO WAY!
YOU'LL GET ONE MINUTE TO DISCUSS YOUR FORMATION.
WITH TWO KEEPERS, IT'LL BE IMPOSSIBLE TO SCORE.
THIS IS AN *IDIOTIC TEST.*

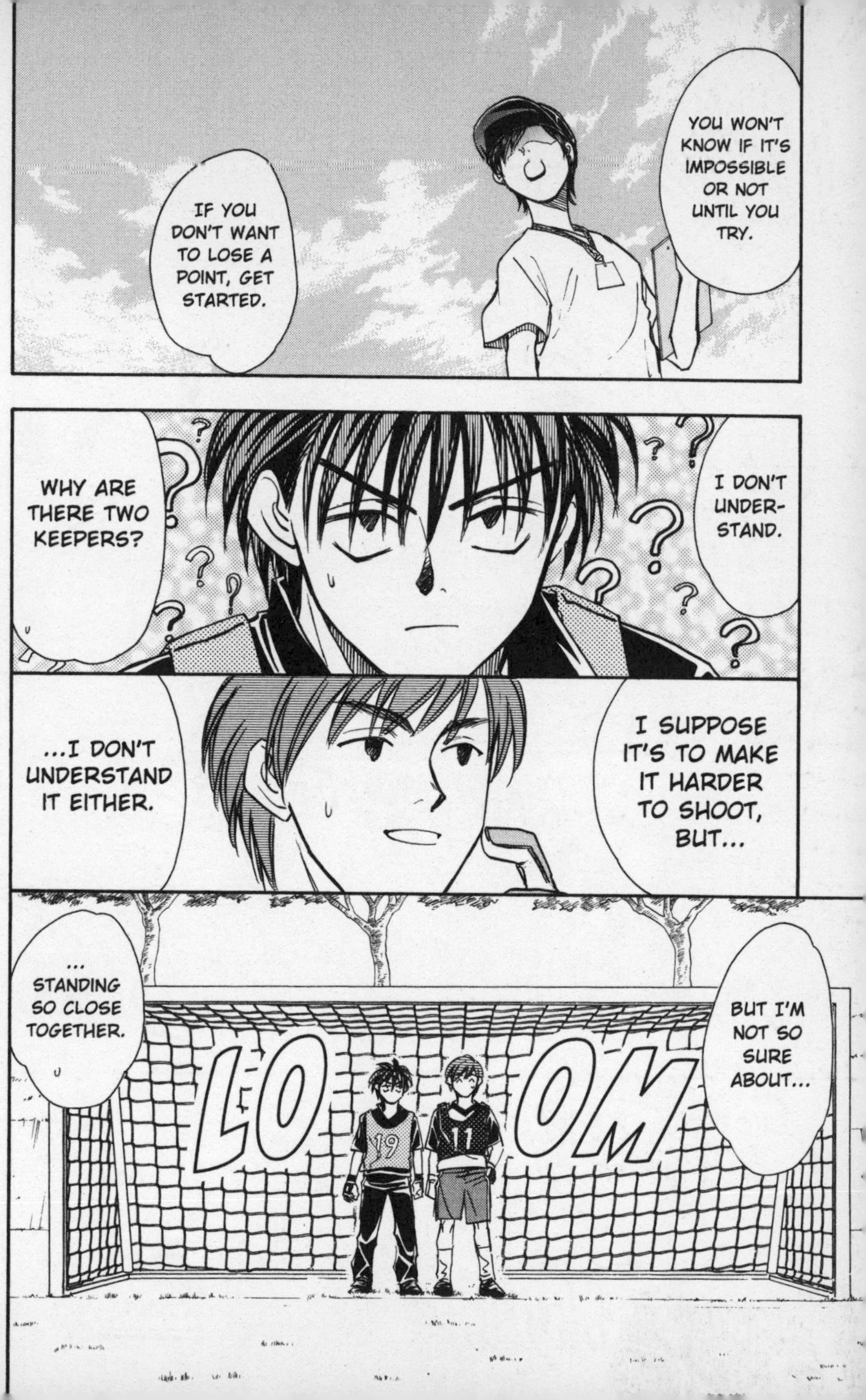

YOU WON'T KNOW IF IT'S IMPOSSIBLE OR NOT UNTIL YOU TRY.
IF YOU DON'T WANT TO LOSE A POINT, GET STARTED.
I DON'T UNDER-STAND.
WHY ARE THERE TWO KEEPERS?
I SUPPOSE IT'S TO MAKE IT HARDER TO SHOOT, BUT...
...I DON'T UNDERSTAND IT EITHER.
BUT I'M NOT SO SURE ABOUT...
... STANDING SO CLOSE TOGETHER.
LO OM

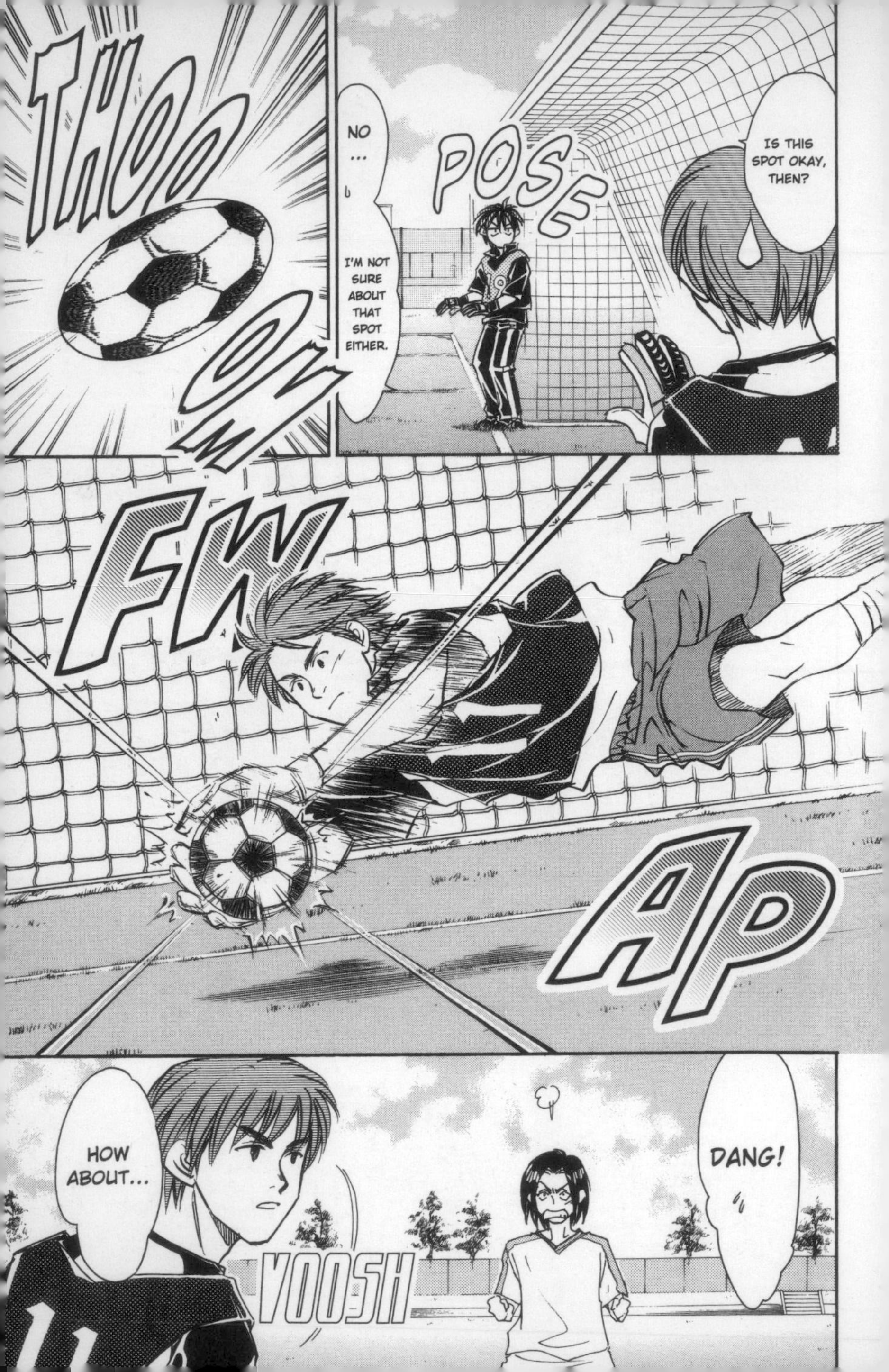

IS THIS SPOT OKAY, THEN?
POSE
NO ...
I'M NOT SURE ABOUT THAT SPOT EITHER.
THOOOOM
FWAP
DANG!
VOOSH
HOW ABOUT...

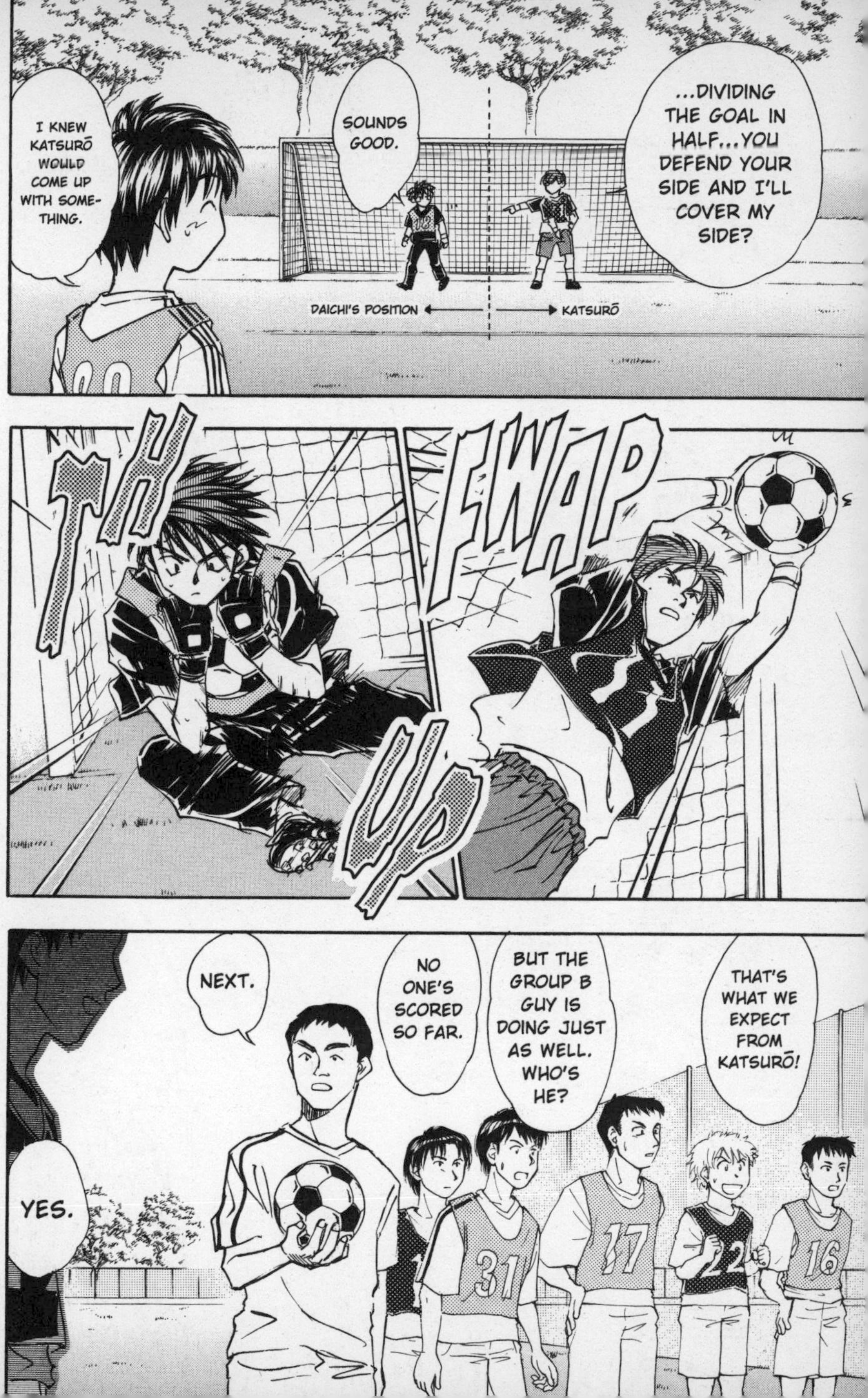
...DIVIDING THE GOAL IN HALF...YOU DEFEND YOUR SIDE AND I'LL COVER MY SIDE?
SOUNDS GOOD.
DAICHI'S POSITION
KATSURŌ
I KNEW KATSURŌ WOULD COME UP WITH SOME-THING.
FWAP
TH
UP
THAT'S WHAT WE EXPECT FROM KATSURŌ!
BUT THE GROUP B GUY IS DOING JUST AS WELL. WHO'S HE?
NO ONE'S SCORED SO FAR.
NEXT.
YES.

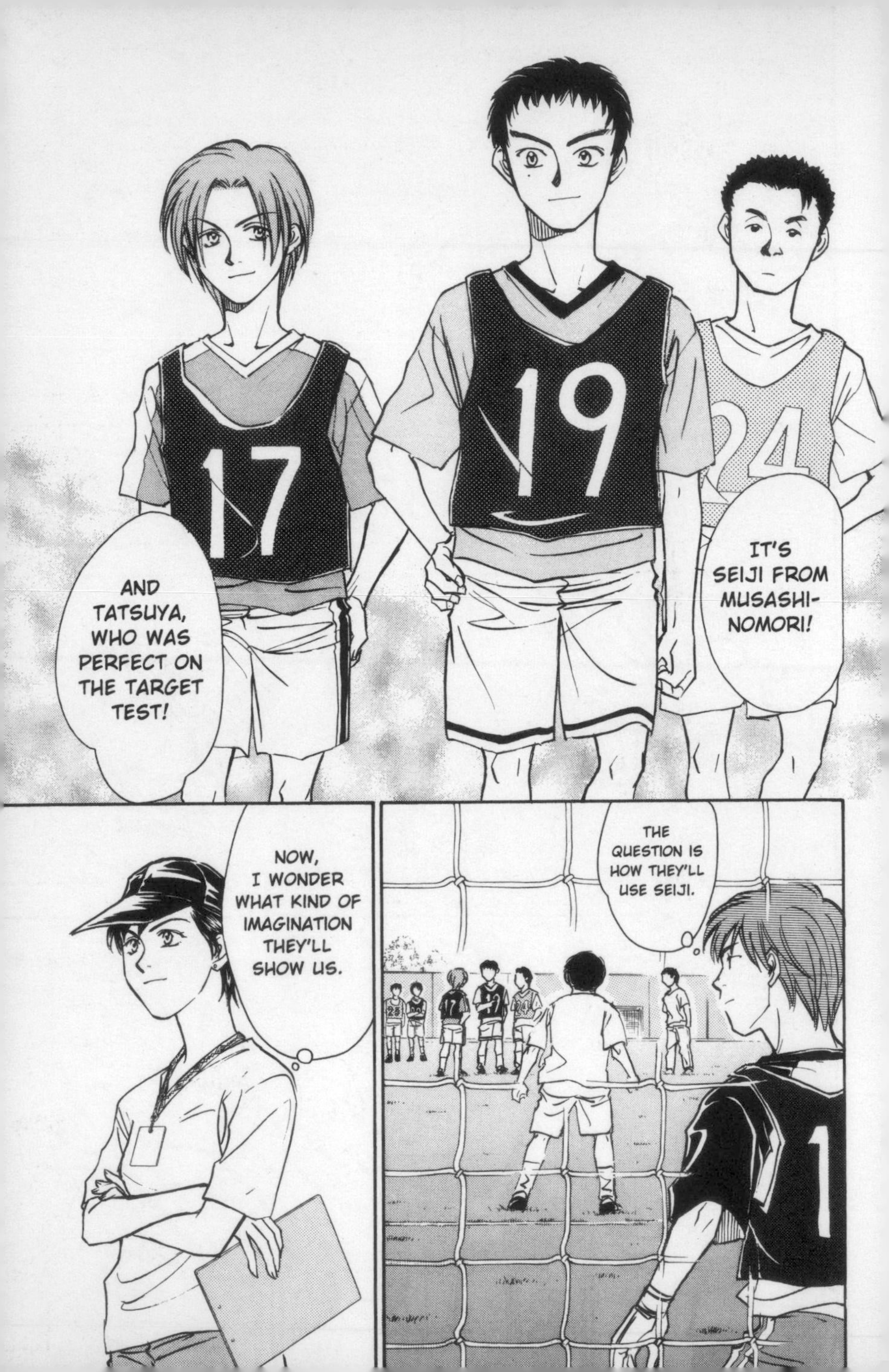
IT'S SEIJI FROM MUSASHI-NOMORI!
AND TATSUYA, WHO WAS PERFECT ON THE TARGET TEST!
THE QUESTION IS HOW THEY'LL USE SEIJI.
NOW, I WONDER WHAT KIND OF IMAGINATION THEY'LL SHOW US.

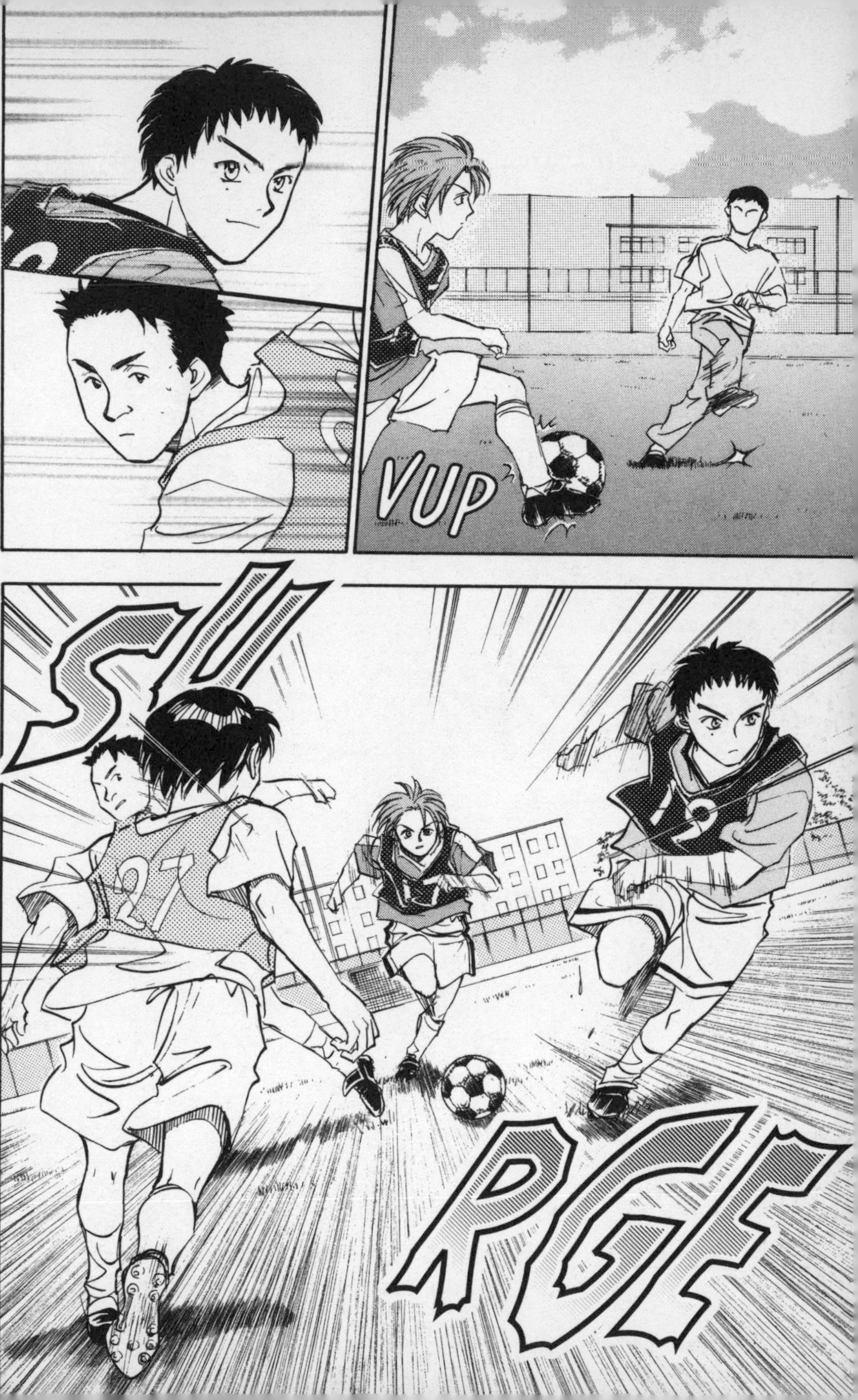
VUP
SU
RGF

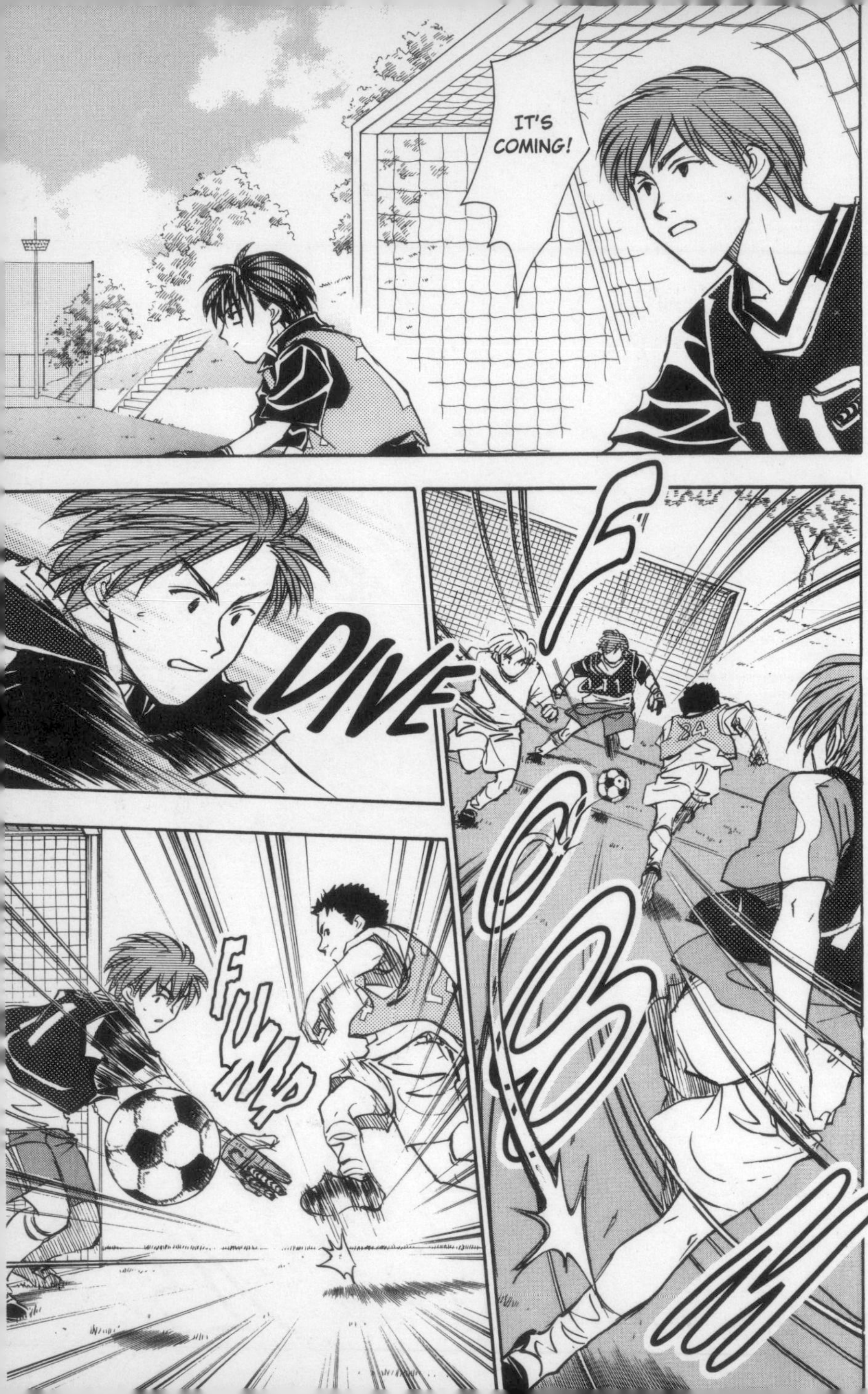
IT'S COMING!
FOOM
DIVE
FLUMP

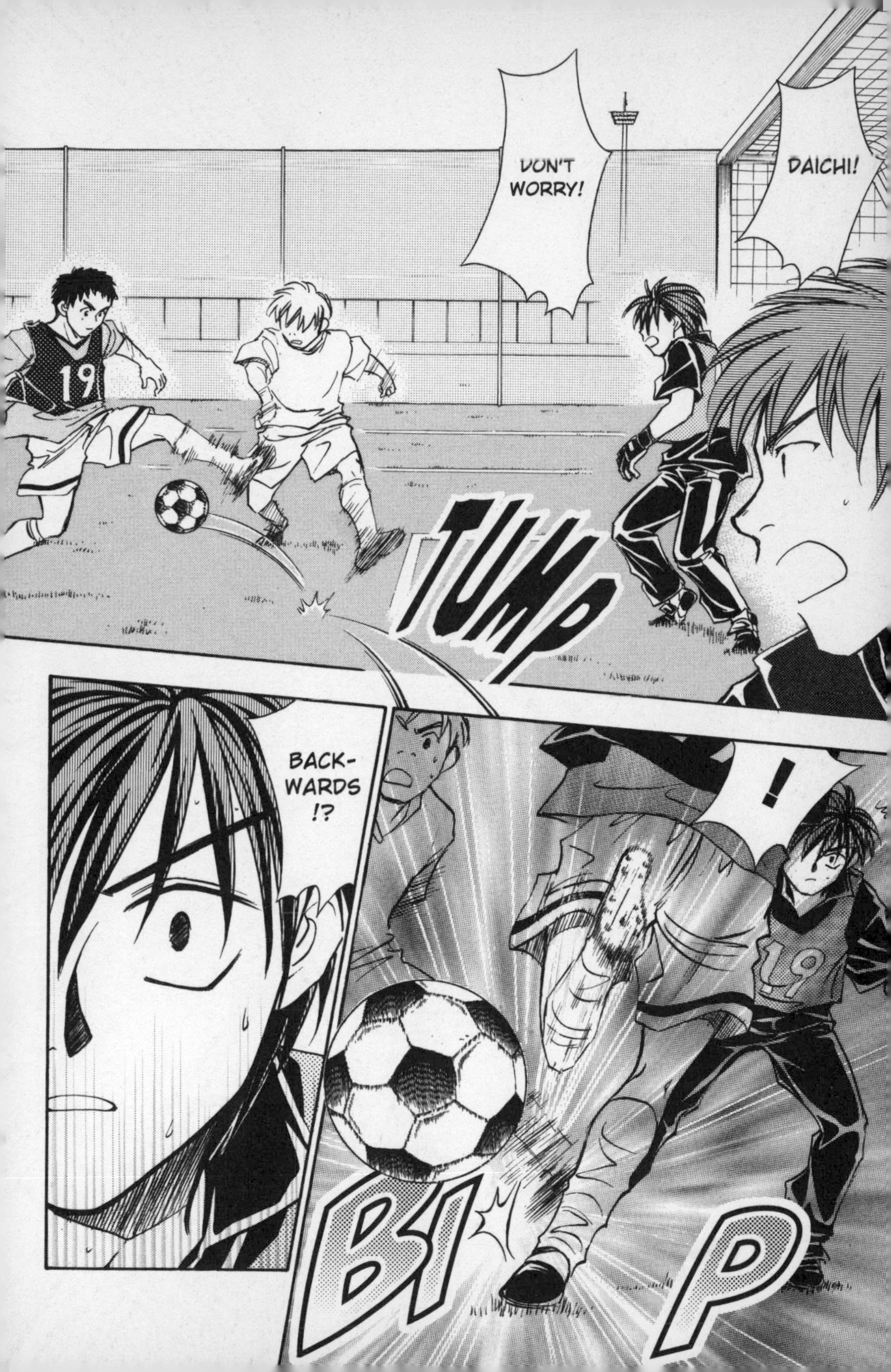
DAICHI!
DON'T WORRY!
TUMP
!
BIP
BACK-WARDS !?

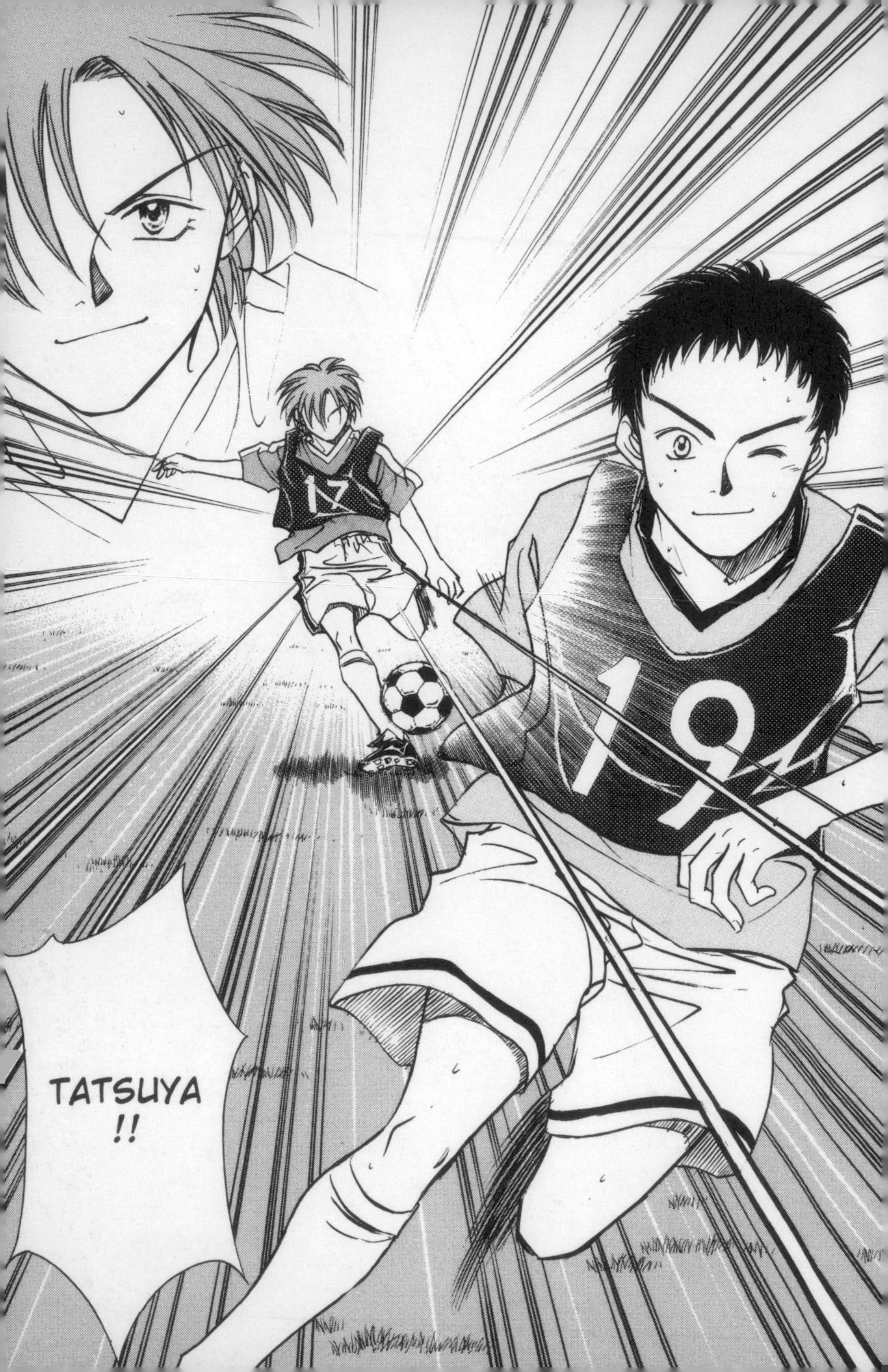
TATSUYA
!!

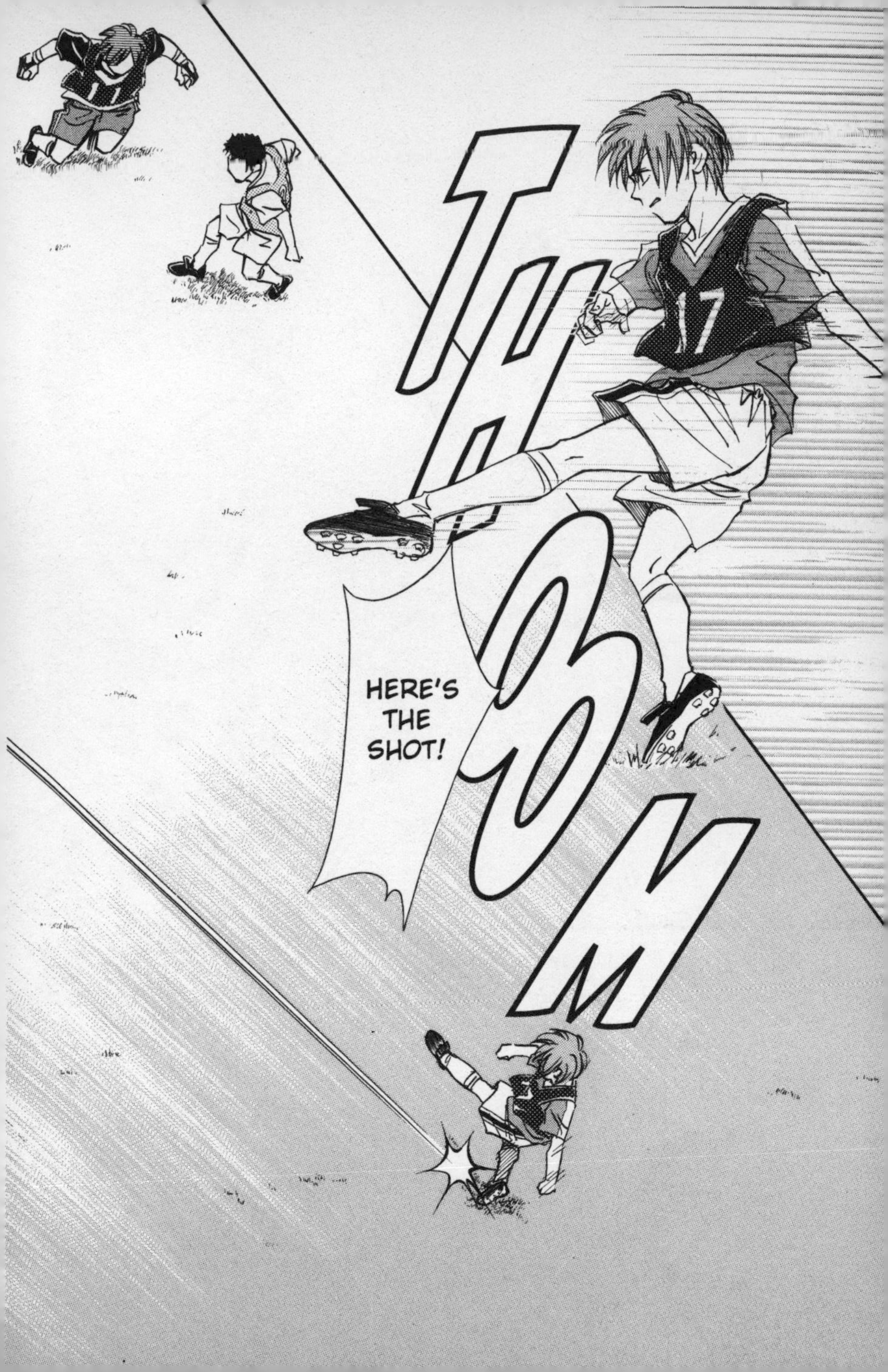
THOOM
HERE'S THE SHOT!

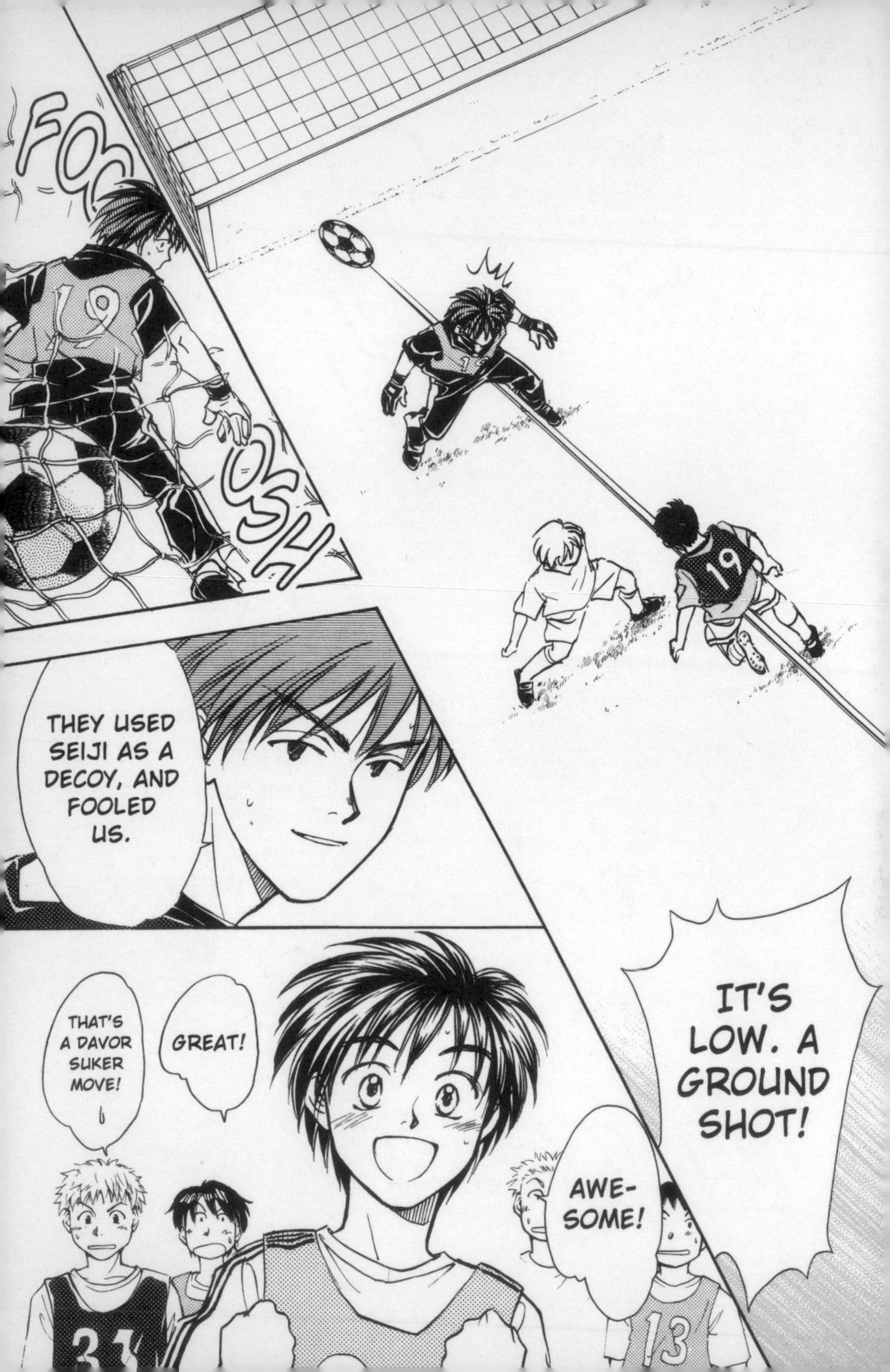

FOOOSH
THEY USED SEIJI AS A DECOY, AND FOOLED US.
IT'S LOW. A GROUND SHOT!
AWE-SOME!
GREAT!
THAT'S A DAVOR SUKER MOVE!

WHISTLE!™

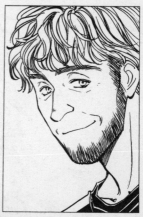

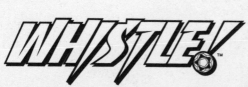

STAGE.105
Skill Test (Last Episode)

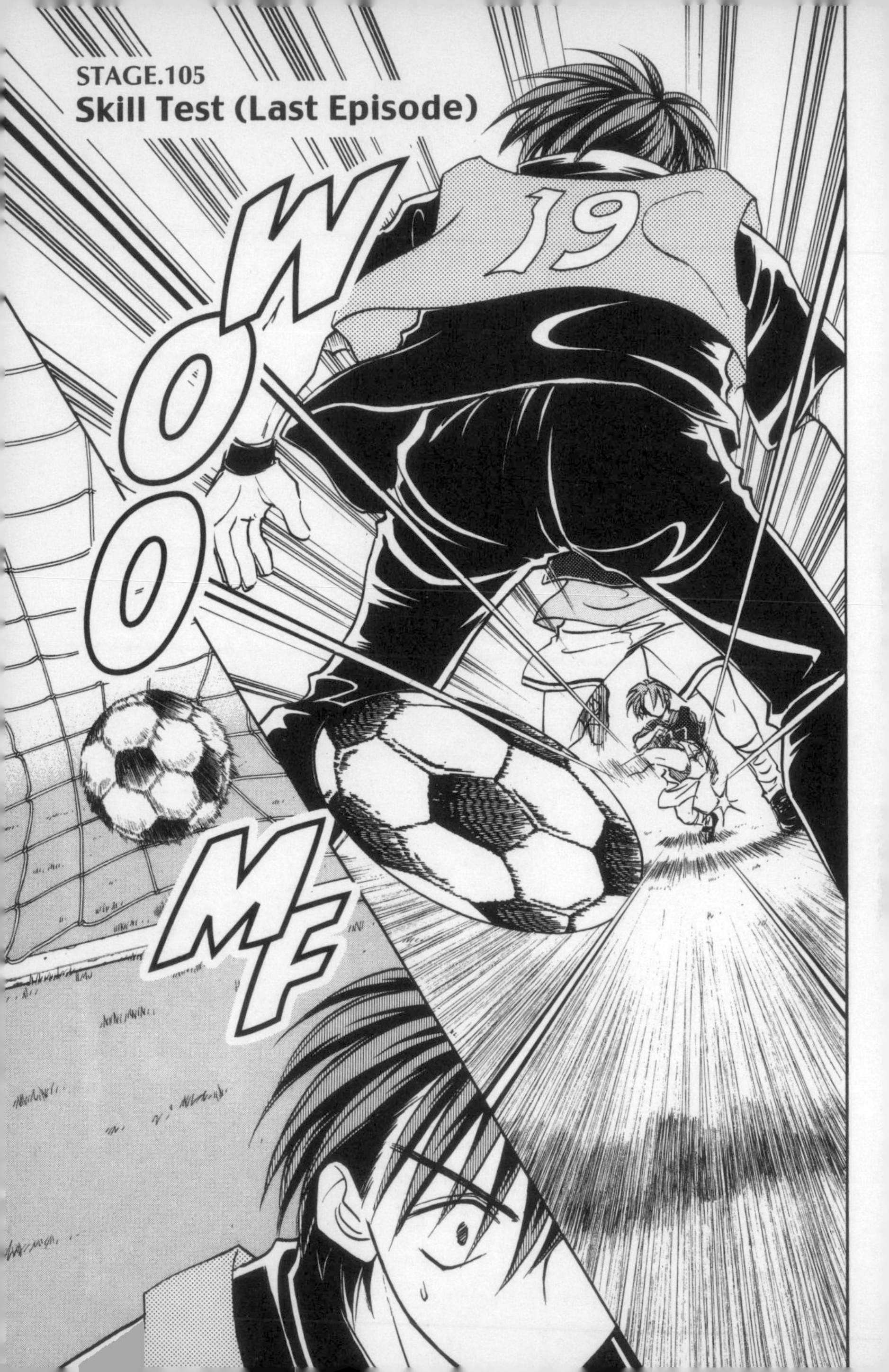
WOOMF

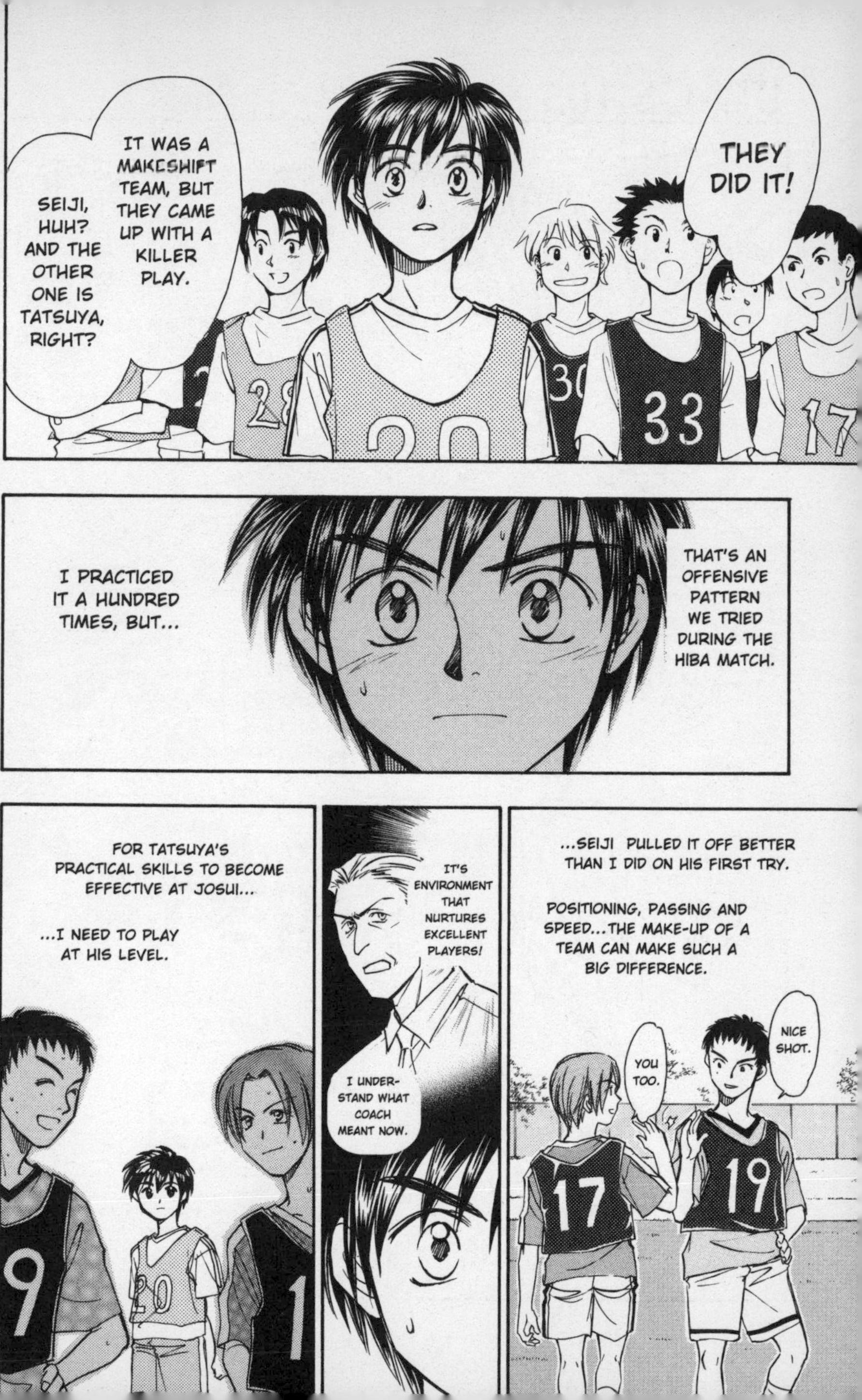
THEY DID IT!
IT WAS A MAKESHIFT TEAM, BUT THEY CAME UP WITH A KILLER PLAY.
SEIJI, HUH? AND THE OTHER ONE IS TATSUYA, RIGHT?
THAT'S AN OFFENSIVE PATTERN WE TRIED DURING THE HIBA MATCH.
I PRACTICED IT A HUNDRED TIMES, BUT...
...SEIJI PULLED IT OFF BETTER THAN I DID ON HIS FIRST TRY.
POSITIONING, PASSING AND SPEED...THE MAKE-UP OF A TEAM CAN MAKE SUCH A BIG DIFFERENCE.
NICE SHOT.
YOU TOO.
IT'S ENVIRONMENT THAT NURTURES EXCELLENT PLAYERS!
I UNDER-STAND WHAT COACH MEANT NOW.
FOR TATSUYA'S PRACTICAL SKILLS TO BECOME EFFECTIVE AT JOSUI...
...I NEED TO PLAY AT HIS LEVEL.

STAGE.105

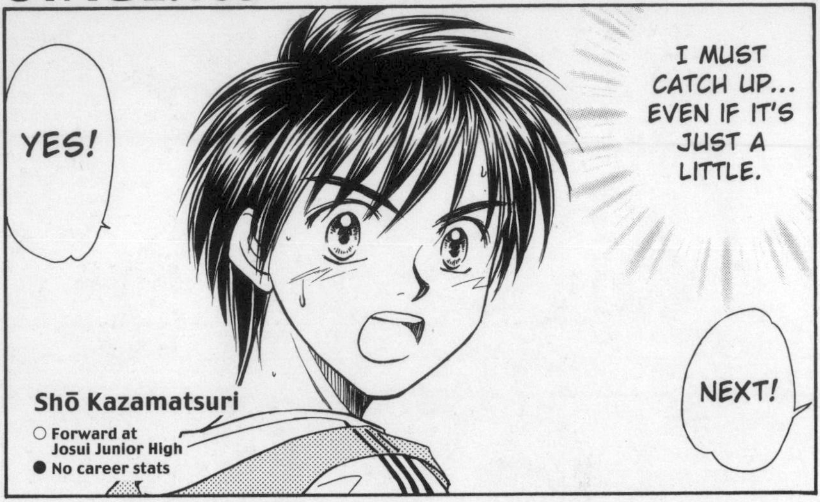
I MUST CATCH UP... EVEN IF IT'S JUST A LITTLE.
NEXT!
YES!
Shō Kazamatsuri
○ Forward at Josui Junior High
● No career stats

Skill Test (Last Episode)

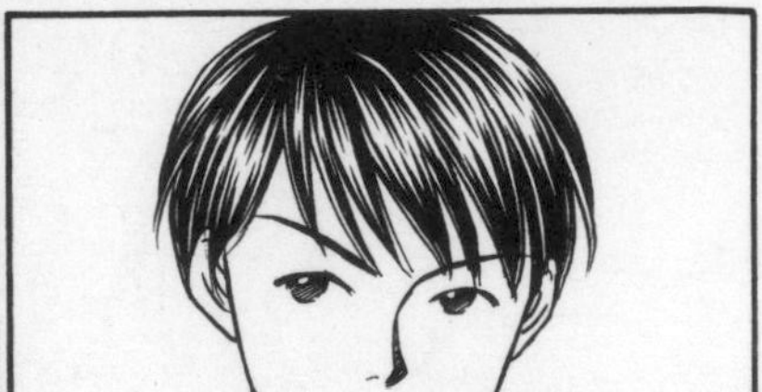
Kaku Eishi
○ Midfielder at Zōshigayaminami Junior High
● U-14 (Under-14 Circuit)

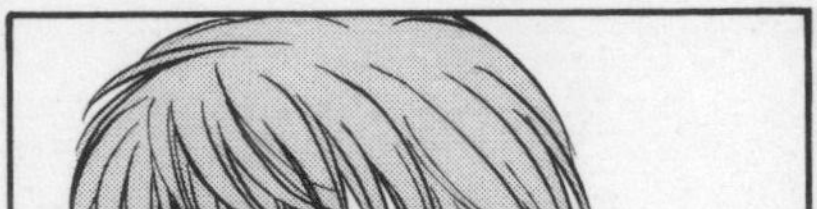
Yūto Wakana
○ Midfielder/Captain at Seta Third Junior High
● U-14 (Under-14 Circuit)

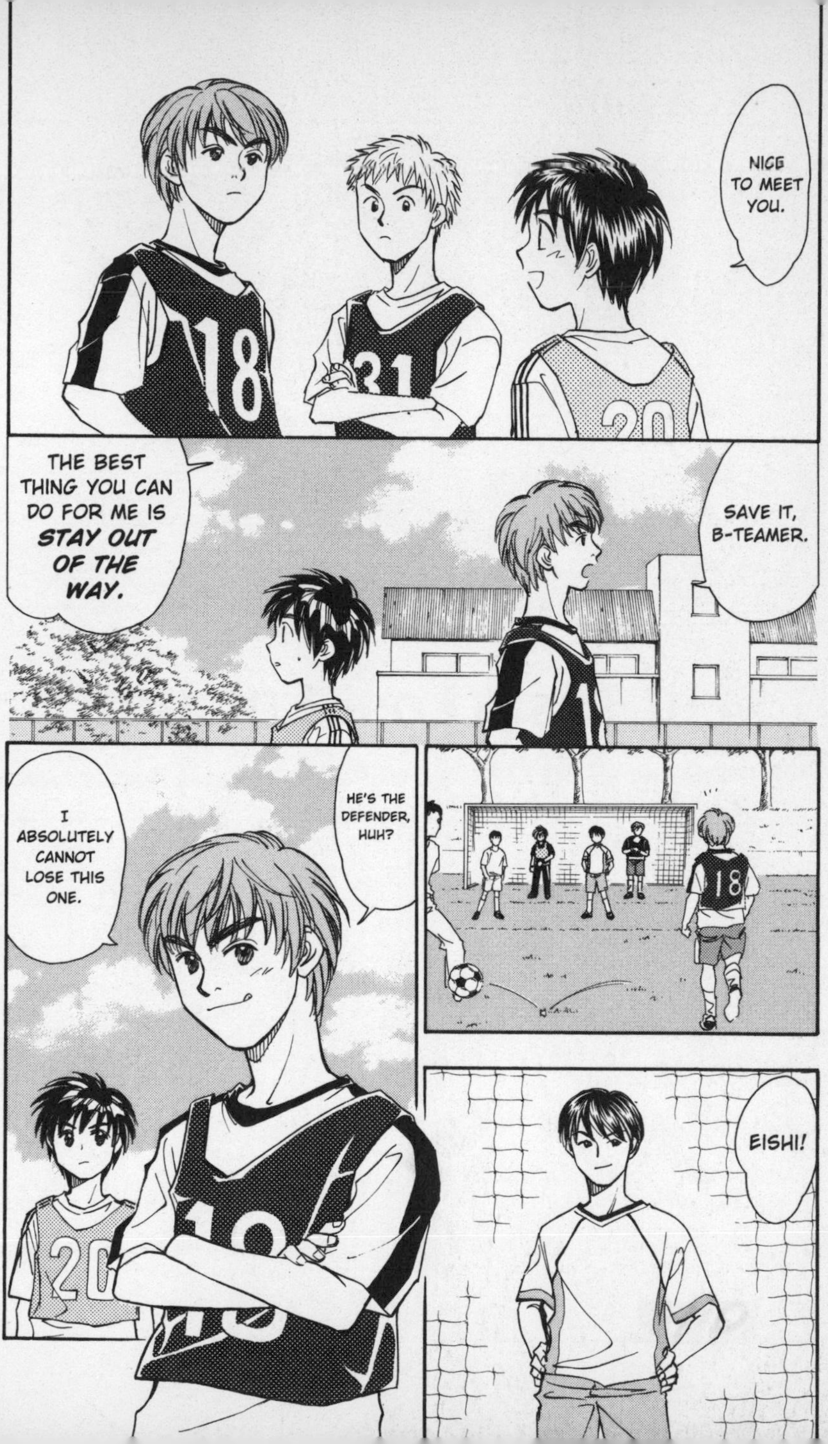
NICE TO MEET YOU.
SAVE IT, B-TEAMER.
THE BEST THING YOU CAN DO FOR ME IS *STAY OUT OF THE WAY.*
EISHI!
HE'S THE DEFENDER, HUH?
I ABSOLUTELY CANNOT LOSE THIS ONE.

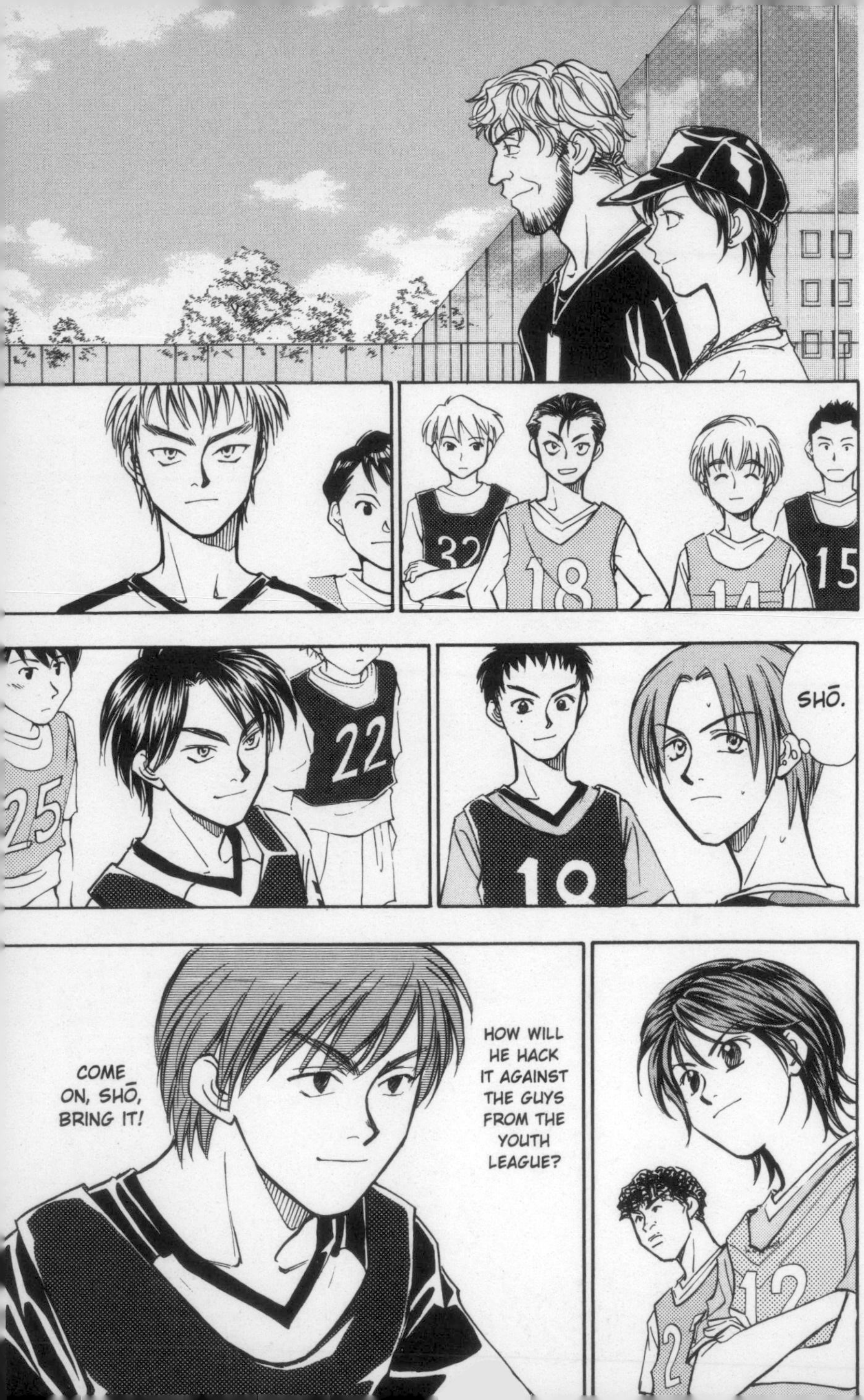
SHŌ.
HOW WILL HE HACK IT AGAINST THE GUYS FROM THE YOUTH LEAGUE?
COME ON, SHŌ, BRING IT!

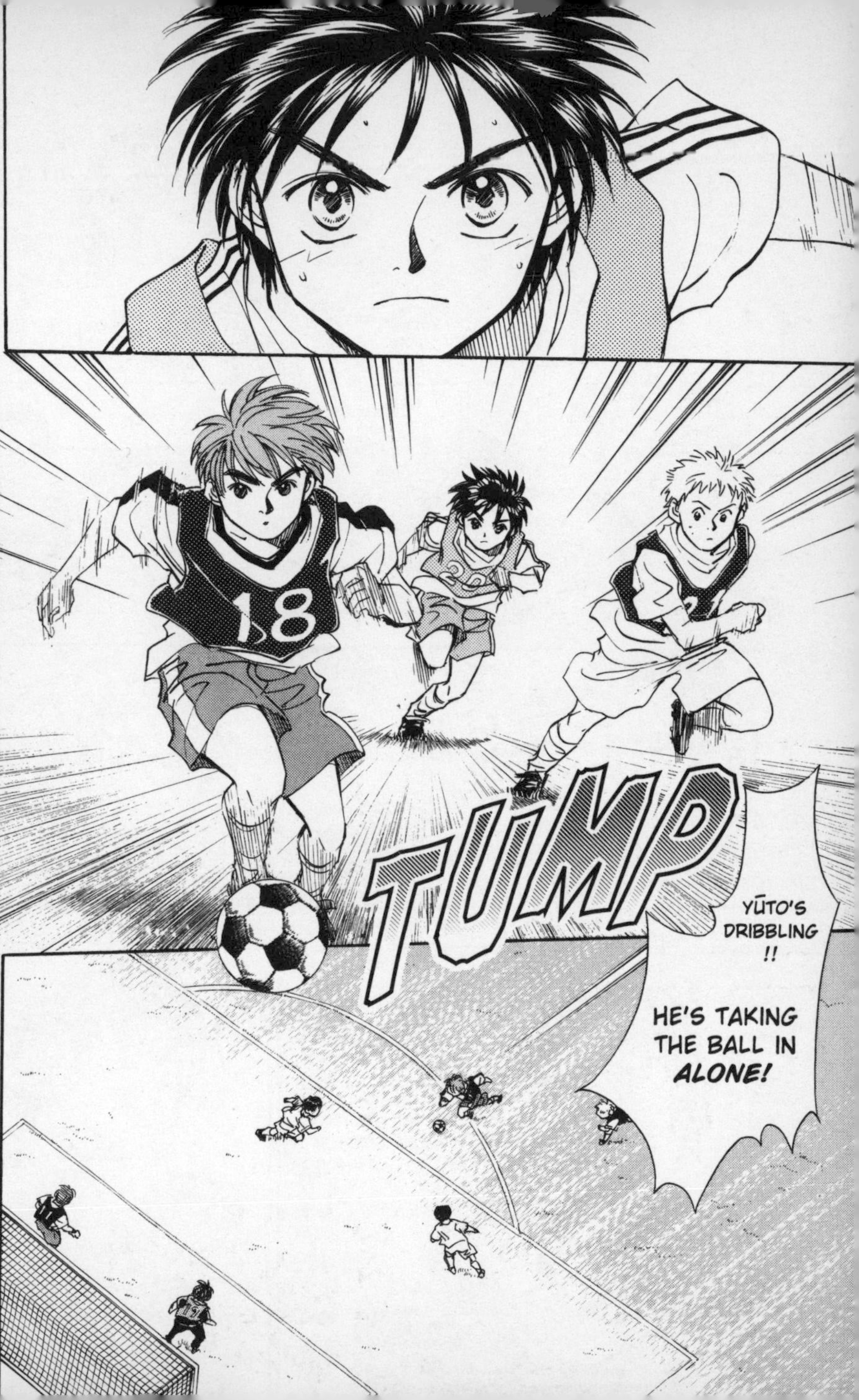
18
TUMP
YŪTO'S DRIBBLING !!
HE'S TAKING THE BALL IN ALONE!

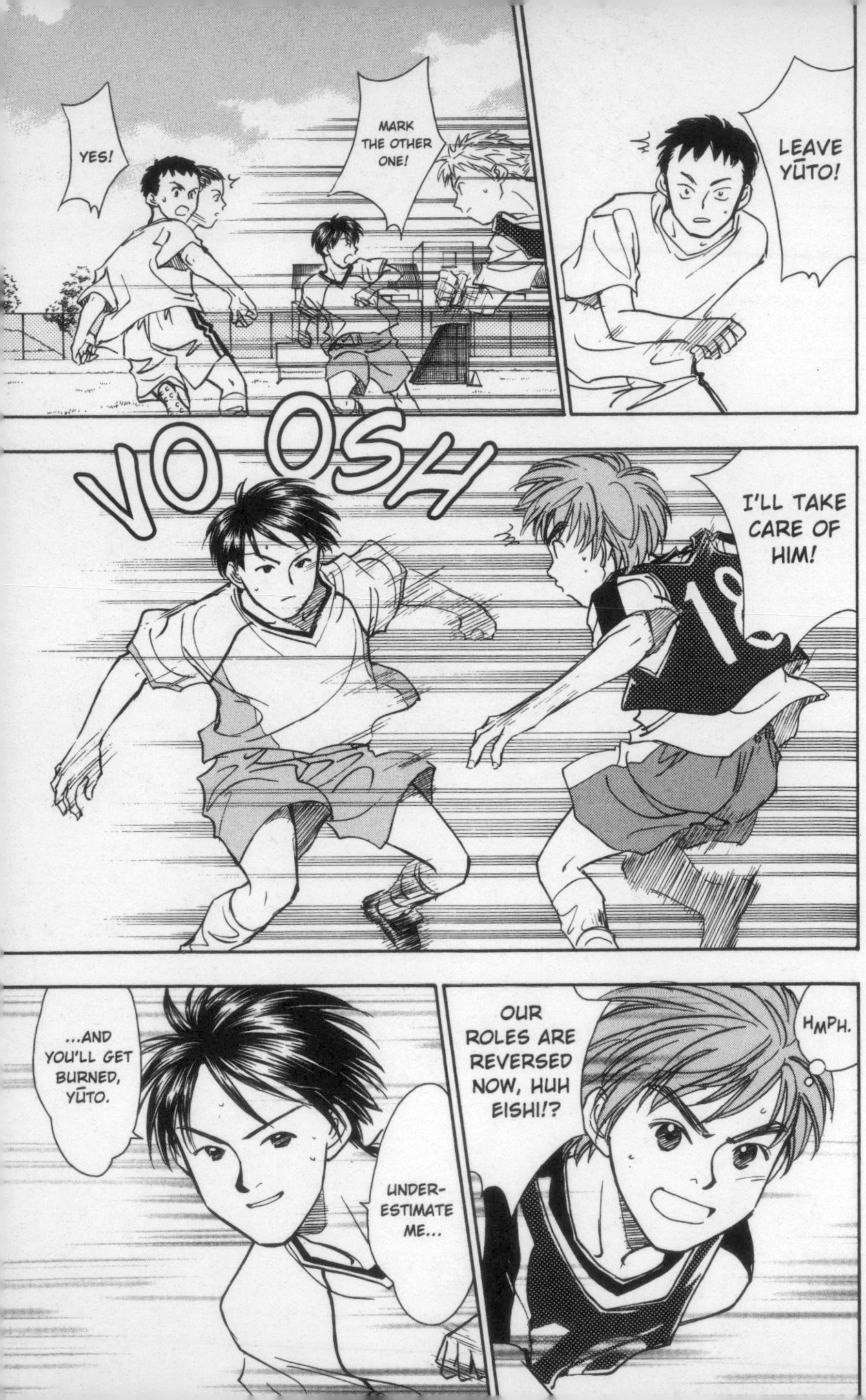
LEAVE YŪTO!
MARK THE OTHER ONE!
YES!
I'LL TAKE CARE OF HIM!
VOOSH
HMPH.
OUR ROLES ARE REVERSED NOW, HUH EISHI!?
UNDER-ESTIMATE ME...
...AND YOU'LL GET BURNED, YŪTO.

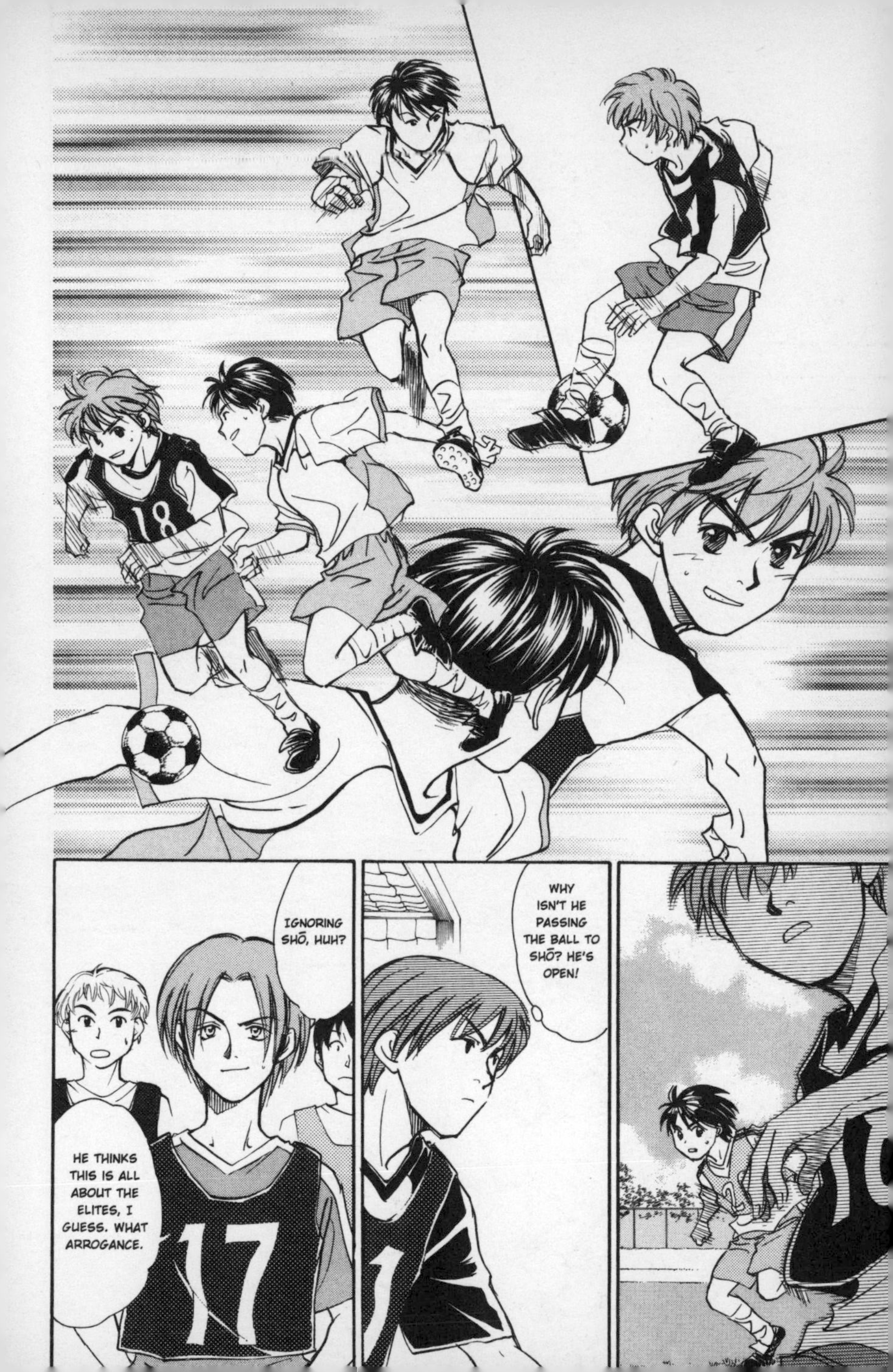
WHY ISN'T HE PASSING THE BALL TO SHŌ? HE'S OPEN!
IGNORING SHŌ, HUH?
HE THINKS THIS IS ALL ABOUT THE ELITES, I GUESS. WHAT ARROGANCE.

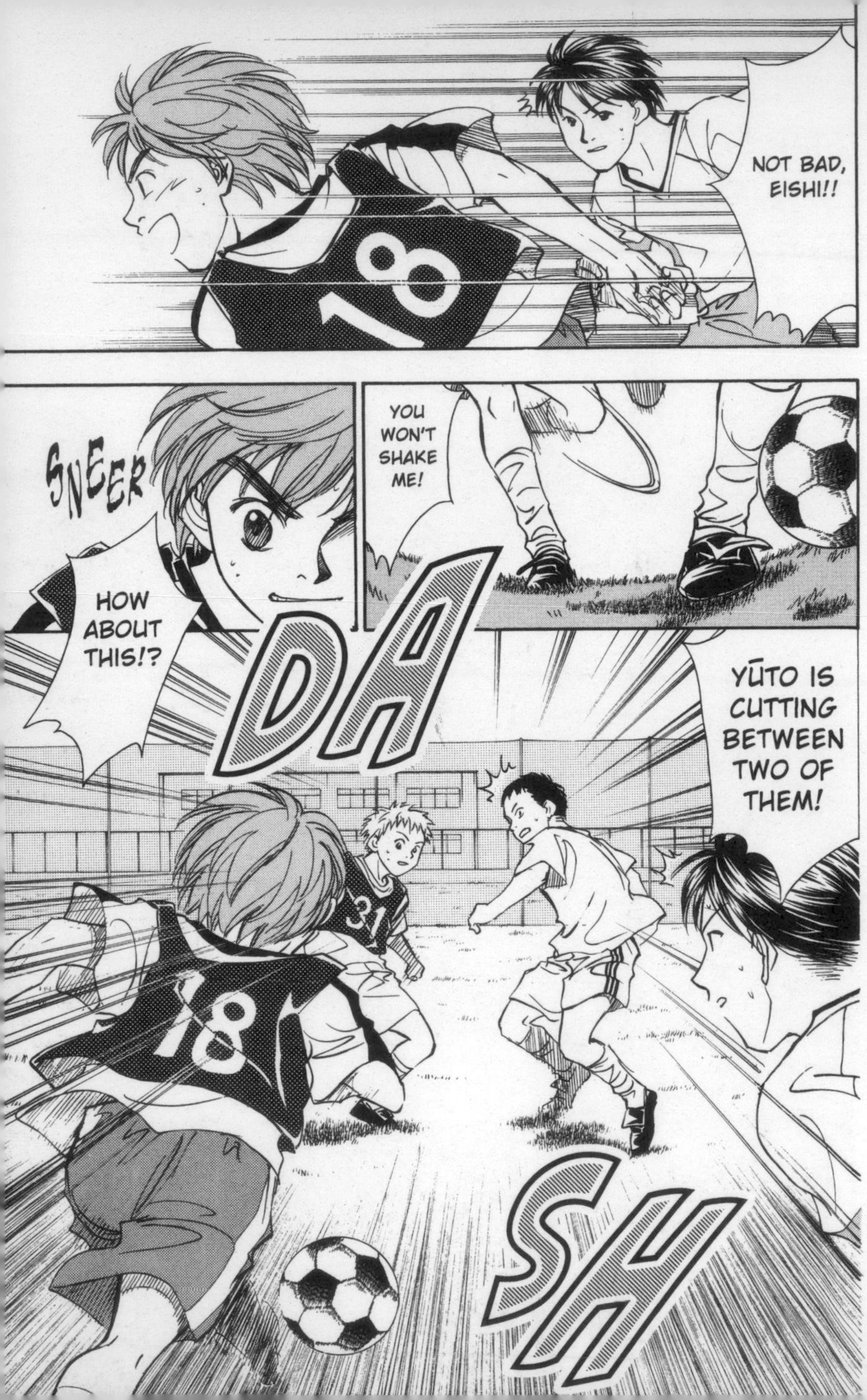
NOT BAD, EISHI!!
YOU WON'T SHAKE ME!
SNEER
HOW ABOUT THIS!?
YŪTO IS CUTTING BETWEEN TWO OF THEM!
DA
SH

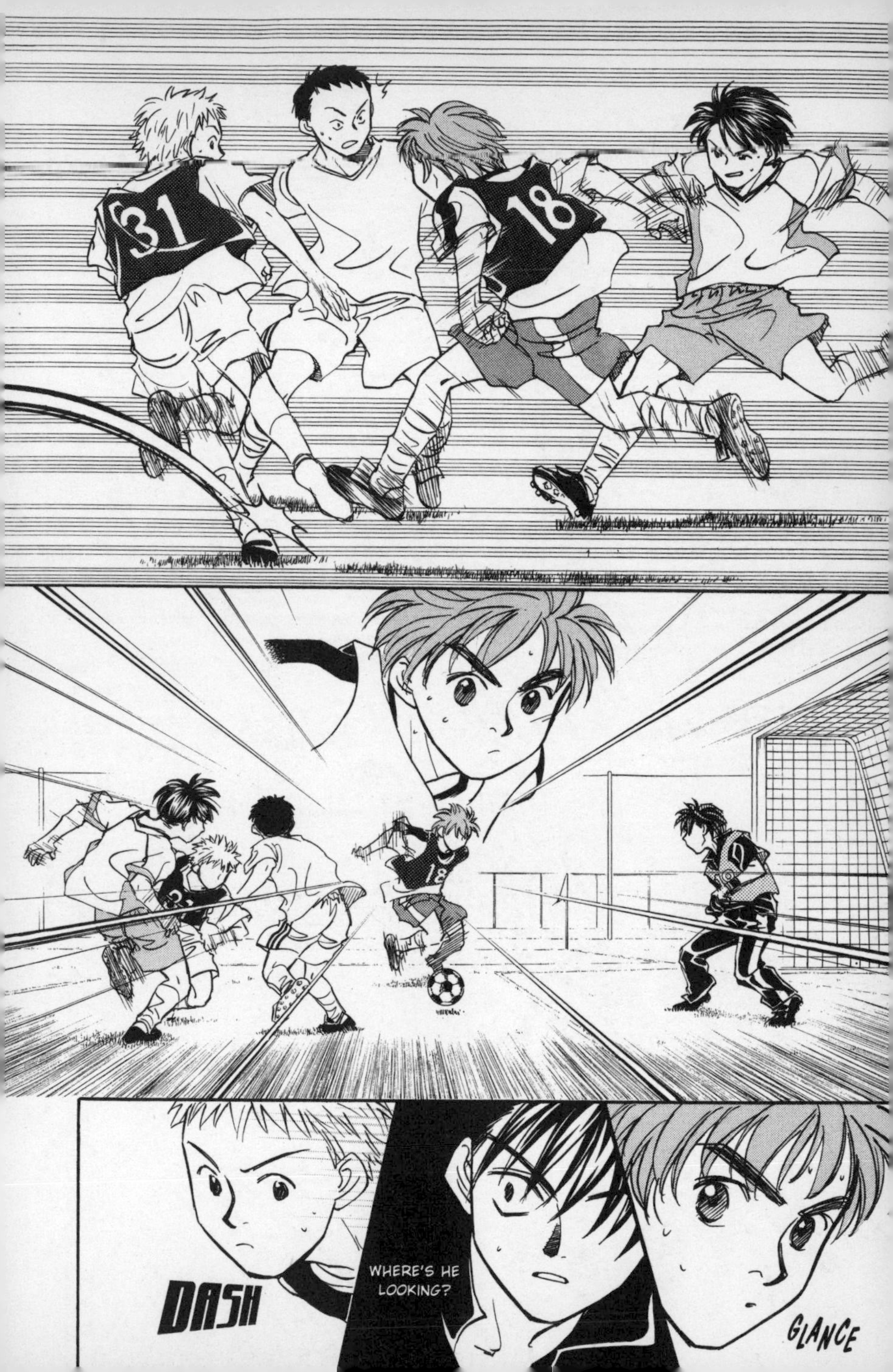

GLANCE
WHERE'S HE LOOKING?
DASH

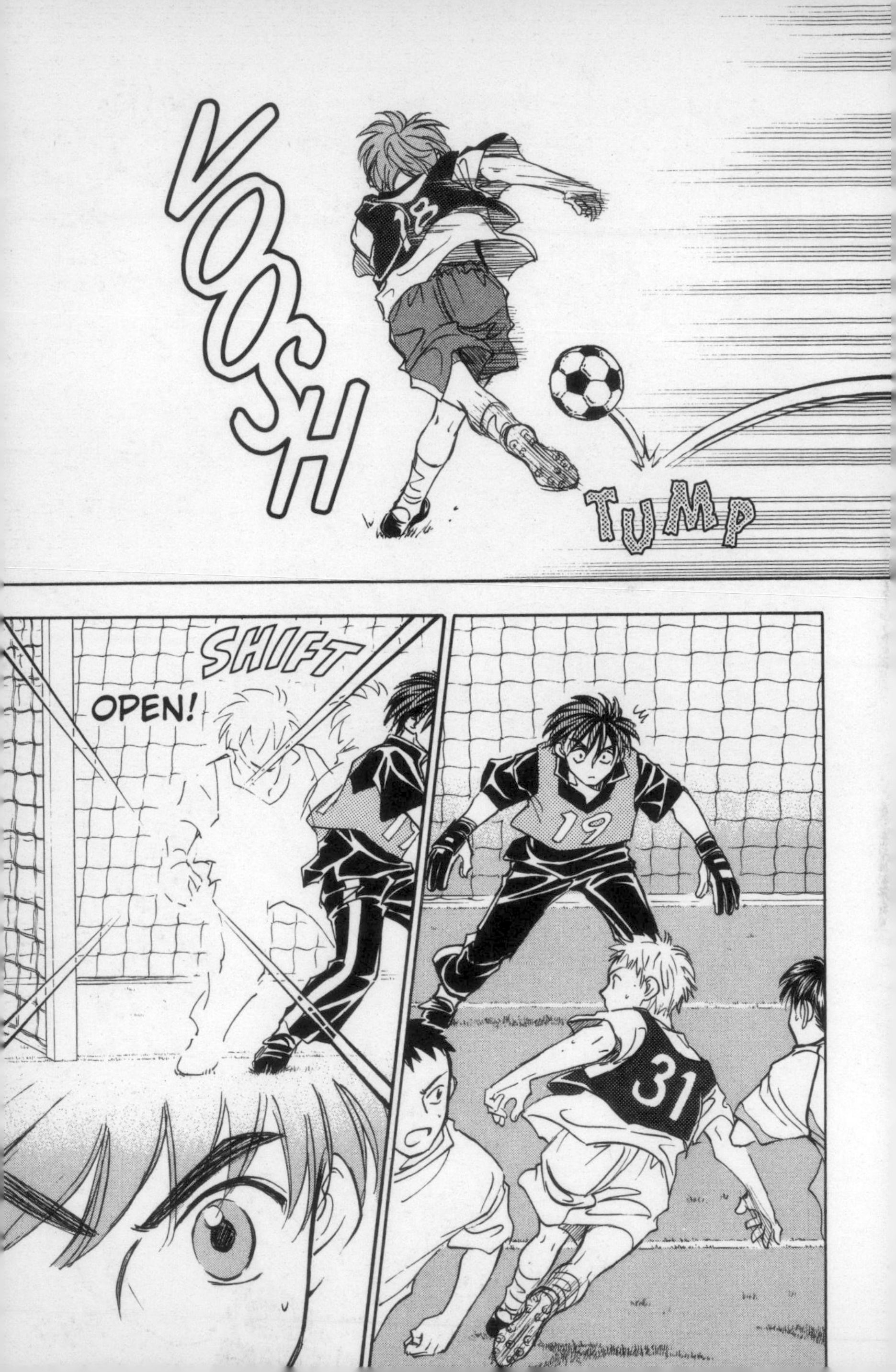
VOOSH
TUMP
SHIFT
OPEN!

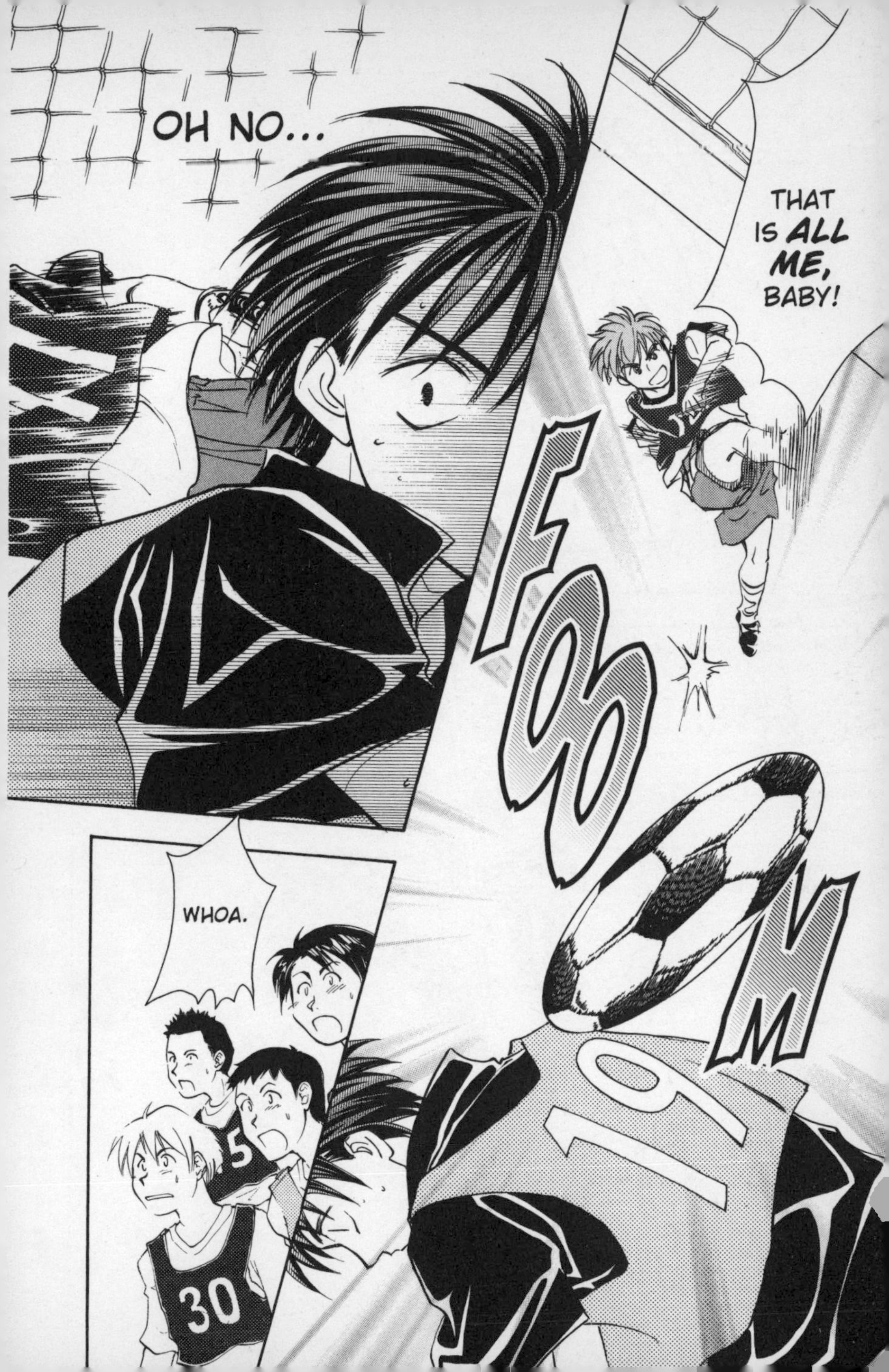
THAT IS ALL ME, BABY!
OH NO...
WHOA.

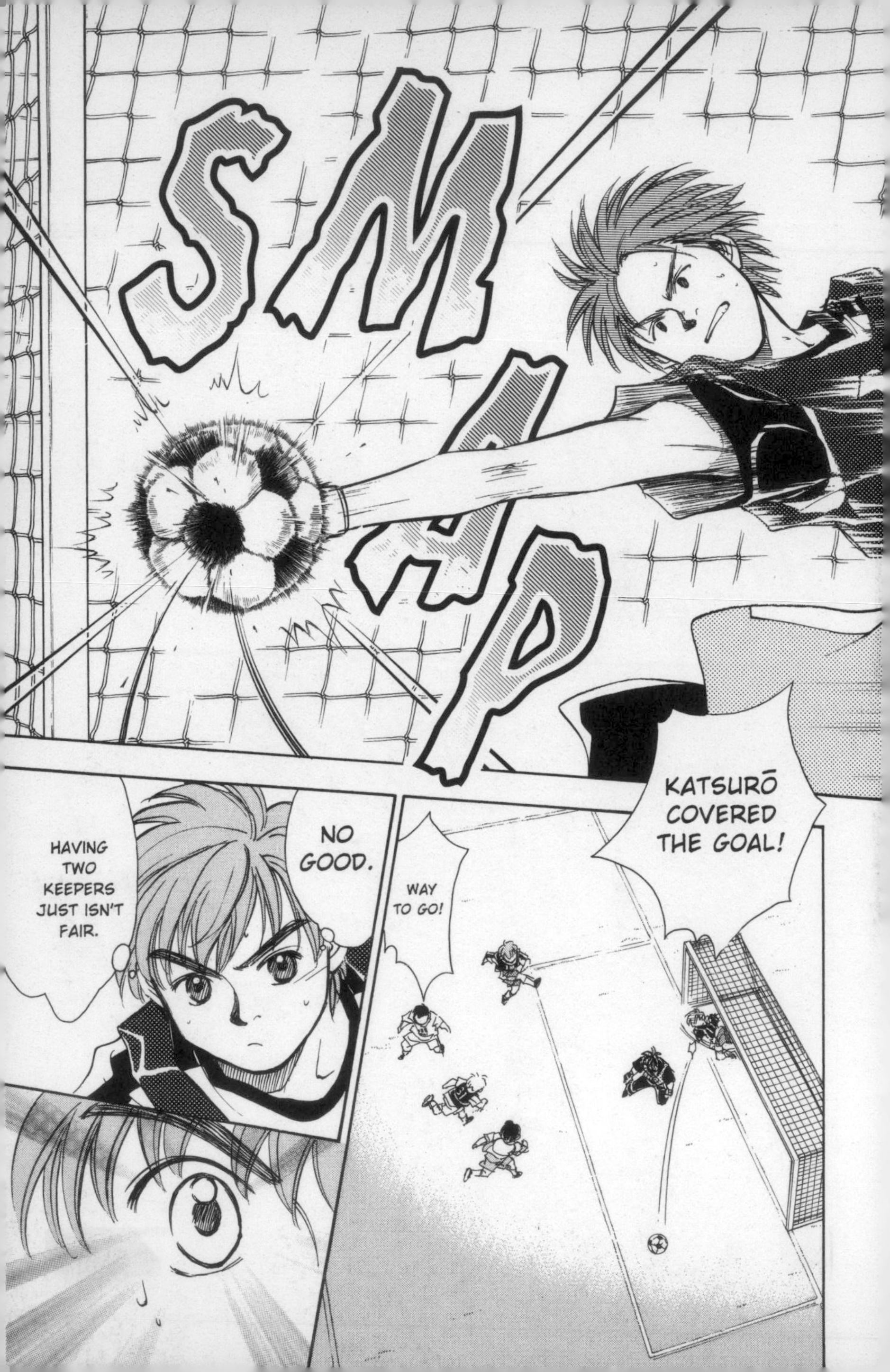
SMAP
KATSURŌ COVERED THE GOAL!
WAY TO GO!
NO GOOD.
HAVING TWO KEEPERS JUST ISN'T FAIR.

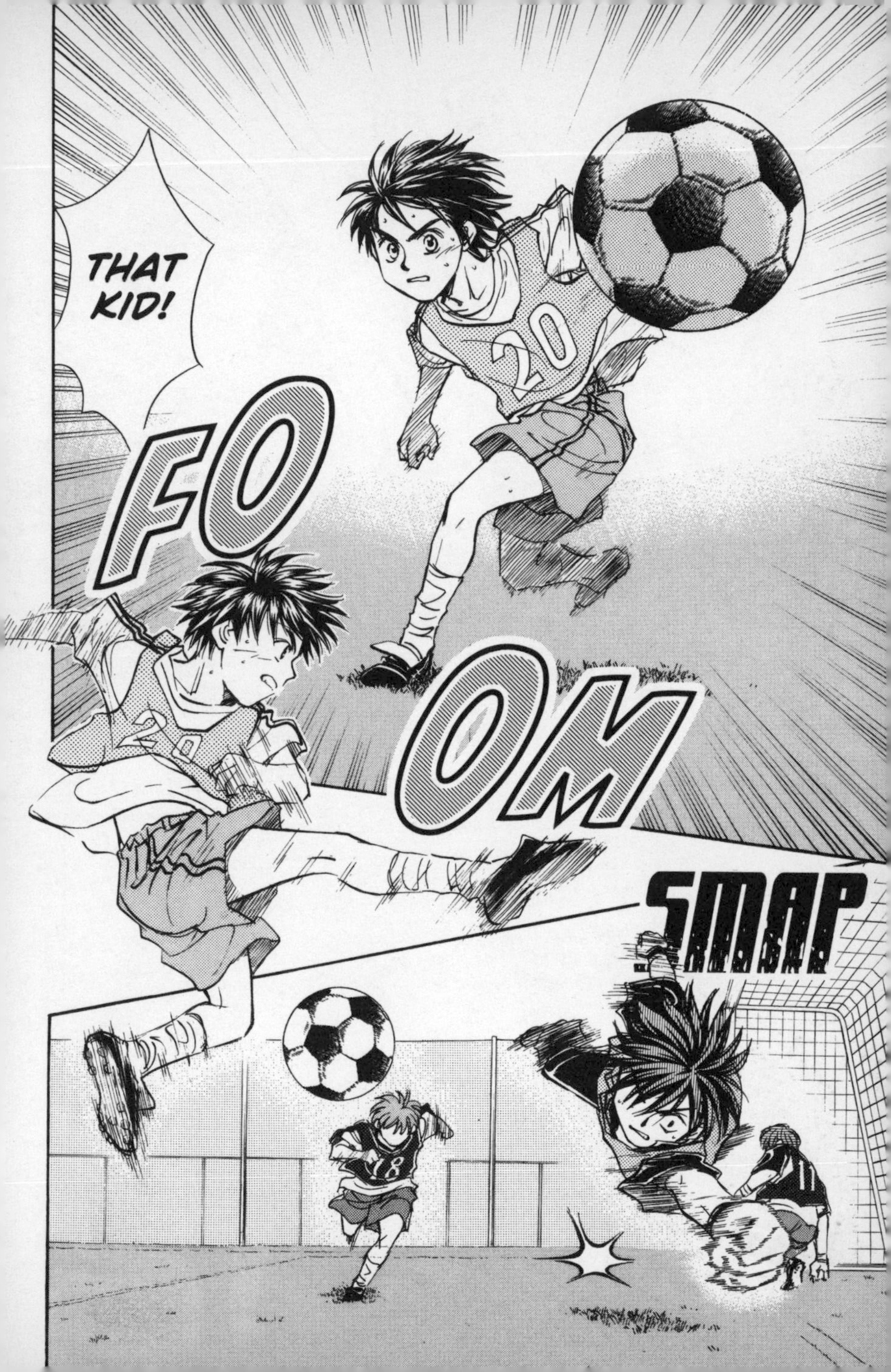
THAT KID!
FOOM
SNAP

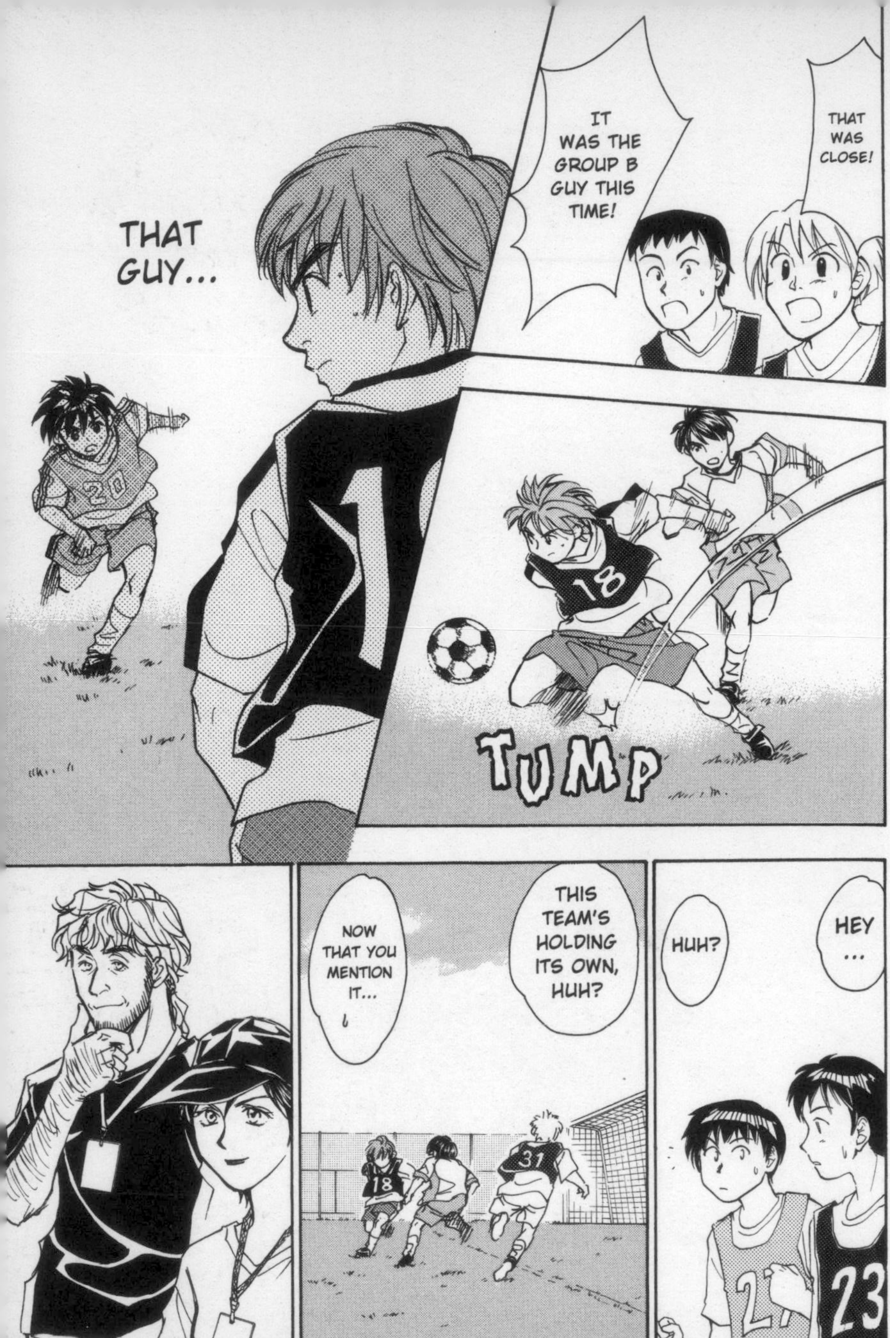
THAT WAS CLOSE!
IT WAS THE GROUP B GUY THIS TIME!
TUMP
THAT GUY...
HEY ...
HUH?
THIS TEAM'S HOLDING ITS OWN, HUH?
NOW THAT YOU MENTION IT...

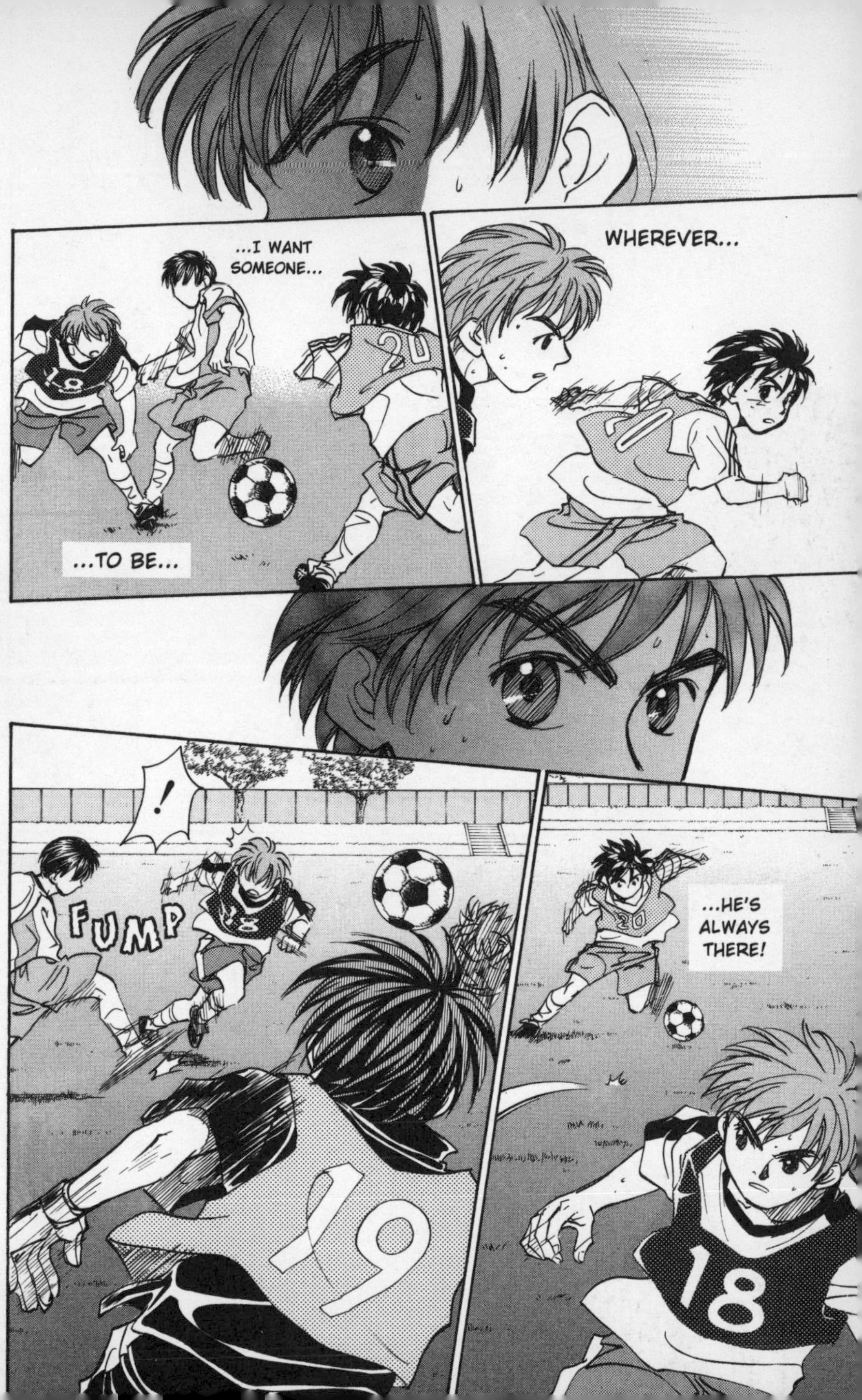
WHEREVER...
...I WANT SOMEONE...
...TO BE...
...HE'S ALWAYS THERE!
!
FUMP

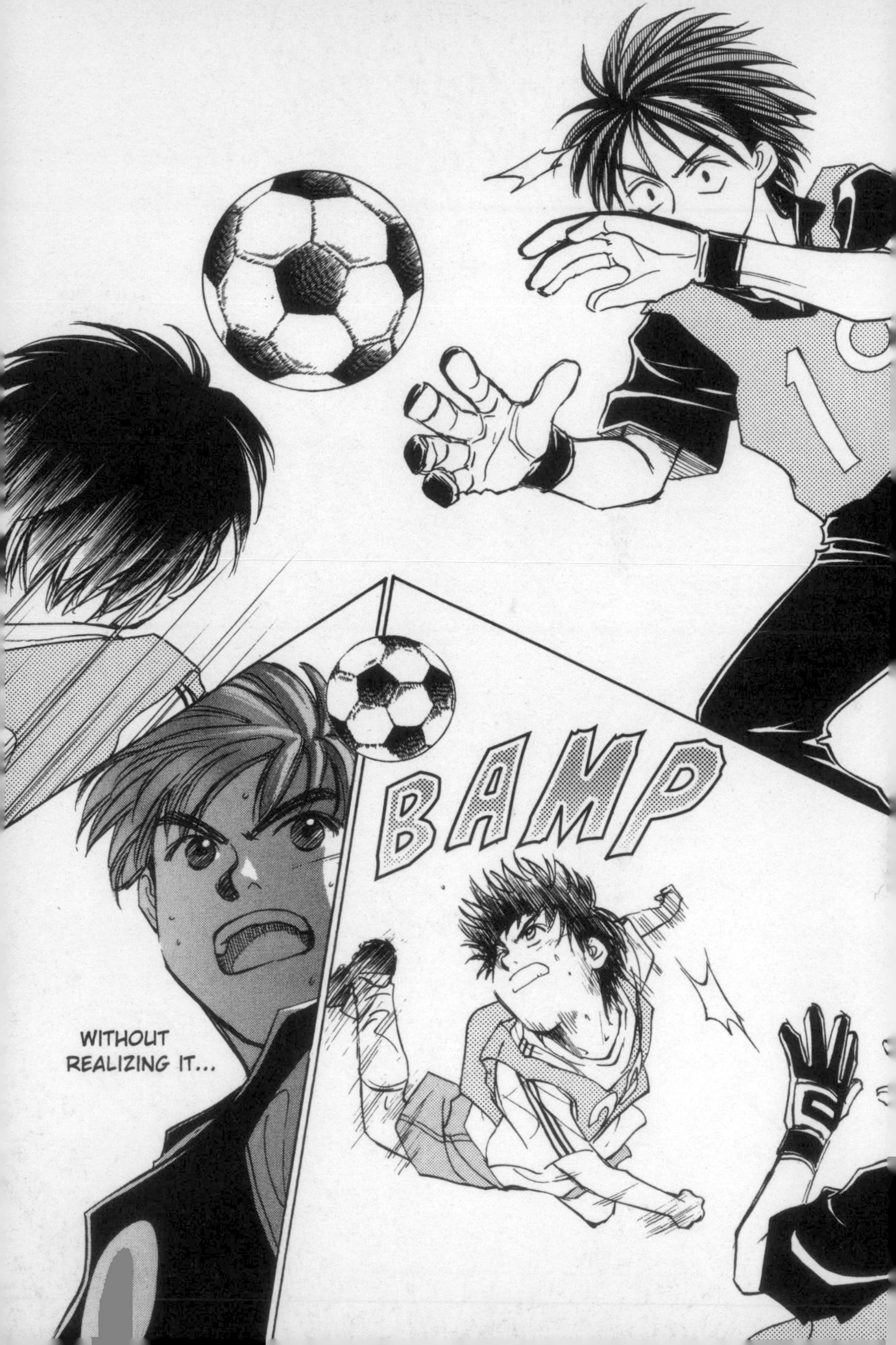
BAMP
WITHOUT REALIZING IT...

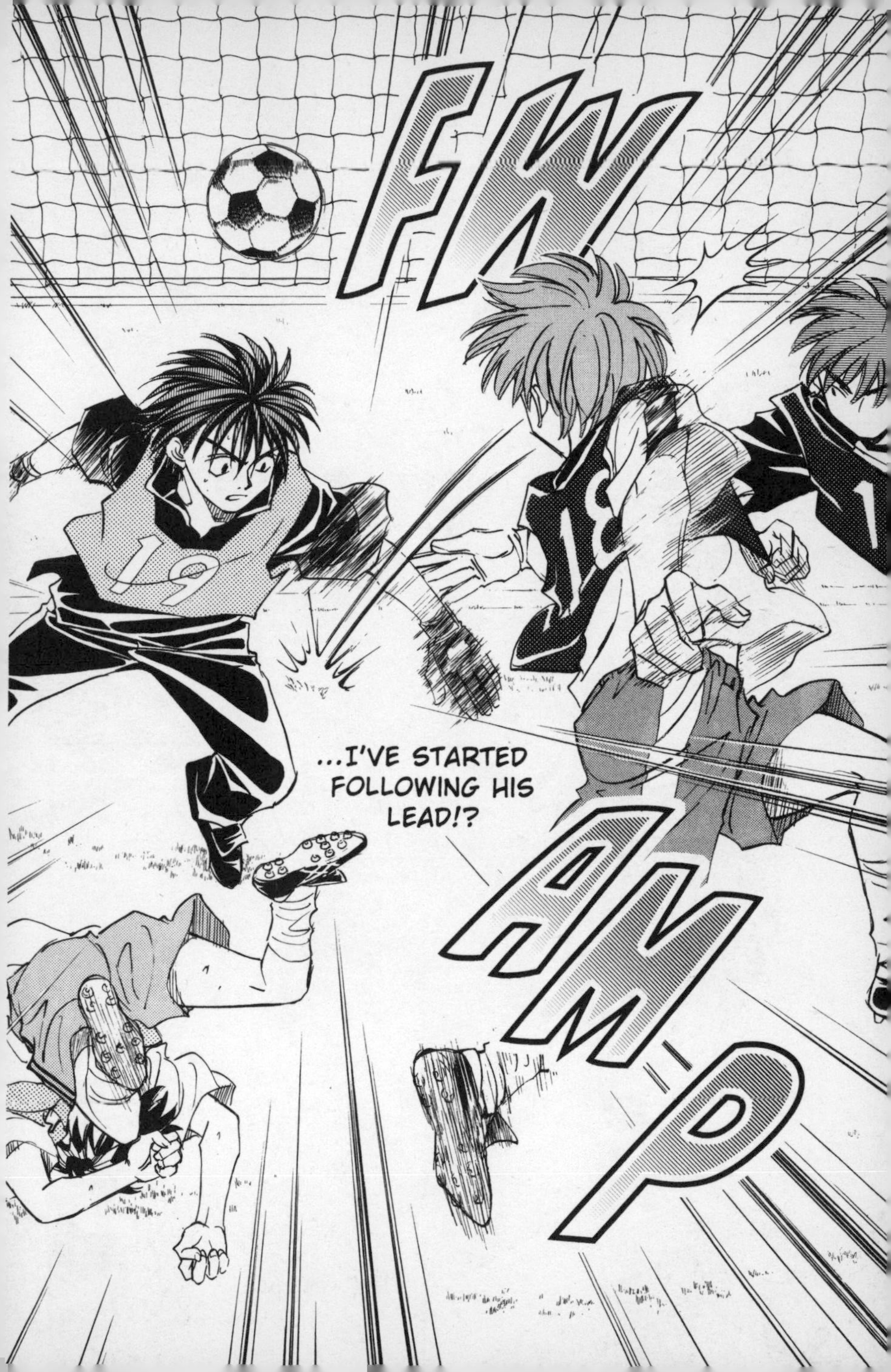
FW
...I'VE STARTED FOLLOWING HIS LEAD!?
WAMP

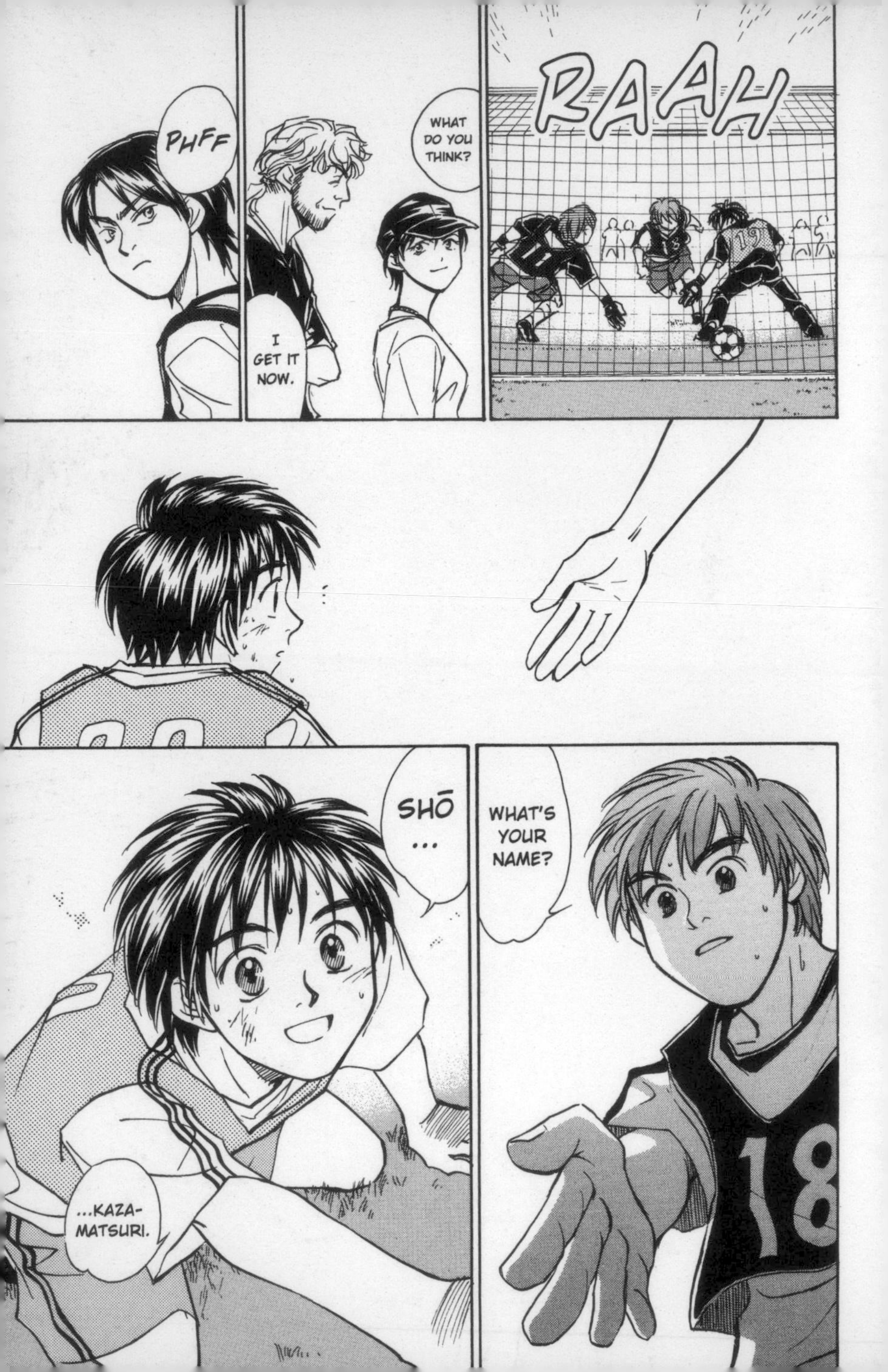
RAAH
WHAT DO YOU THINK?
I GET IT NOW.
PHFF
WHAT'S YOUR NAME?
SHŌ...
...KAZA-MATSURI.

WHISTLE!™

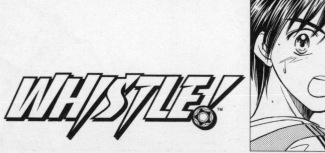

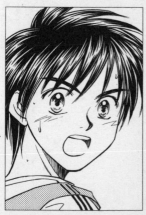

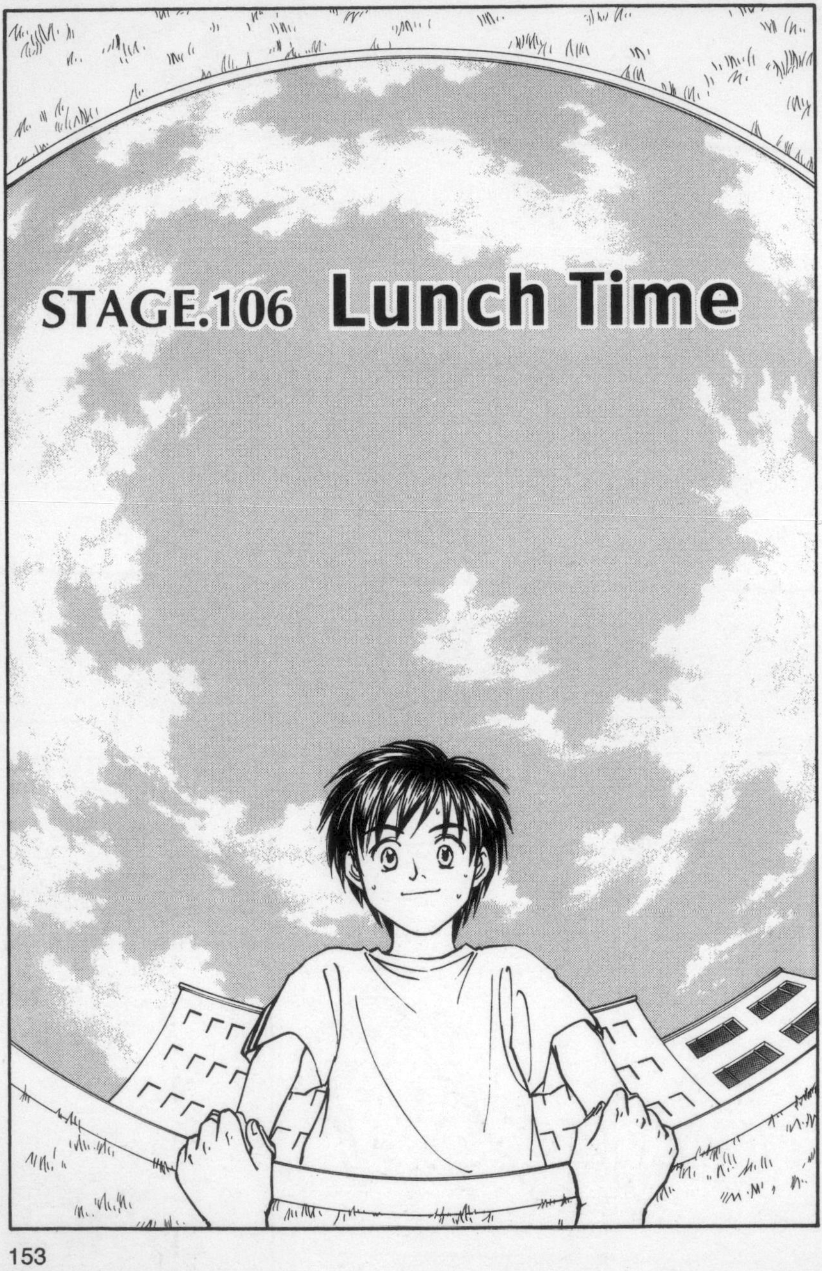
STAGE.106 Lunch Time

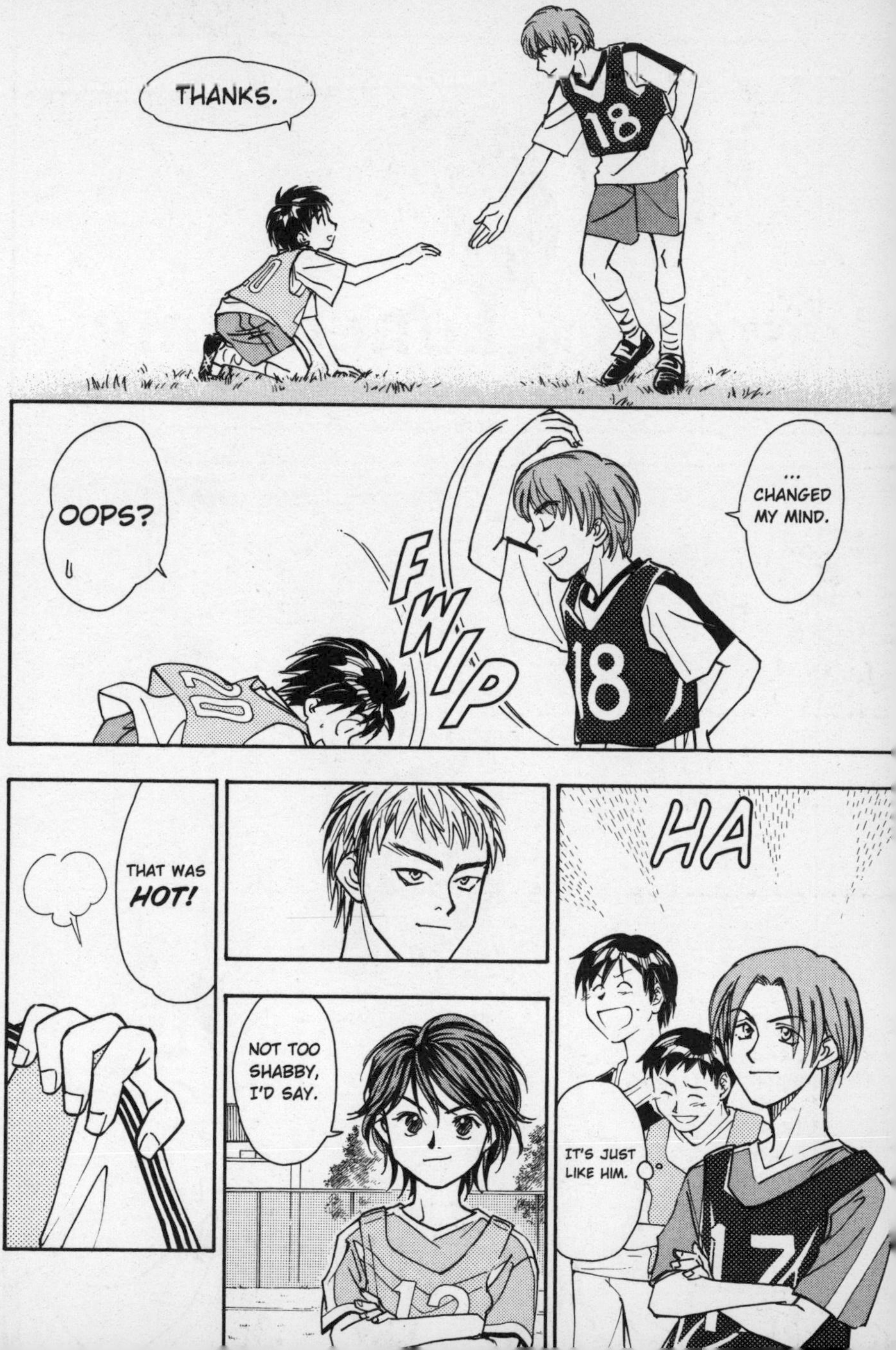
THANKS.
... CHANGED MY MIND.
FWIP
OOPS?
HA
IT'S JUST LIKE HIM.
NOT TOO SHABBY, I'D SAY.
THAT WAS HOT!

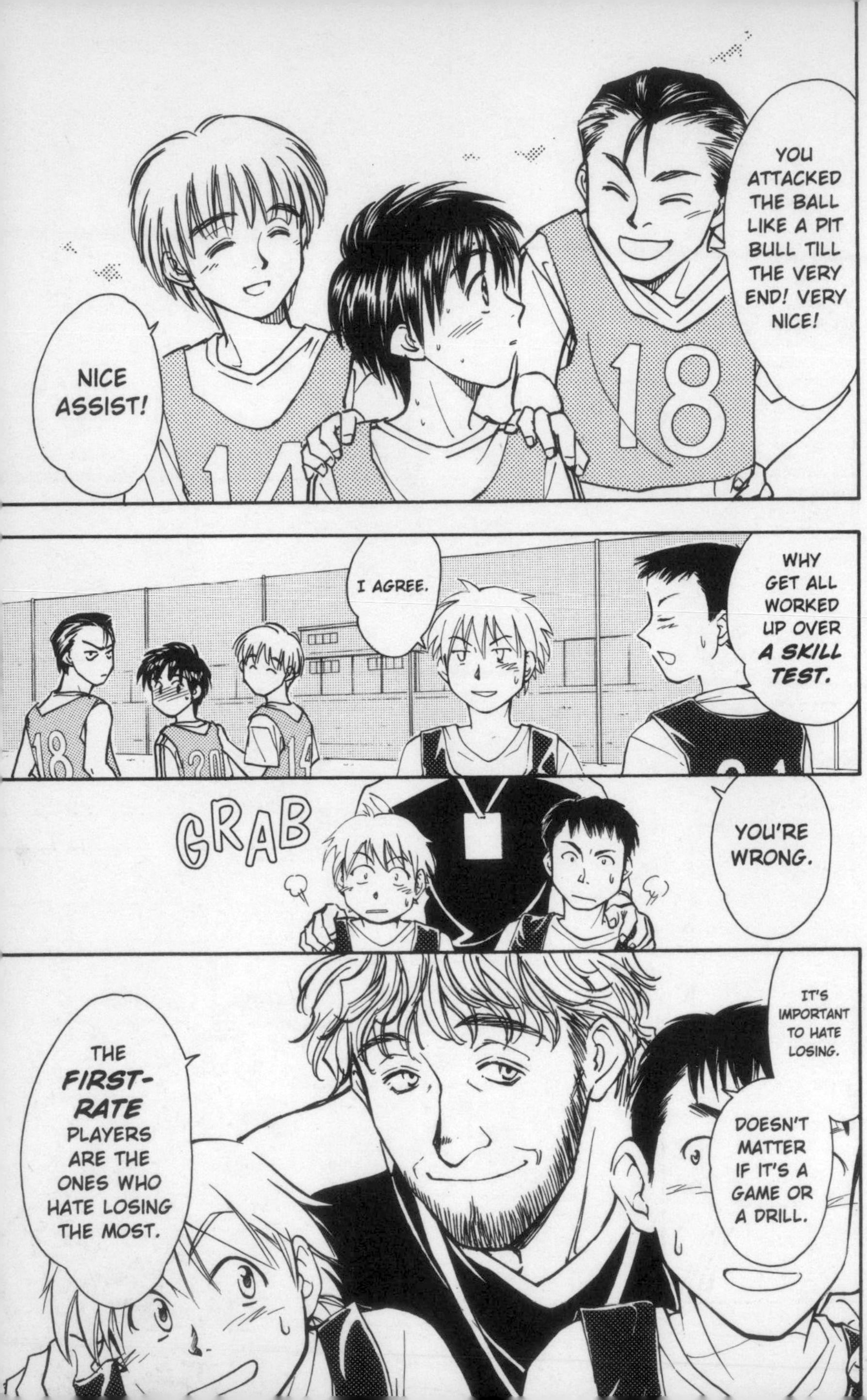
YOU ATTACKED THE BALL LIKE A PIT BULL TILL THE VERY END! VERY NICE!
NICE ASSIST!
WHY GET ALL WORKED UP OVER A SKILL TEST.
I AGREE.
YOU'RE WRONG.
GRAB
IT'S IMPORTANT TO HATE LOSING.
DOESN'T MATTER IF IT'S A GAME OR A DRILL.
THE FIRST-RATE PLAYERS ARE THE ONES WHO HATE LOSING THE MOST.

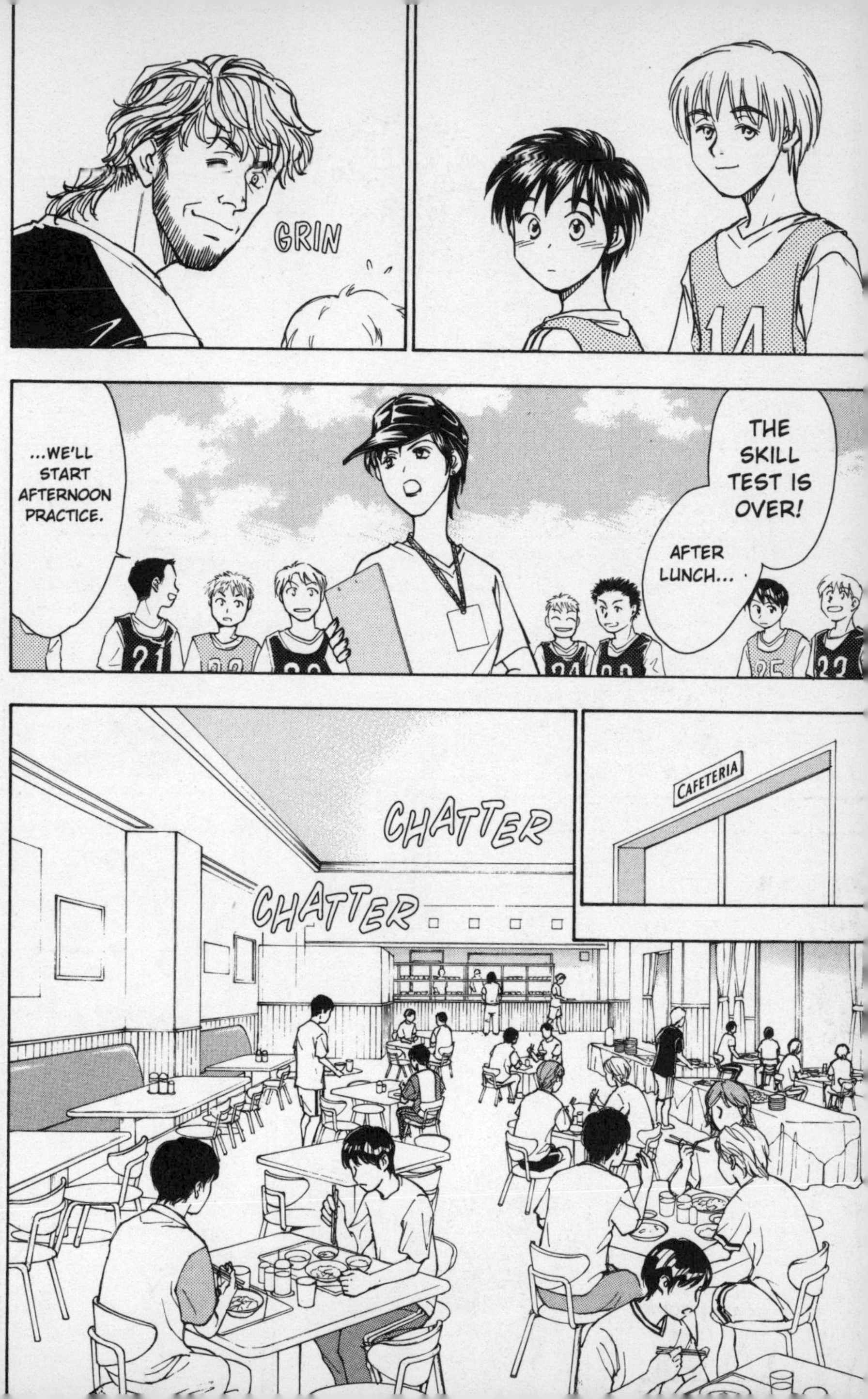
GRIN
THE SKILL TEST IS OVER!
AFTER LUNCH...
...WE'LL START AFTERNOON PRACTICE.
CAFETERIA
CHATTER
CHATTER

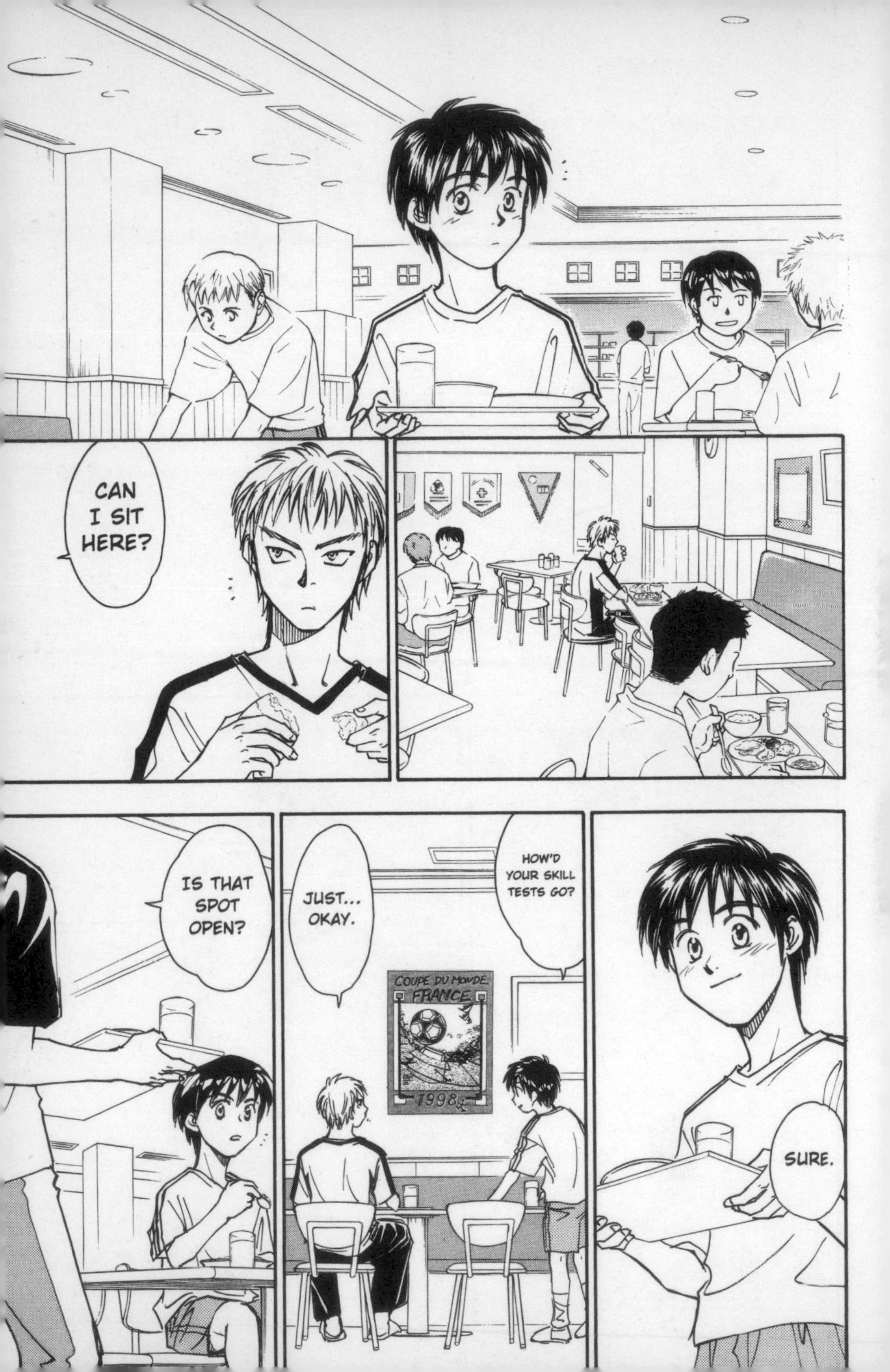
CAN I SIT HERE?
SURE.
HOW'D YOUR SKILL TESTS GO?
JUST... OKAY.
COUPE DU MONDE FRANCE
1998
IS THAT SPOT OPEN?

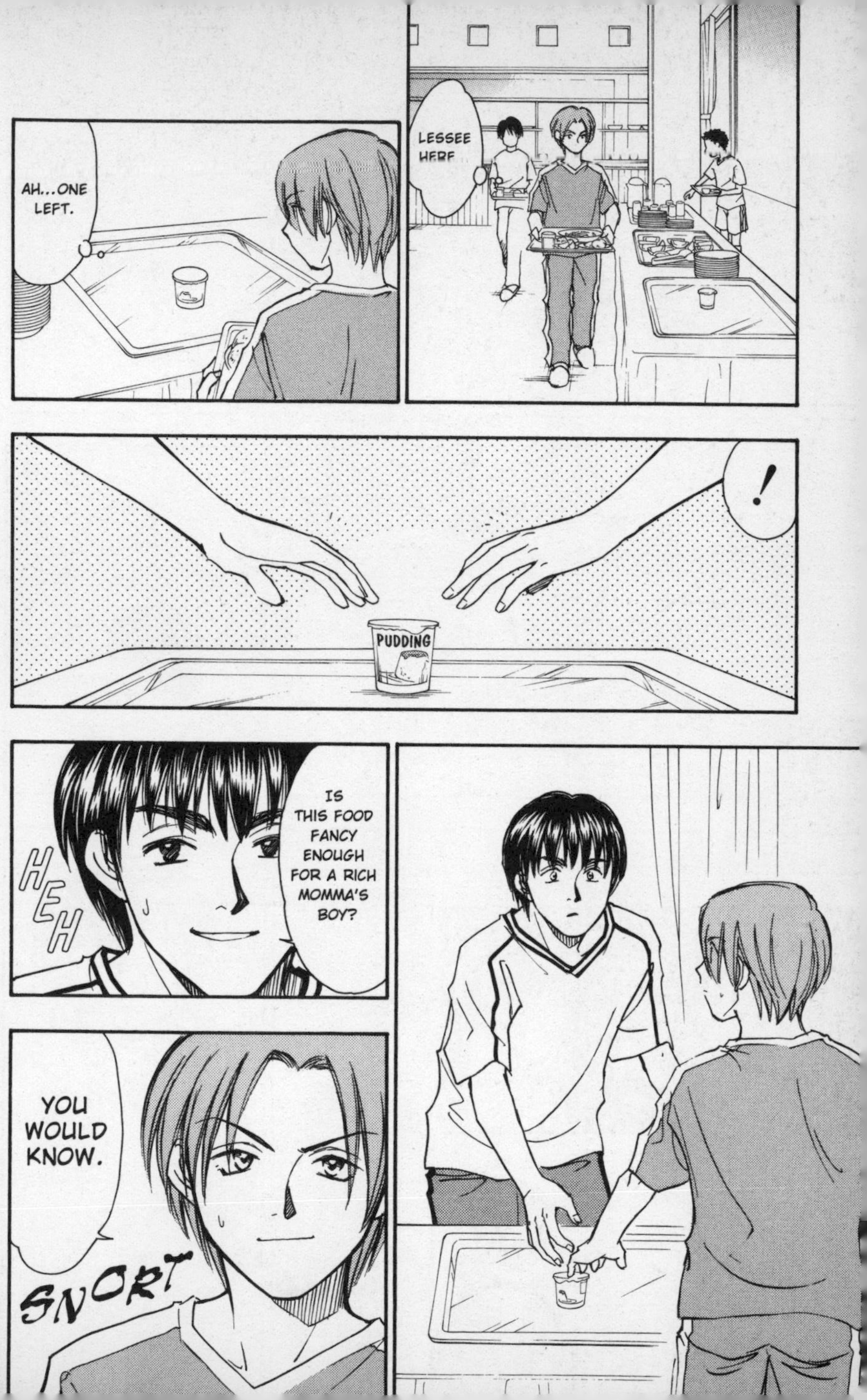
LESSEE HERE...
AH...ONE LEFT.
!
PUDDING
IS THIS FOOD FANCY ENOUGH FOR A RICH MOMMA'S BOY?
HEH
YOU WOULD KNOW.
SNORT

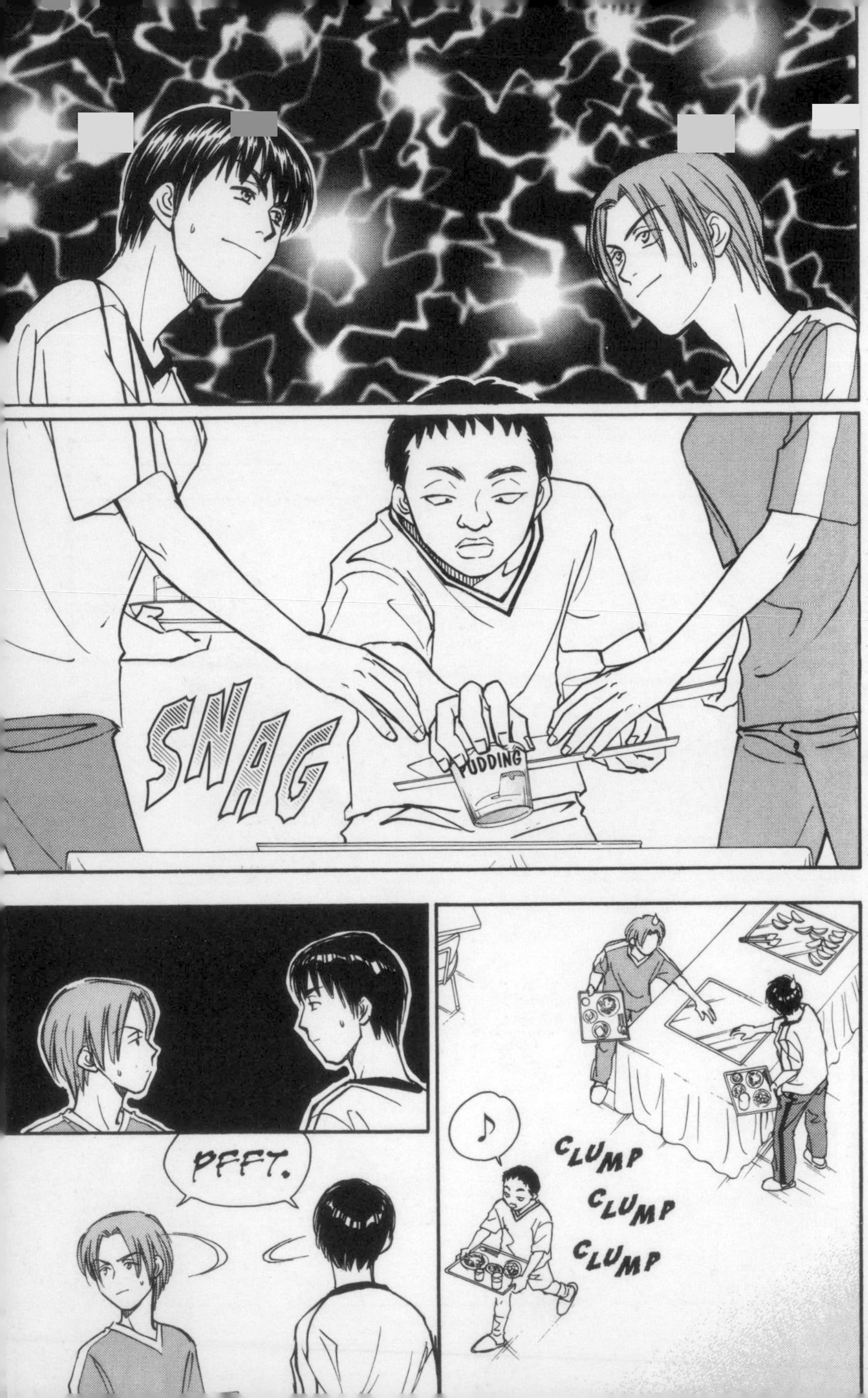
SNAG
PUDDING
♪
CLUMP
CLUMP
CLUMP
PFFT.

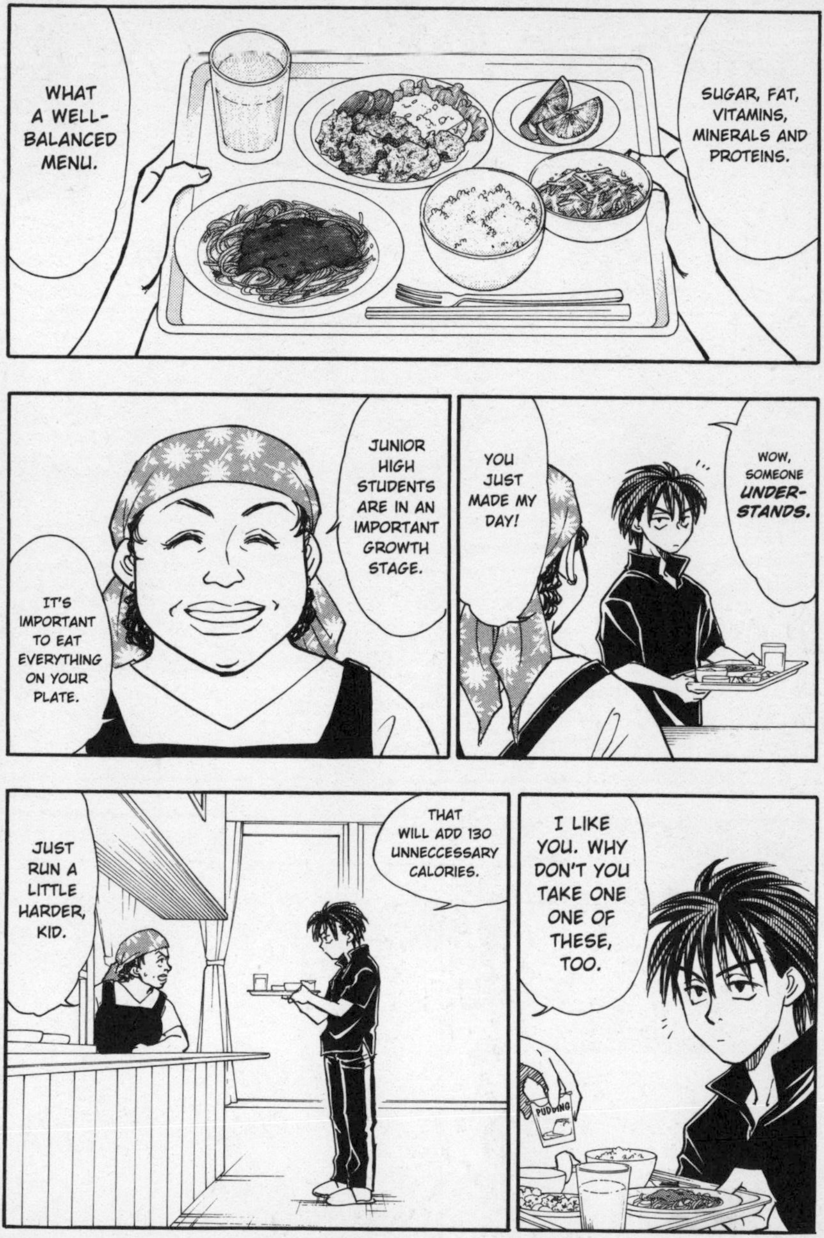
SUGAR, FAT, VITAMINS, MINERALS AND PROTEINS.
WHAT A WELL-BALANCED MENU.
WOW, SOMEONE *UNDERSTANDS.*
YOU JUST MADE MY DAY!
JUNIOR HIGH STUDENTS ARE IN AN IMPORTANT GROWTH STAGE.
IT'S IMPORTANT TO EAT EVERYTHING ON YOUR PLATE.
I LIKE YOU. WHY DON'T YOU TAKE ONE ONE OF THESE, TOO.
PUDDING
THAT WILL ADD 130 UNNECCESSARY CALORIES.
JUST RUN A LITTLE HARDER, KID.

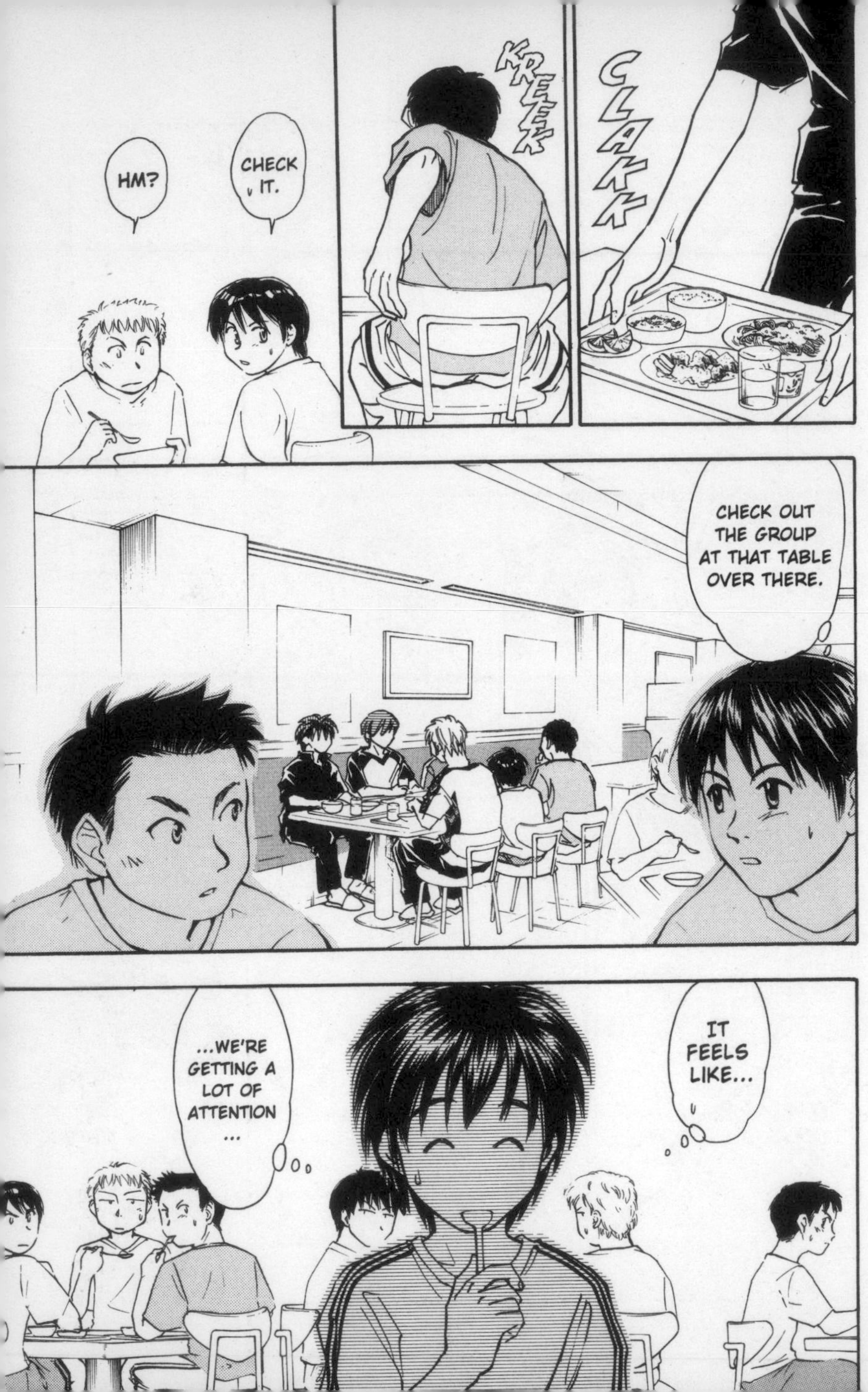
CLAKK
KREEK
CHECK IT.
HM?
CHECK OUT THE GROUP AT THAT TABLE OVER THERE.
IT FEELS LIKE...
...WE'RE GETTING A LOT OF ATTENTION...

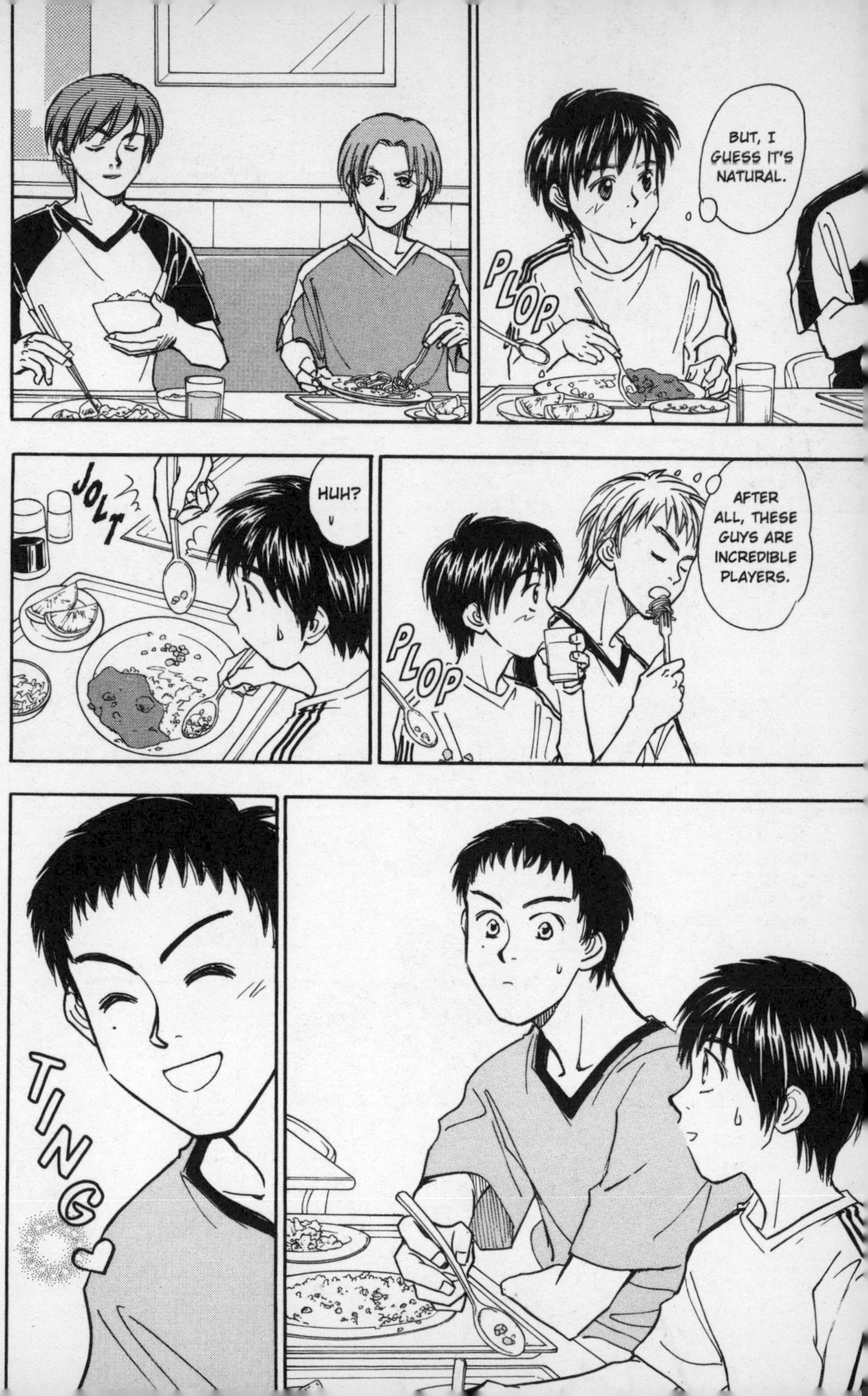
BUT, I GUESS IT'S NATURAL.
PLOP
AFTER ALL, THESE GUYS ARE INCREDIBLE PLAYERS.
PLOP
HUH?
JOLT
TING

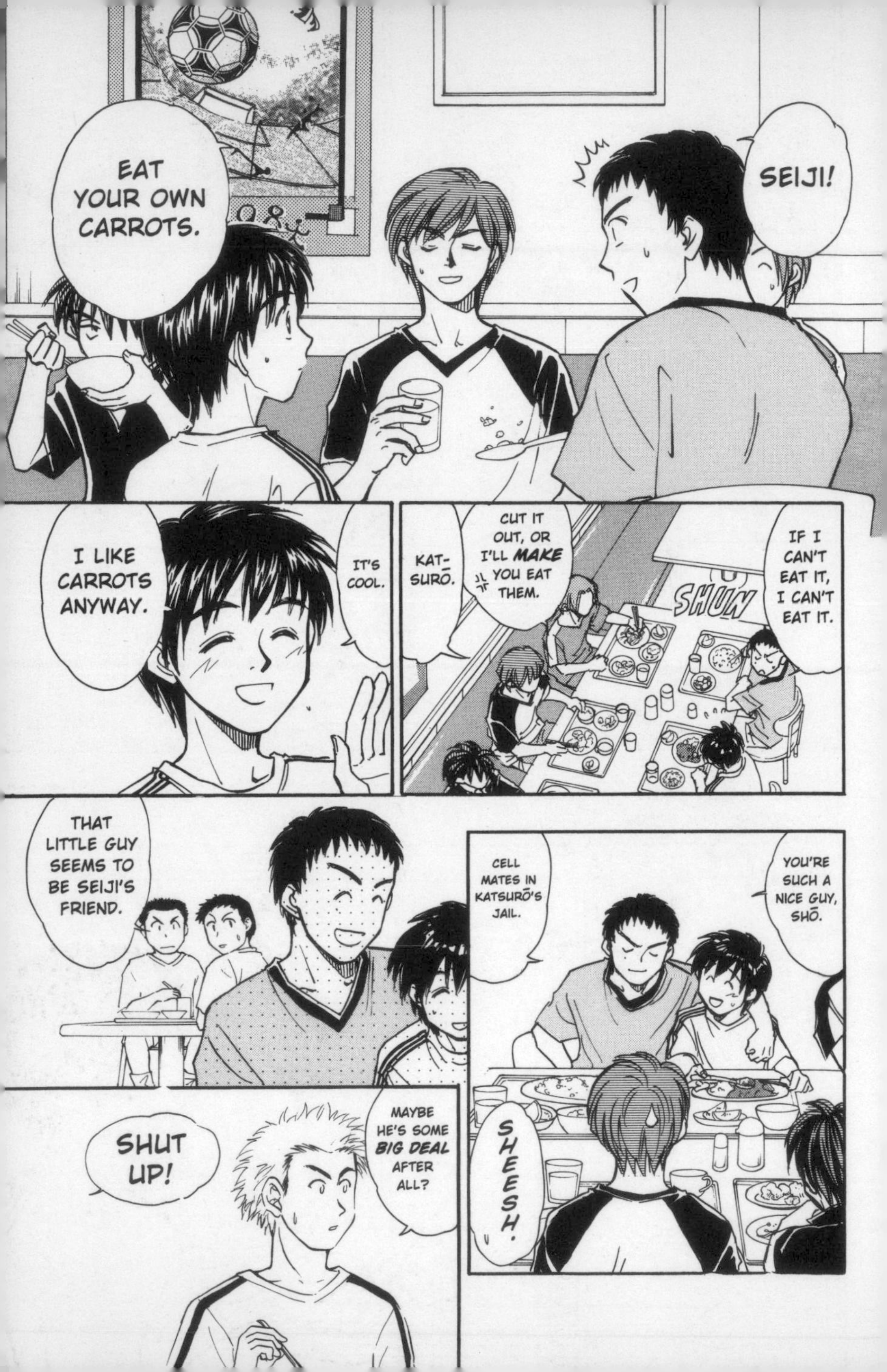
SEIJI!
EAT YOUR OWN CARROTS.
IF I CAN'T EAT IT, I CAN'T EAT IT.
SHUN
CUT IT OUT, OR I'LL MAKE YOU EAT THEM.
KATSURŌ.
IT'S COOL.
I LIKE CARROTS ANYWAY.
YOU'RE SUCH A NICE GUY, SHŌ.
CELL MATES IN KATSURŌ'S JAIL.
SHEESH.
THAT LITTLE GUY SEEMS TO BE SEIJI'S FRIEND.
MAYBE HE'S SOME BIG DEAL AFTER ALL?
SHUT UP!

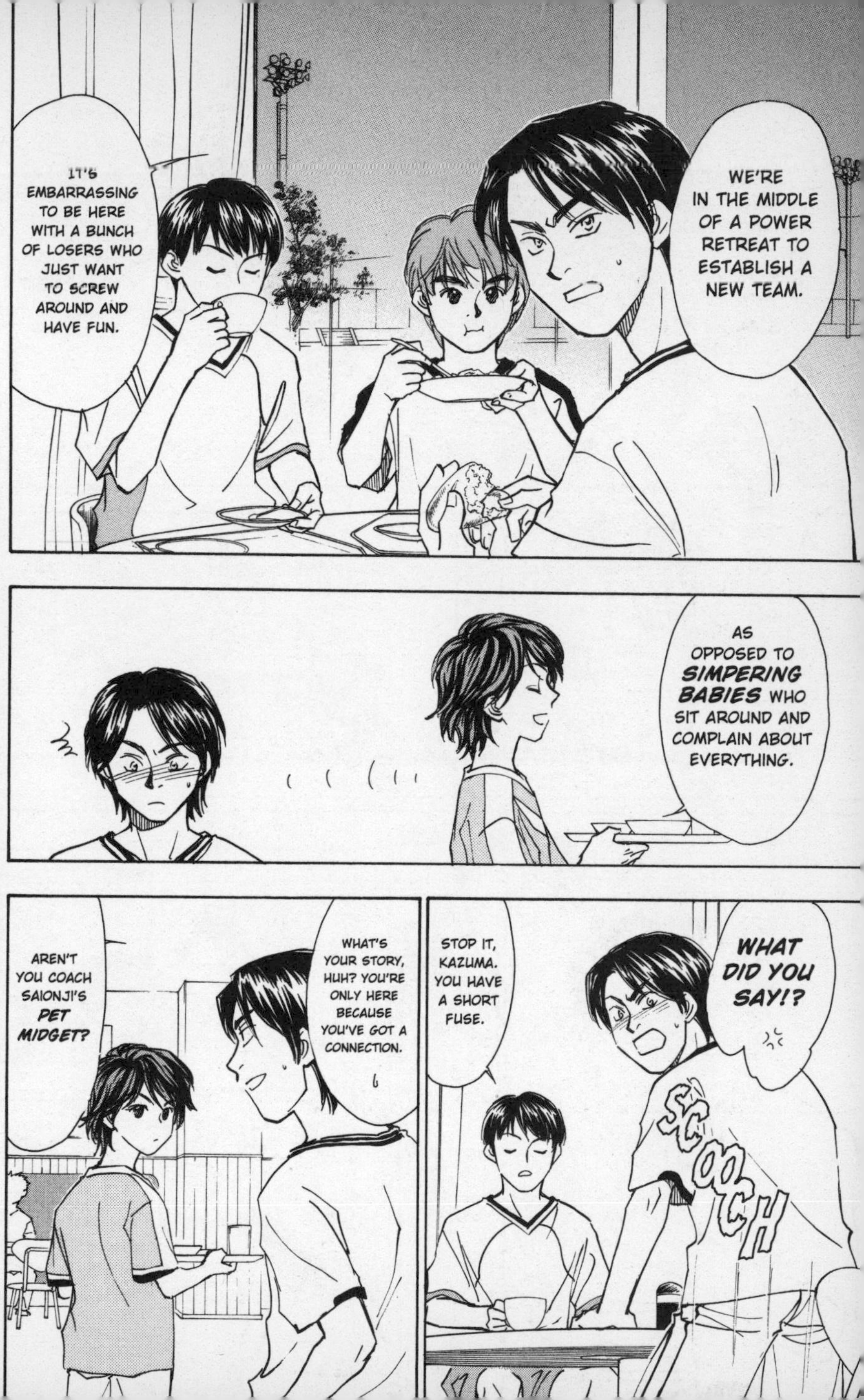
WE'RE IN THE MIDDLE OF A POWER RETREAT TO ESTABLISH A NEW TEAM.
IT'S EMBARRASSING TO BE HERE WITH A BUNCH OF LOSERS WHO JUST WANT TO SCREW AROUND AND HAVE FUN.
AS OPPOSED TO ***SIMPERING BABIES*** WHO SIT AROUND AND COMPLAIN ABOUT EVERYTHING.
WHAT DID YOU SAY!?
STOP IT, KAZUMA. YOU HAVE A SHORT FUSE.
SCOOCH
WHAT'S YOUR STORY, HUH? YOU'RE ONLY HERE BECAUSE YOU'VE GOT A CONNECTION.
AREN'T YOU COACH SAIONJI'S ***PET MIDGET?***

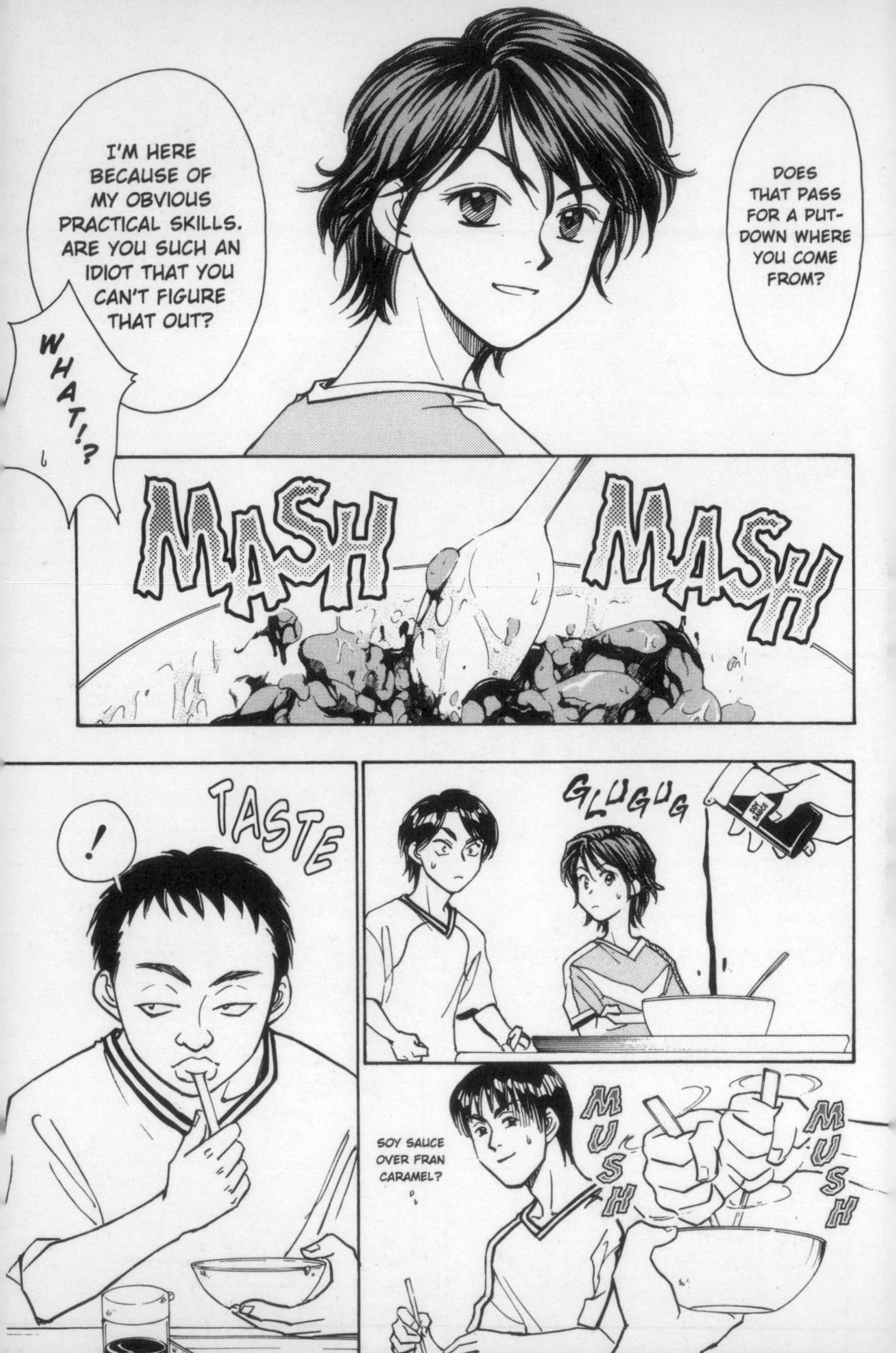
DOES THAT PASS FOR A PUT-DOWN WHERE YOU COME FROM?
I'M HERE BECAUSE OF MY OBVIOUS PRACTICAL SKILLS. ARE YOU SUCH AN IDIOT THAT YOU CAN'T FIGURE THAT OUT?
WHAT!?
MASH
MASH
GLUGUG
SOY SAUCE
MUSH
MUSH
SOY SAUCE OVER FRAN CARAMEL?
!
TASTE

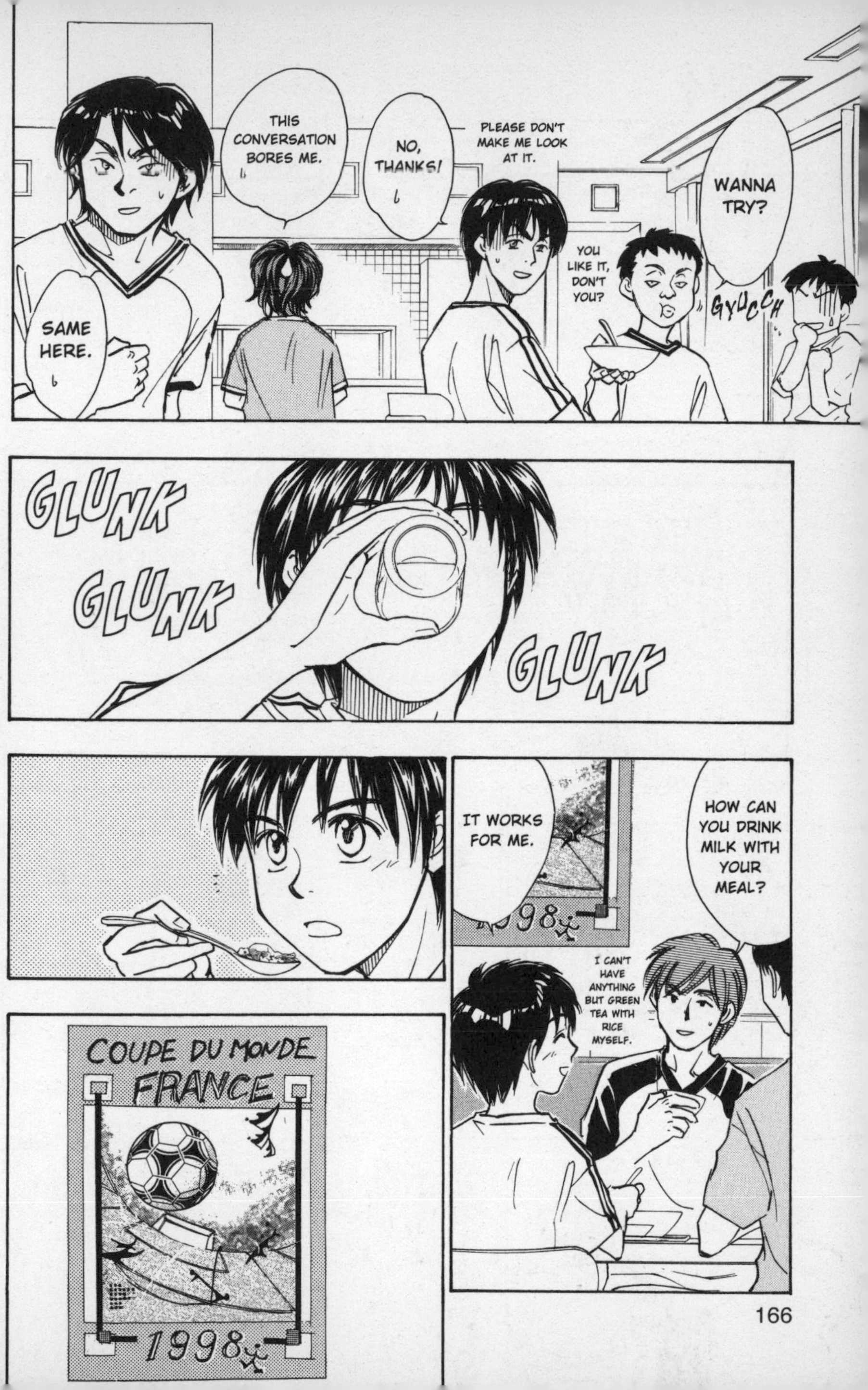
WANNA TRY?
YOU LIKE IT, DON'T YOU?
GYUCCH
PLEASE DON'T MAKE ME LOOK AT IT.
NO, THANKS!
THIS CONVERSATION BORES ME.
SAME HERE.
GLUNK
GLUNK
GLUNK
HOW CAN YOU DRINK MILK WITH YOUR MEAL?
I CAN'T HAVE ANYTHING BUT GREEN TEA WITH RICE MYSELF.
IT WORKS FOR ME.
COUPE DU MONDE FRANCE
1998

READ THIS WAY

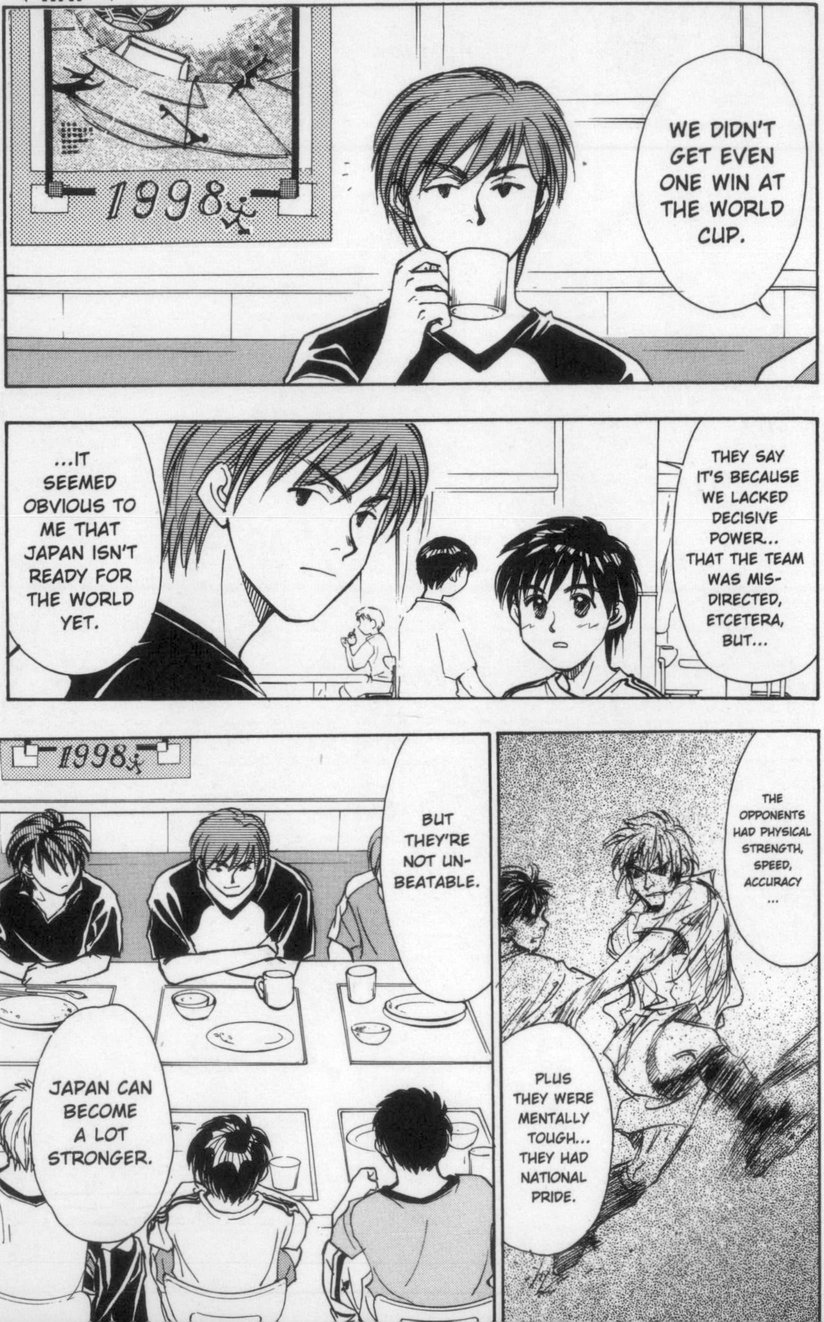
1998
WE DIDN'T GET EVEN ONE WIN AT THE WORLD CUP.
THEY SAY IT'S BECAUSE WE LACKED DECISIVE POWER... THAT THE TEAM WAS MIS-DIRECTED, ETCETERA, BUT...
...IT SEEMED OBVIOUS TO ME THAT JAPAN ISN'T READY FOR THE WORLD YET.
THE OPPONENTS HAD PHYSICAL STRENGTH, SPEED, ACCURACY ...
PLUS THEY WERE MENTALLY TOUGH... THEY HAD NATIONAL PRIDE.
1998
BUT THEY'RE NOT UN-BEATABLE.
JAPAN CAN BECOME A LOT STRONGER.

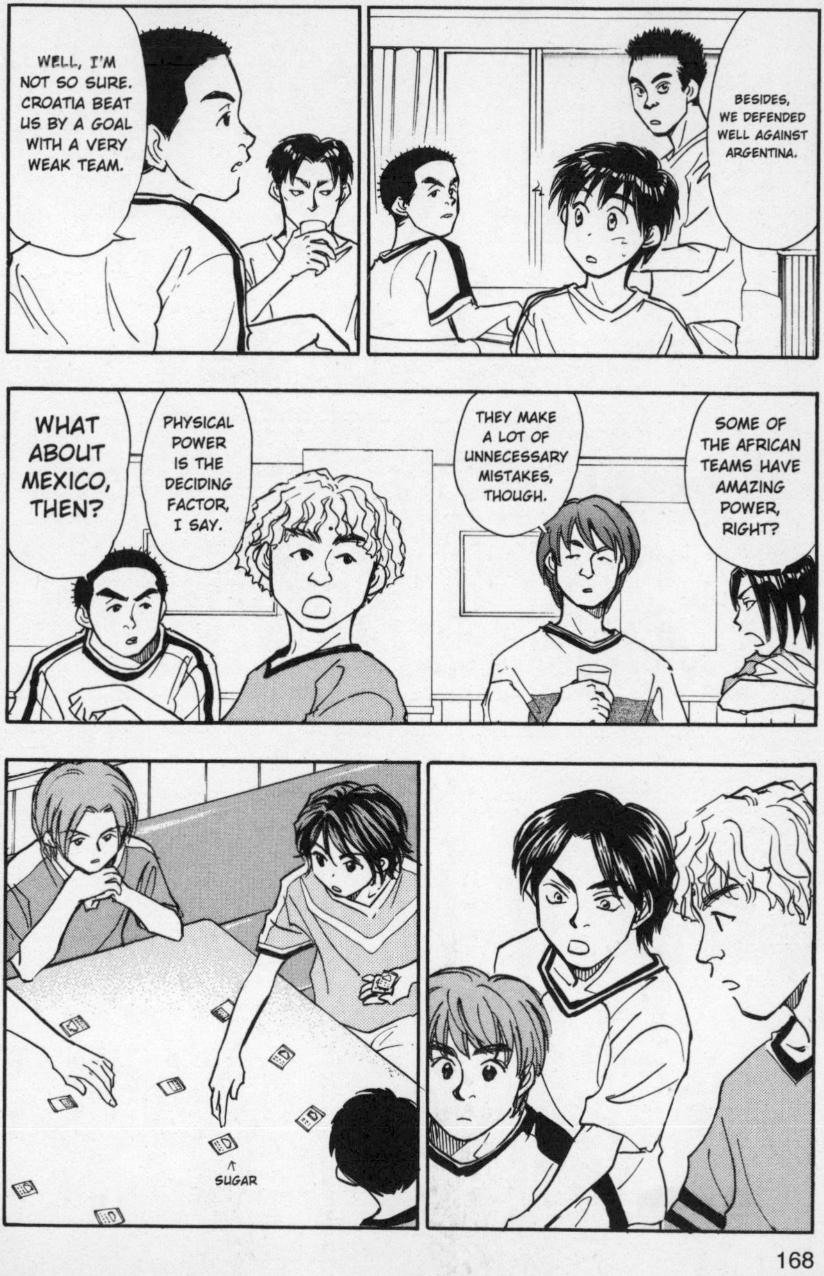
BESIDES, WE DEFENDED WELL AGAINST ARGENTINA.
WELL, I'M NOT SO SURE. CROATIA BEAT US BY A GOAL WITH A VERY WEAK TEAM.
SOME OF THE AFRICAN TEAMS HAVE AMAZING POWER, RIGHT?
THEY MAKE A LOT OF UNNECESSARY MISTAKES, THOUGH.
PHYSICAL POWER IS THE DECIDING FACTOR, I SAY.
WHAT ABOUT MEXICO, THEN?
SUGAR

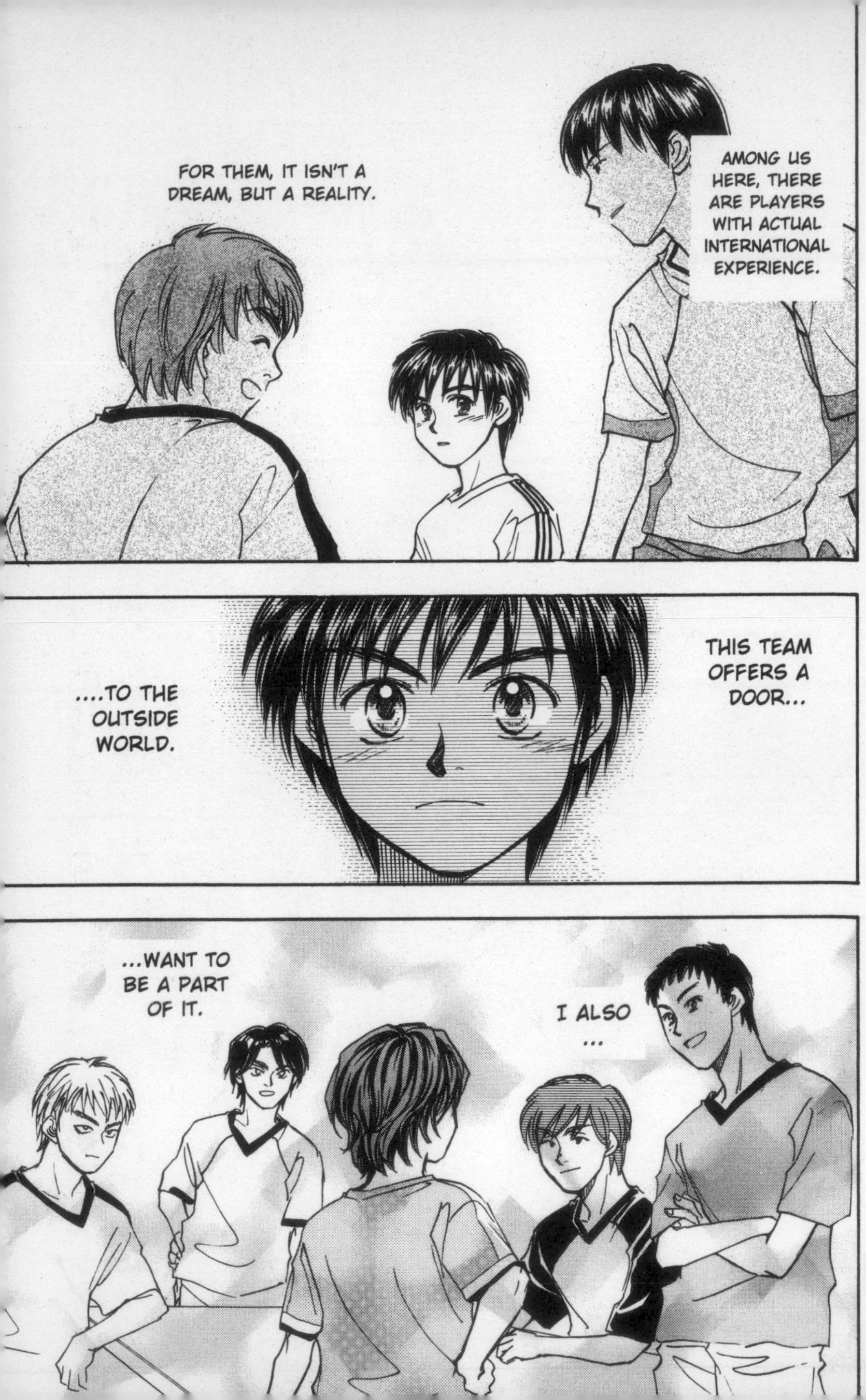
AMONG US HERE, THERE ARE PLAYERS WITH ACTUAL INTERNATIONAL EXPERIENCE.
FOR THEM, IT ISN'T A DREAM, BUT A REALITY.
THIS TEAM OFFERS A DOOR...
....TO THE OUTSIDE WORLD.
I ALSO ...
...WANT TO BE A PART OF IT.

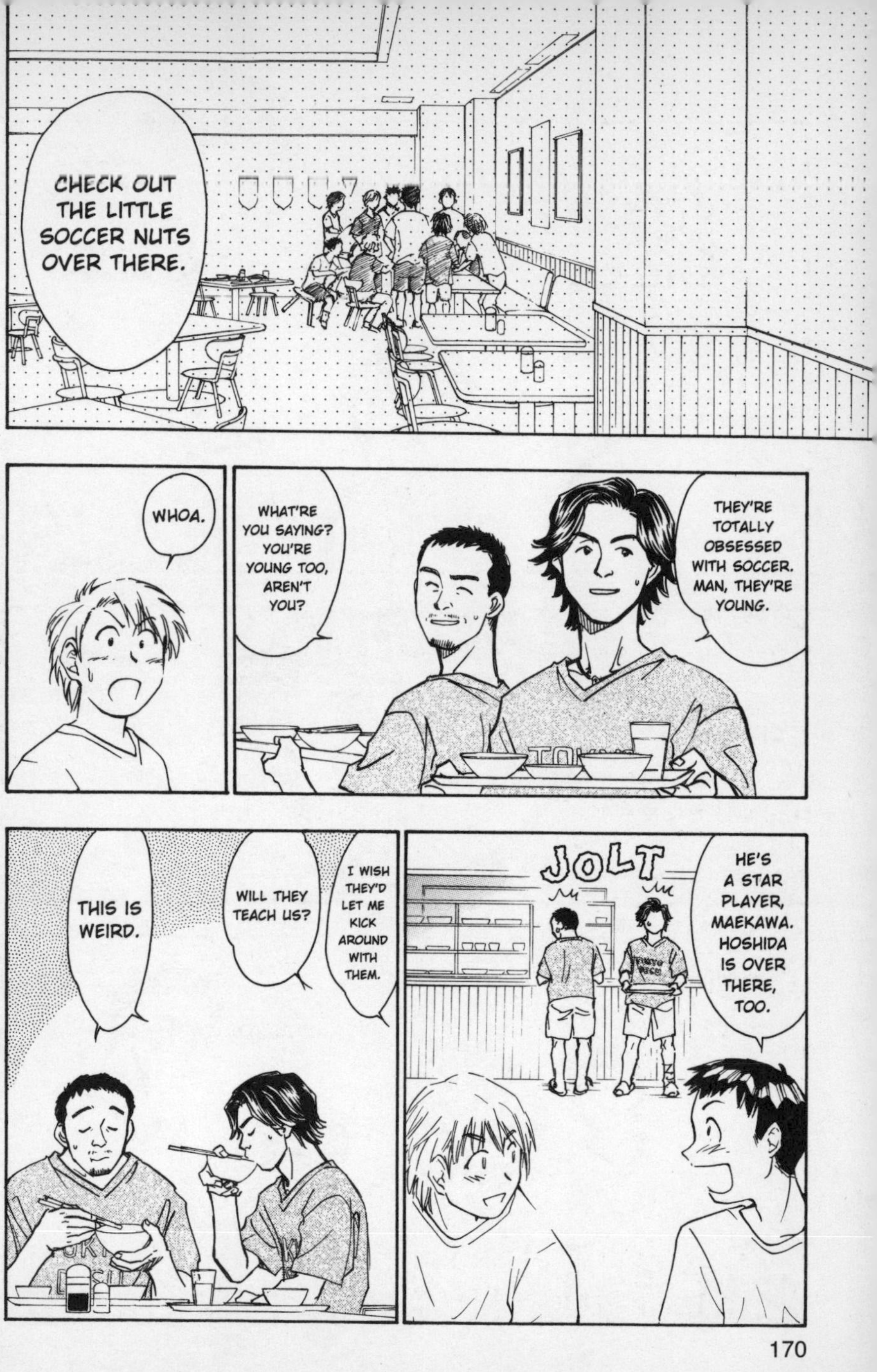
CHECK OUT THE LITTLE SOCCER NUTS OVER THERE.
THEY'RE TOTALLY OBSESSED WITH SOCCER. MAN, THEY'RE YOUNG.
WHAT'RE YOU SAYING? YOU'RE YOUNG TOO, AREN'T YOU?
WHOA.
HE'S A STAR PLAYER, MAEKAWA. HOSHIDA IS OVER THERE, TOO.
JOLT
I WISH THEY'D LET ME KICK AROUND WITH THEM.
WILL THEY TEACH US?
THIS IS WEIRD.

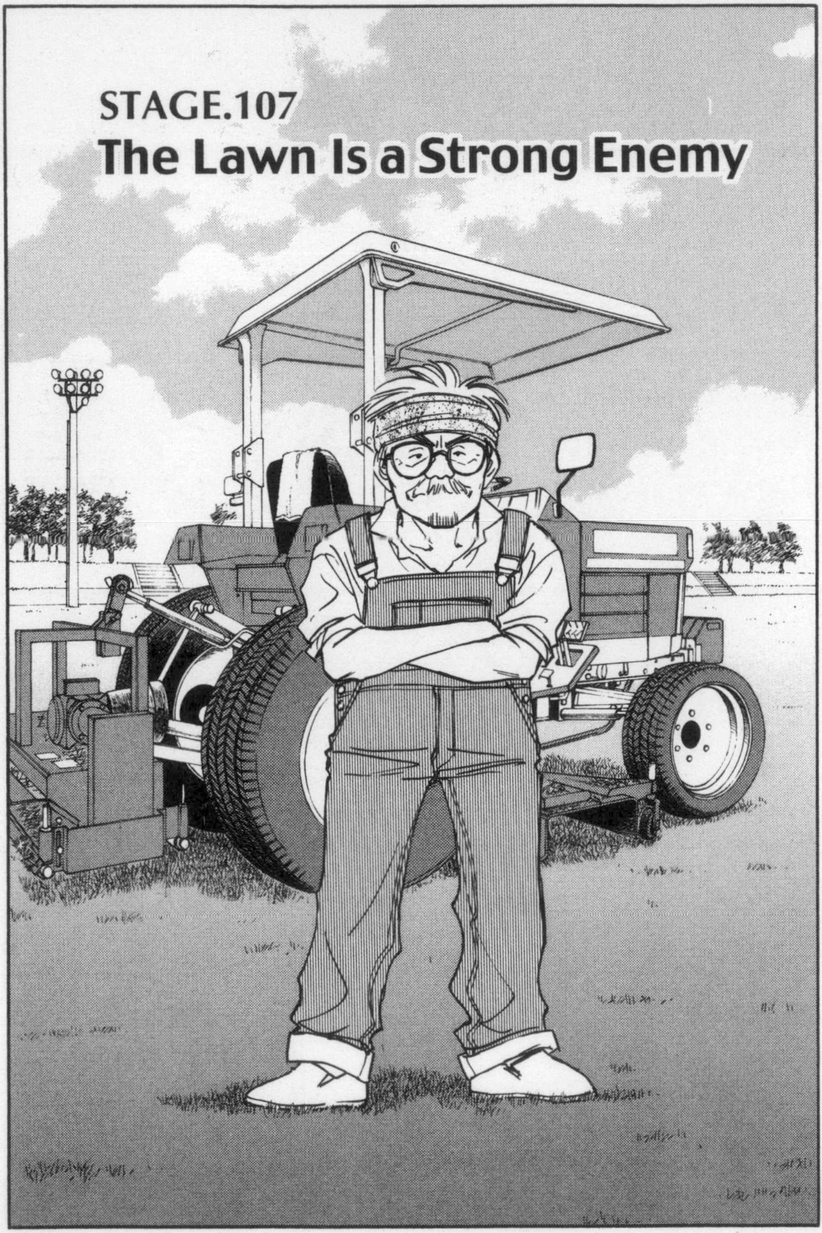
STAGE.107
The Lawn Is a Strong Enemy

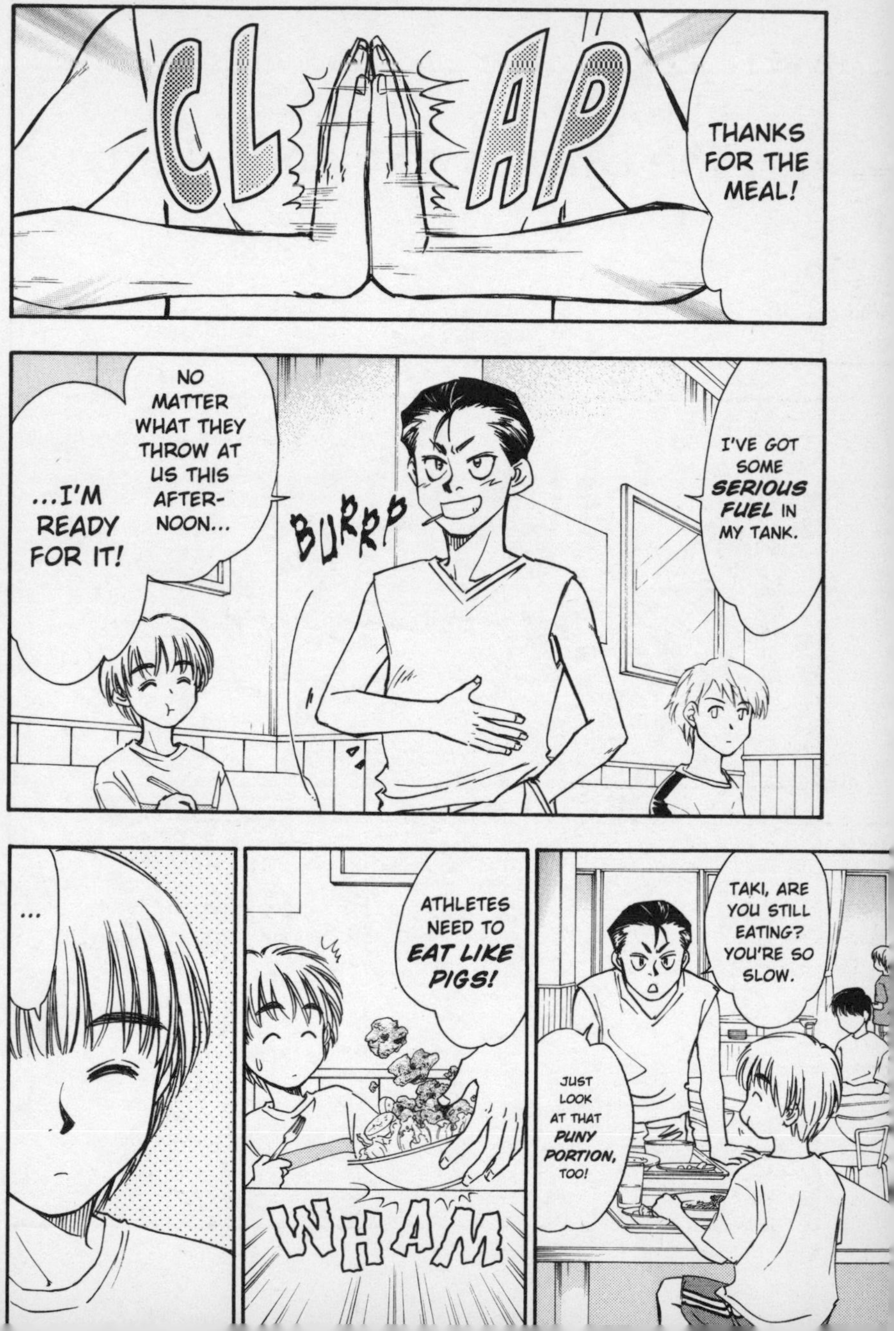
CLAP
THANKS FOR THE MEAL!
I'VE GOT SOME SERIOUS FUEL IN MY TANK.
BURRP
NO MATTER WHAT THEY THROW AT US THIS AFTERNOON...
...I'M READY FOR IT!
TAKI, ARE YOU STILL EATING? YOU'RE SO SLOW.
JUST LOOK AT THAT PUNY PORTION, TOO!
ATHLETES NEED TO EAT LIKE PIGS!
WHAM
...

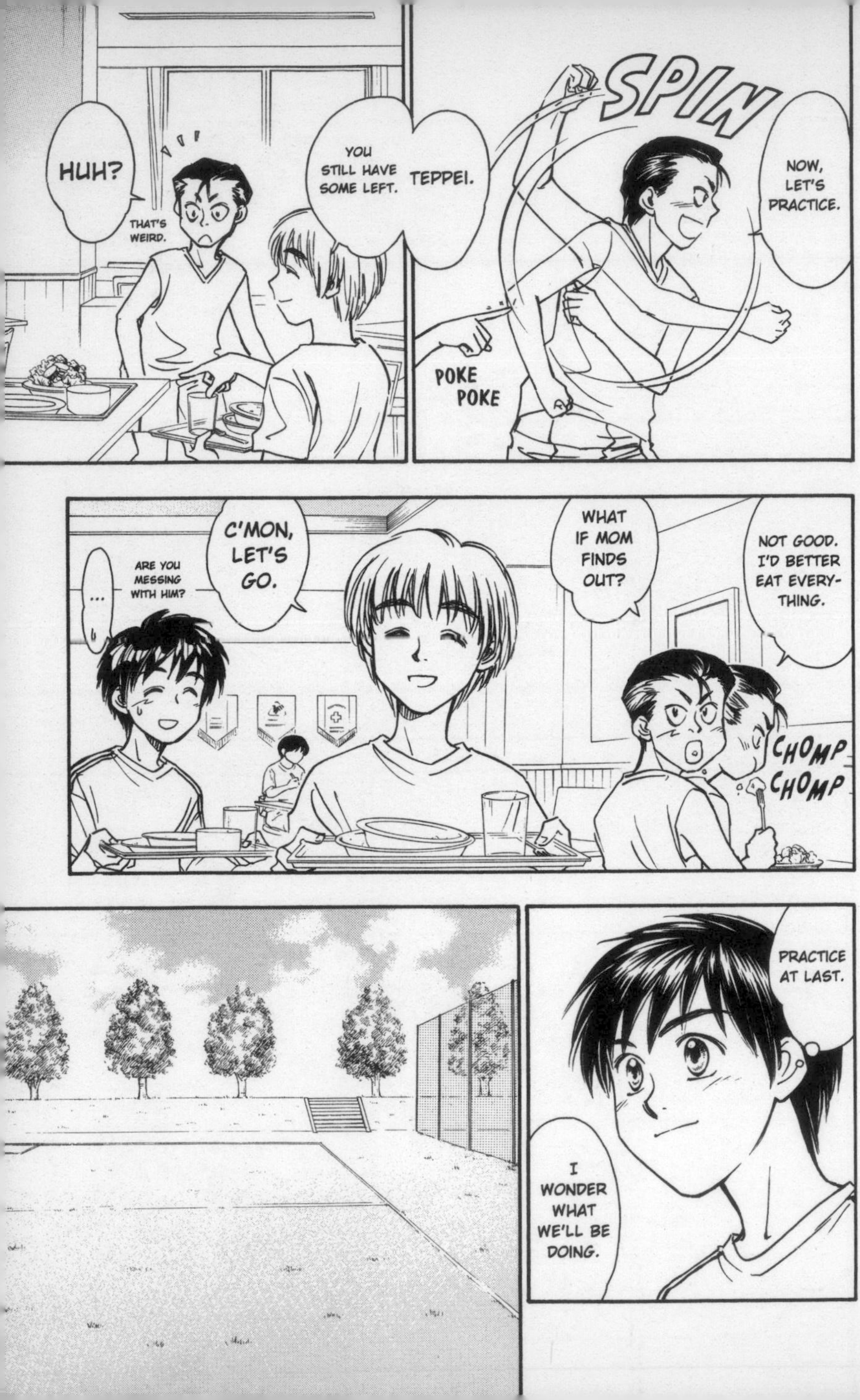
SPIN
NOW, LET'S PRACTICE.
POKE POKE
TEPPEI.
YOU STILL HAVE SOME LEFT.
HUH?
THAT'S WEIRD.
NOT GOOD. I'D BETTER EAT EVERY-THING.
WHAT IF MOM FINDS OUT?
CHOMP CHOMP
C'MON, LET'S GO.
ARE YOU MESSING WITH HIM?
...
PRACTICE AT LAST.
I WONDER WHAT WE'LL BE DOING.

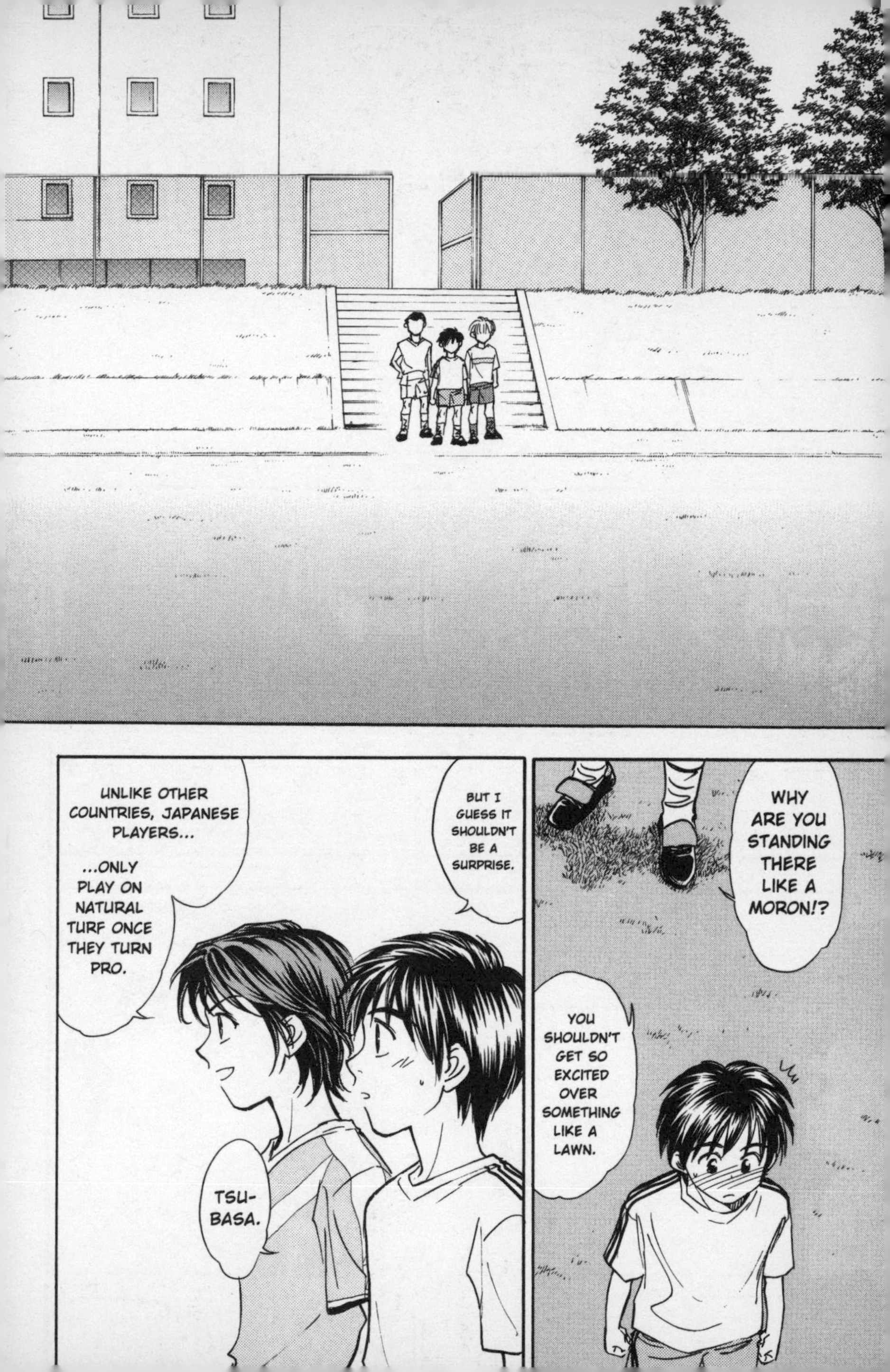
WHY ARE YOU STANDING THERE LIKE A MORON!?
YOU SHOULDN'T GET SO EXCITED OVER SOMETHING LIKE A LAWN.
BUT I GUESS IT SHOULDN'T BE A SURPRISE.
UNLIKE OTHER COUNTRIES, JAPANESE PLAYERS...
...ONLY PLAY ON NATURAL TURF ONCE THEY TURN PRO.
TSU-BASA.

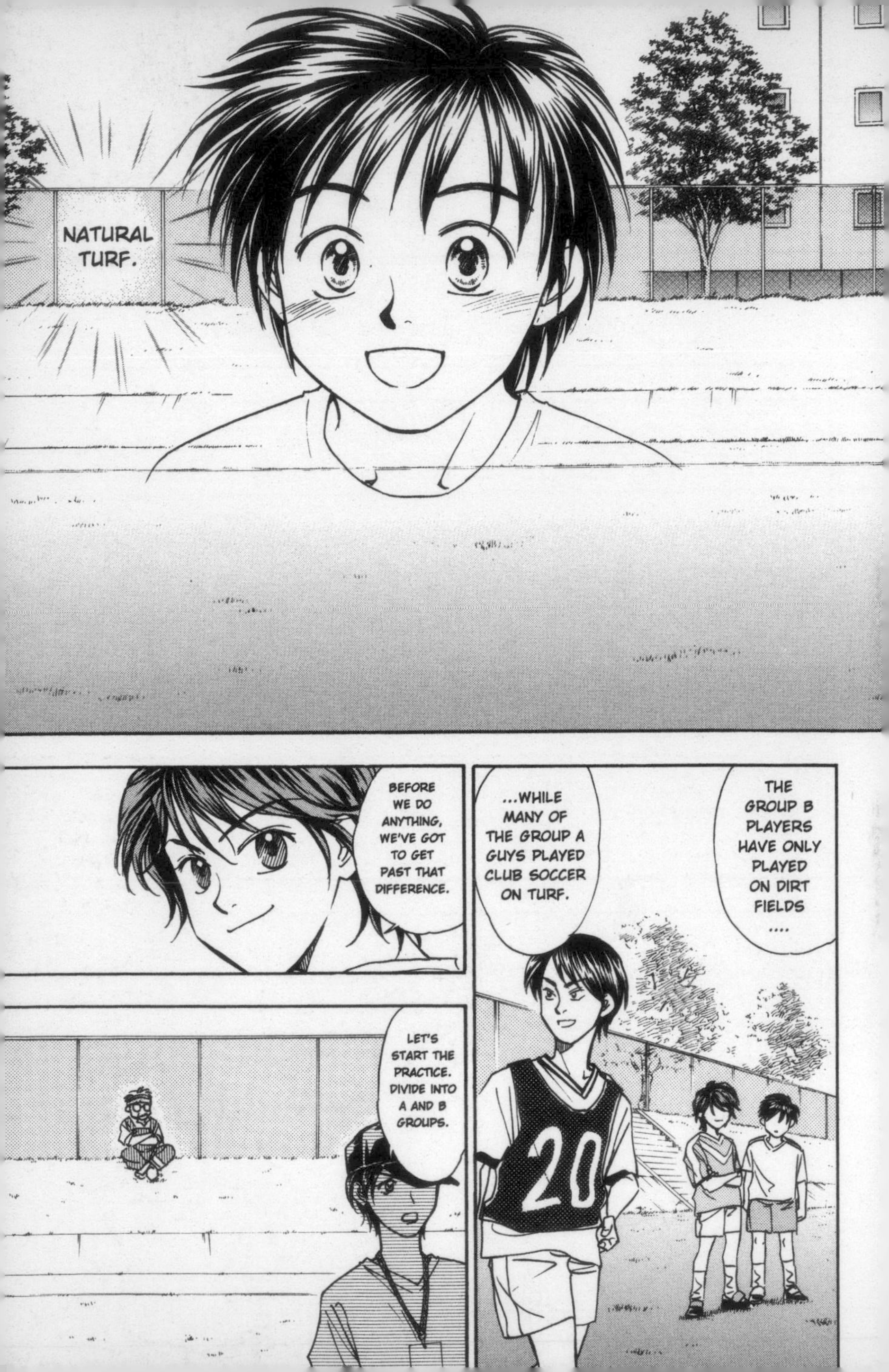
NATURAL TURF.
THE GROUP B PLAYERS HAVE ONLY PLAYED ON DIRT FIELDS ....
...WHILE MANY OF THE GROUP A GUYS PLAYED CLUB SOCCER ON TURF.
BEFORE WE DO ANYTHING, WE'VE GOT TO GET PAST THAT DIFFERENCE.
LET'S START THE PRACTICE. DIVIDE INTO A AND B GROUPS.
20

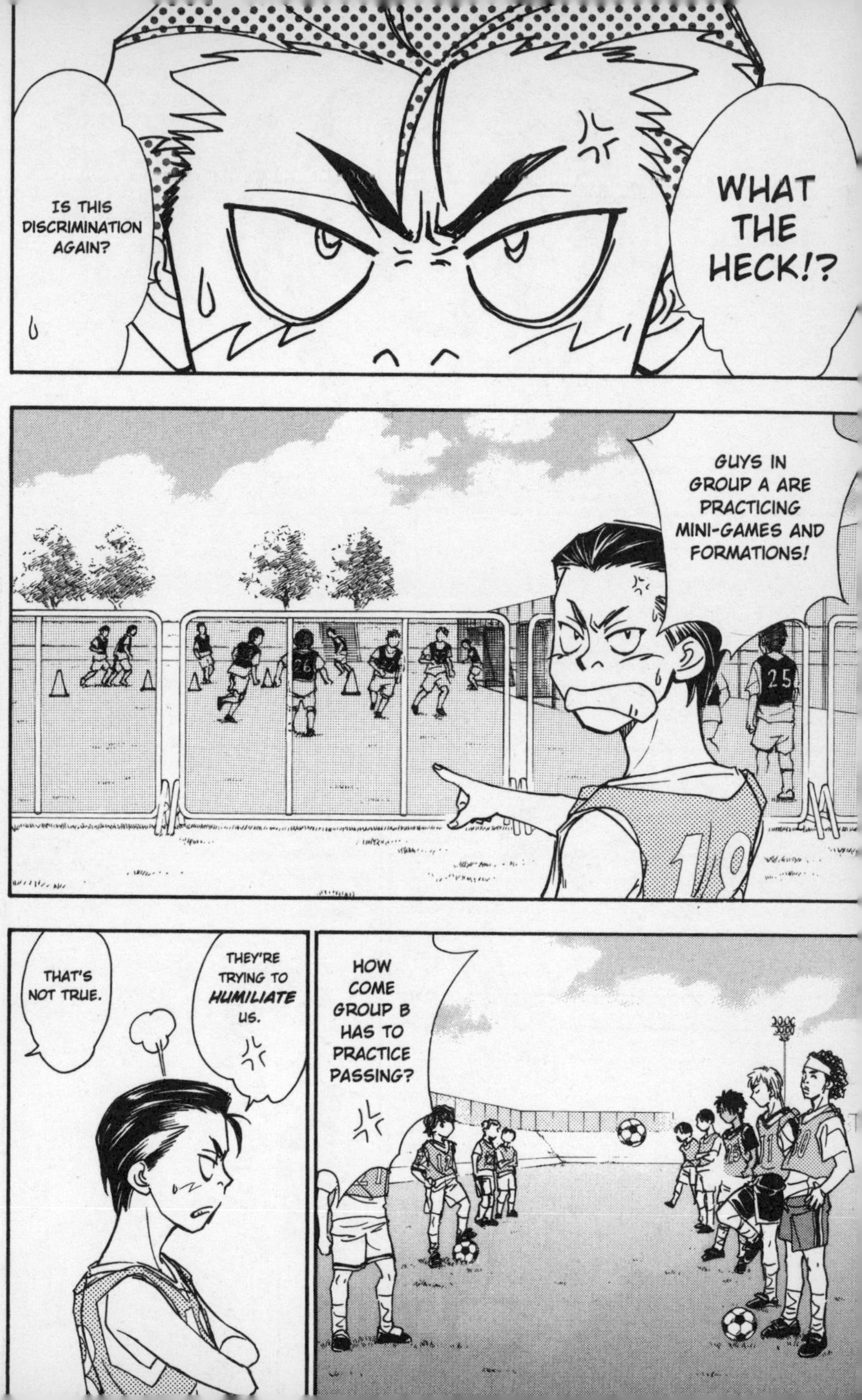
WHAT THE HECK!?
IS THIS DISCRIMINATION AGAIN?
GUYS IN GROUP A ARE PRACTICING MINI-GAMES AND FORMATIONS!
HOW COME GROUP B HAS TO PRACTICE PASSING?
THEY'RE TRYING TO *HUMILIATE* US.
THAT'S NOT TRUE.

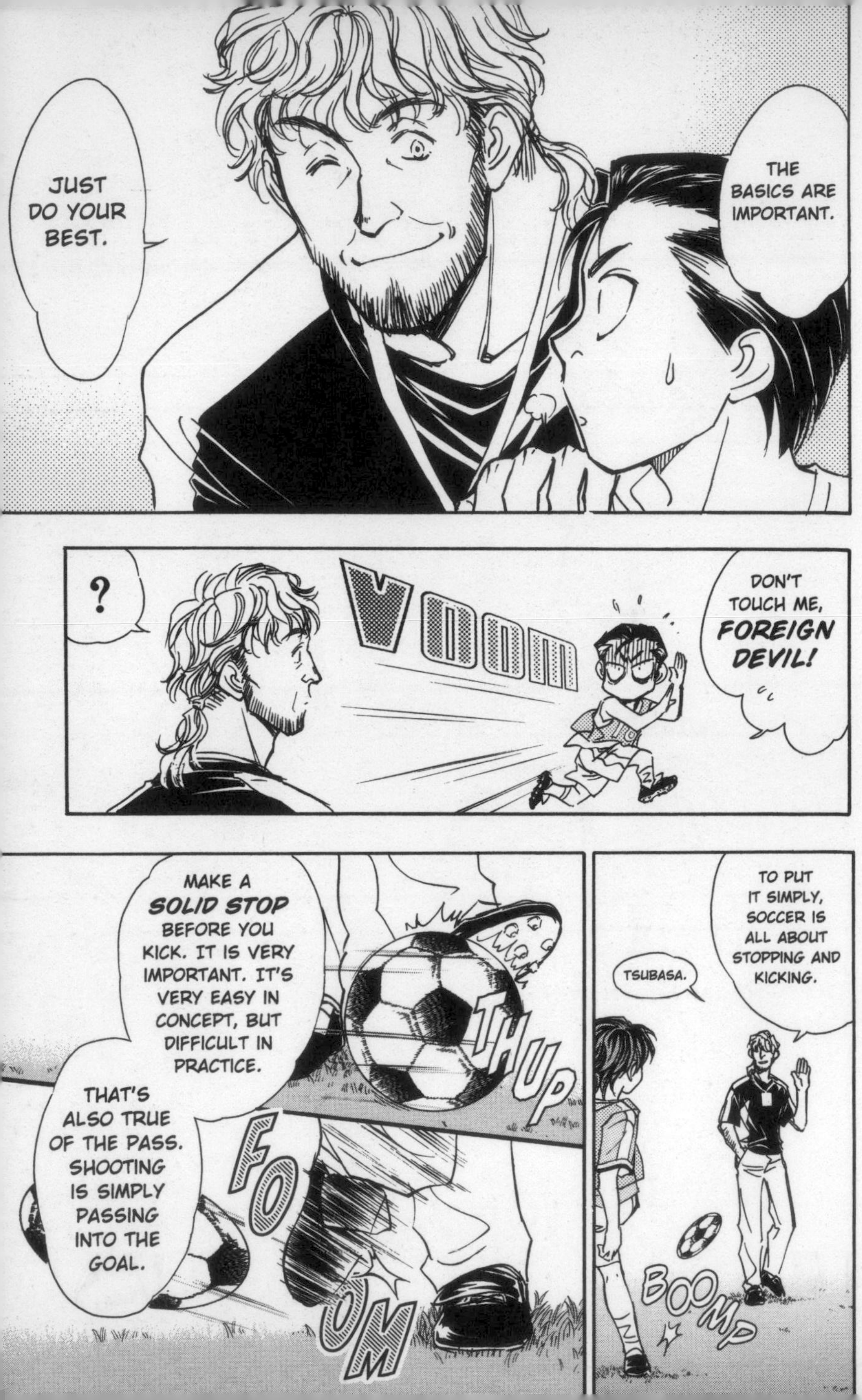
THE BASICS ARE IMPORTANT.
JUST DO YOUR BEST.
DON'T TOUCH ME, FOREIGN DEVIL!
VOOM
?
TO PUT IT SIMPLY, SOCCER IS ALL ABOUT STOPPING AND KICKING.
TSUBASA.
BOOMP
MAKE A SOLID STOP BEFORE YOU KICK. IT IS VERY IMPORTANT. IT'S VERY EASY IN CONCEPT, BUT DIFFICULT IN PRACTICE.
THUP
THAT'S ALSO TRUE OF THE PASS. SHOOTING IS SIMPLY PASSING INTO THE GOAL.
FOOM

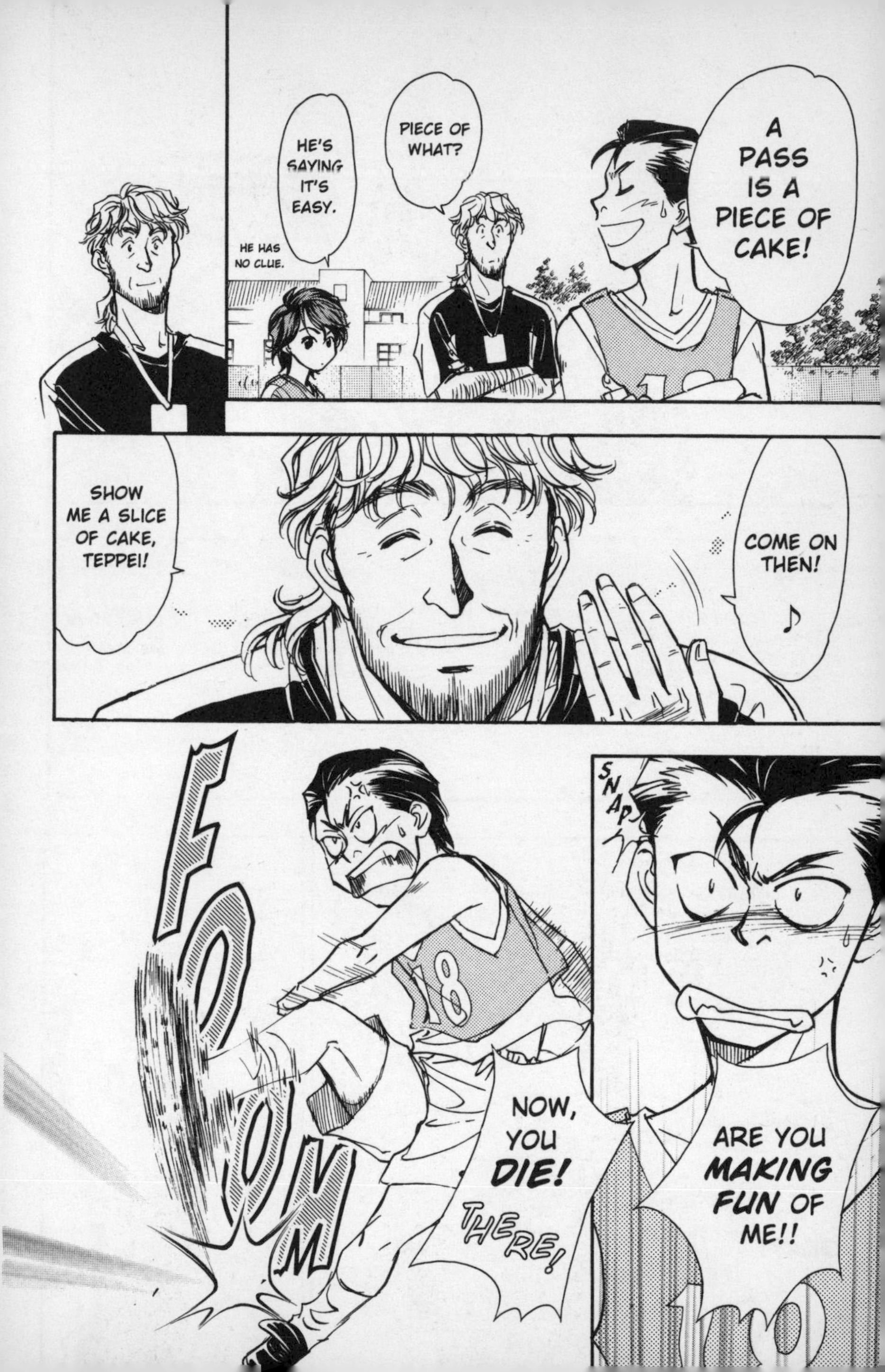
A PASS IS A PIECE OF CAKE!
PIECE OF WHAT?
HE'S SAYING IT'S EASY.
HE HAS NO CLUE.
COME ON THEN! ♪
SHOW ME A SLICE OF CAKE, TEPPEI!
SNAP
ARE YOU MAKING FUN OF ME!!
NOW, YOU DIE!
THERE!
FOOM

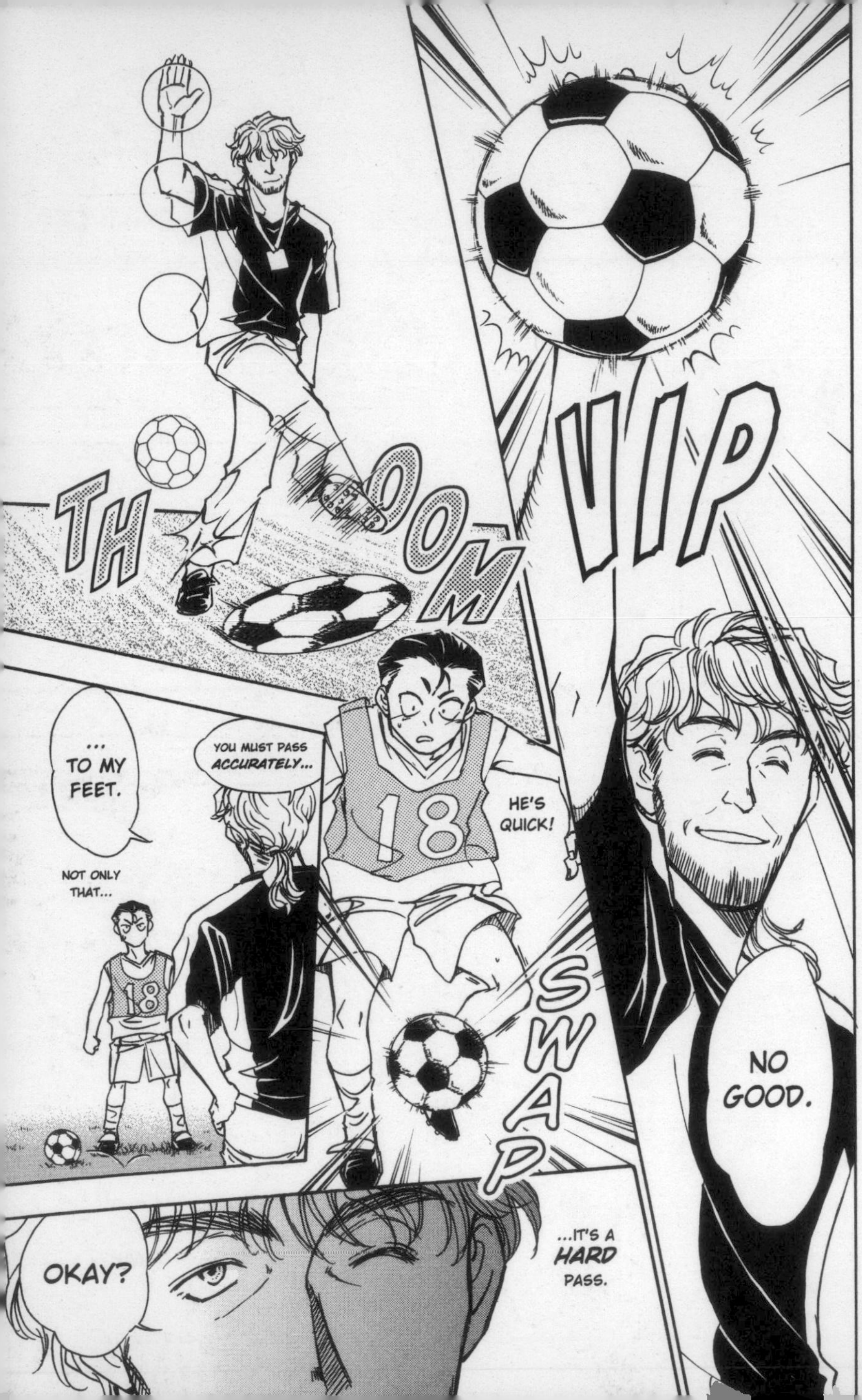
VIP
THOOM
NO GOOD.
HE'S QUICK!
SWAP
YOU MUST PASS ACCURATELY...
... TO MY FEET.
NOT ONLY THAT...
...IT'S A HARD PASS.
OKAY?

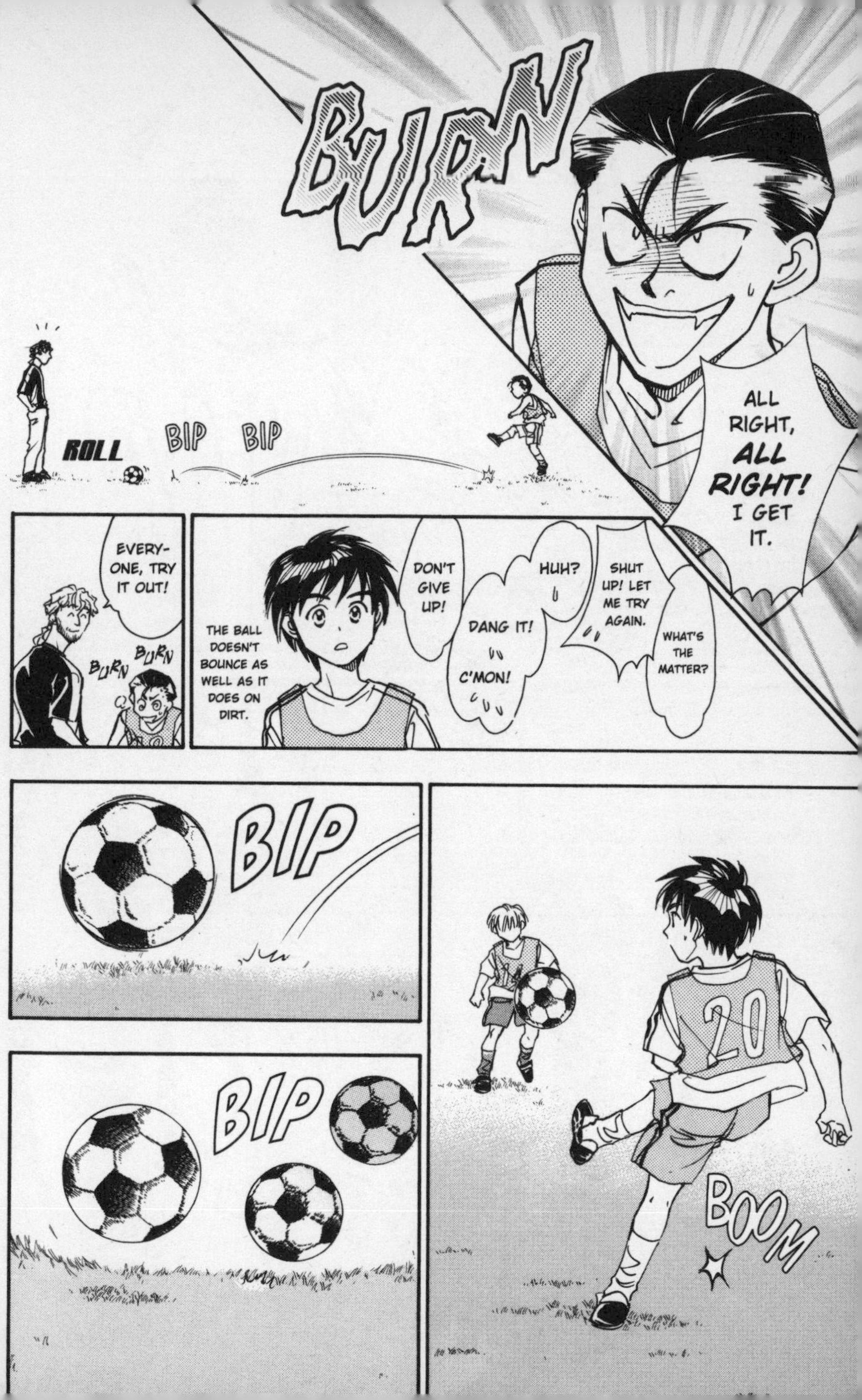
BURN
ALL RIGHT, ALL RIGHT! I GET IT.
BIP
BIP
ROLL
WHAT'S THE MATTER?
SHUT UP! LET ME TRY AGAIN.
HUH?
DANG IT!
C'MON!
DON'T GIVE UP!
THE BALL DOESN'T BOUNCE AS WELL AS IT DOES ON DIRT.
EVERY-ONE, TRY IT OUT!
BURN
BURN
BOOM
BIP
BIP

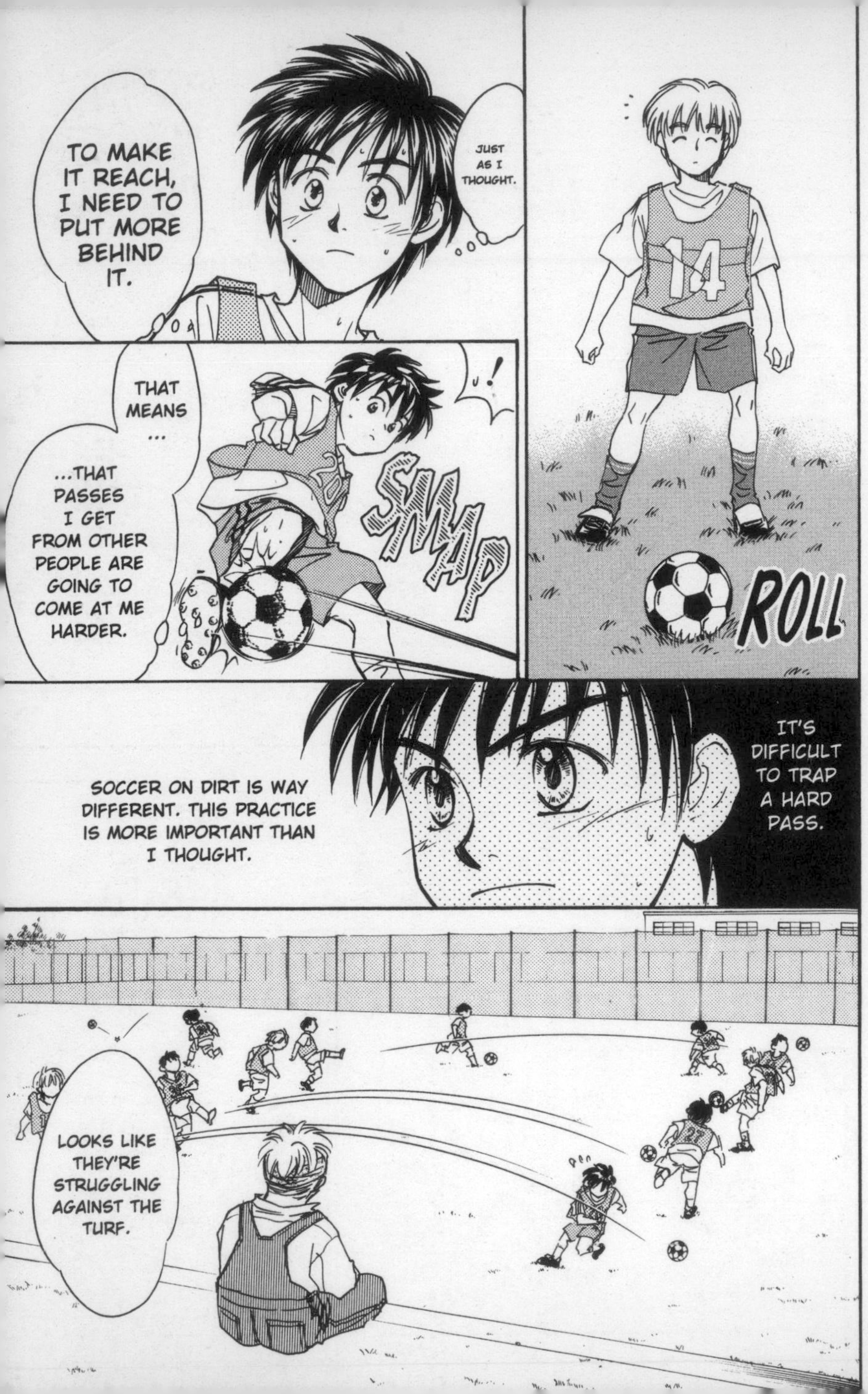
ROLL
JUST AS I THOUGHT.
TO MAKE IT REACH, I NEED TO PUT MORE BEHIND IT.
!
SMAP
THAT MEANS ...
...THAT PASSES I GET FROM OTHER PEOPLE ARE GOING TO COME AT ME HARDER.
IT'S DIFFICULT TO TRAP A HARD PASS.
SOCCER ON DIRT IS WAY DIFFERENT. THIS PRACTICE IS MORE IMPORTANT THAN I THOUGHT.
LOOKS LIKE THEY'RE STRUGGLING AGAINST THE TURF.

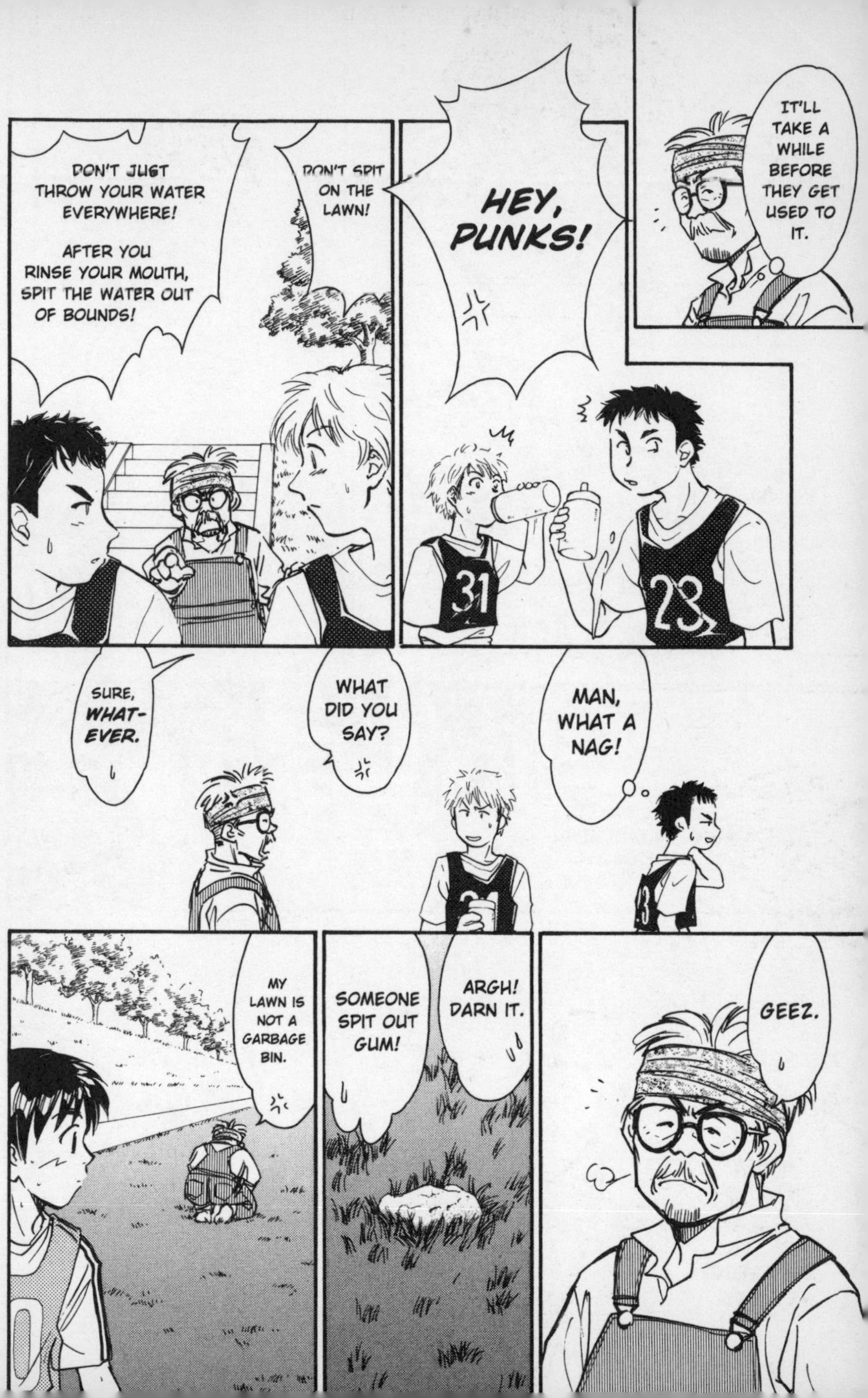
IT'LL TAKE A WHILE BEFORE THEY GET USED TO IT.
HEY, PUNKS!
DON'T SPIT ON THE LAWN!
DON'T JUST THROW YOUR WATER EVERYWHERE!
AFTER YOU RINSE YOUR MOUTH, SPIT THE WATER OUT OF BOUNDS!
MAN, WHAT A NAG!
WHAT DID YOU SAY?
SURE, WHATEVER.
GEEZ.
ARGH! DARN IT.
SOMEONE SPIT OUT GUM!
MY LAWN IS NOT A GARBAGE BIN.

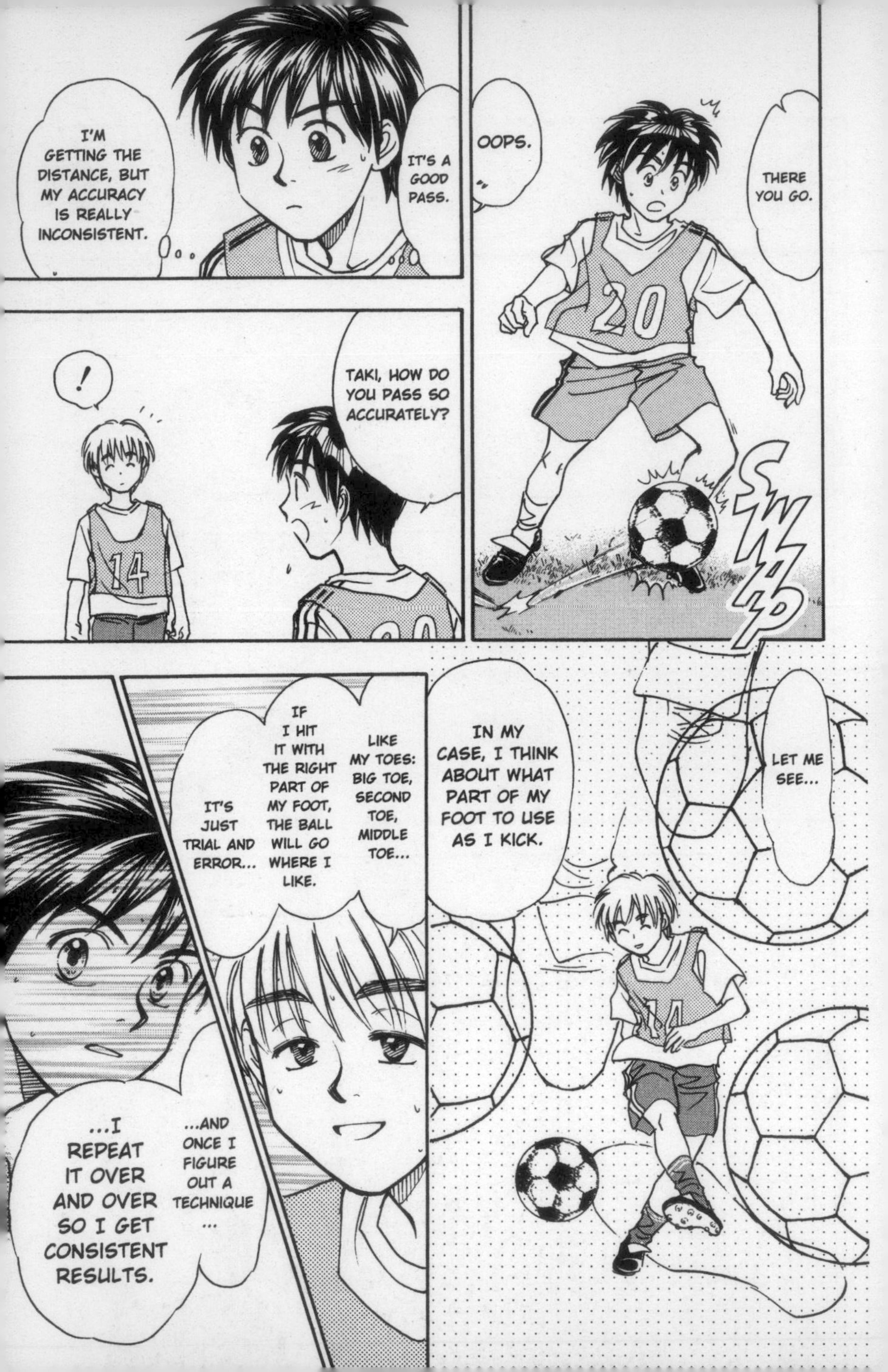
THERE YOU GO.
OOPS.
SWAP
IT'S A GOOD PASS.
I'M GETTING THE DISTANCE, BUT MY ACCURACY IS REALLY INCONSISTENT.
TAKI, HOW DO YOU PASS SO ACCURATELY?
!
LET ME SEE...
IN MY CASE, I THINK ABOUT WHAT PART OF MY FOOT TO USE AS I KICK.
LIKE MY TOES: BIG TOE, SECOND TOE, MIDDLE TOE...
IF I HIT IT WITH THE RIGHT PART OF MY FOOT, THE BALL WILL GO WHERE I LIKE.
IT'S JUST TRIAL AND ERROR...
...AND ONCE I FIGURE OUT A TECHNIQUE ...
...I REPEAT IT OVER AND OVER SO I GET CONSISTENT RESULTS.

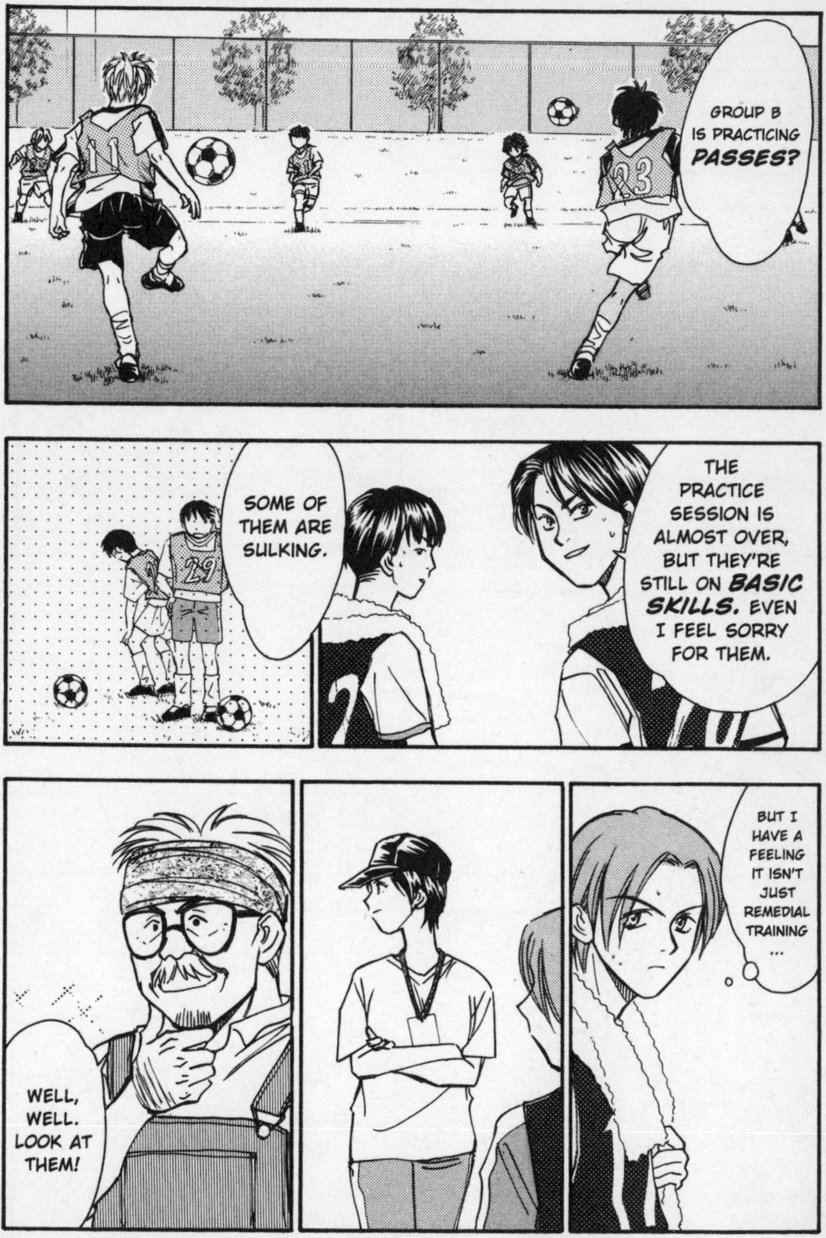
GROUP B IS PRACTICING PASSES?
THE PRACTICE SESSION IS ALMOST OVER, BUT THEY'RE STILL ON BASIC SKILLS. EVEN I FEEL SORRY FOR THEM.
SOME OF THEM ARE SULKING.
BUT I HAVE A FEELING IT ISN'T JUST REMEDIAL TRAINING ...
WELL, WELL. LOOK AT THEM!

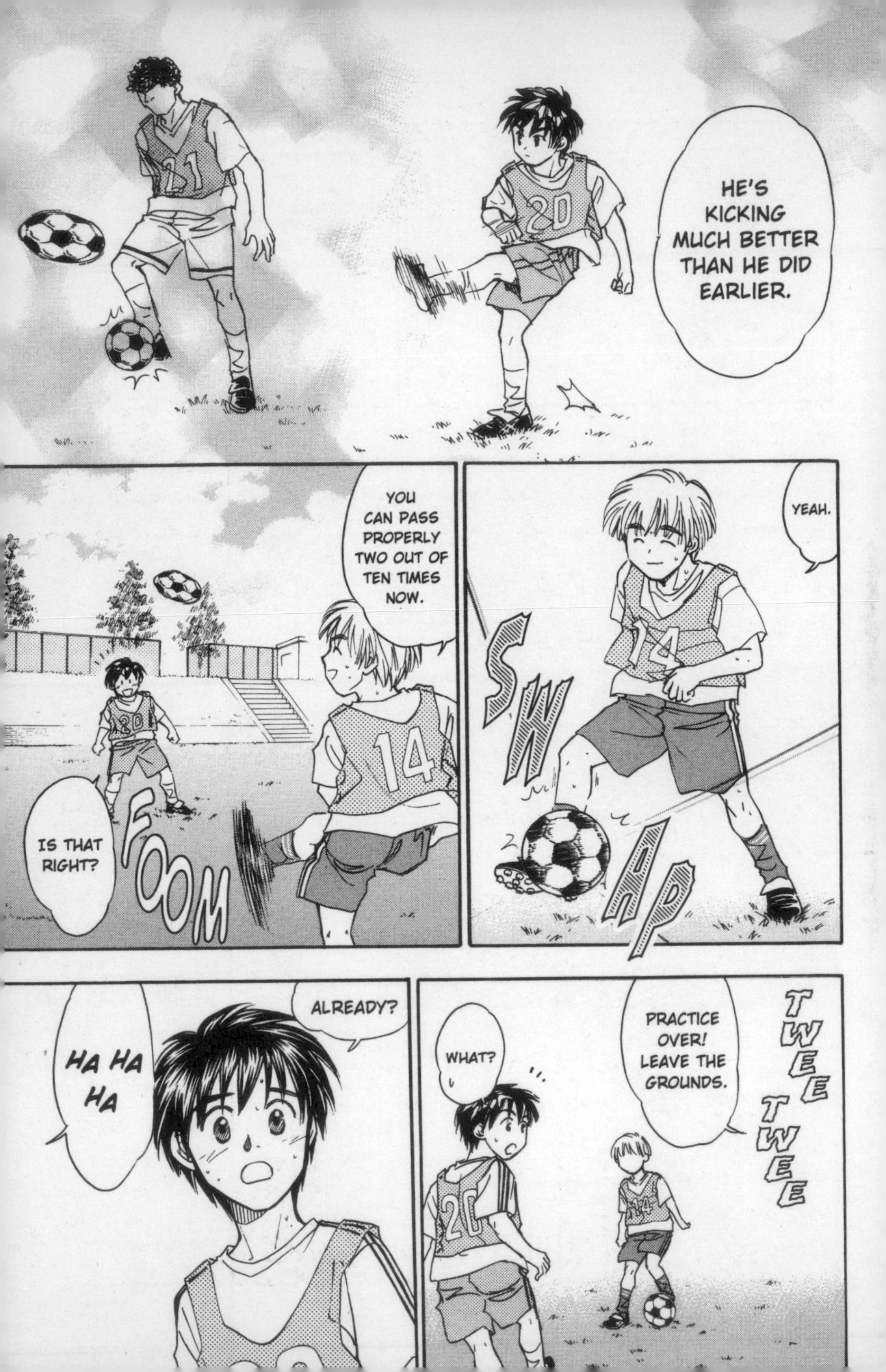
HE'S KICKING MUCH BETTER THAN HE DID EARLIER.
YEAH.
SWAP
YOU CAN PASS PROPERLY TWO OUT OF TEN TIMES NOW.
IS THAT RIGHT?
FOOM
TWEE TWEE
PRACTICE OVER! LEAVE THE GROUNDS.
WHAT?
ALREADY?
HA HA HA

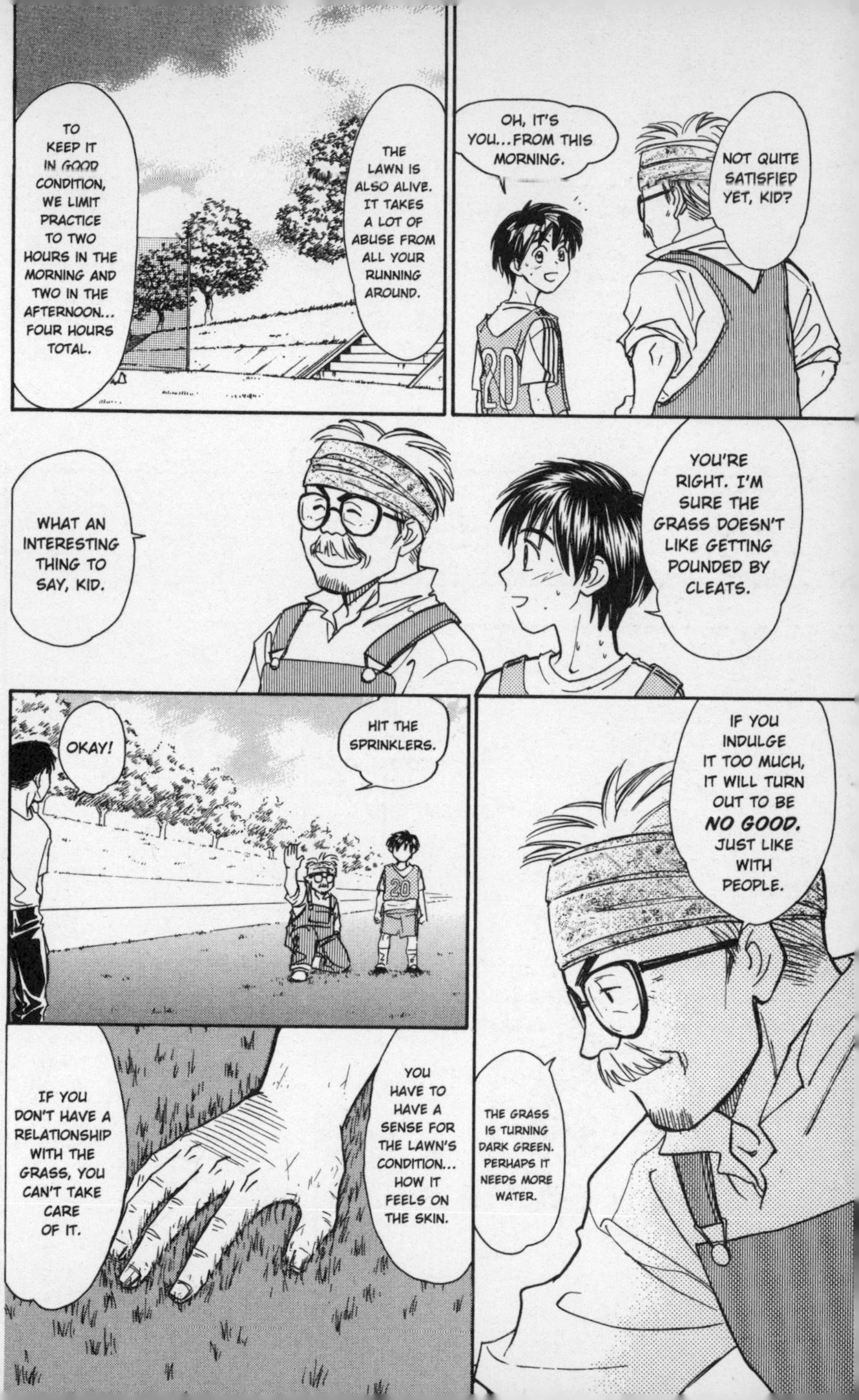
NOT QUITE SATISFIED YET, KID?
OH, IT'S YOU...FROM THIS MORNING.
THE LAWN IS ALSO ALIVE. IT TAKES A LOT OF ABUSE FROM ALL YOUR RUNNING AROUND.
TO KEEP IT IN GOOD CONDITION, WE LIMIT PRACTICE TO TWO HOURS IN THE MORNING AND TWO IN THE AFTERNOON... FOUR HOURS TOTAL.
YOU'RE RIGHT. I'M SURE THE GRASS DOESN'T LIKE GETTING POUNDED BY CLEATS.
WHAT AN INTERESTING THING TO SAY, KID.
IF YOU INDULGE IT TOO MUCH, IT WILL TURN OUT TO BE **NO GOOD.** JUST LIKE WITH PEOPLE.
THE GRASS IS TURNING DARK GREEN. PERHAPS IT NEEDS MORE WATER.
HIT THE SPRINKLERS.
OKAY!
YOU HAVE TO HAVE A SENSE FOR THE LAWN'S CONDITION... HOW IT FEELS ON THE SKIN.
IF YOU DON'T HAVE A RELATIONSHIP WITH THE GRASS, YOU CAN'T TAKE CARE OF IT.

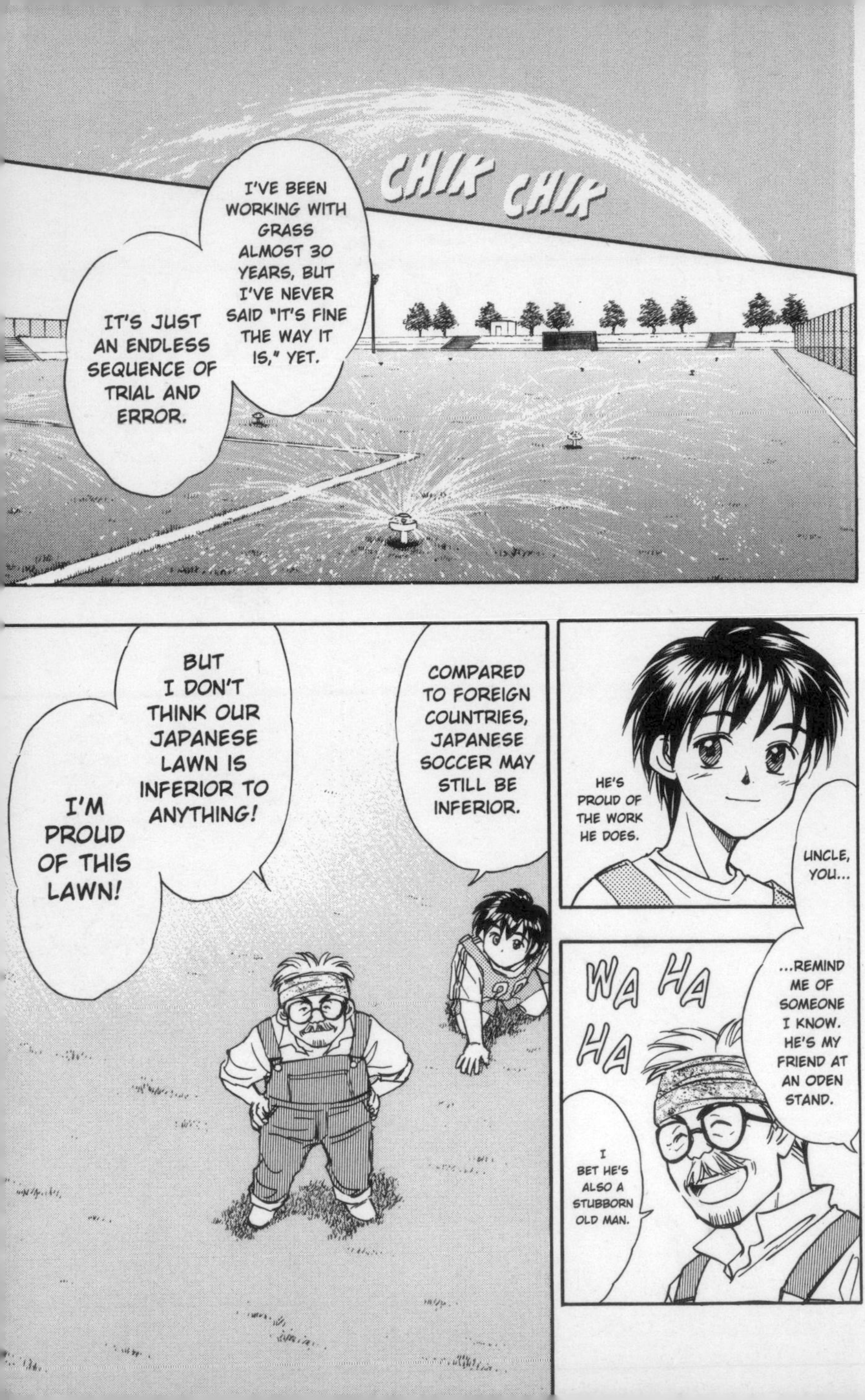
CHIK CHIK
I'VE BEEN WORKING WITH GRASS ALMOST 30 YEARS, BUT I'VE NEVER SAID "IT'S FINE THE WAY IT IS," YET.
IT'S JUST AN ENDLESS SEQUENCE OF TRIAL AND ERROR.
HE'S PROUD OF THE WORK HE DOES.
UNCLE, YOU...
...REMIND ME OF SOMEONE I KNOW. HE'S MY FRIEND AT AN ODEN STAND.
WA HA HA
I BET HE'S ALSO A STUBBORN OLD MAN.
COMPARED TO FOREIGN COUNTRIES, JAPANESE SOCCER MAY STILL BE INFERIOR.
BUT I DON'T THINK OUR JAPANESE LAWN IS INFERIOR TO ANYTHING!
I'M PROUD OF THIS LAWN!

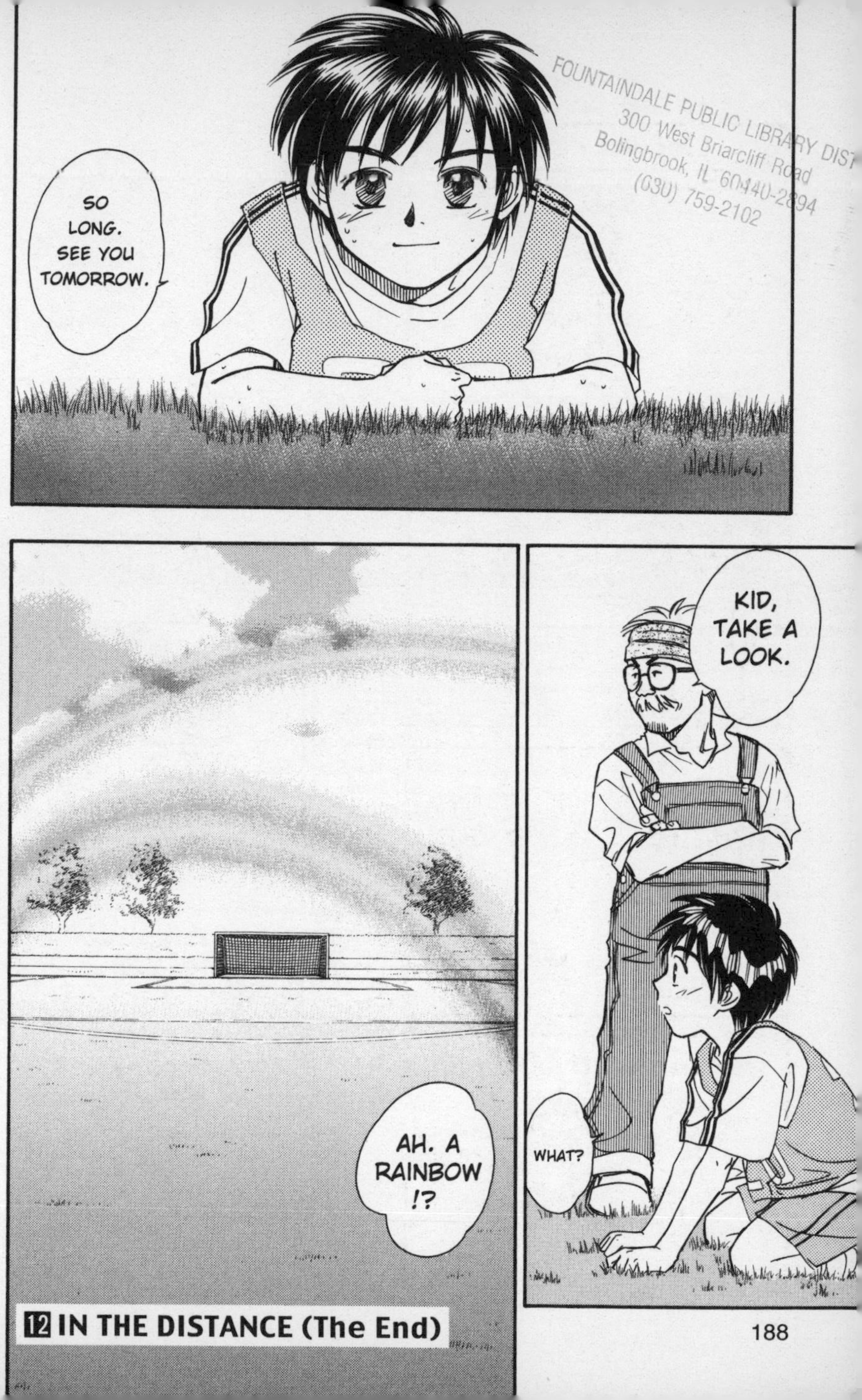
SO LONG. SEE YOU TOMORROW.
KID, TAKE A LOOK.
WHAT?
AH. A RAINBOW !?

12 IN THE DISTANCE (The End)

WHISTLE! THEATRE !!

ORIGAMI? OH, IT'S DELICIOUS!!
I THINK YOU MEAN "EDAMAME," MARCO.

MANGA BY SEKI, ASSISTANT S

Elegant People
HE'S DELICATELY BREAKING OFF A SMALL PIECE.
THEY RADIATE CHARM AND GRACE...
SMALL BITES.
A DAINTY GRIP.
SOY SAUCE IN FLAN CARAMEL.
BUT THIS ONE IS OBVIOUSLY DIFFERENT.
I DON'T WANT TO BE SEEN WITH YOU...

Will you wait for him?

PLOP
PLOP
DEADLY SERIOUS
WHOOSH
WHOOSH
NOW, I CAN EAT!!
LET'S EAT.
ALMOST FINISHED
...
FINISHED
FINISHED

FRAN CARAMEL.
BUT "RARE CHEESE CAKE" IS MY NO. 1 ♡

--Previously on "The Young and the Clueless"--

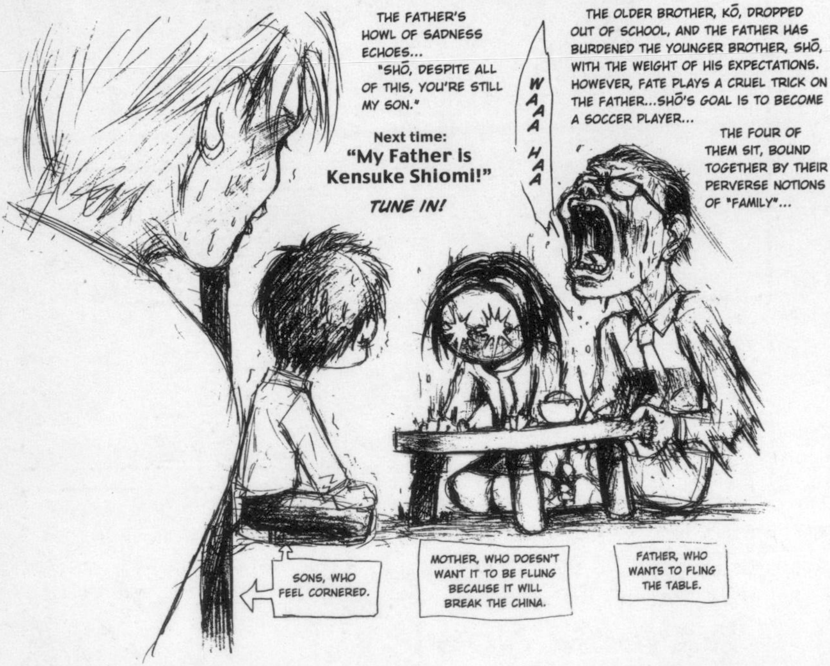
THE OLDER BROTHER, KŌ, DROPPED OUT OF SCHOOL, AND THE FATHER HAS BURDENED THE YOUNGER BROTHER, SHŌ, WITH THE WEIGHT OF HIS EXPECTATIONS. HOWEVER, FATE PLAYS A CRUEL TRICK ON THE FATHER...SHŌ'S GOAL IS TO BECOME A SOCCER PLAYER...
THE FOUR OF THEM SIT, BOUND TOGETHER BY THEIR PERVERSE NOTIONS OF "FAMILY"...
WAAA HAA
THE FATHER'S HOWL OF SADNESS ECHOES...
"SHŌ, DESPITE ALL OF THIS, YOU'RE STILL MY SON."
Next time:
"My Father Is Kensuke Shiomi!"
TUNE IN!
FATHER, WHO WANTS TO FLING THE TABLE.
MOTHER, WHO DOESN'T WANT IT TO BE FLUNG BECAUSE IT WILL BREAK THE CHINA.
SONS, WHO FEEL CORNERED.

By MESO AIKO

Next in Whistle!

IN THE DISTANCE

Shô, Tatsuya and Daichi have been invited to try out for an all-star team that will compete on an international level. New and old rivals alike gather to vie for spots on the select team, but for Shô, it's gut-check time when he realizes that his technical skills are on the bottom end of the curve. Will he be able to make the cut?

Available Now!

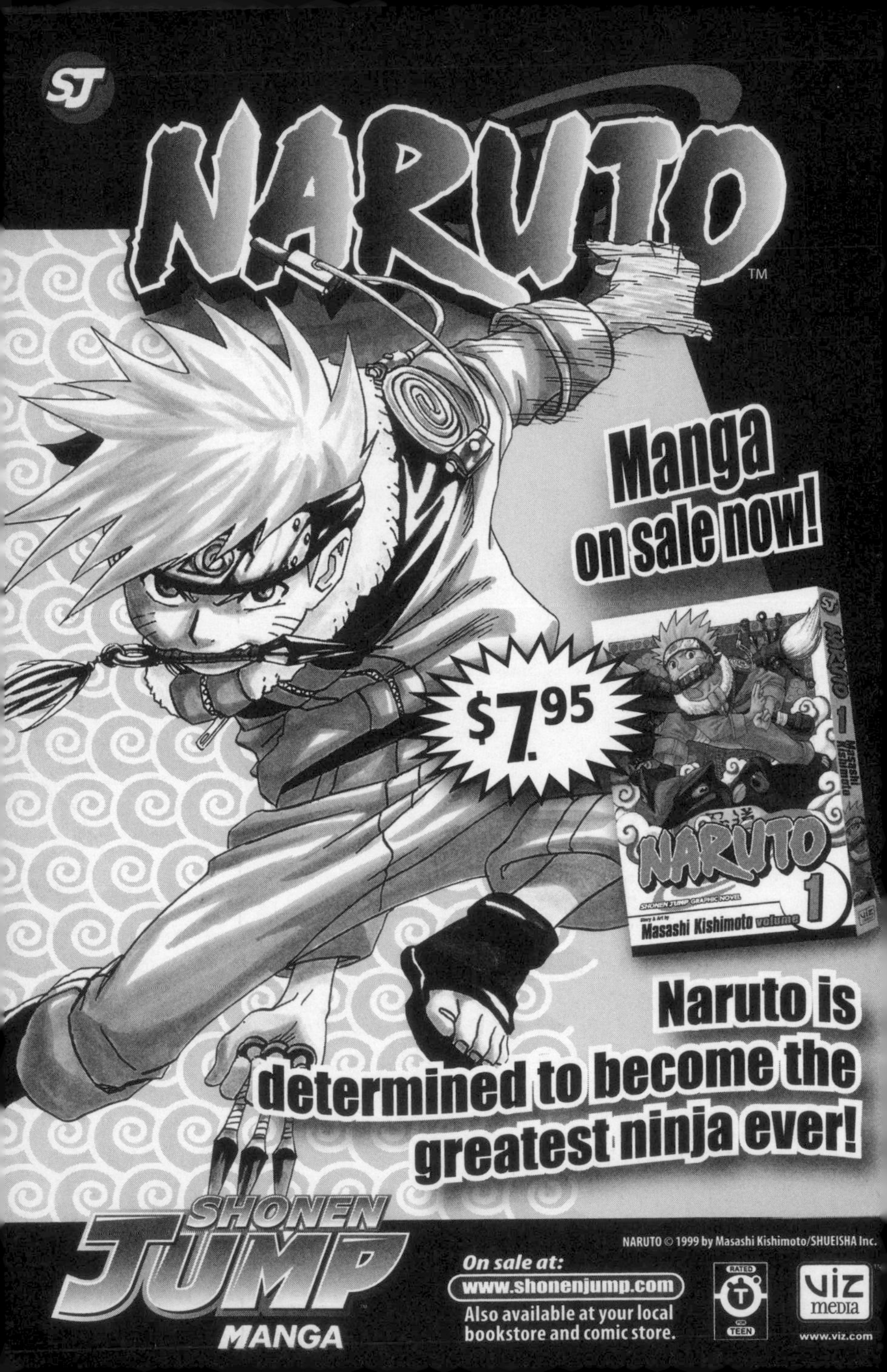
SJ
NARUTO™
Manga on sale now!
$7.95
NARUTO
SHONEN JUMP GRAPHIC NOVEL
Masashi Kishimoto volume 1
Naruto is determined to become the greatest ninja ever!
SHONEN JUMP MANGA
NARUTO © 1999 by Masashi Kishimoto/SHUEISHA Inc.
On sale at:
www.shonenjump.com
Also available at your local bookstore and comic store.
RATED T TEEN
viz media
www.viz.com

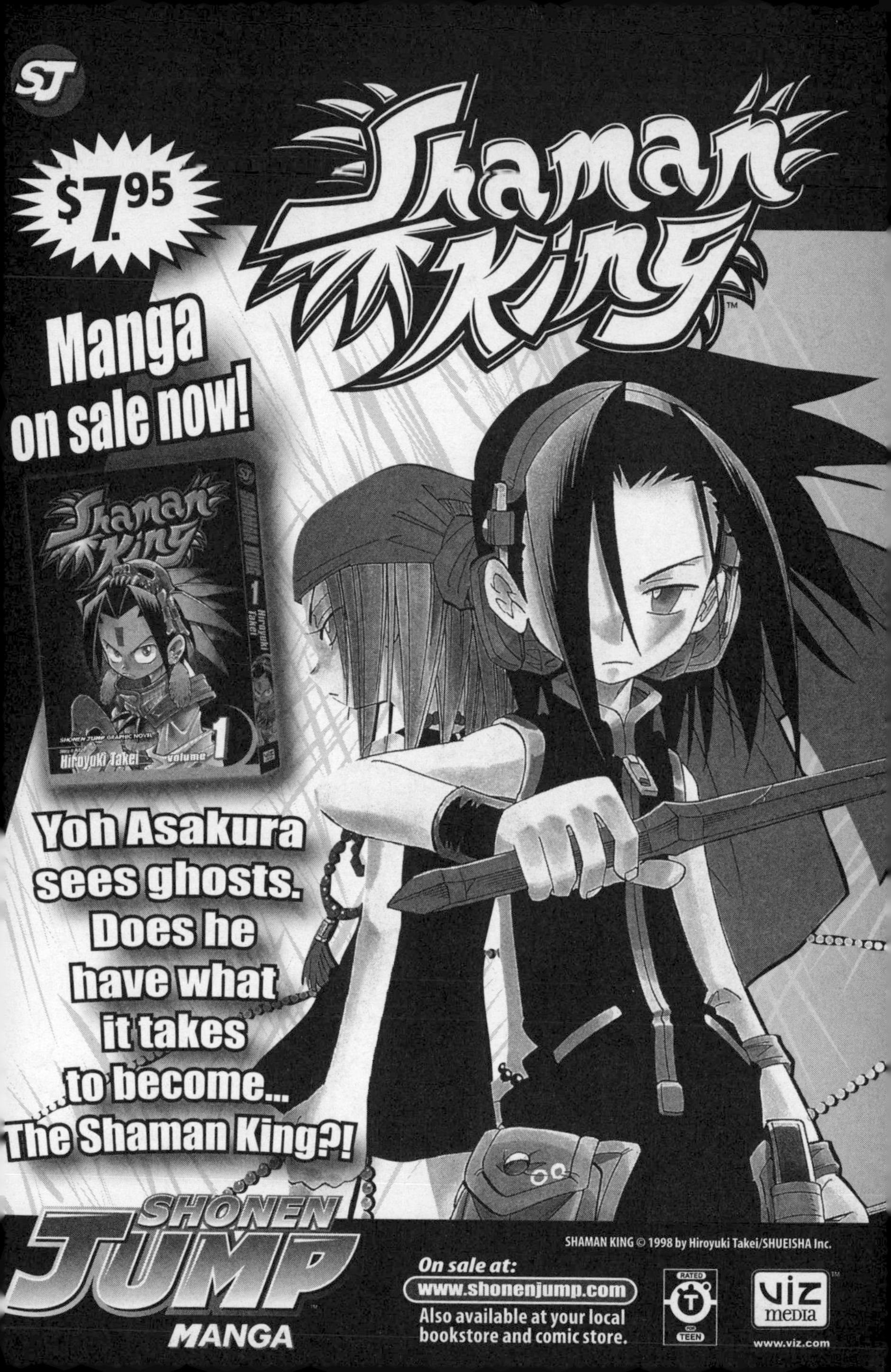
SJ
$7.95
Shaman King™
Manga on sale now!
Shaman King
1
Hiroyuki Takei
Shonen Jump Graphic Novel
Hiroyuki Takei
volume 1
Yoh Asakura sees ghosts. Does he have what it takes to become... The Shaman King?!
SHONEN JUMP MANGA
SHAMAN KING © 1998 by Hiroyuki Takei/SHUEISHA Inc.
On sale at:
www.shonenjump.com
Also available at your local bookstore and comic store.
RATED T TEEN
viz media
www.viz.com

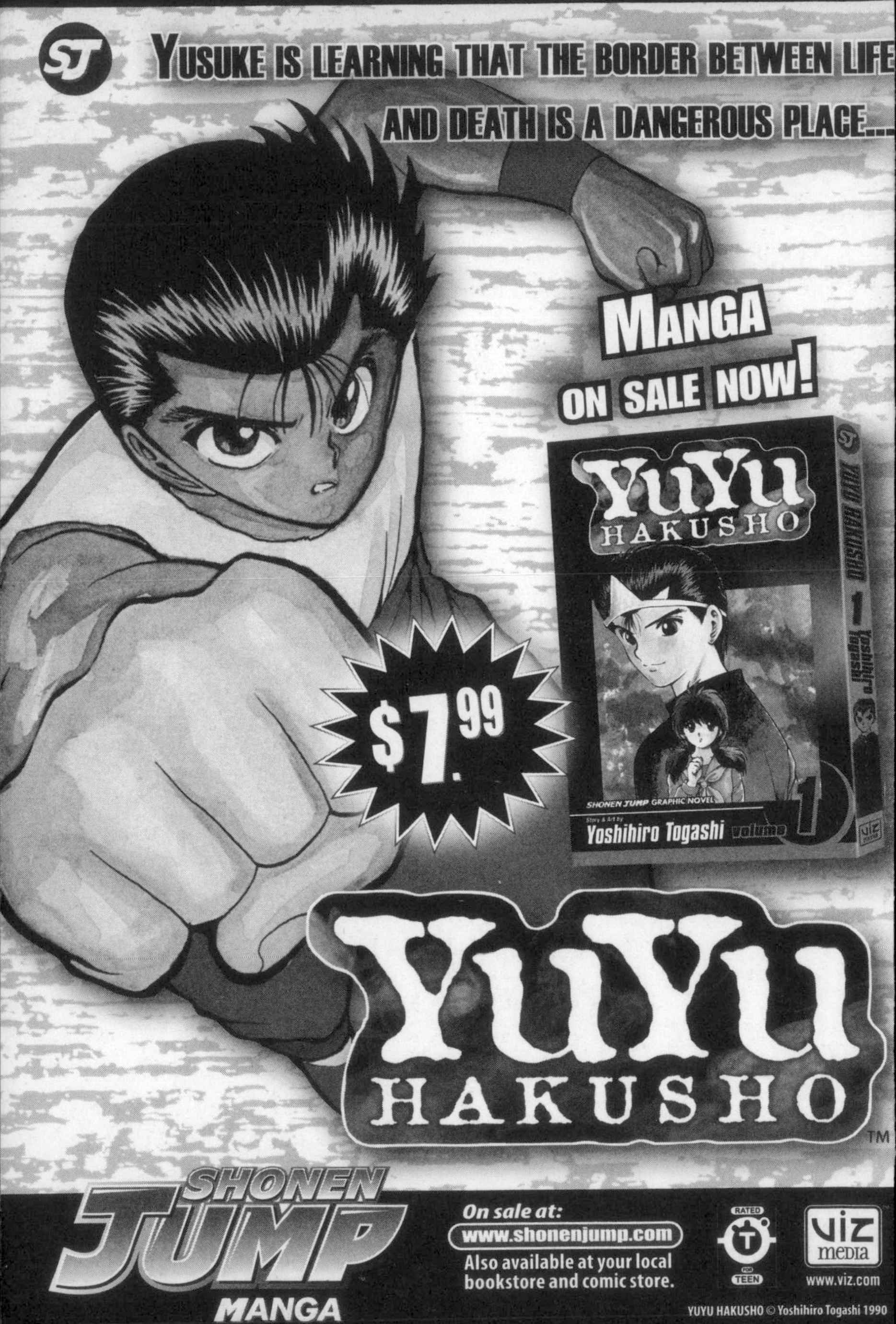
SJ
YUSUKE IS LEARNING THAT THE BORDER BETWEEN LIFE AND DEATH IS A DANGEROUS PLACE...
MANGA ON SALE NOW!
$7.99
YUYU HAKUSHO
SHONEN JUMP GRAPHIC NOVEL
Story & Art by Yoshihiro Togashi volume 1
YUYU HAKUSHO™
SHONEN JUMP MANGA
On sale at:
www.shonenjump.com
Also available at your local bookstore and comic store.
RATED T FOR TEEN
VIZ media
www.viz.com
YUYU HAKUSHO © Yoshihiro Togashi 1990

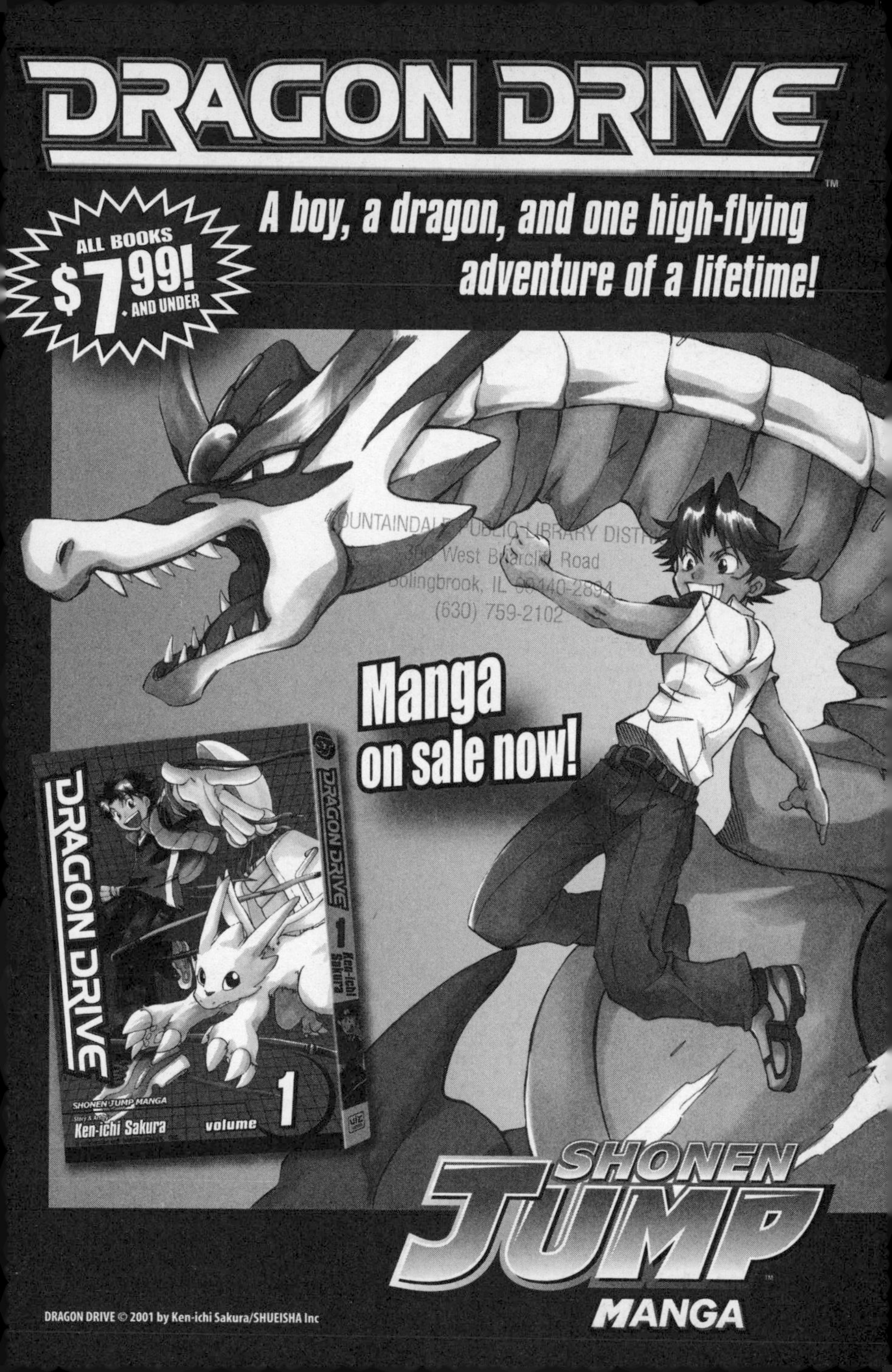
DRAGON DRIVE™
ALL BOOKS $7.99! AND UNDER
A boy, a dragon, and one high-flying adventure of a lifetime!
Manga on sale now!
DRAGON DRIVE
SHONEN JUMP MANGA
Story & Art by Ken-ichi Sakura
volume 1
SHONEN JUMP™ MANGA
DRAGON DRIVE © 2001 by Ken-ichi Sakura/SHUEISHA Inc

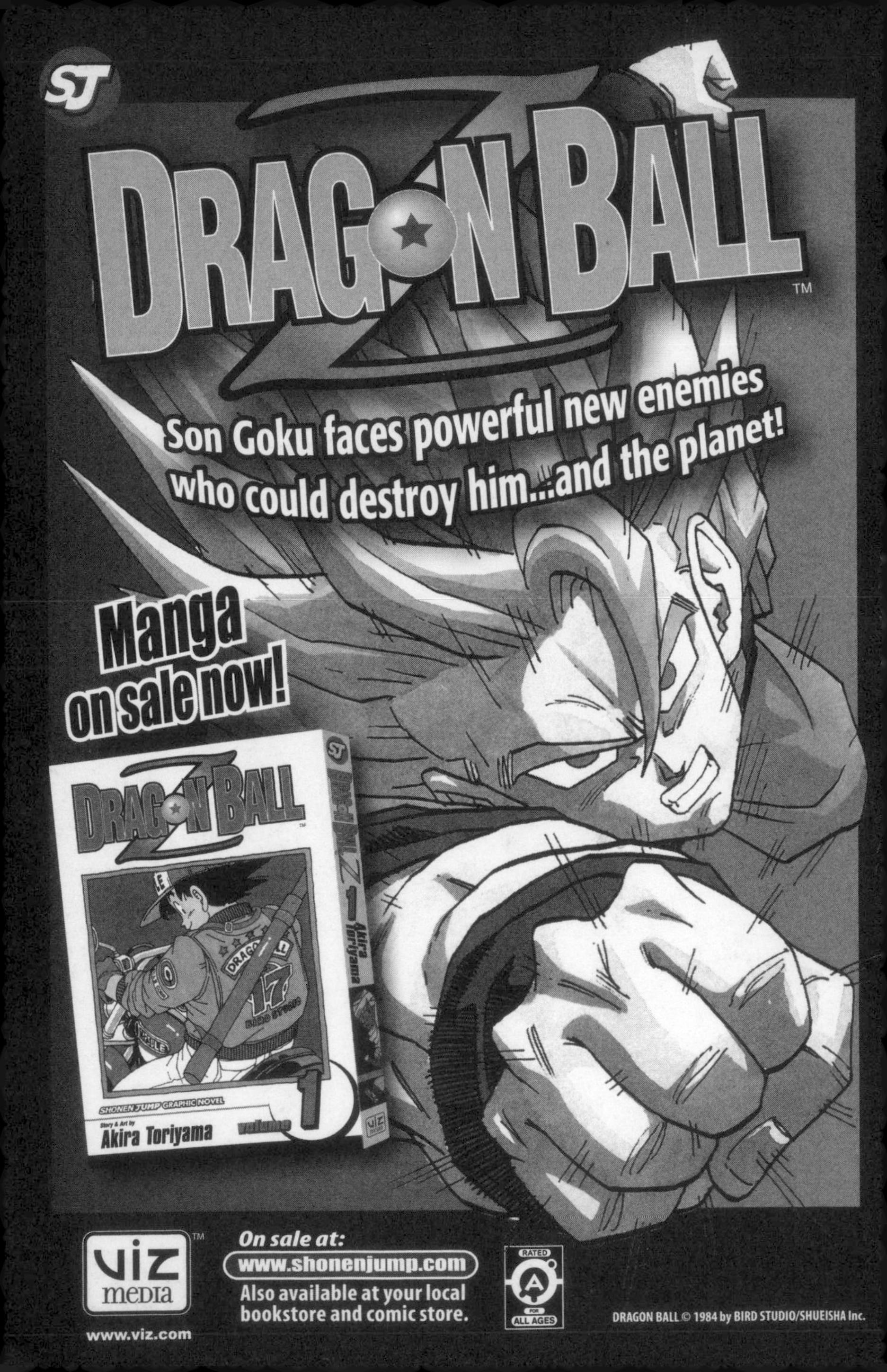

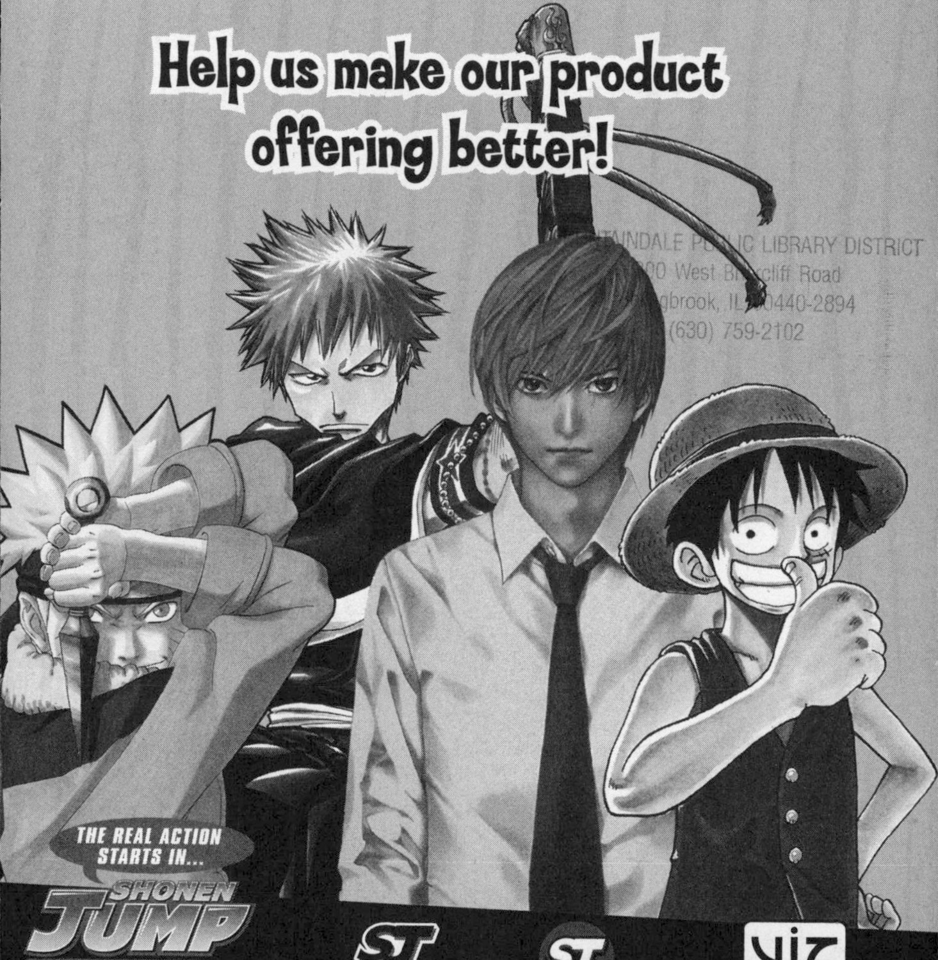

THE REAL ACTION STARTS IN...
SHONEN JUMP
THE WORLD'S MOST POPULAR MANGA
www.shonenjump.com
SJ ADVANCED
SJ
VIZ media